Rufus William Bailey

Scholar's Companion

Containing Exercises in the Orthography, Derivation, and Classification of English

Works

Rufus William Bailey

Scholar's Companion

Containing Exercises in the Orthography, Derivation, and Classification of English Works

ISBN/EAN: 9783337178277

Printed in Europe, USA, Canada, Australia, Japan

Cover: Foto ©Paul-Georg Meister /pixelio.de

More available books at **www.hansebooks.com**

THE

SCHOLAR'S COMPANION;

CONTAINING

EXERCISES

IN THE

Orthography, Derivation, and Classification

OF

ENGLISH WORDS.

WITH

AN INTRODUCTION AND A COPIOUS INDEX,

BY

RUFUS W. BAILEY.

A NEW EDITION, THOROUGHLY REVISED.

PHILADELPHIA:
PUBLISHED BY E. H. BUTLER & CO.
1870.

OFFICE OF THE CONTROLLERS OF PUBLIC SCHOOLS,
FIRST SCHOOL DISTRICT OF PENNSYLVANIA.
Philadelphia, May 28th, 1863.

At a meeting of the Controllers of Public Schools, First District of Pennsylvania, held at the Controllers' Chamber, on Friday, January 2d, 1863, the following Resolution was adopted:—

Resolved, That THE SCHOLAR'S COMPANION shall be the only Text-Book on the subject of Etymology to be used in the Schools of the District; and that the study of Definitions, and the Questions to be asked at the High School Examinations, shall be confined to words derived from roots, to be found in said work, and that all technical terms shall be excluded.

From the Minutes.
JAMES D. CAMPBELL,
Secretary.

DEPARTMENT OF PUBLIC INSTRUCTION,
Baltimore, Md., July 22d, 1865.

At a meeting of the State Board of Education, held this day, "THE SCHOLAR'S COMPANION" was adopted as a Text-Book to be used in the Public Schools throughout the State.

W. HORACE SOPER,
Clerk.

Entered, according to Act of Congress, in the year 1841, by HENRY PERKINS, in the Clerk's Office of the District Court of the United States, in and for the Eastern District of Pennsylvania.

Entered, according to Act of Congress, in the year 1854, by CLARK & HESSER, in the Clerk's Office of the District Court of the United States, in and for the Eastern District of Pennsylvania.

Entered, according to Act of Congress, in the year 1854, by E. H. BUTLER & Co., in the Clerk's Office of the District Court of the United States, in and for the Eastern District of Pennsylvania.

Entered, according to Act of Congress, in the year 1863, by
E. H. BUTLER & CO.,
In the Clerk's Office of the District Court of the United States, in and for the Eastern District of Pennsylvania.

CAXTON PRESS OF
SHERMAN & CO., PHILADELPHIA.

INTRODUCTION.

The "Scholar's Companion" has been too long before the public, and too widely endorsed, to require a labored defence as a text-book for schools. The sale of half a million of copies in more than a hundred editions, with an increasing demand, is sufficient indication of the estimate in which it is held. In revising it for a new edition, it has not been thought best to attempt any alteration in the plan or arrangement of the text. This, besides the doubtful utility, would render the new edition unfit to be used with those already in extensive use in the schools. Some more marked distinctions in the old arrangement, with a copious index for easy reference, with an improved typography and style of mechanical execution, is all the Publishers deem necessary to meet the wishes of its numerous patrons. These improvements have been effected at considerable expense, and it is hoped they will be acceptable.

Part I. embraces a large and judicious selection of cognate words, requiring the particular attention of the learner to their orthography and orthoepy; also a list of equivocal words, or words spelled and pronounced alike, but used in different significations, and a corrected list of others that are improperly spelled and used. These selections are not unnecessarily multiplied, and yet they are fully sufficient for all practical purposes.

Part II. treats of the composition and the derivation of words. The learner who makes himself familiar with the prefixes and suffixes, as here presented in a few pages, will hardly need more for all practical purposes to enable him to recognise readily their proper force and effect.

The etymology of words derived from the Latin and the Greek is of leading importance, because such words are the most numerous.

Language, in its principles and its structure, is necessarily, and everywhere, the same. The Latin and Greek scholar has the advantage of the mere English scholar in this only, a facility in tracing the etymology of a large class of our words which have been derived from those languages. Yet by a careful study of the etymology of the words whose derivation is traced in the following pages, the English scholar will find his only compensation for the lack of that classical learning which can be obtained only by a long course of study. To the classical scholar, these exercises will be doubly useful and interesting.

Part III. embraces the important study of synonyms. The importance of this branch of the study of words can be duly appreciated only by those who have pursued it critically. It is indispensable to a correct use of language, and has contributed essentially to place the few who have attained the highest eminence in scholarship above the others of high position. Augustine said of Cicero, "Ille verborum vigilantissimus appensor ac mensor"—*a skilful mint-master, a subtle watcher and weigher of words.* Of all masters of the English language, none perhaps deserves so nearly a comparison with Cicero as Daniel Webster. All who have ever aided him in placing his thoughts upon paper—and he was often obliged to employ amanuenses—can testify how critically he watched and weighed his words, how accurately he discriminated, how he would discourse on the nice shades of distinction when he required the change of a word, how he was capable of showing clearly, etymologically, historically, eloquently, and convincingly, a difference where ordinary scholars had discerned only a simple synonym. This made his definitions and opinions of authority, and will for ever place his written discussions in every department among the most cherished classics of English literature.

The subject is fairly opened in these pages, and enough is here collated for a class-book; enough, too, to awaken an interest which may lead the inquiring mind to pursue the subject in more elaborate treatises. These may be found at hand in "Roget's Thesaurus of English words," revised and edited by Dr. Sears, a work of sterling merit and priceless value to the scholar who would attain to accuracy in writing or speaking his mother-tongue. "Trench on the Study of Words" may also be recommended as a book which unites the interest of a novel with a most critical and discriminating philological discussion.

"How often," says Trench, "do the great masters of style in every tongue,—perhaps none so often as Cicero, the greatest of all,—pause to discriminate between the words they are using; how much care and labor, how much subtlety of thought they have counted well bestowed on the operation; how much importance do they avowedly attach to it! Not to say that his works, even where he does not intend it, will be a continual lesson in this respect, a great writer, merely in the accuracy with which he employs words, will always be exercising us in synonymous discrimination.

INTRODUCTION.

"Nor is this habit of discrimination valuable only as a part of our intellectual training; but what a positive increase is it of mental wealth when we have learned to discern between things which really differ, but have been hitherto confused in our minds; and have made these distinctions permanently our own in the only way by which they can be secure, that is. by assigning to each its appropriate word and peculiar sign.

"What a help, moreover, will it prove to the writing of a good English style, if instead of having many words before us, and choosing almost at random and hap-hazard from among them, we at once know which, and which only, we ought in the case before us to employ, which will be the exact vesture of our thoughts. It is the first characteristic of a well-dressed man that his clothes fit him; that they are not too small and shrunken here, too large and loose there. Now it is precisely such a prime characteristic of a good style that the words fit close to the thoughts: they will not be too big here, hanging like a giant's robe on the limbs of a dwarf; nor too small there, as a boy's garment into which the man has with difficulty and ridiculously thrust himself. We do not feel in one place that the writer means more than he has succeeded in saying; in another, that he has said more than he means; in a third, something beside what his intention was—and all this from a want of dexterity in employing the instrument of language, of precision in knowing what words would be the exactest correspondents and fittest exponents of his thought."

Words are to be considered principally in two relations, viz.: in their definite meaning, and in their grammatical construction. In their latter aspect, we learn the structure of language, the different classes of words with their philosophical uses and relative importance—in the former, the force and distinct signification of each separate word. This requires an accurate knowledge of their origin and authorized use.

In tracing the etymology of words, we go first to the original words in the language where they have been first employed, or to their first formation, if original, in our own language. Thence we trace their related meanings, the modified uses to which they have been applied, and the new significations which, in process of time, have been assigned to them. Sometimes a word is entirely changed from its original meaning, and is used not only in varied but in opposite senses. Words are constantly manufactured too for the times, for the new things that are made the subject of thought, or for the new modes of thought that are entertained. They are also formed by the combination of different words; by affixes and suffixes. They are thus, at different periods, changed or modified in meaning, and new words are invented.

Language, the first necessity of the mind, is not only the instrument but the nutriment of thought, "essential to the activity of our speculative powers, modifying, by its changes, the growth and complexion of the faculties it feeds."

The importance of language, then, is readily perceived in its necessity, its controlling influence, and its uses. It is necessary to the development of mind and to civilization. The language of a nation or of an individual tests the character as accurately as the thermometer tests the elevation of the temperature, or as the consols of England indicate the value of money in the market.

Thought is the capital deposit of the mind; Language the medium of exchange and intercommunication. The consols of the race man consist of the united stock of all these separate deposits, where the value of each is set forth and certified in language, the instrument of thought. Books written become the indentures of a common partnership. Here, the treasures "unhedged, lie open in one common field, and bid all welcome to the vital feast."

The study of language as a mental discipline, is, perhaps, of greater influence than any other study: not generally so considered, only, perhaps, because like everything common, its true position and true influence are lost in the subtle involution of its power with any study that is new, startling, or difficult. We must analyze the mind's operations in the solution of problems in science, or labored results in philosophy, before we can detect the nice distinctions required, and sought out, and discovered in the words and forms of speech which we use to define our propositions and elucidate our arguments. Here is a field for philosophy, for logic, for mental enterprise, for keen analysis, and nice discrimination. Here, in the clear exhibition of results to others—requiring the logic, the philosophy, the illumination of language—a mental activity is exercised more important to a healthful discipline than in most, perhaps than in any, other profound investigations prosecuted in thought.

The study of words is the study of philosophy, of history, of morals. We may read a nation's history in a nation's words. Mind is there stereotyped in form and feature like the reality of life. There is often more of true history to be learned in a Dictionary, which cannot lie, than in written annals, which may be framed by prejudice, pride, affectation, misconception, or intended falsehood. Tradition is shadowy; memories may be partial; history, even, is often poetic, mixed with fiction. But a nation's language is itself, the record of the day and the hour, and the honest reality of its acting, thinking, speaking. Words are things. In everything, therefore, which they fairly indicate, they are reliable.

The study of words, then, becomes something more than a detail of vocables, a tissue of sounds: "'Tis food, 'tis strength, 'tis life."

INTRODUCTION.

The study of words has never yet had its proper place in the educational course. If pursued at all, it has been a study of definitions merely, disconnected with etymology. We here trace the stream to its sources, explore its fruitful branches and its delta, where, by a hundred mouths, it brings down accumulated treasures to a common reservoir of human thought, whence, as from the ocean, is exhaled a healthful influence that refreshes the whole face of the earth.

"Word warriors" have caused more bloodshed and misery than all the executioners of martyrs to truth and principle. Books have been written, treasures squandered, controversies exasperated, eternal hatred engendered, armies brought into deadly conflict, and nations revolutionized or destroyed, for *a word:* more than this,—for a word *misunderstood*, for an illusion.

> "One word interposed
> Makes enemies of nations that had else,
> Like kindred drops, been mingled into one."

Theological controversies, political asperities, judicial litigations, personal animosities, have their origin and vitality most often in the misunderstanding of words. This, unperceived by the contending parties, is often obvious to the disinterested observer—sometimes apparent to the combatants themselves after all the mischief has been done, past remedy.

That which is so often fatal to truth and to right in social life, is also injurious to the individual mind in all its own inquiries and activities. We think in words. Hence these words must truly represent their antitypes, else the mind deceives itself, and is at war with its own opinions. Thus the mind becomes its own tormentor, biting and devouring itself; or urged on to conflict without an object, it builds a man of straw, applies the faggot, and is consumed by the fire it has wantonly kindled; or like the viper bites itself to death, a suicide without a cause.

Thus it is not without a philosophical reason the Saviour said to the Pharisees: "By thy *words* thou shalt be justified, and by thy *words* thou shalt be condemned." The connection between the words we utter and the moral emotions, is palpable to every man who has studied the mental processes of his own consciousness. Physiologically, the connection between the vocal organs and the brain is known to be delicately sensitive and powerfully reciprocal. The same may be true, metaphysically, between the verbal definitions in our mental activities and the permanent impressions of principles on the mental and moral emotions. In the spiritual state, these verbal mental processes place in permanent forms what words, uttered or written, stereotype in vocables.

They are then ours, adopted, attach to the mind as a part of itself, and become permanently operative. A man's thoughts, which are words uttered in himself, are the record by which he may read himself as truly as the opinion, written or spoken and defended, reveals him to others. Habits of thinking are as important, often more important, on permanent forms of character than habits of speaking. Hence the wisdom of that caution, "Be careful of thy words, whether in thought or utterance."

Definitely, the *study of words* is the object of this treatise, intended to initiate the young learner early into the habit of a critical definition of the language he uses. Beyond mere orthography and correct pronunciation, it is designed to introduce the young mind into the inner life of words, and thus into the inner life of the soul. It is a spelling-book, but that is not all. It teaches correct pronunciation, but that is not all. It is a defining Dictionary,—but still more, it discriminates the nicest shades of difference in words, in thought, and contributes eminently to form the mind to truth, and the character to uprightness, and the soul for its immortal destiny.

If we may have contributed to awaken the minds of Teachers and educationists to the true dignity, importance, and influence of the *study of words*, we have installed our subject in its proper place, and accomplished the object of this brief Introduction to the SCHOLAR'S COMPANION.

R. W. BAILEY.

CONTENTS.

PART I.

CLASSIFICATION OF WORDS ACCORDING TO ORTHOGRAPHY AND PRONUNCIATION.

	PAGE
CHAP. I.—Words pronounced exactly alike, but spelled differently; arranged according to the sound of the principal vowel,	9

CHAP. II.—Words of similar pronunciation.
1. The first of each pair having the sound of *s*, the second of *z*, ... 19
2. The first of each pair ending in *ts*, ... 20
3.   ending in *le*, ... 21
4.   having an *f*, the latter a *v*, . . 21
5.   ending in *er* or *or*, the second in *ure* or *eur*, ... 21
6. The second of each pair aspirated, ... 22
7.   beginning with *h*, . . . 22
8. The first of each pair having the sound of *a* in *mat*; the second of *e* in *met*, ... 23
9. Several sounds of *a* and *e* compared, ... 24
10. The first of each pair having the sound of *e* in *mete*, . 24
11. Sounds of *e* and *i* compared, ... 25
12. The first of each pair having the sound of *o* in *more*, . 25
13. Several sounds of *o* and other vowels compared, . . 26
14. The first of each pair having the sound of *o* in *move*, . 26
15. Words to be carefully distinguished, ... 26
16. Words often confounded from improperly introducing or omitting the sound of *r*, ... 29
17. Dissyllables differing in accent, ... 30
18. Words spelled alike but pronounced differently, . . 33

CHAP. III.—Equivocal words, ... 35
CHAP. IV.—Improprieties heard in conversation, . . . 44
CHAP. V.—Rule in orthography, ... 46

PART II.

DERIVATION.

Chap. I. General account of derivation and composition,	48
Prefixes,	50
Suffixes,	53
Chap. II.—Words derived from the Latin,	57
Chap. III.—Words derived from the Greek,	171
Chap. IV.—Miscellaneous tables,	202
1. Corresponding derivatives,	202
2. Greek and Latin plurals,	203
3. Latin words and phrases,	205
4. French words and phrases,	209
5. Abbreviations,	213
6. Words derived chiefly from classical proper names,	216

PART III.

ENGLISH SYNONYMS, ... 223

THE

SCHOLAR'S COMPANION.

PART I.

CLASSIFICATION OF WORDS ACCORDING TO ORTHOGRAPHY AND PRONUNCIATION.

To the Teacher.—In using Part I., various modes of study and recitation may be employed, and it will usually be found best to pursue no one mode exclusively. But it is earnestly recommended to the teacher to employ a variety of *written*, as well as oral exercises, in the classes which are studying this Part. Let the pupils be required (for instance), to form sentences which shall contain the words of the lesson; and let the plan of the composition be simple or more difficult, according to the age and attainments of the class. Written exercises of this kind may be varied to almost any extent, and will be found on many accounts advantageous in the prosecution of such studies.

CHAPTER I.

Words pronounced exactly *alike, but spelled differently; arranged according to the sound of the principal vowel.*

A as in *mate.*
ALE, a malt liquor.
AIL, to affect unpleasantly.
ATE, did eat.
  AIT, a small island in a river.
EIGHT, a number.
A'TE, the goddess of mischief.
  EIGH'TY, fourscore.
BA'CON, smoked pork.
  BAK'EN, cooked in an oven.
BALE, a pack of goods.
  BAIL, a surety.
BATE, to deduct.
  BAIT, an allurement.
BAY, a color; a tree.
  BEY, a Turkish governor.

BAYS, [pl. of Bay] a garland.
  BAIZE, a kind of cloth.
BRAID, to plait.
  BRAYED, did bray.
BRAKE, fern; a thicket.
  BREAK, to part by force.
CANE, a walking stick.
  CAIN, a man's name.
CHASTE, pure.
  CHASED, pursued.
DANE, a native of Denmark.
  DEIGN, to condescend.
DAY, a period of time.
  DEY, the governor of Algiers
FAINT, languid; weak.
  FEINT, a pretence.

(9)

FANE, a temple.
  FAIN, willingly; gladly.
  FEIGN, to pretend.
FRAYS, quarrels.
  FRAISE, a kind of fortification.
  PHRASE, a mode of speech.
GAGE, a pledge.
  GAUGE, a measuring rod.
GATE, a sort of door.
  GAIT, manner of walking.
GRATE, a range of bars.
  GREAT, large.
GRA'TER, a sort of rasp.
  GREAT'ER, larger.
HALE, strong; healthy.
  HAIL, frozen rain; to salute.
HAY, dried grass.
  HEY! an exclamation.
LADE, to load.
  LAID, placed.
LANE, a narrow road.
  LAIN, remained.
MADE, finished.
  MAID, an unmarried woman.
MALE, a he animal.
  MAIL, armor; a post-bag.
MANE, of a horse.
  MAIN, principal; chief.
  MAINE, name of a state.
MAZE, an intricate place.
  MAIZE, Indian corn. [wheel.
NAVE, the centre or hub of a
  KNAVE, a rogue.
NAY, no.
  NEIGH, the voice of a horse.
PALE, whitish.
  PAIL, a wooden vessel.
PANE, a square of glass.
  PAIN, uneasiness.
PLACE, a situation.
  PLAICE, a flat fish.
PLANE, a carpenter's tool.
  PLAIN, manifest; even.
PLATE, a shallow dish.
  PLAIT, a fold.

PRAY, to beseech.
  PREY, plunder; booty.
RAIN, water from the clouds.
  REIN, of a bridle.
  REIGN, to rule.
RAZE or RASE, to demolish.
RAYS, sunbeams.
  RAISE, to lift; to elevate.
RA'ZOR, a shaving tool.
  RAIS'ER, a lifter.
SALE, a selling.
  SAIL, the canvas of a vessel.
SAIL'ER, a sailing vessel.
  SAIL'OR, a seaman.
SANE, sound in mind.
  SEINE, a river in France.
SETA'CEOUS, set with bristles.
  CETA'CEOUS, of the whale
SLAY, to kill.   [kind.
  SLEIGH, a vehicle on runners.
  SLEY, a weaver's reed.
STAKE, a small post.
  STEAK, broiled meat.
STA'TIONARY, fixed.
  STA'TIONERY, paper, pens,&c.
STRAIT, a narrow pass.
  STRAIGHT, not crooked.
TALE, a story.
  TAIL, the end.
VALE, a valley.
  VAIL, or VEIL, a curtain; a
      covering.
VANE, a weathercock.
  VAIN, proud; fruitless.
  VEIN, a blood vessel.
WALE, a ridge.
  WAIL, to lament.
WANE, to decrease.
  WAIN, a wagon.
WASTE, useless expenditure.
  WAIST, a part of the body.
WAIT, to stay for.
  WEIGHT, heaviness.
WAVE, a billow.   [off.
  WAIVE, to relinquish; to put

WORDS PRONOUNCED ALIKE.   11

Way, a manner; a road.
　Weigh, to ascertain weight.
Wade, to walk in water.
　Weighed, did weigh.

A as in *care*.

Air, the atmosphere.
　Heir, an inheritor.
Bare, naked.
　Bear, to support.
Fare, food; price of passage.
　Fair, beautiful; honest.
Glare, splendor.
　Glair, white of an egg.
Hare, an animal.
　Hair, of the head.
Pare, to shave off the outside.
　Pair, a couple.
　Pear, a fruit.
Stare, to gaze.
　Stair, a step.
Tare, an allowance in weight.
　Tear, to rend.
Their, belonging to them.
　There, in that place.
Ware, merchandise.
　Wear, to diminish by use.

A as in *mat*.

Adds, increases.
　Adz, a kind of hatchet.
An, a particle.
　Ann, or Anne, a woman's name.
An'nalist, a writer of annals.
　An'alyst, one who analyses.
An'ker, a liquid measure.
　An'chor, of a vessel.
As'perate, to make rough.
　As'pirate, to give the sound of *h*.　　　　[sure.
Cal'ender, to polish by pres-
　Cal'endar, an almanac.

Cal'lous, hardened; insensible.
　Cal'lus, a hardening of the fibres.
Can'did, frank; ingenuous.
　Can'died, turned to sugar.
Can'non, a large gun.
　Can'on, a law; a rule.
Can'vass, to examine.
　Can'vas, coarse cloth.
Dam, a wall across a stream.
　Damn, to condemn.
Dram, a small weight.
　Drachm, an ancient coin.
Jam, a conserve of fruit.
　Jamb, a supporter.
Lack, to want.
　Lac, a sort of gum.
Man'ner, mode; custom.
　Man'or, the land belonging to a nobleman.
Man'tle, a kind of cloak.
　Man'tel, the chimney piece.
Nag, a little horse.
　Knag, a knot in wood.
Nap, a short sleep.
　Knap, a protuberance.
Pal'let, a little bed.
　Pal'lette, or Pal'let, a painter's board.
Pan'nel, a rustic saddle.
　Pan'el, a square of wainscot.
Rap, to strike.
　Wrap, to fold.
Tacks, small nails.
　Tax, a rate imposed.

A as in *mart*.

Ant, an insect.
　Aunt, a relative.
Ark, a chest.
　Arc, part of a circle.
Bard, a poet.
　Barred, closed with bars.
Cast, to throw.　　　[doos.
　Caste, rank among the Hin-

Cast'er, a small bottle.
Cast'or, a beaver. [tion.
Draught, a drink; a delinea-
Draft, an order for money.
Hart, a sort of stag.
Heart, the seat of life.
Mark, a line; an impression.
Marque, license for reprisals.
Mar'shal, to arrange.
Mare'schal, a chief commander.
Mar'tial, warlike.

A as in all.

All, every one.
Awl, a sharp pointed tool.
Al'ter, to change.
Al'tar, that on which sacrifices were offered.
Au'gur, a soothsayer.
Au'ger, a boring tool.
Aught, anything.
Ought, should.
Ball, a spherical body.
Bawl, to cry out.
Bald, without hair.
Bawled, did bawl.
Call, to name.
Caul, a membrane.
Cauk, a sulphate of barytes.
Caulk, to stop leaks.
Cauf, a box for live fish.
Cough, a convulsion of the lungs.
Claws, talons.
Clause, part of a sentence.
Cord, a small rope.
Chord, a musical harmony.
Gall, bile; bitterness.
Gaul, a Frenchman.
Hall, a large room.
Haul, to pull.
Mall, a wooden hammer.
Maul, to beat; to bruise.

Naught, bad; worthless.
Nought, or Naught, nothing.
Paul, a man's name.
Pall, a covering for the dead.
Paws, a beast's feet.
Pause, a stop.
Psal'ter, a psalm book.
Salt'er, more salt.
Wall, a partition.
Wawl, to cry as a cat.

E as in mete.

Arrear', what is unpaid.
Arriere', last body of an army.
Be, to exist.
Bee, a stinging insect.
Beech, a tree.
Beach, the sea shore.
Beer, malt liquor.
Bier, a carriage for the dead.
Beet, an eatable root.
Beat, to strike.
Breach, a breaking.
Breech, of a gun.
Deer, an animal.
Dear, beloved; expensive.
Discreet', prudent.
Discrete', separate.
Feet, plural of *foot*.
Feat, an exploit.
Flee, to run away.
Flea, a biting insect.
Freeze, to congeal with cold.
Frieze, coarse woollen cloth
Greece, a country of Europe.
Grease, soft fat.
Heel, of the foot.
Heal, to cure.
Hear, to hearken.
Here, in this place.
Key, for a lock.
Quay, a mole, or wharf.

LEA, or LEY, a meadow.
LEE, opposite to the wind.
LEAF, part of a plant.
LIEF, willingly.
LEEK, a sort of onion.
LEAK, a slow escape of fluid.
MEED, reward.
MEDE, a native of Media.
MEAD, a liquor made from honey.
MEAN, paltry; low.
MIEN, air; deportment; aspect.
MEET, to come together.
MEAT, animal food.
METE, to measure.
ME'TER, one who measures.
ME'TRE, or ME'TER, measure; verse.
NEED, want; necessity.
KNEAD, to work dough.
PEACE, quiet; tranquillity.
PIECE, a part.
PEAK, a point; the top.
PIQUE, a grudge.
PEEL, a rind, or skin.
PEAL, a loud sound.
PEER, a nobleman.
PIER, the support of an arch or bridge.
PLEAS, excuses.
PLEASE, to gratify; to delight.
QUEEN, a king's wife.
QUEAN, a worthless woman.
REED, a plant.
READ, to peruse.
REEK, to emit vapor.
WREAK, to inflict.
SEE, to view; to behold.
SEA, the ocean.
SEAL, an impression.
CEIL, to make a ceiling.
SEAL'ING, fixing a seal.
CEIL'ING, of a room.
SEED, of a plant.
CEDE, to give up; to resign.

SEEM, to appear.
SEAM, a joint.
SEEN, viewed; beheld.
SEINE, a fishing net.
SCENE, a sight; a view.
SEER, a prophet.
SEAR, to burn; to wither.
CERE, to cover with wax.
SEIR, name of a mountain.
SEAS, great waters.
SEES, views; beholds.
SEIZE, to lay hold of.
SEN'IOR, elder.
SEIGN'OR, a lord.
SHAGREEN', a sort of fish skin.
CHAGRIN', vexation.
SHEER, pure; unmixed.
SHEAR, to clip.
SHIRE, a county.
SLEEVE, covering of the arm.
SLEAVE, untwisted silk.
STEEL, carbonized iron.
STEAL, to thieve; to pilfer.
SWEET, fitted to gratify the taste.
SUITE, [generally written and pronounced SUIT] retinue.
TEAL, a water fowl.
TEIL, a kind of tree.
TEAR, water from the eye.
TIER, a rank; a row.
TEAS, plural of *tea*.
TEASE, to torment.
TEEM, to abound.
TEAM, animals harnessed together.
THE, the definite article.
THEE, thyself.
WEEK, seven days.
WEAK, feeble; infirm.
WEEN, to think.
WEAN, to alienate.
WHEEL, a circular body.
WHEAL, a pustule.

E as in *met.*

Assent', agreement.
  Ascent', a going up.
Bell, a hollow sounding body.
  Belle, a gay young lady.
Ber'ry, a small fruit.
  Bur'y, to put under ground.
Bet'ter, superior.
  Bet'tor, one who lays wagers.
Bred, brought up.
  Bread, food made from corn.
Cen'sor, a critic.
  Cen'ser, a vessel for incense.
Conses'sion, a sitting together.
  Conces'sion, a yielding.
Fer'rule, a metallic band.
  Fer'ule, a wooden pallet.
Guessed, conjectured.
  Guest, a visitor.
Herd, a drove.
  Heard, did hear.
Inten'tion, design; purpose.
  Inten'sion, the act of straining.
Jes'sy, a woman's name.
  Jes'se, a man's name.
Led, conducted.
  Lead, a metal.
Les'sen, to make less.
  Les'son, a task; a lecture.
Lev'y, to raise money, &c.
  Lev'ee, a concourse; a bank.
Pen'cil, for writing.
  Pen'sile, hanging.
Pen'dent, hanging.
  Pen'dant, a small flag.
Red, a color.
  Read, did read.
Rest, repose.
  Wrest, to take violently.
Sell, to deliver for a price.
  Cell, a small cavity; a hut.
Sel'ler, one who sells.
  Cel'lar, a room under ground.

Sense, feeling; perception.
  Cense, a public tax.
Sent, participle of *send.*
  Cent, a coin.
  Scent, odor.
Ses'sion, a sitting.
  Ces'sion, a yielding.
Weth'er, a sheep.
  Weath'er, state of the air.
Wretch, a worthless person.
  Retch, to attempt to vomit.

I as in *pine.*

Bite, to seize with the teeth.
  Bight, one round of a cable.
By, with; near.
  Buy, to purchase.
Clime, a climate.
  Climb, to mount up.
Die, to expire; a stamp.
  Dye, to color.
Find, to discover.
  Fined, punished by fine.
Guise, appearance.
  Guys, ropes.
Hide, to conceal.
  Hied, did hie.
High, lofty.
  Hie, to make haste.
I, myself.
  Eye, the organ of sight.
I'll, I will.
  Isle, an island.
  Aisle, passage in a church.
Indite', to compose; to write.
  Indict', to accuse.
Lie, a wilful falsehood.
  Lye, liquor from wood ashes.
Li'er, one who lies down.
  Li'ar, one who tells lies.
Mi'ner, a worker in a mine.
  Mi'nor, one under age.
Mite, a little insect.
  Might, power; ability.

WORDS PRONOUNCED ALIKE.

Night, darkness.
Knight, a title of honor.
Pri'er, a close inquirer
Pri'or, former; previous.
Pries, inquires into.
Prize, a reward; a premium.
Pride, self-esteem.
Pried, past tense of *pry*.
Quire, 24 sheets of paper.
Choir, a band of singers.
Rice, a species of grain.
Rise, elevation.
Rime, hoar frost.
Rhyme, agreement of sound.
Rite, a ceremony.
Write, to form letters.
Right, straight; correct.
Wright, a workman.
Rye, a kind of grain.
Wry, crooked; distorted.
Side, the margin.
Sighed, did sigh.
Sine, a geometrical line.
Sign, a mark; a token.
Si'on, name of a mountain.
Ci'on, or Sci'on, a sprout.
Site, a situation.
Cite, to summon; to quote.
Sight, a view; a vision.
Size, bulk, magnitude.
Sighs, expressions of grief.
Slight, to neglect.
Sleight, an artful trick.
Stile, a stairway over a wall.
Style, manner of writing.
Tide, rush of water.
Tied, fastened.
Time, duration; season.
Thyme, an aromatic herb.
Tire, of a wheel; to weary.
Tyre, an ancient city.
Vi'al, or Phi'al, a small bottle.
Vi'ol, a musical instrument.
Vice, sin.
Vise, a kind of press.

I as in *pin*.

Been, participle of *be*.
Bin, a large box.
Brit'on, a native of Britain.
Brit'ain, England and Scotland.
Dis'cous, broad and flat.
Dis'cus, a quoit.
Fil'lip, to hit with the finger.
Phil'ip, a man's name.
Fil'ter, to strain liquors.
Phil'ter, a love charm.
Fis'sure, a cleft; a crack.
Fish'er, one who catches fish.
Gild, to adorn with gold.
Guild, the name of an association.
Gilt, adorned with gold.
Guilt, wickedness; sin.
Gris'ly, frightful; hideous.
Grizz'ly, somewhat gray.
Him, that man.
Hymn, a sacred song.
In, within.
Inn, a public-house.
Kill, to take away life.
Kiln, a sort of stove.
Limb, a member.
Limn, to draw or paint.
Links, connecting rings.
Lynx, an animal.
Mil'linery, goods of a milliner.
Mil'lenary, consisting of a thousand.
Mist, a fine rain.
Missed, did miss.
Nit, an insect's egg.
Knit, to weave with needles.
Rig'ger, one who rigs.
Rig'or, severity; sternness.
Ring, a circle; to sound.
Wring, to twist.
Sig'net, a seal.
Cyg'net, a young swan.

2

SILI′CIOUS, flinty.
  CILI′CIOUS, made of hair.
SIL′LY, simple; foolish.
  SCIL′LY, name of islands.
SIN′GLE, alone.
  CIN′GLE, a girth.
SINK, to fall down.
  CINQUE, five.
SIT, to rest on a seat.
  CIT, a citizen.
STICKS, small pieces of wood.
  STYX, a fabulous river.

O as in *no.*

BLOTE, to dry by smoke.
  BLOAT, to swell.
BOLL, a pod.
  BOLE, a kind of earth.
  BOWL, a basin.
BORE, to make a hole.
  BOAR, a male swine.
BORED, pierced.
  BOARD, a thin plank.
BORNE, carried; supported.
  BOURNE, a limit; a boundary.
BOW, an instrument.
  BEAU, a gay gentleman.
BROACH, to open; to utter.
  BROOCH, a jewel.
COLE, a sort of cabbage.
  COAL, a kind of fuel.
COARSE, rough; gross.
  COURSE, order; progress.
CORE, the inner part.
  CORPS, a body of troops.
DOE, a female deer.
  DOUGH, unbaked bread.
DOZE, to slumber.
  DOES, female deer.
FORE, preceding.
  FOUR, twice two.
FORTH, forward.
  FOURTH, next after the third.
GOURD, a vegetable production.
  GORED, pierced with a horn.

GROAN, to sigh deeply.
  GROWN, increased.
GRO′CER, a dealer in groceries
  GROSS′ER, coarser.
HO, a cry to attend.
  HOE, a garden tool.
HOARD, to lay up.
  HORDE, a tribe.
HOLE, a hollow place.
  WHOLE, entire; unbroken.
HOME, one's dwelling.
  HOLM, the evergreen oak.
LO, behold.
  LOW, not high.
LONE, retired; solitary.
  LOAN, to lend.
MOAN, to lament.
  MOWN, cut down.
MODE, manner.
  MOWED, cut down.
MOTE, a particle of dust.
  MOAT, a ditch.
NO, not so.
  KNOW, to understand.
NOSE, a part of the face.
  KNOWS, understands.
O! or OH! alas!
  OWE, to be indebted.
ODE, a poem.
  OWED, did owe.
ORE, unrefined metal.
  OAR, a pole to row with.
  O′ER, over.
POLE, a long stick.
  POLL, the head.
PORE, a minute tube.
  POUR, to cause to flow.
PORT, a harbor.
  PORTE, the Turkish court.
ROAN, a color.
  ROWN, impelled by oars.
  RHONE, a river in France.
ROADS, highways.
  RHODES, an island in the Levant

WORDS PRONOUNCED ALIKE. 17

Rode, did ride.
  Rowed, did row.
  Road, a way.
Roe, a female deer.
  Row, to impel with oars.
Roes, female deer.
  Rose, a flower.
Rome, a city of Italy.
  Roam, to wander; to rove.
Rote, a round of words.
  Wrote, did write.
Shone, did shine.
  Shown, exhibited.
Sloe, an animal; sort of plum.
  Slow, tardy; not quick.
So, in such manner.
  Sow, to scatter seed.
  Sew, to work with a needle.
Sold, did sell.
  Soled, furnished with a sole.
Sole, only.
  Soul, the immortal part of [man.
Sore, tender; painful.
  Soar, to rise high.
Sword, a weapon.
  Soared, did soar.
Throe, extreme agony.
  Throw, to cast; to heave.
Throne, a seat of state.
  Thrown, cast.
Toe, part of the foot.
  Tow, dressed hemp; to drag.
Told, did tell.
  Tolled, rung.
Tole, to allure.
  Toll, a kind of tax.

O as in *not*.

Cod'ling, a sort of apple.
  Cod'dling, parboiling.
Col'lar, covering for the neck.
  Chol'er, anger; rage.
Com'pliment, a token of respect.
  Com'plement, the full number.

Lock, a tuft of hair; a fastening.
  Loch, or Lough, a lake.
Not, a word of negation.
  Knot, a tie.
On'erary, fit for burdens.
  Hon'orary, conferring honor.
Proph'et, a foreteller.
  Prof'it, gain; advantage.
Sor'rel, a color.
  Sor'el, a buck in the third year.

O as in *move*.

Coom, a species of soot.
  Coomb, a measure.
To, unto; towards.
  Too, likewise.
  Two, a couple.

Oo as in *book*.

Hoop, of a barrel.
  Whoop, a shout.
Wood, the substance of trees.
  Would, was willing.

U as in *tube*.

Blue, a color.
  Blew, did blow.
Brews, does brew.
  Bruise, to hurt.
Brute, a beast.
  Bruit, noise; a report.
Crews, ships' companies.
  Cruise, to sail up and down.
Crew'el, a ball of yarn.
  Cru'el, savage; inhuman.
Due, owed.
  Dew, moisture.
Ewe, a female sheep.
  Yew, an evergreen tree.
Feud, a quarrel.
  Feod, a tenure.
Flue, a chimney pipe.
  Flew, did fly.

Hue, a color, or tint.
Hew, to cut down.
Hugh, a man's name.
Ju'ry, a set of men sworn to give a true verdict.
Jew'ry, the land of Judea.
Lu'sern, a lynx.
Lu'cerne, a sort of clover.
Mu'cous, slimy.
Mu'cus, a viscid fluid.
Mue, or Mew, to moult.
Mew, a fowl; an enclosure.
Mule, a beast.
Mewl, to cry like an infant.
New, fresh; novel.
Knew, understood.
Su'er, one who entreats.
Sew'er, a drain.
Threw, did throw.
Through, from end to end.
Use, to employ.
Ewes, female sheep.

U as in *tub.*

Bur'row, the cell of an animal.
Bor'ough, a corporation.
But, except.
Butt, to push with the head.
Chuff, a blunt clown.
Chough, a sea bird.
Cous'in, a relative.
Coz'en, to defraud; to cheat.
Cull'er, a selector.
Col'or, hue.
Cur'rent, a stream; flowing.
Cur'rant, a fruit.
Dun, to ask for a debt.
Done, finished.
Dust, powdered dirt.
Dost, contraction of *doest.*
Fun'gous, growing as a fungus.
Fun'gus, a spongy excrescence.

Furs, skins of beasts.
Furze, a wild shrub.
Just, honest; upright.
Joust, or Just, a mock fight.
Lump, a shapeless mass.
Lomp, a roundish fish.
Plum, a fruit.
Plumb, a leaden weight.
Ruff, a plaited collar.
Rough, coarse; uneven.
Rung, did ring.
Wrung, twisted.
Skull, the bone of the head.
Scull, a small boat.
Suck'er, a young shoot.
Suc'cor, relief; help.
Sum, the whole; the total.
Some, a part.
Sun, the fountain of light.
Son, a male child.
Sut'ler, a seller of provisions.
Subt'ler, more cunning.
Sut'tle, neat weight.
Subt'le, cunning; artful.
Tun, a large cask.
Ton, 20 hundred weight.
Won, gained.
One, a single thing.

Sound of *u* in *turn.*

Berth, a sleeping place in vessel.
Birth, coming into life.
Col'onel, a military officer.
Ker'nel, the seed.
Fur, soft hair.
Fir, a tree.
Herd, a drove or flock.
Heard, did hear.
Pearl, a precious substance.
Purl, to murmur.
Cir'cle, a round figure.
Sur'cle, a shoot; a twig.

SERGE, a kind of cloth.
  SURGE, a swelling sea.
URN, a vessel.
  EARN, to gain by labor.
WERT, past tense of *be*.
  WORT, an herb.

Sound of *ou* in *out*.

BOW, to bend.
  BOUGH, a branch.

BROWS, brinks, or edges.
  BROWSE, to eat shrubs.
FOUL, unclean.
  FOWL, a large bird.
OUR, belonging to us.
  HOUR, part of the day.
ROUT, a rabble; to defeat.
  ROUTE, a way.
TOUS'ER, one who tears.
  TOW'SER, the name of a dog.

CHAPTER II.

WORDS OF SIMILAR PRONUNCIATION.

1. *In this section, the first of each pair has the sound of* s, *and the other that of* z.

ADVICE', counsel.
  ADVISE', to give advice.
BOD'ICE, a kind of waistcoat.
  BOD'IES, material substances.
CEASE, to leave off.
  SEIZE, to take hold of.
COP'PICE, a wood of small growth.
  COP'IES, imitations.
DACE, a kind of fish.
  DAYS, plural of day.
DECEASE', death.
  DISSEIZE', to dispossess.
  DISEASE', sickness.
DEVICE', contrivance.
  DEVISE', to contrive.
DICE, small cubes.
  DIES, expires.
DIVERSE', different.
  DI'VERS, several.
DOSE, a portion of medicine.
  DOZE, to slumber.
FUSS, a bustle.
  FUZZ, to fly off in particles.

FRAN'CIS, a man's name.
  FRAN'CES, a woman's name.
GLA'CIERS, fields of ice. [glass.
  GLA'ZIERS, workmen who set
GRACE, favor; elegance.
  GRAZE, to eat grass.
GREECE, a country of Europe.
  GREASE, to smear with fat.
GRIST'LY, cartilaginous.
  GRIZZ'LY, somewhat gray.
HEARSE, a carriage for the dead.
  HERS, belonging to her.
HISS, the noise of a serpent.
  HIS, belonging to him.
INSI'TION, a grafting. [thing.
  INCIS'ION, a cut into any
JUICE, the fluid part.
  JEWS, Hebrews.
LEASE, a contract for houses, &c.
  LEES, dregs.
LOOSE, slack; untied.
  LOSE, to be deprived of.
MACE, a sort of spice.
  MAZE, an intricate place.

MUS'CLE, a shell fish.
MUZ'ZLE, to bind the mouth.
PEACE, quiet; tranquillity.
PEAS, a kind of pulse.
PENCE, coins; pennies.
PENS, writing implements.
PRE'CEDENT, an example.
PRES'IDENT, a governor.
PRICE, the estimated equivalent.
PRIZE, reward.
PRIN'CESS, the daughter of a king.
PRIN'CES, plural of *prince*.

RACE, a contest in running.
RAISE, to elevate.
RA'CER, a racing horse.
RA'ZOR, a tool for shaving.
RICE, a sort of grain.
RISE, to get up.
SINK, a drain.
ZINC, a metal.
SI'ON, }
ZI'ON, } the name of a mount.
TRUTH'S, belonging to truth.
TRUTHS, plural of *truth*.
TREA'TISE, an essay.
TREA'TIES, plural of *treaty*.

---

2. *The first of each pair ending in* ts.

AC'CIDENTS, unexpected events.
AC'CIDENCE, rudiments of grammar.
ACTS, deeds.
AXE, a chopping tool.
ADHE'RENTS, partisans.
ADHE'RENCE, fidelity.
ASSIST'ANTS, helpers.
ASSIST'ANCE, help.
ATTEND'ANTS, those who attend.
ATTEND'ANCE, attention; service.
CHANTS, sacred melodies.
CHANCE, fortune; accident.
CORRESPOND'ENTS, persons who correspond. [ment.
CORRESPOND'ENCE, agreeCOURTS, halls of justice.
COURSE, race; career.
DENTS, hollow marks.
DENSE, thick; close.
DEPEND'ENTS, subordinates.
DEPEND'ENCE, connection; reliance.

FAULTS, defects; errors.
FALSE, untrue.
IN'NOCENTS, harmless beings.
IN'NOCENCE, purity.
IN'STANTS, moments.
IN'STANCE, example.
INTENTS', purposes.
INTENSE', powerful.
PARTS, portions.
PARSE, to analyse sentences.
PA'TIENTS, sick people.
PA'TIENCE, forbearance.
PRES'ENTS, gifts.
PRES'ENCE, immediate view.
PRINTS, impressions.
PRINCE, a sovereign, or chief.
SCENTS, perfumes.
SENSE, feeling; reason.
SECTS, parties in religion.
SEX, male, or female.
TAL'ENTS, natural powers.
TAL'ONS, claws.
TENTS, canvas houses.
TENSE, strained to stiffness.

WORDS OF SIMILAR PRONUNCIATION.

3. *The first of each pair ending in* le.

A'BLE, of sufficient power.
A'BEL, a man's name.
BRI'DLE, a curb.
BRI'DAL, relating to marriage.
CHRON'ICLE, a record; history.
CHRON'ICAL, of long duration.
GEN'TLE, mild.
GEN'TILE, one who is not a Jew.
I'DLE, unemployed.
I'DOL, an image.

MED'DLE, to interfere.
MED'AL, a piece of metal stamped like a coin.
MET'TLE, spirit; courage.
MET'AL, iron, silver, &c.
PED'DLE, to sell as a pedler.
PED'AL, a part of an organ.
PRIN'CIPLE, elementary part.
PRIN'CIPAL, chief.
RAD'ICLE, a young root. [root.
RAD'ICAL, pertaining to the

4. *The first of each pair having an* f, *the latter a* v.

BEHOOF', advantage.
BEHOOVE', to be fit.
HALF, one of two equal parts.
HALVE, to part equally.
LEAF, green part of a plant.
LEAVE, permission.

OFF, at a distance.
OF, [sound of *v*,] concerning.
PLAIN'TIFF, the complainant.
PLAIN'TIVE, complaining.
REFEREE', one referred to.
REV'ERIE, irregular musing.

5. *The first ending in* er *or* or; *the latter in* ure *or* eur.

CAP'TOR, one who seizes.
CAP'TURE, a seizure.
CEN'SOR, a critic.
CEN'SURE, blame.
COUL'TER, a plough iron.
CUL'TURE, cultivation.
DICTA'TOR, one with absolute authority. [dictator.
DICTA'TURE, the office of a
FLEX'OR, a contracting muscle.
FLEX'URE, a bending.
GRAND'ER, more grand.
GRAND'EUR, magnificence.
IMPOS'TOR, a deceiver.
IMPOS'TURE, a cheat.
JEST'ER, one who jokes. [tion.
GES'TURE, a significant mo-

JOINT'ER, a long plane.
JOINT'URE, a wife's estate.
LEG'ISLATOR, a law giver.
LEG'ISLATURE, the assembly which enacts laws.
LIQ'UOR, a fluid.
LIQ'UEUR, a spirituous cordial.
OR'DER, method.
OR'DURE, filth.
PAS'TOR, a shepherd.
PAST'URE, grazing land.
SCULP'TOR, a carver.
SCULPT'URE, carved work.
TEN'OR, part in music; purport.
TEN'URE, manner of holding land.

6. *Words pronounced alike, excepting that the latter of each pair is aspirated*

Ar′dor, zeal.
Hard′er, firmer.
Ar′ras, tapestry.
Har′ass, to vex; to plague.
Art′less, without art. [rage.
Heart′less, wanting cou-
Awe, reverence.
Haw, fruit of the hawthorn.
Awl, a sharp pointed tool.
Haul, to pull.
Axe, a chopping tool.
Hacks, plural of *hack*.
Cow′ard, a fearful person.
Cow′herd, one who tends [cows.
Ed′dy, a whirlpool.
Head′y, rash; heedless.
Eight, a number.
Hate, to dislike.
E′ther, a volatile fluid.
Heath′er, the plant heath.
Err, to mistake.
Her, that woman.
Eye, the organ of sight.
High, tall; lofty.
Isl′ands, lands in the sea.
High′lands, elevated regions.

Owe, to be indebted.
Hoe, a gardening tool.
Owes, is indebted.
Hose, stockings, &c.
Own, to acknowledge.
Hone, a whetstone.
Wales, part of Great Britain.
Whales, large sea animals.
Ware, merchandise.
Where, in what place.
Way, a road.
Whey, the thin part of curdled milk.
Weal, prosperity.
Wheel, of a machine.
Weath′er, state of the air.
Wheth′er, which of the two.
Wen, a fleshy excrescence.
When, at what time.
Wet, moist.
Whet, to sharpen.
Wile, a trick.
While, as long as.
Wine, a fermented liquor.
Whine, to moan.
Wit, shrewdness; humor.
Whit, a bit.

---

7. *Words spelled and pronounced alike, excepting that the latter of each pair begins with the sound of H.*

Ail, to affect unpleasantly.
Hail, frozen rain.
Air, the atmosphere.
Hair, covering of the head.
Aft, behind.
Haft, a handle.
Ale, a malt liquor.
Hale, strong; healthy.
All, every one.
Hall, a large room.

Al′ter, to change.
Hal′ter, a rope.
Am, I am.
Ham, a kind of smoked meat.
And, also.
Hand, part of the body.
Ank′er, a liquid measure.
Hank′er, to long after.
Ar′bor, a bower.
Har′bor, a shelter.

ARK, a chest.
  HARK! listen.
ARM, a limb; a branch.
  HARM, hurt; mischief.
AR'ROW, a pointed weapon.
  HAR'ROW, a farming implement.
ART, skill; a trade.
  HART, a male deer.
AS, like.
  HAS, possesses.
ASH, a timber tree.
  HASH, minced meat.
ASP, a serpent.
  HASP, a fastening.
AT, in; near to.
  HAT, cover for the head.
ATE, did eat.
  HATE, to dislike.
AUNT, a relative.
  HAUNT, to frequent.
EAR, the organ of hearing.
  HEAR, to hearken.
EAT, to consume.
  HEAT, warmth.
EAVES, the edges of the roof.
  HEAVES, throws.
EDGE, the sharp border.
  HEDGE, a fence of bushes.
EEL, a fish.
  HEEL, part of the foot.

ELL, a measure of length.
  HELL, the eternal abode of the wicked.
ELM, a tree.
  HELM, that by which a vessel is steered.
EW'ER, a kind of pitcher.
  HEW'ER, one who cuts down.
IDES, a Roman term of time.
  HIDES, skins of animals.
ILL, badly; unwell.
  HILL, a mount.
IRE, rage; anger.
  HIRE, wages.
IS, it is.
  HIS, belonging to him.
IT, that thing.
  HIT, to strike.
OAR, a pole to row with.
  HOAR, white.
OLD, aged; ancient.
  HOLD, to keep; to possess.
O'RAL, delivered by mouth.
  HO'RAL, relating to the hour.
O'SIER, a sort of willow.
  HO'SIER, a dealer in hosiery.
OT'TER, an amphibious animal.
  HOT'TER, warmer.
OWL, a bird.
  HOWL, to cry as a dog.

---

8 *The first of each pair having the sound of* **a** *in* **mat**; *the second that of* **e** *in* **met**.

ABOLI'TION, an abolishing.
  EBULLI'TION, a boiling.
ACCEPT', to take; to receive.
  EXCEPT', to leave out.
ACCESS', an approach.
  EXCESS', more than enough.
AF'FABLE, ready to converse.
  EF'FABLE; utterable.

AFFECT', to move the passions.
  EFFECT', consequence.
ASSAY', to test or try.
  ESSAY', to attempt.
AR'RANT, infamous.
  ER'RANT, wandering.
CAR'AT, a small weight.
  CA'RET, a mark in writing.

Catch, to seize.
  Ketch, a kind of vessel.
Expanse′, an extension.
  Expense′, cost; charge.
Extant′, in being.
  Extent′, space; length.
Mus′cat, a sweet grape.
  Mus′ket, a small gun.

Par′ish, a district.
  Perish, to die.
Rad′ish, an eatable root.
  Red′dish, somewhat red.
Sal′ary, wages.
  Cel′ery, a vegetable.
Tar′rier, a delayer.
  Ter′rier, a sort of dog.

---

9. *Several sounds of* a *and* e *compared.*

Apprize′, to set a price on.
  Apprise′, to give notice.
Car′at, a small weight.
  Ca′ret, a mark in writing.
Chair, a movable seat.
  Cheer, to encourage.
Command′, to order.
  Commend′, to praise.
Du′al, expressing two.
  Du′el, combat between two.
Fair, beautiful.
  Fear, dread.
Ha′lo, a bright circle.
  Hal′low, to make holy.
Ha′ven, a harbor.
  Hea′ven, the state of the blessed.
Med′lar, a fruit.
  Med′dler, a busy-body.

Mo′dal, formal.
  Mod′el, a pattern.
Pal′ace, a princely house.
  Pal′las, a heathen deity.
Pal′ate, the roof of the mouth.
  Pal′let, a little bed.
Par′sonage, the house of a par-[son.
  Per′sonage, an important person.
Rai′sin, a dried grape.
  Rea′son, a faculty; a cause.
Rare, scarce.
  Rear, the hinder troop.
Star′ling, a bird.
  Ster′ling, genuine.
Wear, to consume by use.
  Were, past tense of *be.*
Yarn, spun wool. [thy.
  Yearn, to feel strong sympa-

---

10. *The first of each pair having the sound of* e *in* mete.

Bea′con, a kind of signal.
  Beck′on, to make signs.
Cavalier′, a horseman.
  Cav′iller, a captious person.
Ce′rate, salve made of wax.
  Ser′rate, formed like a saw.
Cleav′er, a butcher's tool.
  Clev′er, expert.

Creek, a small bay.
  Crick, a cramp.
Critique′, a criticism.
  Crit′ic, a judge of literature.
Deform′ity, unsightly shape.
  Difform′ity, variety of form.
Descent′, a going down.
  Dissent′, disagreement.

WORDS OF SIMILAR PRONUNCIATION.

Eas'ter, the anniversary of our Lord's resurrection.
Es'ther, a woman's name.
Elic'it, to draw out.
Illic'it, unlawful.
Elude', to escape from.
Illude', to deceive.
Erup'tion, a breaking out.
Irrup'tion, a breaking into.
Impe'rial, of an emperor.
Empyr'eal, pure; aerial.

Inge'nious, skilful.
Ingen'uous, open; candid.
Least, smallest.
Lest, for fear.
Leap'er, a jumper.
Lep'er, a leprous person.
Nei'ther, not either.
Neth'er, lower.
Tierce, [sometimes pronounced like *terse*,] a kind of cask.
Terse, neat; elegant.

---

11. *Sounds of* e *and* i *compared.*

Coun'sel, advice.
Coun'cil, an assembly.
Def'erence, respect.
Dif'ference, disagreement.
Em'inent, conspicuous; noted.
Im'minent, threatening.
Posses'sion, property.
Posi'tion, situation.

Rab'bet, a joint in carpentry.
Rab'bit, a small animal.
Set, to place.
Sit, to take seat.
Shell'ing, taking off shells.
Shil'ling, twelve pence.
Wheth'er, which of the two.
Whith'er, to what place.

---

12. *The first in each pair having the sound of* o *in* more.

Board'er, one who boards.
Bor'der, a boundary.
Boat, a small vessel.
Bought, purchased.
Borne, carried; supported.
Born, brought into life.
Bin'ocle, a kind of telescope.
Bin'nacle, a compass box.
Boar, a male swine.
Boor, a clownish person.
Cola'tion, the act of straining.
Colla'tion, a repast. [hair.
Comb, an instrument for the
Coomb, a corn measure.
Doe, a female deer.
Do, to perform.
Doge, a magistrate of Venice.
Dodge, to start aside.

Do'lor, grief.
Dol'lar, a coin.
Dome, an arched roof.
Doom, a sentence.
Folks, people.
Fox, a cunning animal.
Grope, to feel about.
Group, a cluster.
Grove, a small wood.
Groove, a channel.
Hoarse, having a rough voice.
Horse, an animal.
Loam, a rich earth.
Loom, a weaver's frame.
Mourn, to lament.
Morn, morning.
Poul'try, fowls.
Pal'try, mean.

13. *Several sounds of o and other vowels compared.*

Bar′on, a nobleman.
  Bar′ren, unfruitful.
Car′rot, a root.
  Car′at, a weight.
Cof′fer, a chest.
  Cough′er, one who coughs.
Con′sort, a companion. [tion.
  Con′cert, union; combina-
Cap′itol, a public edifice.
  Cap′ital, principal; chief.
Conforma′tion, shape.
  Confirma′tion, strengthening.
Depos′itory, a place of safe keeping.
  Depos′itary, a person to whom any thing is committed. [spirits.
Ex′orcise, to cast out evil
  Ex′ercise, employment.
Fond′ling, one caressed.
  Found′ling, an infant found.

Glut′tonous, greedy.
  Glu′tinous, sticky.
Grot, a pleasant cave.
  Groat, four pence.
Gam′bol, a frolic.
  Gam′ble, to practise gaming.
Hol′low, a cavity; not solid.
  Hal′low, to make holy.
I′dol, an image; a favorite.
  I′dle, not industrious.
Op′posite, contrary.
  Ap′posite, suitable; proper.
Or′acle, counsel supernaturally given.
  Au′ricle, the external ear.
Pi′lot, he who guides a ship.
  Pi′late, a man's name.
Rot, to decay.
  Wrought, worked.
Sym′bol, a sign; a type.
  Cym′bal, a musical instrument.

---

14. *The first in each pair having the sound of o in move.*

Brood, to sit over.
  Brewed, did brew.
Choose, to select.
  Chews, masticates.
Do, to perform.
  Due, owed. [knot.
Noose, to catch with a running
  News, tidings.

Poor, not rich; lean.
  Pure, clear; innocent.
Rood, a measure of land.
  Rude, rustic.
Boot′y, plunder. [ance.
  Beau′ty, pleasing appear-
Sho′er, a fastener of shoes.
  Sure, certain.

---

15. *Words which have some similarity in pronunciation, but which ought to be carefully distinguished.*

Arraign′, to bring to trial.
  Arrange′, to put in order.
Harangue′, a formal oration.

Ar′rant, infamous; bad in a high degree.
  Er′rand, a message.

WORDS OF SIMILAR PRONUNCIATION. 27

BAL'LAD, a song.
BAL'LOT, secret voting.
BEE'TLE, an insect.
BEA'DLE, a parish officer.
BEA'GLE, a small hound.
BILE, a liquid substance.
BOIL, to bubble by heat.
BREATH, respiration.
BREADTH, width.
CAREER', a course.
CAR'RIER, one who carries.
CEN'TAURY, a plant.
CEN'TURY, a hundred years.
SEN'TRY, a guard.
CHOKE, to suffocate.
JOKE, a jest.
CLOSE, to shut; to end.
CLOTHES, garments.
CLOTH, a texture of wool, &c.
CLOTHE, to dress.
COALS, plural of *coal.*
COLDS, plural of *cold.*
COAT, a garment.
QUOTE, to cite.
COL'ORS, plural of *color.*
COLURES', geographical circles.
COM'EDY, a play.
COM'ITY, civility.
COMMIT'TEE, a body of managers.
COM'FORT, convenience; ease.
COM'FIT, a dry sweetmeat.
CONCUR', to agree.
CON'QUER, to overcome.
COR'PORAL, an officer.
CORPO'REAL, not spiritual.
CUR'RIER, a leather-dresser.
COU'RIER, a messenger.
CUR'RANT, a small berry.
COURANT', a newspaper.
DESCENT', going down.
DE'CENT, becoming.
DESERT', to forsake.
DESSERT', fruit, &c. after dinner.

DILU'TION, making weaker.
DELU'SION, a deception.
DIRE, dismal.
DY'ER, one who dyes.
DISEASE', a disorder.
DECEASE', death.
DISA'BLE, to weaken.
DISHABILLE', an undress.
DOE, a female deer.
DAW, a chattering bird.
DRONE, an idle bee.
DROWN, to suffocate in water.
DRAWN, pulled.
EAR, a member.
YEAR, a twelvemonth.
EAST, where the sun rises.
YEAST, barm.
EI'THER, one of the two.
E'THER, a volatile fluid.
E'RA, a fixed point of time.
HEAR'ER, one who hears.
EX'ECUTER, one who performs.
EXEC'UTOR, a trustee.
ELIS'ION, act of cutting off.
ELYS'IAN, very delightful.
EW'ER, a kind of pitcher.
YOUR, belonging to you.
EM'ANANT, flowing from.
EM'INENT, high; exalted.
FILE, a rasping tool.
FOIL, to defeat.
VILE, base; wicked.
FLOUR, meal.
FLOWER, a blossom.
FOUGHT, contended.
FAULT, error; mistake.
GAUL, a Frenchman.
GOAL, a starting place.
GAOL, a prison.
GE'NIUS, a peculiar talent.
GE'NUS, a kind.
HIRE, wages.
HIGH'ER, loftier.
HOAR, white.
HO'ER, one who hoes.

Ho′ly, free from sin.
　Whol′ly, entirely.
　Hol′ly, an evergreen tree.
I′dol, an image.
　I′dle, unemployed.
　I′dyl, a pastoral poem.
Im′potent, weak; powerless.
　Im′pudent, insolent.
　Imper′tinent, intrusive.
Isle, an island.
　Oil, an unctuous matter.
Incide′, to cut into.
　In′side, within.
Incite′, to urge.
　In′sight, discernment.
Jest, a joke.
　Just, nearly.
Kine, cows.
　Coin, stamped money.
　Quoin, a kind of wedge.
Lease, a kind of contract.
　Leash, a line, or strap.
　Leech, a bloodsucker.
Lick′erish, dainty; nice.
　Lic′orice, a sweet root.
Line, a string; a row.
　Loin, part of the body.
Lin′eament, a feature.
　Lin′iment, an ointment.
Light′ning, the flash which precedes thunder.
　Light′ening, unloading.
Liv′er, one of the entrails.
　Li′vre, a French coin.
Loath, unwilling.
　Loathe, to dislike.
Luke, a man's name.
　Look, to see.
　Luck, chance or fortune.
Lore, learning.
　Low′er, deeper.
Lyre, a musical instrument.
　Li′ar, a teller of lies.
Marsh, a swamp.
　Mash, to crush.
　Mesh, the opening in a net.

Mar′vel, to wonder.
　Mar′ble, a sort of stone.
Mat′in, belonging to the morning.
　Mat′ting, stuff for mats.
Mes′sage, an errand.
　Mess′uage, a house and grounds.
Me′tre, verse.
　Me′teor, a fiery body.
Min′ister, an agent.
　Min′ster, a monastery.
Mis′sile, thrown by hand.
　Mis′sal, a mass book.
　Mis′le, to rain in small drops.
More, a greater quantity.
　Mow′er, one who mows.
Mount′ain, a great hill.
　Moun′ting, rising.
Mus′lin, fine linen.　[mouth.
　Muz′zling, tying up the
Mus′cat, a sweet grape.
　Musk′cat, an animal.
Nick, a notch.
　Niche, a hollow for a statue.
Oft′en, frequently.
Or′phan, a parentless child.
Or′dinance, a law.
　Ord′nance, cannon.
　Or′donnance, disposition of figures in a picture.
Or′ison, a prayer.
　Hori′zon, the line which bounds the sight.
Pelisse′, a coat, or habit.
　Police′, internal government.
Petrifac′tion, conversion into stone.
　Putrefac′tion, decomposition.
Pint, a measure.
　Point, the small end.
Pistole′, a Spanish coin.
　Pis′tol, a small hand gun.
Pop′ulace, the common people.
　Pop′ulous, full of people.

Precedents

PRE′SCIOUS, foreknowing.
  PREC′IOUS, of great value.
PROPH′ECY, a prediction.
  PROPH′ESY, to predict.
PUM′ACE, ground apples.
  PUM′ICE, a kind of cinder.
RE′AL, true; genuine.
  RAIL, a bar.
  REEL, to stagger.
REL′ICT, a widow.
  REL′IC, that which remains.
RID′ICULE, derision.
  RET′ICULE, a net bag.
ROAR, to cry with great voice.
  ROW′ER, one who rows.
RUM, an alcoholic liquor.
  RHOMB, a quadrangular figure.
SAT′YR, a sylvan god.
  SAT′IRE, pointed remark.
SE′RIES, succession; order.
  SE′RIOUS, solemn; grave.
  SIR′IUS, the dog-star.
SHAWL, a garment.
  SHALL, will.
SMILE, a look of pleasure.
  SIM′ILE, a comparison.
SOAR, to rise.
  SOW′ER, one who sows.

STAT′UTE, a law.
  STAT′UE, an image.
  STAT′URE, height of a person.
SUR′PLUS, remainder.
  SUR′PLICE, a white robe.
TALC, a transparent mineral.
  TALK, to converse.
TOW′ER, a strong building.
  TOUR, a journey.
TRACK, a path.
  TRACT, a short treatise.
TIN′CAL, a mineral.
  TIN′KLE, a sharp quick noise.
TREBLE, a part in harmony.
  TRIPLE, or TREBLE, consisting of three.
TROUGH, a long vessel.
  TROTH, faith; fidelity.
  THROUGH, from side to side.
  THOR′OUGH, complete.
VER′DURE, greenness.
  VER′GER, a mace bearer.
VIR′GIN, a girl.
  VERG′ING, tending.
YOU, thyself.
  YEW, a tree.

---

16. *Words often confounded either from giving the sound of* r *where it does not belong, or omitting it where it should be given.*

AH! an exclamation.
  ARE, plural of is.
ALMS, gifts to the poor.
  ARMS, weapons.
AWE, reverence.
  OR, a conjunction.
BAA, the cry of a sheep.
  BAR, an obstacle.
BALM, a plant.
  BARM, yeast.
BO′A, a sort of serpent.
  BOAR, a male swine.

BUST, a half-length statue.
  BURST, to break open.
CALVE, to bring forth a calf.
  CARVE, to cut.
CIN′NA, a Roman consul.
  SIN′NER, an evil doer.
DUST, powdered substances.
  DURST, dared.
FA′THER, a male parent.
  FAR′THER, more distant.
FEL′LOW, a companion.
  FELL′ER, one who cuts down.

Foment', to excite.
Ferment', to work as beer.
For'mally, ceremoniously.
For'merly, in times past.
Fust, a mouldy smell.
First, foremost.
Gnaw, to eat by degrees.
Nor, neither.
Go'a, an Indian island.
Gore, clotted blood.
Laud, to praise.
Lord, a nobleman.
La'va, discharge from a volcano.
La'ver, a washing vessel.
Lawn, fine linen.
Lorn, forsaken.
Ma, mamma.
Mar, to spoil.
Man'na, a kind of gum.
Man'ner, method.
Moss, a vegetable.
Morse, a sea-horse.
No'ah, a man's name.
Nore, the entrance of the Thames.

Pa, papa.
Par, equality.
Palm'er, a pilgrim.
Par'ma, a city of Italy.
Pass, a passage.
Parse, to analyse grammatically
Peti'tion, supplication.
Parti'tion, separation.
Pil'low, a cushion for the head
Pil'lar, a column.
Pus, purulent matter.
Purse, a money bag.
Quar'tan, fourth day ague.
Quar'tern, a fourth of a pint.
Quo'ta, a proper share.
Quo'ter, one who quotes.
Sought, searched after.
Sort, a kind.
Stalk, a stem.
Stork, a bird.
Stra'ta, layers.
Straight'er, less crooked.
Taught, instructed.
Tort, mischief.

There is an error, which may be noticed in this connection, that should be carefully avoided; it consists in inserting an *r* between words, when the former ends and the latter begins with a vowel. Thus the sentence, "a boa is a sort of serpent," would be read by some as if it were, "a *boar* is a sort of serpent."

---

17. *Dissyllables spelled alike, but differing in accent.*

Signification when the accent is on the first syllable.		Signification when the accent is on the second syllable.
Not present.	Absent,	To keep away.
An abridgment.	Abstract,	To take from.
Stress of voice.	Accent,	To mark the accents.
A particle added to a word.	Affix,	To subjoin.
An increase.	Augment,	To increase.
The eighth month.	August,	Grand.
A great gun.	Bombard,	To attack with bombs.
A partner.	Colleague,	To unite with.
A short prayer.	Collect,	To gather.

WORDS OF SIMILAR PRONUNCIATION.

Signification when the accent is on the first syllable.		Signification when the accent is on the second syllable.
An agreement.	COMPACT,	Firm; solid.
A confederacy.	COMPLOT,	To conspire.
Behavior.	COMPORT,	To suit.
A mixture.	COMPOUND,	To mingle.
A bolster of linen used in surgery.	COMPRESS,	To force together.
A musical performance.	CONCERT,	To contrive together.
A mass formed of parts.	CONCRETE,	To unite into one body.
Behavior.	CONDUCT,	To manage; to guide.
A boundary.	CONFINE,	To limit; to restrain.
A struggle.	CONFLICT,	To contest.
A sweetmeat.	CONSERVE,	To candy fruit.
Companion.	CONSORT,	To associate with.
Thing contained.	CONTENT,	Satisfied.
A dispute.	CONTEST,	To dispute.
A bargain.	CONTRACT,	To shorten; to bargain.
Opposition.	CONTRAST,	To put in opposition.
Discourse.	CONVERSE,	To talk.
One who embraces a new opinion.	CONVERT,	To turn from one condition to another.
A person found guilty.	CONVICT,	To prove guilty.
Attendance for defence.	CONVOY,	To accompany by sea.
A tune.	DESCANT,	To discourse.
A compend.	DIGEST,	To concoct.
A body guard.	ESCORT,	To guard on a journey.
An attempt.	ESSAY,	To endeavor.
Commodity sent out.	EXPORT,	To carry out of the country.
Essence drawn out.	EXTRACT,	To draw out.
A tumult.	FERMENT,	To be in commotion.
Contrivance.	FORECAST,	To form schemes.
Anticipation.	FORETASTE,	To taste before.
Happening often.	FREQUENT,	To visit often.
Signification.	IMPORT,	To bring into.
Mark; stamp.	IMPRESS,	To print.
Printer's name in the title of a book.	IMPRINT,	To fix in the mind.
A kind of perfume.	INCENSE,	To enrage.
Wood formed to inlay.	INLAY,	To insert.
Natural impulse.	INSTINCT,	Animated.
Insolence	INSULT,	To treat with contempt.
A thing acted on.	OBJECT,	To oppose.
Complete.	PERFECT,	To finish; to complete.

THE SCHOLAR'S COMPANION.

Signification when the accent is on the first syllable.		Signification when the accent is on the second syllable.
A particle put before a word.	Prefix,	To put before.
An introduction.	Prelude,	To introduce.
A prognostic.	Presage,	To forebode.
A declaration against.	Protest,	To declare solemnly.
Passage back.	Regress,	To go back.
Sale by small lots.	Retail,	To sell in small lots.
One under dominion.	Subject,	To put under.
A kind of verbal noun.	Supine,	Negligent; careless.
The family name.	Surname,	To add another name.
A view; measure.	Survey,	To overlook.
Pain; anguish.	Torment,	To vex; to torture.
A conveyance.	Transfer,	To convey; to remove.
A vessel of carriage.	Transport,	To banish; to enrapture.
A negligent dress.	Undress,	To take off the clothes.

Words spelled alike, but different both in accent and sound.

Cem'ent, sticky matter.
   Cement', to agglutinate.
Con'jure, to practise charms.
   Conjure', to intreat.
Des'ert, a wilderness.
   Desert', to forsake.
En'trance, place of entering.
   Entrance', to put into an ecstasy.
Ex'ile, banishment.
   Exile', slender.
Gal'lant, high spirited.
   Gallant', attentive to ladies.
Min'ute, a short space of time.
   Minute', small.

Pres'ent, a gift.
   Present', to offer.
Prod'uce, product.
   Produce', to bring forth.
Prog'ress, motion forward.
   Progress', to advance.
Proj'ect, a scheme.
   Project', to jut out.
Reb'el, a revolter.
   Rebel', to rise against authority.
Rec'ord, a register.
   Record', to put on record.
Rev'el, a noisy feast.
   Revel', to retract.
Traj'ect, a ferry.
   Traject', to cast through.

At'tribute, quality.
   Attrib'ute, to ascribe.
Inval'id, of no force.
   In'valid, a sick person.
O'vercharge, too high a charge.
   Overcharge', to oppress.

Prec'edent, an example.
   Prece'dent, going before.
Prem'ises, positions assumed.
   Premi'ses, explains before.
Sev'erer, one who separates.
   Sever'er, more rigorous.

WORDS OF SIMILAR PRONUNCIATION. 33

'18. *Words spelled alike but pronounced differently.*

1st. *In which* ow *has the sound of* o *in* so, *or of* ou *in* thou.

Bow, an instrument to shoot arrows.
Bow, to bend; to stoop.
Lower, to bring down.
Lower, to appear dark.

Mow, to cut down.
Mow, a heap of hay or grain.
Row, a rank or file.
Row, a tumult; an uproar.
Sow, to scatter seed.
Sow, a female swine.

2d. *In which* s *has the sound of* s *or of* z.

Abuse′, the ill use of a thing.
Abuse′, to use ill.
As, a Roman coin.
As, so; like.
Close, shut fast; narrow.
Close, the conclusion.
Cruise, a small cup.
Cruise, a voyage for plunder.
Dif′fuse, scattered.
Diffuse′, to spread.
Excuse′, an apology.
Excuse′, to pardon.
Grease, soft fat.
Grease, to smear with grease.

House, a place of abode.
House, to shelter.
Lease, a kind of contract.
Lease, to glean.
Misuse′, a bad use.
Misuse′, to misemploy.
Mouse, a little animal.
Mouse, to catch mice.
Ref′use, that which is rejected.
Refuse′, to reject; to deny.
Resign′, to sign again.
Resign′, to relinquish.
Rise, beginning; increase.
Rise, to ascend.
Use, purpose; convenience.
Use, to employ

3d. *Various.*

A′te, the goddess of mischief.
Ate, devoured.
Ax′es, plural of axe.
Ax′es, plural of axis.
Cour′tesy, civility.
Courtesy [*kurt′se*], the reverence made by women.
Deni′er, one who denies.
Denier′, a French coin.

Does, female deer.
Does, [*duz*] doth.
Dove, did dive.
Dove, a bird.
Gill, a quarter of a pint.
Gill, a fish's organ of respiration.
Gout, a disease.
Gout, [*goo*] taste.

Hin′der, to prevent.
Hind′er, backward.
In′timate, to hint.
In′timate, familiar.
I′rony, contrary meaning.
Ir′ony, partaking of iron.
Job, a piece of work.
Job, a man's name.
Lead, to conduct.
Lead, a metal.
Learn′ed, intelligent; skilful.
Learned, did learn.
Live, alive.
Live, to exist.
Lives, plural of life.
Lives, does live.
Manes, plural of mane.
Ma′nes, departed spirits.
Mod′erate, to regulate.
Mod′erate, temperate.
Num′ber, reckoning.
Numb′er, more torpid.
Pol′ish, to brighten.
Po′lish, belonging to Poland.
Poll, the head; a tax.
Poll, a parrot's name.
Put, to place.
Put, a clown.

Ra′ven, a large black bird.
Rav′en, to devour greedily.
Read, to peruse.
Read, perused.
Read′ing, perusing.
Read′ing, a town.
Sep′arate, to part.
Sep′arate, disjoined.
Sew′er, one who sews.
Sew′er, a drain.
Sing′er, one who sings.
Sin′ger, one who singes.
Slough, a deep miry place.
Slough, to fall off.
Staves, plural of staff.
Staves, parts of a cask.
Tar′ry, to wait; to stay.
Tar′ry, smeared with tar.
Tear, water from the eye.
Tear, to rend.
Ti′er, one who ties.
Tier, a long row.
Wind, air in motion.
Wind, to twist.
Wound, twisted.
Wound, a hurt.
Wors′ted, woollen yarn.
Worst′ed, defeated.

CHAPTER III.

EQUIVOCAL WORDS: *or words whose different significations have either no connection with each other, or none which can be easily traced.*

NOTE.—As the words of our language have been derived from various other languages, it has often happened that two or more words entirely distinct in their origin and signification, have taken the same spelling and pronunciation in English. Thus, from the Saxon word *beorcan*, is derived the English word *bark*, signifying to make the noise of dogs; from the French word *barque*, is derived *bark*, a vessel; and from the Danish word *bark*, is derived *bark*, the covering of a tree. Words which thus have the same form while they are of different derivation and signification, are sometimes called *paronymous*. Many of the words in the following chapter are of this class. The remaining words are such as have significations which are very different, although they are to be traced to a common origin.

☞ The abbreviation *a.* before a word, stands for adjective; *adv.* for adverb; *conj.* for conjunction; *part.* for participle; *prep.* for preposition; *pron.* for pronoun; *s.* for substantive; and *v.* for verb.

ADDRESS', *v.* to accost.—*s.* deportment; dexterity, direction of a letter; a speech.
AIR, a melody; that which we breathe; appearance.
AN'GLE, *s.* a corner.—*v.* to fish with a rod and hook.
APPA'RENT, plain, visible; seeming, not real.
ARCH, *s.* a curved roof.—*a.* mirthful; chief.
ART, *s.* skill.—*v.* thou art.
AX'IS, that on which any thing revolves; an animal.
BACH'ELOR, an unmarried man; a university degree.
BAIL, a surety; the handle of a bucket, or kettle.
BAIT, *s.* a temptation; refreshment.—*v.* to worry with dogs.
BALL, a sphere; an entertainment of dancing.
BANK, a heap of earth; a financial institution.
BAR, a rail used to stop a passage; the place where the criminal stands in court.
BARK, *s.* the rind of a tree; a stout vessel.—*v.* to make the noise of dogs.
BASTE, to pour the dripping over roasting meat; to sew slightly.
BASE, *a.* vile, worthless; *s.* the foundation.
BAT, a stick to strike a ball; a flying animal.
BAY, *s.* a tree; a small gulf; a color.—*v.* to bark.
BEAM, a large piece of timber; a ray of light.
BEAR, *v.* to carry.—*s.* a rough savage animal.
BECOME', to enter into a new condition; to befit.

Bee'tle, an insect; a heavy mallet.
Bill, the beak of a bird; an account of money.
Bil'let, a small stick of wood; a note.
Bit, a small piece; the iron put into a horse's mouth; a boring tool.
Blade, the cutting part of a tool; a leaf of grass.
Blow, *s.* a stroke.—*v.* to puff; to blossom.
Board, *s.* a thin plank.—*v.* to live with another for a certain price.
Boot, covering for the leg; profit; advantage.
Bound, *s.* a limit; a leap.—*v.* did bind.
Bowl, *s.* a concave dish; a ball.—*v.* to roll.
Box, *s.* a tree; a case, or chest; a slap on the ear.—*v.* to fight with the fists.
Brace, *v.* to strengthen, to make firm.—*s.* a couple.
Brake, a fern; a thicket; an instrument for breaking flax, or hemp; the lever by which a pump is worked; the lever by which the wheels of a carriage, or railway car, are checked.
Brazier, or Brasier, a worker in copper; a pan to hold coals.
Brook, *s.* a rivulet.—*v.* to endure.
Butt, *s.* a liquid vessel; a kind of hinge; a person made the object of sport.—*v.* to strike with the head.
Calf, the young of a cow; the thick part of the leg.
Can, *s.* a metallic cup, or bottle.—*v.* to be able.
Cape, a headland; a collar-piece.
Ca'per, *v.* to skip and jump.—*s.* a bud of a plant.
Card, *s.* a piece of stiff paper; a kind of advertisement.—*v.* to comb wool.
Case, a covering; state of things; variation of nouns.
Cast, *v.* to throw; to form in a mould.—*s.* a moulded form.
Cat'aract, a waterfall; a disease of the eye.
Charge, care; command; accusation; expense; attack.
Chase, to hunt.—[Enchase] to engrave with punches.
Chord, a line connecting the extremities of an arch; harmony of sounds; the string of a musical instrument.
Cleave, to adhere; to separate; to split off.
Club, a heavy stick; an association.
Cock'le, a shell fish; a weed.
Colla'tion, comparison; a repast between full meals.
Comb, an instrument for the hair; the crest of a cock; the waxen structure in which bees put honey.
Commit', to intrust; to be guilty of a crime; to send to prison.
Concord'ance, agreement; an index to words in the Bible.
Consist'ency, agreement with one's self; thickness.
Cop'y, a model to be imitated; an imitation.
Cord, a small rope; a measure of wood.

Corn, *s.* grain; a hard substance on the foot.—*v.* to salt.
Count, *v.* to reckon.—*s.* an earl; a point in an indictment.
Count'er, *s.* a table in a shop.—*a.* contrary.
Court, *v.* to solicit.—*s.* seat of justice; space before a house; residence of a prince; a little street.
Crab, a shell fish; a wild apple.
Craft, cunning; small sailing vessels.
Crane, a long legged bird; an engine to raise weights; a bent tube to draw liquor out of a cask.
Crick'et, a chirping insect; a game with bat and ball.
Crop, *s.* the harvest; the craw of a bird.—*v.* to cut short.
Cross, *s.* a straight body laid at right angles over another.—*a.* peevish.—*v.* to thwart; to pass over.
Crow, a large black bird; an iron lever; the voice of a cock.
Cry, *v.* to proclaim loudly; to lament aloud.—*s.* the call of an animal.
Cue, a braid of hair; a suggestion; a turn of mind.
Dam, the mother of an animal; a bank to confine water.
Date, a time; the fruit of the date tree.
Deal, *s.* quantity; a kind of timber.—*v.* to traffic; to treat with; to distribute.
Dear, beloved; expensive.
Deck, *s.* the floor of a ship.—*v.* to dress.
Desert', *s.* merit.—*v.* to forsake.
Despatch', *s.* hasty execution.—*v.* to put to death.
Die, *v.* to pass from life; to tinge.—*s.* a stamp; a little cube.
Di'et, course of food; an assembly of states.
Di'vers, *s.* they who plunge under water.—*a.* several.
Dock, *s.* a place where ships are built, or moored; an herb.—*v.* to cut off.
Down, *s.* soft feathers; an open plain.—*adv.* not up.
Draw, to drag; to let out a liquid; to delineate.
Drill, to bore holes; to exercise recruits.
Drug, a medicinal substance; an unsaleable thing.
Dun, *a.* dark colored.—*v.* to call for payment.
Ear, the organ of hearing; a spike of corn.
Eld'er, *a.* older.—*s.* the name of a shrub.
Ellip'sis, an omission of words; an oval.
Engross', to occupy the whole; to copy law writings.
Entertain', to amuse; to hold in the mind.
E'ven, *a.* level; equal.—*s.* evening.—*adv.* so much as.
Exact', *a.* accurate.—*v.* to require authoritatively.
Express', *v.* to utter; to squeeze out.—*a.* definite.
Fair, *a.* beautiful; just; favorable.—*s.* a sale.
Fare, price of passage by land, or water; provisions.

Fast, *a.* firm; swift.—*s.* abstinence from food.
Fawn, *s.* a young deer.—*v.* to court servilely.
Feed, *v.* to supply with food.—*part.* rewarded.
Fell, *v.* did fall; to cut down.—*a.* cruel.
Fel'low, an associate; one of a pair; a mean wretch; a trustee of a college.
Fel'on, a criminal; a whitlow.
Felt, *v.* perceived.—*s.* a substance of which hats are made.
Fer'ret, a sort of weasel; a kind of narrow ribbon.—*v.* to drive out of a lurking place.
Fig'ure, shape; a statue; a numerical character; a kind of simile.
File, a rasping tool; a line on which papers are put; a line of soldiers; a series.—*v.* to exhibit officially.
Fil'let, a band; the thick part of a leg of veal.
Fine, *a.* thin; clear; splendid.—*s.* a forfeit; the end.
Firm, *a.* strong; steady.—*s.* the name of a house of trade.
Fit, *a.* proper; suitable.—*s.* a paroxysm.—*v.* to suit.
Flag, *s.* a water plant; a paving stone; an ensign, or standard. —*v.* to hang loose; to grow spiritless.
Flat'ter, *a.* more flat.—*v.* to praise falsely.
Fleet, *s.* a navy.—*a.* nimble.
Flock, a company of birds, or beasts; a lock of wool.
Flue, a chimney; soft fur, or down.
Foil, leaf metal; a blunt sword.—*v.* to defeat.
Fold, an enclosure for sheep; a double.
Foot, a member of the body; a measure of twelve inches.
For, *prep.* instead of; on account of.—*conj.* because.
Forge, *v.* to form by the hammer; to counterfeit.—*s.* a furnace
For'mer, *a.* before in time.—*s.* a maker.
Fort, a fortified place; a strong side.
Found'er, *s.* one who establishes; a caster.—*v.* to sink to the bottom; to fall.
Frieze, a term in architecture; the nap on cloth.
Fret, to be peevish; to wear away by rubbing.
Fry, *s.* a swarm of young fishes.—*v.* to cook food in a pan.
Full'er, *a.* nearer full.—*s.* a cleanser of cloth.
Gall, an excrescence on the oak; a secretion of the body; malignity.
Game, sport; a single match of play; animals chased.
Gin, a snare; an alcoholic liquor.
Gloss, superficial lustre; a comment.
Gore, *s.* clotted blood.—*v.* to pierce with a horn.
Grain, corn; any minute particle; a small weight.
Grate, *s.* a range of bars.—*v.* to wear away by rasping; to make a harsh noise.

EQUIVOCAL WORDS.   39

GRATE'FUL, thankful; agreeable, pleasing.
GRAVE, s. the place of burial.—a. not acute in sound; serious.—v. to carve figures.
GRAZE, to feed on grass; to touch lightly in passing.
GREEN, colored like grass; fresh; immature.
GROSS, a. large; coarse.—s. the chief part; twelve dozen.
GROUND, s. earth; the first coat of paint.—v. to found.—part. sharpened by grinding; reduced to powder.
HAB'IT, state of a thing; custom; dress.
HAIL, s. frozen rain; an exclamation.—v. to salute.
HAM'PER, s. a large packing basket.—v. to perplex.
HAUT'BOY, a wind instrument; a sort of strawberry.
HEAV'EN, the eternal abode of the good; the sky.
HELP, to assist; to avoid.
HIDE, v. to conceal.—s. the skin of an animal.
HIND, a. backward.—s. a female deer; a peasant.
HOP, v. to jump.—s. a climbing plant.
HOST, the master of a feast; landlord of an inn; an army; any great number; the sacrifice of the mass.
HUE, a color; a clamor.
IN'STANCE, a case occurring; suggestion; urgency.
IN'STANT, a. urgent; immediate; s. a moment.
JAM, s. a conserve of fruits.—v. to wedge in.
JAR, a kind of vessel; a rattling sound; discord; the state of a door not quite shut.
JET, s. a black fossil; a spout of water.—v. to jut out.
JUST, a. right.—adv. exactly; nearly.
KEN'NEL, a cot for dogs; a watercourse of a street.
KEY, an instrument to open a lock; that which solves a difficulty; a finger-piece on a musical instrument.
KIND, a. ready to confer favors.—s. a sort.
KITE, a bird of prey; a paper toy to fly.
LACE, a string; fine net work.
LAKE, a large body of inland water; a color.
LAP, v. to lick up; to fold.—s. the part formed by the knees in a sitting posture.
LAST, a. latest.—v. to endure.—s. the mould on which shoes are made; a corn measure.
LAWN, an open space between woods; a linen fabric.
LAY, v. to place down; to wager; did lie.—s. a song.—a. not clerical.
LEAGUE, a confederacy; a distance of three miles.
LEAN, v. to incline.—s. muscular part of flesh.—a. thin.
LEAVE, s. permission.—v. to forsake; to suffer to remain; to intrust; to refer for decision.

LEFT, *a.* pertaining to the left hand.—*part.* not taken.
LET, *v.* to permit; to lease.—*s.* hindrance.
LET'TER, a vowel, or consonant; an epistle; one who lets.
LIE, *v.* to rest; to utter wilful falsehoods.—*s.* a fiction. [settle.
LIGHT, *s.* illumination.—*a.* not heavy; bright.—*v.* to kindle; to
LIKE, *a.* resembling.—*v.* to approve.—*adv.* as.
LIME, an alkali; a sort of lemon; a sticky substance.
LINE, *s.* a string; a single verse.—*v.* to cover inside.
LINK, *s.* a single ring of a chain; a torch.—*v.* to connect.
LIT'TER, a portable bed; straw laid under animals; a number of things in disorder; a birth of animals.
LOCK, a complicated fastening; a quantity of hair, or wool; a contrivance to raise barges in canals.
LONG, *a.* protracted.—*v.* to desire earnestly.
LOT, fortune; a parcel; a field.
LUTE, a stringed musical instrument; a sort of cement.
MACE, an ensign of authority; a kind of spice.
MAIL, armor; a post-bag.
MAIN, *a.* chief.—*s.* strength; the ocean; the continent.
MALL, a heavy beetle; a public walk.
MAN'GLE, to smooth linen; to cut and tear.
MARCH, *s.* the third month.—*v.* to walk in procession.
MASS, a lump; the service of the Latin church.
MAST, the pole to which the sails of a ship are fixed; the fruit of the oak or beech.
MATCH, a thing that easily inflames; an equal; a thing that suits; a marriage alliance.
MAT'TER, material substance; subject of discourse; consequence.
MEAD, a meadow; honey-wine.
MEAL, a repast; the flour of corn. [to signify.
MEAN, *a.* base; niggardly; middling.—*s.* medium.—*v.* to intend;
MEET, *v.* to encounter.—*a.* proper, suitable.
MEW, *s.* a sea-fowl.—*v.* to cry as a cat; to shut up; to change the appearance.
MINE, *s.* a cavern dug for minerals.—*pron.* belonging to me.
MINT, a plant; the place where money is coined.
MIN'UTE, the sixtieth part of an hour; a short record.
MOLE, a little animal; a spot on the skin; a mound.
MOOR, *s.* a marsh, or fen; a negro.—*v.* to make fast a vessel to the shore.
MOR'TAR, a vessel in which substances are pulverized; cement for bricks; a short wide cannon for bombs.
MOULD, the ground in which plants grow; the shape in which things are cast; a substance which gathers on bodies in a damp place.

Must, *v.* to be compelled; to grow musty.—*s.* new wine.
Nail, the horny substance at the end of the fingers and toes; a metal spike; two inches and a quarter.
Nap, a short sleep; the down on cloth, &c.
Neat, *s.* an ox, or cow.—*a.* elegant; cleanly.
Nerv'ous, vigorous; having weak nerves.
No, *a.* not any.—*adv.* the word of refusal, or denial.
Oblige', to compel; to please.
Or'der, regularity; a command; a class.
Or'gan, a natural instrument of sense; a musical wind instrument.
Ounce, a small weight; an animal like a panther.
Page, one side of a leaf; a young attendant on a prince.
Pale, *a.* wanting color; dim.—*s.* a rail to enclose grounds; a space enclosed, or limited. [insipid.
Pall, *s.* a mantle of state; a covering for the dead; *v.* to become
Pal'let, a small bed; a painter's board.
Palm, *s.* a tree; victory; the inner part of the hand.—*v.* to impose upon by fraud.
Pan'el, a small board set in a frame; a list of jurors.
Pan'ic, sudden fright; a plant.
Par'tial, biassed to one side, or individual; affecting only a part.
Paste, a mixture of flour and water; imitations of precious stones.
Pa'tient, *a.* enduring.—*s.* a sick person.
Peck, *s.* a quarter of a bushel.—*v.* to pick up food with the beak; to strike with a pointed instrument.
Peer, an equal; a nobleman.
Pen, a writing instrument; a small enclosure.
Perch, a kind of fish; a roosting place; 5½ yards.
Pet, a slight passion; a favorite.
Pike, a fish; a long lance.
Pile, a beam driven into the ground; a heap; nap; the head of an arrow.
Pine, *s.* a tree.—*v.* to languish.
Pin'ion, *s.* a wing; fetters for the arms; a small toothed-wheel on the same axis with a larger one.—*v.* to shackle.
Pink, *s.* a flower; a color; the highest quality.
Pitch, *s.* thickened tar; degree of elevation.—*v.* to fix; to throw; to fall headlong; to alight.
Plate, a shallow dish; wrought silver; flatted metal.
Poach, to boil slightly; to steal game; to tread soft ground.
Pole, a long piece of timber; 5½ yards in length; the extremity of the earth's axis; a native of Poland.
Pol'lard, a tree lopped; a mixture of bran and meal.
Port, a harbor; a gate; the gun-hole in a ship; a sort of wine from Oporto.

Por'ter, a door-keeper; one who carries loads; strong beer.
Post, *s.* a piece of timber set upright; a messenger; office; a station.—*v.* to travel quickly; to transcribe into a leger.
Pound, *s.* twenty shillings; a weight; a prison for stray beasts.—*v.* to reduce to powder.
Prefer', to choose before another; to advance.
Pretend', to represent falsely; to lay claim.
Pri'or, former; the chief monk of a convent.
Prune, *v.* to lop trees.—*s.* a dried plum.
Pulse, the throbbing of an artery; leguminous plants.
Pump, an engine to raise water; a light shoe.
Punch, an instrument for cutting holes; a mixed liquor.
Pu'pil, the apple of the eye; a scholar; a ward.
Pur'chase, *v.* to buy.—*s.* convenience for using force.
Quar'ter, *s.* fourth part; mercy shown by a conqueror; eight bushels.—*v.* to lodge soldiers.
Race, a generation; a contest in running.
Rail, *s.* a bar.—*v.* to speak contemptuously.
Ram, *s.* a male sheep.—*v.* to drive in violently.
Rank, *a.* luxuriant; rancid.—*s.* a row; dignity.
Rash, *a.* hasty; *s.* a breaking out.
Rear, *s.* the hinder part.—*v.* to raise up; to educate.
Refu'sal, a denial; the right of choice.
Ren'der, *s.* one who tears.—*v.* to restore; to yield.
Rent, *s.* a tear; revenue.—*v.* tore.—*part.* torn.
Resolu'tion, act of separating into parts; determination.
Rest, repose; remainder.
Right, *a.* correct; straight; not left.—*s.* justice; just claim.
Ring, *s.* a circle.—*v.* to sound; to fit with rings.
Road, a way; a place where ships may anchor at a distance from the land.
Rock, *s.* a vast mass of stone.—*v.* to move backwards and forwards.
Roe, a female deer; the eggs of fish.
Rose, *s.* a sweet scented flower.—*v.* did rise.
Row, *v.* to impel with the oar; a rank, or file.
Rue, *s.* a plant.—*v.* to regret.
Rush, *s.* a plant.—*v.* to move with violence.
Sack, *s.* a bag; a sort of wine.—*v.* to pillage.
Sage, *s.* a plant.—*a.* wise.
Sash, a silken band; a window frame.
Saw, *s.* a toothed instrument for cutting; a proverb.—*v.* did see.
Scale, *s.* the dish of a balance; graduation; a little shell on a fish's skin.—*v.* to climb; to peel off in thin pieces.
Seal, the sea-calf; a stamp.

SEA'SON, *s.* one of the four parts of the year; a fit time.—*v.* to give a relish to.
SEE, *s.* the jurisdiction of a bishop.—*v.* to view.
SET, *v.* to place; to bring to a fine edge; to fall below the horizon.—*s.* a number of things suited to each other. [riage.
SHAFT, an arrow; a narrow perpendicular pit; the pole of a car-
SHED, *s.* a slight covered building.—*v.* to let fall, to spill.
SHEER, *a.* unmingled.—*v.* to deviate.
SHOAL, *s.* a great multitude; a sand bank.—*a.* shallow.
SHORE, the coast; a prop or support under a building.
SHRUB, a bush; an alcoholic mixture.
SINK, *s.* a drain; a reservoir.—*v.* to go down.
SIZE, bulk; a sticky substance.
SMELT, *s.* a small sea-fish.—*v.* to melt ore; did smell.
SOLE, *s.* the bottom of the foot; a small sea-fish.—*a.* only.
SOUND, *s.* a noise; a shallow sea; a probe.—*a.* hearty; uninjured.—*v.* to try depth.
SPIR'IT, the soul of man; courage; an inflammable distilled liquor.
SPRING, *s.* one of the four seasons; an elastic body; a leap; a fountain.—*v.* to arise; to grow.
STEEP, *a.* precipitous.—*v.* to soak.
STEER, *s.* a young bullock.—*v.* to direct a course.
STEM, *s.* a stalk.—*v.* to oppose a current.
STERN, *a.* severe.—*s.* the hind part of a ship.
STICK, *s.* a slender piece of wood.—*v.* to adhere; to stab.
STILL, *a.* quiet.—*v.* to calm.—*s.* a vessel for distilling.—*adv.* to this time.—*conj.* notwithstanding.
STRAIN, *v.* to filter; to sprain; to force.—*s.* style; a passage of music.
SUCCEED', to follow; to prosper.
SUF'FER, to permit, to allow; to endure, to bear.
SUIT, *s.* a set; courtship; prosecution.—*v.* to 'fit.
SWAL'LOW, *s.* a bird.—*v.* to take down the throat.
TA'BLE, an article of furniture; an index, or list of particulars methodically arranged.
TACK, *v.* to join; to turn a ship.—*s.* a little nail.
TAIL, the extremity; a limited estate.
TA'PER, *s.* a wax candle; conical form.
TEN'DER, *s.* an attendant.—*a.* soft.—*v.* to offer.
TILL, *v.* to cultivate.—*s.* a money box.—*conj.* to the time.
TIRE, *s.* a head dress; the hoop of a wheel.—*v.* to weary.
TOLL, *s.* a tax on passengers, &c.—*v.* to ring a bell.
TONE, sound; elasticity, or vigor.
TOP, the highest part of any thing; a toy.
TREAT, *v.* to negotiate; to discourse.—*s.* a feast.

Tum′bler, a posture master; a large drinking glass.
Tur′tle, a species of dove; the sea tortoise.
Ush′er, *v.* to introduce.—*s.* an under-teacher.
Ut′ter, *v.* to speak; to put forth.—*a.* entire.
Vault, *s.* a cellar.—*v.* to leap.
Vice, wickedness.—*as a prefix,* in the place of.
Wa′ges, *s.* stipulated compensation for labor.—*v.* carries on.
Wear, *s.* the act of wearing; a kind of dam.—*v.* to impair by friction; to carry upon the person.
Well, *s.* a deep narrow pit of water.—*a.* in good health.
Yard, an enclosure by the side of a building; a measure of three feet; the support of the sails of a ship.

CHAPTER IV.

IMPROPRIETIES HEARD IN CONVERSATION.

Some of the following improprieties are heard in the conversation of those who are regarded as persons of refinement; while others of them are heard only among the most uneducated classes. Improprieties of the latter kind are often imitated by children who do not hear them from the lips of their parents.

Acrost, for *across.*
Actyve, for *active.*
Afeard, for *afraid.*
Agin, for *again* [agen].
Agur, for *ague.*
Aint, for *are not.*
All′ez, for *always.*
Arethmetic, for *arithmetic.*
Arriv, for *arrived.*
Arter, for *after.*
Ax, for *ask.*
Bachelder, for *bachelor.*
Bagonet, for *bayonet.*
Begrutch, for *grudge.*
Bellusses, for *bellows.*
Bettermost, for *best.*
Beyend, for *beyond.*
Bile, for *boil.*
Bimeby, for *by-and-by.*
Blowed, for *blew.*

Bran, for *brand.*
Brustle, for *bristle.*
Bust, or Busted, for *burst.*
Catechise, for *catechism.*
Cause, for *because.*
Chaw, for *chew.*
Cheer, for *chair.*
Chimbly, for *chimney.*
Chist, for *chest.*
Chuse, for *choose.*
Cly, for *cloy.*
Clumb, for *climbed.*
Cornish, for *cornice.*
Cowcumber, for *cucumber.*
Critter, for *creature.*
Cupelow, for *cupola.*
Dare′snt, for *dare not.*
Dater, [*a* as in *far*] for *daughter.*
Done, for *did.*

IMPROPRIETIES. 45

DRAWED, for *drew*.
DREAN, for *drain*.
DROWNDED, for *drowned*.
EEND, for *end*.
EEN-A-MOST, for *almost*.
FAIRM, for *firm*.
FELLER, for *fellow*.
FIFT, for *fifth*.
FORRUD, for *forward*.
FOR'T-I-NUR, for *for aught I know*.
FRIND, for *friend*.
FUR, for *far*.
FURDER, for *further*.
FUST, for *first*.
GAL, for *girl*.
GETHER, for *gather*.
GIN, for *gave*.
GINERAL, for *general*.
GINSANG, for *ginseng*.
GIM-ME, for *give me*.
GIT, for *get*.
GOWND, for *gown*.
GUARDEEN', for *guar'dian*.
HAINT, for *have not*.
HANDIRON, for *andiron*.
HANKERCHER, for *handkerchief*.
HENDER, for *hin'der*.
HERN, for *hers*.
HERTH, for *hearth* [harth.]
HIS'N, for *his*.
HOSS, for *horse*.
HOUSEN, for *houses*.
HOWSOMEVER, for *however*.
HUM, for *home*.
HUMBLY, for *homely*.
HUSBANT, for *husband*.
IDEE, for *idea*.
ILE, for *oil*.
INGIN, for *Indian* [Ind'yan.]
INGINE, for *engine*.
INWITE, for *invite*.
JANDERS, for *jaundice*.
JEST, for *just*.
JICE, for *joists*.

JINE, for *join*.
JINUARY, for *January*.
KETCH, for *catch*.
KITTLE, for *kettle*.
KIVER, for *cover*.
KNOWED, for *knew*.
LARNING, for *learning*.
LEAST, for *lest*.
LEM-ME, for *let me*.
LESS, for *let us*.
LETTIS, for *lettuce*.
LEVEN, for *eleven*.
LICKERISH, for *licorice*.
LINE, for *lion*.
LINNING, for *linen*.
LUTH'ER, for *leather*.
LOOM, for *loam*.
MAINT, for *may not*.
MASSACREE, for *massacre*.
MEDDLE, for *medal*.
MILED, for *mile*.
MORE'N, for *more than*.
MORNIN, for *morning*.
MOST, for *almost*. [ous.
MOUNTANEOUS, for *mountain-*
MOUNTING, for *mountain*.
MUSHMELON, for *muskmelon*.
NARY, for *neither*.
NIGGER, for *negro*.
NORWEST, for *northwest*. [ous.
OBSTROPOLOUS, for *obstreper-*
ONCE'T, for *once*.
ORNERY, for *ordinary*.
OURN, for *ours*.
OUTCH, for *Oh!*
PARDNER, for *partner*.
PLETE, for *plait*.
POME, for *poem*.
POOTY, for *pretty*.
POPPLE, for *poplar*. [ciation.
PRONOUNCEATION, for *pronun-*
QUATE, for *quoit*.
RALY, for *really*.
REMARKABLE, for *remarkably*.
RENSE, for *rinse*.

RHEUMATIZ, for *rheumatism*.
RIBBET, for *rivet*.
RIZ, for *risen*.
ROZZUM, for *rosin*.
RUTHER, for *rather*.
SAFT, for *soft*.
SARCER, for *saucer*.
SARMON, for *sermon*.
SASSAGE, for *sausage*.
SAXAFRAX, for *sassafras*.
SCURSE, for *scarce*.
SECT, for *sex*.
SEEN, for *saw*.
SENCE, or SEN, for *since*.
SET, for *sit*.
SHAWL, for *shall*.
SHAY, for *chaise*.
SHEER, for *share*.
SHET, or SHOT, for *shut*.
SHUE, for *shoe*.
SICH, for *such*.
SILE, for *soil*.
SITHE, for *sigh*.
SIXT, for *sixth*.
SKEERED, for *scared*.
SKROUGE, for *crowd*.
SMUDDER, for *smother*.
SOME'RS, for *somewhere*.
SPARROW-GRASS, for *asparagus*.
SPERE, for *spire*.
SPERIT, for *spirit*.
SQUINCE, for *quince*.
STIDDY, or STUDY, for *steady*.
STUN, for *stone*.

STUNTED, for *stinted*.
SULLER, for *cellar*.
SURRINGE, for *syringe*.
SUT, for *soot*.
SUTHING, for *something*.
TAINT, for *it is not*.
TENANT, for *tenon*.
THAT-ARE, for *that*.
THEIRN, for *theirs*.
THIS-ERE, for *this*.
TOTHER, for *the other*.
TOWER, for *tour*.
TURCLE, or TORTLE, for *turtle*.
TWICE'T, for *twice*.
UMBERIL, or UMBERILLA, for *umbrella*.
VYAGE, for *voyage*.
WANT, for *was not*.
WARNUT, for *walnut*.
WATERMILLION, for *watermelon*.
WEAL, for *veal*.
WEEK, for *wick*.
WEN, for *when*.
WICH, for *which*.
WIDDER, for *widow*.
WILLER, for *willow*.
WINDER, for *window*.
WINE, for *vine*.
WINEGAR, for *vinegar*.
WINEPIPE, for *windpipe*.
WRASTLE, for *wrestle*.
YENDER, for *yonder*.
YOURN, for *yours*.

CHAPTER V.

RULE IN ORTHOGRAPHY.

WORDS of one syllable, ending with a single consonant preceded by a single vowel, double that consonant when they take an additional syllable beginning with a vowel. Words of more than one

RULE IN ORTHOGRAPHY.

syllable, ending in the same manner, follow the same rule, when they are accented on the last syllable. General usage allows some words to double the final consonant on taking an additional syllable, though the accent is not on the last syllable: as *travel, traveller; worship, worshipping,* &c.

In the following table, the several columns contain specimens of the several classes of words which do, or do not double their final consonant.

BAR,	Bare,	Bait,	Bark,	BEFIT',	Bal'lot.
BARRED,	Bared,	Baited,	Barking,	BEFITTING,	Balloting.
CHIP,	Chime,	Cheat,	Cart,	COMMIT',	Cur'pet.
CHIPPING,	Chiming,	Cheating,	Carting,	COMMITTED,	Carpeted.
DIP,	Dire,	Dear,	Damp,	DEFER',	Dif'fer.
DIPPING,	Direr,	Dearer,	Damper,	DEFERRING,	Differing.
DIG,	Dive,	Deal,	Dark,	DISTIL',	Discom'fit.
DIGGER,	Diver,	Dealer,	Darker,	DISTILLER,	Discomfited.
DOT,	Date,	Deaf,	Dart,	DETER',	Dis'mal.
DOTTED,	Dated,	Deafer,	Darting,	DETERRING,	Dismally.
FAT,	Fade,	Jail,	Ink,	IMPEL',	Inhab'it.
FATTED,	Faded,	Jailer.	Inky,	IMPELLING,	Inhabiting.
IN,	Ice,	Fail,	Find,	FORGET',	Fer'ret.
INNER,	Iced,	Failing.	Finder,	FORGETTING,	Ferreting.
JUT.	Jade,	Join,	Jolt,	JAPAN',	Jab'ber.
JUTTING,	Jaded,	Joiner,	Jolted,	JAPANNING,	Jabberer.
RUN,	Race,	Rain,	Rend,	REBEL',	Ri'pen.
RUNNER,	Racer,	Raining,	Rending,	REBELLING,	Ripening.
RED,	Ride,	Rail,	Rest,	REMIT',	Rea'son.
REDDER,	Riding,	Railing,	Rested,	REMITTED,	Reasoner.
RAP,	Rise,	Roar,	Rust,	REBUT',	Recov'er.
RAPPING,	Rising,	Roaring,	Rusted,	REBUTTING,	Recovering
RAG,	Rage,	Read,	Right,	REFER',	Rob'ber.
RAGGED,	Raging,	Reading,	Righter,	REFERRING,	Robbery.
TAN,	Tune,	Tear,	Tight,	TREPAN',	Tam'per.
TANNER,	Tuner,	Tearing,	Tighter,	TREPANNING,	Tampering.
UP,	Use,	Vain,	Urn,	UNSHIP',	Ut'ter.
UPPER,	Using,	Vainer,	Urned,	UNSHIP'PED,	Uttering.

When *ed* is added to those words which double the consonant, the *e* may be omitted in writing, and an apostrophe supply its place; but when the consonant is not doubled, the *e* should be written; thus, *robb'd* for *robbed;* but not *rob'd* for *robed.*

PART II.

DERIVATION.

DIRECTIONS FOR USING PART II.—The pupil should study Chapter I., so as to be able to recite it readily, (i. e. to state the substance of each of the preliminary observations, and to give an account of each of the Prefixes and Suffixes, with the examples which illustrate their use,) before proceeding further.

The figures included in parentheses refer to the paragraphs of Chapters II. and III.; and in Chapter I., the references to Latin and Greek words are distinguished by the letters L. and G.

It is desirable that Part II. should be *studied, as a distinct exercise,* before it is used as a reference book. The pupils will thus become accustomed to tracing the etymology of words, and will be prepared to discover, without referring to the book, the derivation and signification of many words, on meeting with them for the first time. Not only should the practice of tracing English words to their Latin or Greek primitives be continued by all pupils who have studied this Part, but those who are studying Latin or Greek should be in the habit of ascertaining, and stating in their recitations, what English words are derived from the Latin or Greek words which occur in their lessons.

CHAPTER I.

GENERAL ACCOUNT OF THE DERIVATION AND COMPOSITION OF ENGLISH WORDS.

1. THE words of the English language may be separated into two principal classes, viz.: *words of Saxon origin,* and *words of Latin origin.* Words derived from the ancient Greek, belong, in this general division, to the latter of the two classes; although they will be arranged by themselves, for the sake of convenience, in the following pages.

Note. For an account of such words as are neither of Saxon nor Latin origin, let the student consult Dr. Webster's large Dictionary.

2. A great part of the words which are classed as words of Latin origin, were introduced into the English, not directly from the Latin itself, but from the French, or from some other of those modern languages which sprung from the Latin, and strongly resemble it. For example, the word *finish* may have come into our language from the French word *finir;* but both are to be traced back to the Latin word *finis,* (L. 176), signifying an *end* or *limit.*

DERIVATION AND COMPOSITION. 49

3. By learning the derivation of a word, we often obtain a clearer notion of its signification than we could obtain in any other way. This is true of the following examples, viz.: *contact*, which is from the Latin particle *con*, together, and the verb *tango*, (participle *tactus*), (L. 526), to touch; *Federal*, from *fœdus*, (L. 162,) a league, or treaty; *Gradual* from *gradus*, (L. 207), a step; *Induce* from *in*, into, and *duco*, (L. 133), to lead.

4. As Latin and Greek words often vary considerably in form, in their different cases, tenses, &c., and as the English word is not always formed from that case or tense which is considered the foundation of the others, it is often necessary to know more than one of the forms which the Latin or Greek word may assume. Thus, the word *fluent* is derived from the Latin verb *fluo*, (L. 185), to flow; while *influx* is from *fluxum*, the supine of the same verb, and the preposition *in*. So the Latin adjective *felix*, (L. 163), which has in its genitive case *felicis*, gives rise to the English word *felicity*.

5. In arranging English words in *families* under the Latin or Greek words from which they are derived, it is proper to place under the several Latin or Greek words, not only the English words derived *immediately* from them, but also those derived from *their derivatives*. For example, under the Latin word *nascor*, (L. 324), (part. *natus*), to be born, should be classed the English words *nascent*, *natal*, *natural*, *nativity*, and *nation*; although, with the exception of the first, they are derived more immediately from words in the Latin which are derivatives of *nascor*, viz.:— *natalis*, *naturalis*, *nativitas*, and *natio*.

6. Many English words are formed from other English words, by means of *prefixes* and *suffixes*. A letter, syllable, or word joined to the beginning of a word is called a *prefix*; a letter or syllable joined to the end is called a *suffix*. Thus, from *tell* is formed *foretell*, by joining a prefix; and from *do* is formed *doer*, by joining a suffix. A word may take two or more prefixes or suffixes at the same time. Thus, *re*produce contains two prefixes, *re* and *pro*; wonder*fully* contains two suffixes, *ful* and *ly*; rogu*ishness* two suffixes, *ish* and *ness*.

7. Some of the prefixes and suffixes are of Saxon origin, and others are of Latin origin. Some of them are words which may be used separately, while the greater part are *inseparable*, i. e. are never used by themselves. Many of the prefixes which are inseparable in English, are separable in the languages from which they are derived.

8. In learning our own language, we become so familiar with the signification of most of the prefixes and suffixes, (although it is not always easy to *state* that signification), that as soon as we

have ascertained the meaning of any word which is new to us, we can tell what would be the meaning of the several words formed from it by such additions. Thus, after learning the meaning of the word *confirm*, we know what must be the meaning of the words *confirmed*, *confirmation*, *confirmatory*, *confirmer*, *confirmedly*, *unconfirmed*, &c., from the manner in which they are varied from the word *confirm*. In some cases, the prefixes or suffixes seem not to affect the signification of the word to which they are joined.

9. When a prefix ends with a consonant, that consonant is often changed or omitted, in order that the prefix may unite easily with the word to which it is to be joined. In the words a*ff*ix, *co*here, (L. 217), *i*mplant, and *suf*fix, (for example), the prefixes *ad*, *con*, *in*, and *sub*, are changed, for the sake of producing a more agreeable sound.

PREFIXES.

The following is a list of the most important prefixes used in forming English words. The abbreviation (Lat.) shows that the prefix is from the Latin; (Gr.) that it is from the Greek. Prefixes which are *inseparable* in the languages from which they are derived, (as above explained, § 7,) are denoted by the abbreviation (insep.)

A, (when of English or Saxon origin), signifies *in*, *on*, or *at;* as in the words *a*bed, *a*board, *a*loft, *a*shore, *a*side.

A, or AB, (Lat.), *from;* as, *a*vert, (L. 579), to turn from; *ab*solve, (L. 497), to release from.

A, or AN, (Gr. insep.), *destitute of;* as, *a*theist, (G. 216), one without a God; *an*archy, (G. 18), want of government.

AD, (Lat.), which may become, in composition, (§ 9), a, ac, af, ag, al, an, ap, ar, as, or at, signifies *to;* as *ad*here, (L. 216), to stick to; *a*scend, (L. 465), to mount to; *al*lot, to assign to; *at*test, (L. 538), to bear witness to.

AM, or AMB, (Lat. insep.) *round* or *about;* as, *am*bient (L. 142), going round; surrounding.

ANA, (Gr.) *throughout, up;* as, *ana*lysis, (G. 129), a loosening throughout; the solution of any compound; *ana*tomy, (G. 217), a cutting up.

PREFIXES.

ANTE, (Lat.) *before;* as *ante*cedent, (L. 57), going before.

ANTI, or ANT, (Gr.), *against;* as, *anti*christian, (G. 52), *against* or opposed to Christianity; *ant*arctic, (G. 19), *against* or opposite to the north; southern.

APO, or AP, (Gr.), *from;* as, *apo*stle, (G. 205), one sent out; *ap*helion, (G. 105), *from* the sun.

BE, (from the word *by*), signifies *upon, over, about;* as, *be*sprinkle, to sprinkle *on* or *over*. In some words, the prefix *be* seems to be one of a different origin; as in *be*head, *be*siege.

CATA, (Gr.), *down, against;* as, *cata*rrh, (G. 195), a flowing *down;* *cata*ract, a dashing down.

CIRCUM, (Lat.), *around,* or *about;* as, *circum*navigate, (L. 326), to sail around; *circum*jacent, (L. 238), lying around.

CON, (in Lat., CUM), *with,* or *together*. It takes several forms, viz., *co, cog, col, com,* and *cor;* as, *con*nect, (L. 327), to bind together; *co*here, (L. 216), to stick together; *com*press, (L. 410), to press together.

CONTRA, (Lat.), *against;* as, *contra*dict, (L. 117), to speak in opposition. In many words it takes the form *counter;* as, *counter*act, (L. 3), to act against.

DE, (Lat.), *from,* or *down from;* as, *de*duct, (L. 133), to take from; *de*scend, (L. 465), to go down from.

DIA, (Gr.), *through;* as, *dia*meter, (G. 137) the measure *through*.

DIS, and the forms *di* and *dif,* (Lat. insep.), *asunder, apart, away;* as, *dis*sent, (L. 476), to be of a different opinion; *di*vert, (L. 579), to turn one aside. This prefix often has a kind of negative meaning; as in *dis*advantageous, not advantageous.

E, or EX, (Lat. & Gr.), *out,* or *out of;* as, *e*ject, (L. 239), to cast out; *ex*clude, (L. 77), to shut out. It also takes the forms *ec,* and *ef;* as *ec*centric, (G. 44), out of the centre; *ef*flux, (L. 185), a flowing out.

EN, or EM. See IN.

EPI, or EP, (Gr.), *upon, over, for;* as, *epi*demic, (G. 67), upon a people; *ep*hemeral, (G. 108), lasting *for* a day.

EXTRA, (Lat.), *beyond;* as, *extra*ordinary, (L. 351), beyond what is ordinary.

FORE, *before;* as, *fore*tell, to tell beforehand.

HYPER, (Gr.), *above, beyond;* as, *hyper*critical, (G. 61), critical beyond reason.

HYPO, (Gr.), *under;* as, *hypo*thesis, (G. 215), a supposition taken as the basis of a theory.

IN, or EN, (Lat. & Gr.), *in, on,* or *into;* as, *insert,* (L. 480), to put in; *in*cubation, (L. 99), sitting on; *in*duce, (L. 133), to lead into; *en*grave, (G. 99), to cut upon, or in. *In* may become *ig, il, im,* or *ir;* and *en* may become *em*. *In* and its equivalents often denote privation or negation; as, *in*decent, (L. 110), not decent; *il*legal, (L. 256), not legal. Some words are written with *in* or *en* indifferently; as, *en*close, or *in*close.

INTER, (Lat.), *between,* or *among;* as, *inter*pose, (L. 399), to place between. It sometimes takes the form *enter;* as, *enter*tain, (L. 530).

INTRO, (Lat.), *within;* as, *intro*duce, (L. 133), to lead within.

META, or MET, (Gr.), *after, beyond, from one to another;* as, *meta*physics, (G. 180), the science which is after or beyond physics; *met*onymy, (G. 156), a putting of one word or name for another.

MIS, signifies *wrong, erroneous, defective;* as, *mis*conduct, (L. 133), wrong conduct; *mis*conception, (L. 47), an erroneous notion.

NON, (Lat.), *not;* as, *non*descript, (L. 468), not described.

OB, (Lat.) denotes *opposition;* as, *ob*ject, (L. 239), to cast against. In composition it may become *oc, of,* or *op*.

OUT, *beyond;* as, *out*do, to surpass.

PARA, or PAR, (Gr.), *by the side of;* as, *para*site, (G. 201), that which grows or feeds at the side of something; *par*ish, (G. 75).

PER, (Lat.), *through;* as, *per*vade, (L. 565), to extend through.

PERI, (Gr.), *around;* as, *peri*meter, (G. 137), the outer line, or measure around anything.

POST, (Lat.), *after;* as, *post*script, (L. 468), something written after.

PRE, (Lat.), *before;* as, *pre*cede, (L. 57), to go before; *pre*judge, (L. 241), to judge before.

PRETER, (Lat.), *beyond;* as, *preter*natural, (L. 324), beyond nature.

PRO, (Lat.), *for, forth, forward;* as, *pro*noun, (L. 334), a word used instead of a noun; *pro*voke, (L. 596), to call forth; *pro*pel, (L. 373), to drive forward. It takes the form of *pur*, in *pur*pose, and *por*, in *por*tray.

RE, or RED, (Lat. insep.), *back again, anew;* as, *re*call, to call back; *re*commence, to begin anew; *re*deem, (L. 140), to buy back; to ransom.

RETRO, (Lat.), *backward;* as, *retro*spect, (L. 504), a looking backwards.

SE, (Lat. insep.), *aside, apart;* as, *se*cede, (L. 57), to withdraw; *se*clude, (L. 77), to shut away, or apart.

SUB, or SUBTER, (Lat.), *under;* as, *sub*scribe, (L. 468), to write under; *subter*fuge, (L. 197), a flying under. It also takes the forms *suc, suf, sug, sup,* and *sus.*

SUPER, (Lat.), *above, over, more than enough;* as, *super*natural, (L. 324), above nature; *super*vision, (L. 586), overseeing. It often takes the form *sur;* as, *sur*charge, to overload.

SYN, (Gr.), *with, together;* as, *syn*thesis, (G. 215), putting together. It also takes the forms *sy, syl,* and *sym.*

TRANS, or TRA, (Lat.), *over, through, beyond;* as, *trans*gress, (L. 207), to go over a law, or rule; *trans*parent, (L. 362), clear like glass; *tra*verse, (L. 579), to pass over.

UN, denotes *privation* or *negation,* (see IN); as, *un*bind, to take off a band; *un*certain, (L 67), not certain.

UNDER, as, *under*mine; *under*rate, (L. 439).

WITH, as a prefix, usually denotes *opposition,* or *separation;* as, *with*stand, (L. 491), to stand against; *with*draw, to retire.

SUFFIXES.

IN the following list of suffixes, examples are given, under each suffix, of the several parts of speech which that suffix is used to form. Thus, under Ate, the example preceded by the abbreviation *a.* illustrates the manner in which *ate* is used to form adjectives; the example marked *s.* illustrates its use in forming substantives.

The signification of the suffixes must be learned by observation. In many cases, it is impossible so to state it, that the pupil can use the statement as a general definition, in analyzing words. Should the teacher desire something like a general definition, the words italicized in the explanations of the examples given in this list, may be used for this purpose, as the sentences are constructed with a view to such a use of the italicized portion. In analyzing words, with reference to their derivation, the pupil should be accustomed to state what part of the word constitutes the suffix,—what part or parts of speech it is used to form—and how it affects the signification of the word in question. A careful study of the examples here adduced and explained, will give the pupil facility in expressing the signification of the suffixes in other cases.

AC; *a.* demoni*ac, like* a demon; cardi*ac,* (G. 43), *pertaining to* the heart.

ACEOUS; *a.* sapon*aceous,* (L. 462), *having the qualities of* soap.

ACY; *s.* obstin*acy,* (L. 491), the *state* or *condition* of being obstinate.

AGE; *s.* bond*age,* the *condition* of one bound; coin*age,* the *doing* of the work upon coins.

AL; *a.* person*al,* (L. 379), *relating to* person.—*s.* remov*al,* (L. 316), *the act of* removing.

AN, or IAN; *a.* a republic*an,* (L. 441), *belonging to* a republic; barbar*ian, belonging to* a barbarous people.—*s.* histor*ian, one who* writes history.

ANCE, or ANCY; *s.* ignor*ance,* (G. 97), *the state of being* ignorant; const*ancy,* (L. 491), *the being* constant.

ANT; *a.* abund*ant,* (L. 561), *being* in abundance.—*s.* disput*ant,* (L. 422), *one who does the act or work* of disputing.

AR; *a.* lun*ar,* (L. 274), *belonging to* the moon; annu*lar,* (L. 15), *resembling* a ring.—*s.* li*ar, one who does* the act of lying.

ARD; *s.* drunk*ard, one who does,* or is guilty of intemperate drinking.

ARY; *a.* rot*ary,* (L 448), *resembling* a wheel; planet*ary,* (G. 182), *pertaining to* the planets.—*s.* avi*ary,* (L. 32), *a place*

SUFFIXES.

where birds are kept; mission*ary*, (L. 805), *one who does* the work, or bears the responsibilities of a mission.

ATE; *a.* accur*ate*, (L. 102), *having the quality of* accuracy.— *s.* a magistr*ate*, (L. 277), *one who does* the duties of a ruler.— *v.* abbrevi*ate*, (L. 39), *to make* short; nav*i*g*ate*, *to perform the act* of sailing.

BLE; *a.* ara*ble*, (L. 26), *that can be* plowed; lauda*ble*, (L. 251), *that may be* praised.

CLE; *s.* vesi*cle*, *a little* cavity, or vessel; corpus*cle*, *a little* body.

CULE, *s.* animal*cule*, (L. 13), *a minute* animal.

DOM; *s.* free*dom*, *the condition of* being free; king*dom*, *the realm of* a king.

EE; *s.* refer*ee*, (L. 167), *one who is* referred to for a decision.

EER; *s.* engin*eer*, *one who does* the work of managing an engine.

EN; *v.* black*en*, *to make* black.

ENCE, or ENCY; *s.* pres*ence*, (L. 520), *the state of being* present; tenden*cy*, (L. 529), *the act or quality* of tending towards.

ENT; *a.* prud*ent*, (L. 586), *having the quality of* prudence.— *s.* stud*ent*, *the person who* studies.

ER; *s.* carri*er*, *one who does* the work of carrying.—*a.* broad*er*, *more* broad.

ERY; *s.* distill*ery*, (L. 511), *a place where* distilling is carried on.

ESCENCE; *s.* convale*scence*, (L. 567), *state of growing or becoming* healthy.

ESCENT; *a.* putre*scent*, *becoming* putrid.

ESS; a suffix denoting feminine gender; as, *s.* lion*ess*, a female lion.

FUL; *a.* joy*ful*, full of joy.

HOOD; *s.* widow*hood*, *the condition of* being a widow.

IC; *a.* hero*ic*, *like* a hero, or *having the quality of* heroism.

ICE; *s.* coward*ice*, *the quality of* being cowardly.

ICS; *s.* opt*ics*, (G. 157), *the science of* vision; mathemat*ics*, (G. 133), the science of quantity.

ID; *a.* frig*id*, (L. 194), *having the quality of* coldness.

ILE; *a.* frag*ile*, (L. 191), *that may be* broken; puer*ile*, (L. 417), *like*, or *pertaining to* a boy.

INE; *a.* can*ine*, (L. 45), *pertaining to* dogs; alkal*ine*, *like*, or *having the qualities of* an alkali.

ION; *s.* rebell*ion*, (L. 35), *the act of* rebelling; expan*sion*, (L. 358), *the act of* expanding, or *state of being* expanded.

ISH; *a.* whit*ish*, *somewhat* white; boy*ish*, *like* a boy.—*v.* publ*ish*, (L. 400), *to make* public; van*ish*, *to do* the thing denoted by the word disappear.

ISM, or ASM; *s.* hero*ism*, *the state of being* a hero; critic*ism*, (G. 61), *the practice of* criticising; Hebra*ism*, *an idiom of* the Hebrew language.

IST; *s.* art*ist*, (L. 27), *one who does* work in any branch of art; flor*ist*, (L. 184), *one who practises* the art of cultivating flowers; Calvin*ist*, *one who is a follower of* Calvin.

ITE; *s.* favor*ite*, *one who is* beloved; Israel*ite*, *one belonging to* the nation of Israel.

IVE; *a.* instruct*ive*, (L. 515), *fitted* to give instruction; act*ive*, (L. 3), *having power or fitness* to act.

IZE, or ISE; *v.* fertil*ize*, (L. 167), *to make or render* fertile.

LESS; *a.* fear*less*, *without* fear; penni*less*, *destitute of* a penny.

LET; *s.* stream*let*, *a little* stream.

LIKE; *a.* war*like*, *resembling* war.

LING; *s.* a suffix denoting *littleness*, as in sap*ling*, year*ling*, lord*ling*.

LY; *a.* beast*ly*, *like* a beast.—*adv.* proud*ly*, *in a manner* exhibiting pride; fixed*ly*, (L. 172), *in a manner* unchanging or unmoved.

MENT; *s.* banish*ment*, *the state of being* banished, or *the act of* banishing; accompani*ment*, *that which* accompanies.

MONY; *s.* acri*mony*, (L. 1), *the quality of* sharpness or severity. In the words *testimony*, (L. 538), *matrimony*, (L. 284), *patrimony*, (367), &c., the suffix *mony* is used with a singular variety of signification.

NESS; *s.* firm*ness*, (L. 177), *the state of being* firm; little*ness*, *the quality or circumstance of* being little.

Or; *s.* govern*or*, (L. 213), *one who does* that which is denoted by the word govern.

Ory; *a.* preparat*ory*, (L. 364), *fitted or designed* to prepare.— *s.* observat*ory*, (L. 483), *a place where* observations are taken.

Ose; *a.* verb*ose*, (L. 575), *abounding in* words.

Ous; *a.* danger*ous*, *partaking of* danger; courage*ous*, (L. 86), *having the quality of* courage.

Ship; *s.* clerk*ship*, *the place, or office* of a clerk; friend*ship*, *the condition or relation* of being a friend.

Some; *a.* quarrel*some*, *characterized by* a disposition to quarrel; burden*some*, *having the quality or character* of oppressiveness.

Ster; *s.* team*ster*, *one whose business it is* to drive a team.

Tude; *s.* servi*tude*, (L. 483), *the condition* of slavery; forti*tude*, (L. 189), *the quality of* bravery.

Ty; *s.* abili*ty*, (L. 215), *the condition or state of* being able.

Ure; *s.* depart*ure*, (L. 365), *the act of* departing; post*ure*, (399), *the condition* of being in a particular position; furnit*ure*, *the thing* furnished.

Ward; *adv.* east*ward*, *in the direction* of the east.—*a.* awk*ward*, *having the quality of* uncouthness.

Y; *a.* dew*y*, *covered with* dew; water*y*, *partaking of* water. —*s.* modest*y*, (L. 306), *the quality or state of* being modest.

CHAPTER II.

WORDS DERIVED FROM THE LATIN.

Pronunciation. Latin words are usually pronounced in this country, in accordance with the general principles of English pronunciation. The following directions, however, are necessary for those who have not studied Latin, and should be carefully observed.

1. Every Latin word has as many syllables as there are vowels or diphthongs in it. Thus, in the expression *bona fide*, in good faith, the word *fide* has two syllables, the *e* being sounded as *e*

in *me*. In like manner the words *voce, jure, parte, lege*, &c., are pronounced each with two syllables.

2. Words of *two* syllables have the accent always on the first syllable; as *a'cer, a'go, ar'bor*. In this book the accented syllable is marked, in all Latin words of more than one syllable; and the manner in which the word is divided will generally show what sound is to be given to the vowel of the accented syllable.

3. When a word of more than one syllable ends with *a*, that letter is sounded as *a* in *ah*, except that the sound is not prolonged; as *cau'sa, cate'na*.

4. The diphthongs *œ* and *æ* are sounded as simple *e* would be in the same place; thus, *fœ'dus* and *æm'ulus*, are pronounced as if written *fe'dus, em'ulus*.

5. *C* and *g* are hard before *a, o,* and *u,* and soft before *e, i,* and *y;* thus, in the words *ca'no, co'lo,* and *cu'ra,* the *c* has the sound of *k;* in *ce'do* and *ci'vis* it has the sound of *s*. So *g*, in the words *fuga'tus, li'go,* and *lon'gus,* has the sound of *g* in *give;* in the words *ge'ro* and *gig'no* it has the sound of *g* in *gentle*.

6. *Ch* always sounds like *k*.

For a full account of Latin pronunciation, see Andrews's and Stoddard's Latin Grammar.

☞ In the following chapter, a Latin word placed in a parenthesis immediately after another Latin word, as (*acris*) after *Acer*, shows the form which that word assumes in the *genitive case*, if it be a substantive or adjective; or in the supine, or some other inflection, if it be a verb.

In the several paragraphs, the words are not always arranged in exact alphabetical order, because it is desirable that words formed immediately and obviously from the Latin word should be placed before those whose derivation is more remote.

1. *A'cer*, (*a'cris*), sour; pungent. *Acu'tus*, sharp.

ACER'BITY, sharpness of disposition.
AC'RID, of a biting taste.
AC'RIMONY, sharpness; ill-nature.
ACID'ULATE, to flavor with acid.

ACID'ITY, sourness; tartness.
ACUTE', sharp-witted; pointed.
ACU'MEN, (Lat. *acumen*, a sharp point), intellectual penetration; quickness of perception.

WORDS DERIVED FROM THE LATIN. 59

2. *A'ger*, (*a'gri*), a field.

AGRA'RIAN, relating to lands.*
AG'RICULTURE, (82), the cultivation of the ground.

AGRICUL'TURIST, a farmer.
PER'EGRINATE, to travel in foreign lands.

* The agrarian laws of ancient Rome, which caused so much civil commotion, related to the distribution of public lands among the people.

3. *A'go*, (*ac'tum*), to do; to perform.

ACT, to behave; to perform.
AC'TION, a performance.
ACTIV'ITY, AGIL'ITY, quickness of motion.
AC'TUAL, real; existing in act.
AC'TUATE, to put into action.
AC'TUARY, a register or clerk.
A'GENT, a doer; one intrusted with business.
AG'ITATE, to put into motion or excitement.

CO'GENT, forcible.
DAM'AGE, (107), injury.
ENACT', to decree.
EXACT', *v.* to take by authority or force.
EXACT', *a.* accurate.
EX'IGENCY, pressing necessity.
MAN'AGE, (282), to carry on.
PROD'IGAL, wasteful.
TRANSACT', to conduct or perform.

4. *A'lius*, other; another. *Alie'nus*, foreign.

AL'IEN, foreign; estranged.
AL'IENATE, to transfer to another; to estrange.

ALIENA'TION, estrangement.
INAL'IENABLE, that cannot be transferred or alienated.

5. *A'lo*, (*al'itum*, or *al'tum*), to feed; to nourish.

AL'IMENT, nourishment.
ALIMENT'ARY, pertaining to food.

COALESCE', (Lat. *coales'co*), to grow together; to unite.
COALI'TION, combination; union.

6. *Al'ter*, the other. *Alter'nus*, one after the other.

ALTERCA'TION, quarrelling; disputing.
ALTERN'ATELY, one after the other.

ALTERNA'TION, succession; performance by turns.
ALTERN'ATIVE, a choice of two things.

7. *Al'tus*, lofty.

AL'TITUDE, height.

EXALT', to raise up.

8. *Am'bulo, (ambula'tum), to walk.*

AM'BULATORY, pertaining to the act of walking.

AM'BLE, to walk or run in an artificial manner. [through.
PERAM'BULATE, to walk

9. *A'mo, (ama'tum), to love.*

AMATEUR', (Fr.), a lover of the fine arts.
A'MIABLE, lovely; worthy to be loved.
AMIABIL'ITY, loveliness.
AM'ICABLE, friendly, peaceable.
AM'ITY, friendship; good-will.

ENAM'ORED, inflamed with love; fond.
EN'EMY, one hostile to another; a foe.
EN'MITY, hatred; hostility.
INIM'ICAL, unfriendly; opposed.

10. *Am'plus, large.*

AM'PLE, large; liberal.
AM'PLY, largely.
AM'PLIFY, (152), to enlarge.

AMPLIFICA'TION, enlargement; extension.
AM'PLITUDE, largeness.

11. *An'go, (anx'i), to vex.*

AN'GER, wrath.
AN'GUISH, extreme pain.

ANXI'ETY, solicitude.
ANX'IOUS, solicitous.

12. *An'gulus, a corner.*

AN'GLE, a corner.
AN'GULAR, having corners.
RECT'ANGLE, (438), a right-angled, four-sided figure.
TRI'ANGLE, (549), a three cornered figure.

QUAD'RANGLE, (426), a square.
EQUIAN'GULAR, (144), having equal angles.
MULTAN'GULAR, (317), many cornered.

13. *An'ima, the life, or spiritual principle. An'imus, the mind.*

AN'IMAL, a living creature.
ANIMAL'CULE, a minute animal.
AN'IMATE, to make alive.
ANIMADVERT', (579), to consider or criticize.
INAN'IMATE, lifeless.
ANIMA'TION, liveliness.
ANI'MOSITY, violent hatred.

UNANIM'ITY, (563), agreement in opinion.
UNAN'IMOUS, of one mind.
EQUANIM'ITY, (144), evenness of mind. [of mind.
MAGNANIM'ITY, (278), greatness of mind.
PUSILLANIM'ITY, (Lat. *pusil'lus*, weak), cowardice.

14. *An'nus, a year.*

AN'NUAL, happening yearly.
ANNU'ITY, a yearly income.

ANNU'ITANT, one who receives an annuity.

ANNIVER'SARY, (579), a stated day, returning with the revolution of the year.
AN'NALS, yearly records.
BIEN'NIAL, (37), of two years.
TRIEN'NIAL, (549), happening every three years.

SEPTEN'NIAL, (478), of seven years.
SUPERAN'NUATED, impaired by old age.
PEREN'NIAL, continuing through the year. [years.
MILLEN'NIUM, (297), a thousand

15. An'nulus, a ring.

AN'NULAR, in the form of a ring.

SEM'I-ANNULAR, having the form of half a ring.

16. An'tiquus, ancient.

AN'TIQUARY, one who seeks ancient things.
AN'TIQUATED, old; out of date.

ANTIQUE', (Fr.), belonging to old times; a relic of ancient
AN'CIENT, old. [times.

17. Ape'rio, to open.

APE'RIENT, laxative.

AP'ERTURE, an opening.

18. Ap'to, to fit or join.

APT, fit; inclined to.
APT'NESS, fitness; quickness of apprehension.

AP'TITUDE, tendency; disposition.
ADAPT', to adjust; to fit one thing to another.

19. A'qua, water.

AQUAT'IC, living in or on the water.
A'QUEOUS, watery.

AQ'UEDUCT, (133), a channel for water.
TERRA'QUEOUS, (536), consisting of land and water.

20. Ar'biter, a judge or umpire.

AR'BITRATOR, a judge appointed by opposite parties to decide between them.
AR'BITRATE, to decide.

ARBITRA'TION, determination by an arbitrator.
AR'BITRARY, capricious; absolute.

21. Ar'bor, a tree.

AR'BOR, a bower.
AR'BORIST, one who cultivates trees and shrubs.

AR'BORICULTURE, (82), the art of cultivating trees and shrubs.

22. *Ar'ceo*, to hinder or restrain.

Coerce', to restrain by force. | Coer'cion, restraint.

23. *Ardeo,* (*ar'si*), to burn.

Ar'dent, burning; passionate. | Ar'son, setting fire to a dwell-
Ar'dor, heat; earnestness. | ing.

24. *Arguo*, to argue.

Ar'gue, to reason; to dispute. | Argumenta'tion, reasoning.
Ar'gument, a reason offered; | Argument'ative, containing
controversy. | argument.

25. *Ar'ma*, arms, weapons.

Arm, *v.* to take arms. | Ar'mory, the place where arms
Arms, weapons; war. | are kept or made.
Disarm', to deprive of weapons. | Ab'mament, Arma'da, (Sp.), a
Ar'my, a number of armed men. | naval warlike force.
Ar'mistice, (491), a cessation | Armo'rial, belonging to the es-
of hostilities. | cutcheon of a family. [in arms.
Ar'morer, one who makes arms. | Armip'otent, (403), powerful
Ar'mor, defensive weapons. | Unarm'ed, without arms.

26. *A'ro*, to plough.

Ar'able, capable of being | Inar'able, not arable.
ploughed.

27. *Ars*, (*ar'tis*), art, skill.

Art, skill, cunning; a trade. | Art'ifice, (152), stratagem.
Art'ist, a professor of an art. | Art'ful, cunning.
Art'isan, Artif'icer; a work- | Art'less, unskilful; without
man, an operative. [genuine. | fraud.
Artific'ial, made by art, not | Inert', dull; motionless.

28. *Artic'ulus*, a joint or limb.

Ar'ticle, a single thing; a part | Artic'ulately, with distinct-
of speech. | ness of sound.
Artic'ulate, *v.* to speak dis- | Articula'tion, a juncture of
tinctly; to join. | bones; the knots in the stalk
Artic'ulate, *a.* distinct; | of a plant; speech.
branched out into joints. | Inartic'ulate, indistinct.

WORDS DERIVED FROM THE LATIN.

29. As'per, rough.

ASPER'ITY, roughness.

EXAS'PERATE, to enrage.

30. Au'dio, (audi'tum), to hear.

AUD'IBLE, that can be heard.
AUD'IENCE, a hearing; the persons assembled to hear.
AUD'IT, (Lat.), to examine an account.

AUD'ITOR, a hearer; an examiner.
AUD'ITORY, an assembly of hearers.
OBE'DIENT, listening to; obey.

31. Au'geo, (aux'i, auc'tum), to increase.

AUGMENT', to increase.
AUGMENTA'TION, enlargement.
AUC'TION, a sale by bidding more and more. [auction.
AUCTIONEER', one who holds an
AU'THORIZE, to give authority.

AU'THOR, (the Latin word is auc'tor), an originator; a writer.
AUTHOR'ITY, legal power; influence.
AUXIL'IARY, helping.

32. A'vis, a bird. Au'gur, Aus'pex, (aus'picis), a soothsayer.

A'VIARY, a place enclosed to keep birds in.
AU'GUR, s. one who predicted by observing birds.
AU'GUR, v. to forebode.
AU'GURY, an omen or prediction.

INAU'GURATE, to invest with an office by solemn rites.
AUS'PICES, (Lat.), (504), the omens of an undertaking.
AUSPIC'IOUS, favorable.
INAUSPIC'IOUS, unfortunate.

33. Bac'chus, in heathen mythology, the god of wine.

BAC'CHANAL, one who indulges in drunken revelry.

BACCHANA'LIAN, pertaining to drunken revelry.

34. Bea'tus, happy; blessed.

BEATIF'IC, (152), fitted to bless or make happy.

BEAT'ITUDE, blessedness; a blessing pronounced.

35. Bel'lum, war.

BELLIG'ERENT, (203), waging war.

REB'EL, one who revolts.
REBELL'ION, insurrection.

36. *Bi'bo,* to drink.

Bib'ber, a tippler.
Biba'cious, fond of drinking.
Bib'ulous, absorbing.
Imbibe', to drink in.

37. *Bis,* twice.

Bisect', (470), to cut into two equal parts.
Bisect'ion, division into two equal parts.
Bis'cuit, (85), hard, dry, flat bread.
Combine', (Lat. *bi'ni,* two by two), to unite.
Bi'ped, (380), an animal having two feet.
Bi'valve, (Lat. *val'væ,* folding-doors), a molluscous animal, having two valves or shells; an oyster; a mussel, &c.

38. *Be'ne,* well.

Boun'ty, (Lat. *bo'nus,* good), generosity.
Benign', kind; favorable.
Benig'nity, graciousness.
Benef'icent, (152), kind; doing good.
Benef'icence, active goodness.
Ben'efit, advantage.
Benefi'cial, advantageous.
Ben'efice, a church living.
Benefac'tion, a benefit conferred.
Benefac'tor, one who confers a benefit.
Benedic'tion, (117), a blessing.
Benev'olence, (598), disposition to do good.

39. *Brev'is,* short.

Brevet', a commission without seal, giving title and rank in the army above that for which pay is received.
Brevet', taking rank by brevet.
Brev'ity, shortness.
Abbre'viate, to shorten.
Brief, *a.* short; concise.
Brief, *s.* a pleader's notes.

40. *Ca'do, (ca'sum),* to fall.

Ca'dence, fall of the voice.
Deca'dence, falling; decay.
Case, state of a thing.
Cas'ual, happening by chance.
Cas'ualty, accident.
Cas'ually, accidentally; by chance.
Cascade', a waterfall.
Ac'cident, that which happens unforeseen. [of conscience.
Cas'uistry, the science of cases
Coincide', to agree.
Coin'cidence, concurrence.
Decay', to fall away.
Decid'uous, falling.
In'cident, *s.* an event.
In'cident, *a.* likely to happen as an attendant event.
Occa'sion, opportunity; time of a particular occurrence.
Oc'cident, the west, where the sun sets.

WORDS DERIVED FROM THE LATIN.

41. *Cæ'do*, (*cæ'sum*), to cut; to kill.

Incis'ion, a cut into any thing.
Excis'ion, a cutting out.
Excise', a duty on goods.
Concise', short, brief.
Decide', to determine.
Decis'ion, determination.
Deci'sive, conclusive.
Precise', exact; strict.
Precis'ion, exact limitation.
Precise'ly, exactly; in exact conformity to truth, or to a model.
Frat'ricide, (192), killing a brother.
Hom'icide, (220), manslaughter; a manslayer.
Infan'ticide, (158), killing an infant.
Par'ricide, (367), killing a father.
Sui'cide, (519), self-murder.
Reg'icide, (438), murder of a king.

42. *Cal'eo*, to be warm or hot.

Cal'dron, a boiler; a large kettle.
Cal'id, hot.
Calor'ic, the element of heat.
Calefac'tor, (152), a small kind of stove. [fluid.
Scald, to burn with a boiling

43. *Calx*, (*cal'cis*), chalk; limestone. *Cal'culus*, a little pebble.

Calcine', to expel all volatile ingredients from a compound by heat, (as water and carbonic acid from limestone in the manufacture of lime;) to reduce to powder or ashes.
Cal'culate, to reckon. [Anciently pebbles were used in numerical computation.]
Incal'culable, that cannot be calculated; beyond calculation.

44. *Can'deo*, to glow with heat.

Can'dle, a tallow or wax light.
In'cense, *s.* perfumes burnt.
Incense', *v.* to enrage.
Incen'tive, inducement.
Incend'iary, one who sets houses, &c., on fire.
Can'dor, sincerity. [This signification is derived figuratively from the light pertaining to a red-hot substance.]
Can'did, open, ingenuous.
Can'didate, one proposed for office, or preferment.*
Can'didly, without disguise.

* Among the Ancient Romans, those who sought the consûlship wore robes of remarkable whiteness, and were thence called *candidati.*

45. *Ca'nis*, a dog.

Ca'nine, pertaining to dogs.
Canic'ular, pertaining to the dog-star.

46. Can'tus, a song.

CHANT, a kind of sacred music.
CHAN'TICLEER, (75), the cock which crows.
CAN'TICLE, a song; the song of Solomon.
CAN'TO, (It.), a section of a poem.
CANT, a set phraseology used to manifest religious zeal.
DESCANT', to discourse in a formal manner.
AC'CENT, a modification of the voice.
ENCHANT', to delight highly.
INCANTA'TION, charms by singing.
RECANT', to recall, to retract.

47. Ca'pio, (cap'tum), to take.

CA'PABLE, able to do or take.
CAPA'CIOUS, large, holding much.
CAPAC'ITATE, to enable; to qualify.
CAPAC'ITY, power of holding.
CAP'TIOUS, peevish; cavilling.
CAP'TIVATE, to take prisoners; to charm.
CAP'TIVE, a prisoner.
CAP'TOR, one who takes a prize.
CAP'TURE, a seizure.
ACCEPT', to receive.
ACCEPT'ABLE, grateful; pleas-[ing.
ANTICIPA'TION, receiving or doing beforehand.
CONCEIVE', to have an idea or notion.
CONCEP'TION, notion, idea.
DECEIVE', to cheat, to mislead.
DECEP'TION, a fraud, a cheat.
EMAN'CIPATE, (282), to set at liberty.
EXCEPT', to take out.
INCIP'IENT, commencing.
INTERCEPT', to seize on the way; to stop.
OCCUPA'TION, possession; employment.
OC'CUPY, to possess.
PARTIC'IPATE, (365), to share.
PAR'TICIPLE, a word partaking of the nature of an adjective and of a verb.
PERCEIVE', to notice.
PERCEP'TIBLE, capable of being perceived.
PRECEP'TOR, a tutor, a teacher.
PRE'CEPT, a rule given.
PRIN'CIPAL, (412), chief, capital.
PRIN'CIPLE, element; ground of action.
RECEIPT', a taking; acknowledgment for money paid.
RECEIVE', to take, to admit.
RECEP'TACLE, a thing which receives or contains.
REC'IPE, a medical prescription.*
RECIP'IENT, one who takes.
SUSCEP'TIBLE, capable of being affected or changed.

* *Recipe* is an imperative form of the verb *recipio*, and would be the first word in a prescription written in Latin—" Take," etc. In books of pharmacy the word is usually represented by R. or some other character.

48. Cap'ut, (cap'itis), the head.

CAP'ITAL, chief; principal.† | CAPITA'TION, counting by heads.

† *Capital* crimes are those which are punishable by loss of the *head* or life.

WORDS DERIVED FROM THE LATIN. 67

CAPIT'ULATE, to surrender on conditions.*
CAPE, a head-land.
CAP'TAIN, a chief commander.
CHAP'TER, a division, or head.
DECAP'ITATE, to behead.
PRECIP'ITATE, v. to tumble headlong; to hurry.
PRECIP'ITATE, a. headstrong; hasty.
PRECIP'ITATELY, headlong, hastily, rashly.
PREC'IPICE, a headlong steep.
RECAPIT'ULATE, to repeat again (as the topics of a discourse.)

* The word arose from the stipulation being drawn up under heads.

49. Car'cer, a prison.

INCAR'CERATE, to imprison. | INCARCERA'TION, imprisonment.

50. Ca'ro (car'nis), flesh.

CAR'NAL, fleshy, not spiritual.
CAR'NAGE, (3), slaughter.
INCARNA'TION, the taking of a body of flesh.
INCAR'NATE, embodied in flesh.
CAR'NIVAL, (567), in Roman Catholic countries, a feast before Lent.
CAR'NALLY, according to the flesh; not spiritually.
CAR'CASS, a dead body.
CARNIV'OROUS, (601), feeding on flesh.
CHAR'NEL-HOUSE, a place for depositing human bodies.

51. Car'po, to pluck.

CARP, to cavil; to find fault.
CARP'ING, captious; fault-finding.
INDISCERPT'IBLE, that cannot be torn in pieces.
EX'CERPT, something culled out.

52. Cas'tigo, to chastise.

CAS'TIGATE, to punish by stripes. | CASTIGA'TION, punishment.

53. Cate'na, a chain.

CONCATENA'TION, a series of links; a successive order of things depending on each other; (as, a *concatenation* of causes.)

54. Cau'sa, a cause.

CAUSE, that which produces an effect.
CAUSE'LESS, having no cause.
ACCUSE', to charge with a crime
ACCUSA'TION, the act of charging with an offence or crime.
EXCUSE', to pardon.
BECAUSE', for this reason.
RECU'SANT, making opposition.

55. Ca'veo, (cau'tum), to beware.

CAU'TION, prudence in respect to danger.
CAU'TIOUS, using caution.

INCAU'TIOUS, heedless.
PRECAU'TION, previous care.

56. Ca'vus, hollow.

CAVE, a hollow place.
CON'CAVE, hollow, opposed to convex.

EX'CAVATE, to hollow out.
EXCAVA'TION, a cavity made by digging.

57. Ce'do, (ces'sum), to yield; to go away.

CEDE, to yield or give up.
CES'SION, a giving up; resignation.
CEASE, to stop; to leave off.
CESSA'TION, a stop, a discontinuance.
ACCEDE', to assent to; to agree.
ACCESS', approach.
ACCES'SION, a coming to; an increase by the addition of something.
AC'CESSORY, rendering aid.
AN'CESTOR, (Lat. anteces'sor), a person from whom one is distantly a descendant.
ANTECE'DENT, going before.
CONCEDE', to admit, to grant.
DECEASE', departure from this world; death.
EXCEED', to go beyond.
EXCESS', more than enough.
EXCES'SIVE, exceeding.
INCES'SANT, without pause.
INTERCEDE', to go between; to request in behalf of another.

INTERCES'SION, the act of interceding.
PRECEDE', to go before.
PREDECEASE', the decease of one before another.
PRECE'DENCE, priority, superiority
PREDECES'SOR, one that was in a place before another.
PREC'EDENT, an example.
PROCEED', to go forward.
PROCE'DURE, manner of proceeding.
PROC'ESS, progressive course.
PROCES'SION, a ceremonious march.
RECEDE', to go back; to retreat.
RECESS', a place or time of retreat.
SECES'SION, a withdrawing from.
SUCCEED', to follow after; to prosper.
SUCCESS', prosperity; the event of an affair.
SUCCES'SION, series.
SUCCES'SIVE, following in order.

58. Cel'eber, renowned, famous.

CEL'EBRATE, to praise; to commend solemnly.
CEL'EBRATED, renowned, famous.

CELEBRA'TION, a distinguishing by ceremonies.
CELEB'RITY, renown; fame.

WORDS DERIVED FROM THE LATIN.

59. Cé′ler, swift.

CE·LER′ITY, swiftness. | ACCEL′ERATE, to hasten forward.

60. Cel′la, a cellar.

CEL′LAR, an underground store.
CEL′LARAGE, charge for storage in a cellar.

CEL′LARIST, a butler; one who has the care of the cellar.

61. Cé′lo, to cover, to hide.

CONCEAL′, to hide. | CONCEAL′MENT, the act, place, or mode of hiding.

62. Cœ′lum, the heaven.

CELES′TIAL, heavenly. | SUBCELES′TIAL, beneath the heavens.

63. Cen′seo, to judge or estimate.

CEN′SOR, an officer who examines the works of authors before they are allowed to be printed.
CENSO′RIOUS, judging severely.
CEN′SURE, blame, reproach.

CEN′SURABLE, blame-worthy.
CEN′SUS, (Lat.), an official enumeration of the inhabitants of a country.
RECEN′SION, a review, or re-examination.

64. Cen′tum, a hundred.

CENTEN′NIAL, (14), occurring once in a hundred years.
CEN′TURY, a hundred years.
CENTU′RION, an officer over a hundred men.

CENTENA′RIAN, a person who is a hundred years old.
PERCENT′AGE, (3), a rate, allowance, or estimate by the hundred.

65. Cer′no, (cre′tum), to separate; to distinguish; to discern.

CER′TAIN, determined; sure.
CER′TIFY, (152), to assure.
CERTIF′ICATE, a written declaration or testimony.
ASCERTAIN′, to find out certainly.
CONCERN′, business; anxiety.
DECREE′, (Lat. decer′no), to ordain or command.
DECREE′, an edict; a rule or law.

DISCERN′, to see; to distinguish.
DISCREET′, discerning, prudent.
DISCRETE′, distinct, separate.
DISCERN′MENT, judgment.
DISCRE′TION, judgment, prudence.
DISCRIMINA′TION, (Lat. discri′men), distinction.
DISCRIM′INATING, acute.

SECRETE', to put aside.
SE'CRET, concealed; private.

SEC'RETARY, one who writes for another.*

* So called from the private or secret affairs intrusted to him.

66. *Cer'to*, to contend; to vie.

CONCERT', to contrive together.
CON'CERT, union; a musical entertainment.

DISCONCERT', to disturb.
PRECONCERT'ED, contrived together beforehand.

67. *Cer'tus*, sure, (see *Cer'no*).

68. *Ci'eo*, (*ci'tum*), to rouse; to call forth.

CITE, to summon into a court; to quote.
CITA'TION, a summoning; a quotation.
EXCITE', to stir up, to encourage.
EXCI'TABLE, easily stirred up.
EXCITE'MENT, agitation.
RESUS'CITATE, to rouse or enliven again.

INCITE', to animate; to urge on.
INCITE'MENT, impulse.
RECITE', to repeat; to tell over.
RECITA'TION, repetition; rehearsal.
RECI'TAL, account; narration; rehearsal.
QUOTE, to repeat a passage from some author.

69. *Cin'go*, (*cinc'tum*), to gird.

CINCT'URE, a belt; a girdle.
PRE'CINCT, a limit or bound.

SUCCINCT', brought into small compass; compact; concise.

70. *Ci'nis*, (*Cin'eris*), ashes.

CIN'DER, a burnt mass.
CINERA'TION, the reduction of anything to ashes.

INCIN'ERATE, to burn to ashes.
INCIN'ERABLE, that may be reduced to ashes.

71. *Cir'cus*, a circle.

CIR'CLE, a round space, also the line enclosing it.
CIR'CLET, a little circle.
CIR'CULAR, round like a circle.
CIR'CULATE, to move in a circle.
CIR'CUIT, (142), extent round about.

CIRCU'ITOUS, going round about; not direct.
CIR'CUS, an open space for sports.
ENCIR'CLE, to surround.
SEM'ICIRCLE, (474), half a circle.

72. *Ci'vis*, a citizen.

CIV'IC, relating to civil honors.

CIV'IL, relating to the community; gentle, well bred.

WORDS DERIVED FROM THE LATIN.

Civil'ian, one versed in law or political affairs. [or city.
Cit'izen, an inhabitant of a state
Cit'y, a large corporate town.
Civil'ity, gentleness, politeness.
Civiliza'tion, the state of a civilized people.
Civ'ilize, to reclaim from a savage state.
Unciv'il, rude, clownish.

73. *Clam*, secretly.

Clandes'tine, secret.
Clandes'tinely, in a secret manner.

74. *Cla'mo*, (*clama'tum*), to cry out; to shout.

Clam'or, outcry; noise.
Clam'orous, noisy; vociferous.
Clam'orer, a noisy person.
Acclama'tion, a shout of applause.
Declama'tion, discourse addressed to the passions; exercise of public speaking.
Claim, to demand.
Claim'ant, one that demands a right.
Disclaim', to deny the possession of any right or character.
Exclaim', to cry out. [ly.
Proclaim', to announce public-
Proclama'tion, publication by authority.
Reclaim', to recall; to reform.

75. *Cla'rus*, clear, bright.

Clar'ion, a shrill trumpet.
Clear, bright; evident.
Declare', to make known; to proclaim.
Clar'ify, (152), to purify.
Declara'tion, a proclamation; open avowal.

76. *Clas'sis*, a class.

Class, a rank of persons, a set.
Clas'sic, Clas'sical, relating to authors of the highest rank, particularly ancient Greek and Roman authors.
Clas'sify, (152), to arrange in classes.
Classifica'tion, arrangement in classes.
Clas'sis, (Lat.), a convention.

77. *Clau'do*, (*clau'sum*), or *Clu'do*, (*clu'sum*), to shut, to close.

Close, to shut.
Clos'et, a small private room.
Conclude', to come to a decision.
Conclu'sive, decisive.
Clause, a subdivision of a sentence. [nery.
Clois'ter, a monastery or nun-
Exclude', to shut out.
Seclude', to shut up apart.
Include', Enclose', to shut in; to bring within certain limits.
Preclude', to hinder or prevent.
Recluse', one who lives in retirement or seclusion.
Seclu'sion, retirement.

78. *Cle'mens, (clemen'tis)*, merciful, kind

CLEM'ENT, merciful, kind.
CLEM'ENCY, mercy.

INCLEM'ENT, unmerciful; harsh.
INCLEM'ENCY, severity.

79. *Cli'no*, to incline or bend.

INCLINE', to bend, to lean.
INCLINA'TION, propensity.
DECLINE', to lean downwards; to refuse.
DECLIV'ITY, (Lat. *cli'vus*), descent; inclination downwards.

ACCLIV'ITY, ascent, inclination upwards.
PROCLIV'ITY, proneness.
RECLINE', to lean back.
CLIN'ICAL, relating to a couch or bed.*

* Clinical lectures are medical lectures given at the bed-side of the patient.

80. *Cli'vus*, an ascent; a hill. See derivatives under *Cli'no*.

81. *Co'dex, (cod'icis)*, the trunk of a tree; a volume or roll.

CODE, a collection or digest of laws.

COD'ICIL, a supplement to a will.

82. *Co'lo, (cul'tum)*, to cultivate.

COL'ONY, a settlement or plantation abroad.
COL'ONIST, a settler in a colony.
COUL'TER, the sharp iron of a plough.
CUL'TIVATE, to improve by labor.

CUL'TURE, improvement by labor.
AG'RICULTURE, (2), husbandry, farming.
HOR'TICULTURE, (222), gardening.

83. *Co'mes, (com'itis)*, a companion.

COM'ITY, kindness of manner.
CONCOM'ITANT, going with.

84. *Concil'ium*, an assembly; a council.

COUN'CIL, an assembly held for consultation.
CONCIL'IATE, (Lat. *concil'io*), to bring together; to win to friendship.

CONCIL'IATORY, fitted to allay angry feelings.
RECONCILE', to conciliate again, to render consistent.

85. *Co'quo, (coc'tum)*, to cook.

CONCOCT', to prepare by digesting; to devise; to plot; (as, to *concoct* a scheme).

DECOC'TION, the act of boiling anything to extract its virtues.
COOK, to prepare food by heat.

WORDS DERIVED FROM THE LATIN.

86. *Cor*, (*cor'dis*), the heart.

CORE, the central part, as of fruit.
COR'DIAL, *a.* sincere, hearty.
COR'DIAL, *s.* anything that gladdens the heart.
CORDIAL'ITY, sincerity.
CON'CORD, agreement.

CONCOR'DANCE, an index of words contained in the Bible.
COUR'AGE, boldness.
DIS'CORD, disagreement.
RECORD', (Lat. *Recor'dor*, to remember, call to mind), to register.

87. *Cor'nu*, a horn.

COR'NET, a musical instrument blown with the mouth; a sort of trumpet.
CORNUCO'PIA, (Lat. *co'pia*, plenty), the horn of plenty.

BICOR'NOUS, (37), having two horns or antlers.
U'NICORN, (563), an animal having a single horn.

88. *Coróna*, a garland, or crown.

CROWN, the head ornament worn by kings.
CORONA'TION, the solemnity of crowning a king.
COR'ONAL, a crown or garland.

COR'ONET, an inferior crown worn by the nobility.
COR'ONER, an officer to inquire into violent deaths.*
COR'OLLARY, an inference.†

* The name was derived from the relation of the office to the crown.
† So called because it *crowns* the leading proposition or argument.

89. *Cor'pus*, (*cor'poris*), a body.

COR'PORAL, the lowest officer over a body of soldiers.
COR'PORATE, united into a body or community.
CORPORA'TION, a body politic.
INCOR'PORATE, to embody.
COR'PUSCLE, a minute body.

CORPO'REAL, having a body; not immaterial; relating to the body.
COR'PULENT, having a bulky [body.
CORPSE, a dead body.
CORPS, (Fr.), (pronounced *core*), a body of soldiers.

90. *Cos'ta*, a rib.

COAST, the margin of the land.
COS'TAL, pertaining to the ribs.

INTERCOS'TAL, lying between the ribs.

91. *Cras*, to-morrow.

PROCRAS'TINATE, to put off. | PROCRASTINA'TION, deferring.

92. Cre'do, (cred'itum), to believe.

CREED, articles of belief.
CRE'DENCE, belief.
CRED'IT, belief; reputation; trust.
CRED'ITABLE, reputable.
CREDEN'TIAL, that which gives title to belief.

CRED'IBLE, worthy of belief.
INCRED'IBLE, not to be believed.
CRED'ITOR, one who trusts another for a debt.
CRED'ULOUS, apt to believe.
DISCRED'IT, to disbelieve. [lief.
INCREDU'LITY, slowness of be-

93. Cre'o, (crea'tum), to create.

CREATE', to cause to exist.
CREA'TION, the act of creating; the universe.
CREAT'URE, a created being.
CREA'TIVE, that can or does create.

CREA'TOR, (Lat.), God, who gives existence.
RECREA'TION, amusement, diversion, (because it re-creates vigor).

94. Cre'po, (crep'itum) to sound; to rattle.

DECREP'IT,* wasted and worn out with age.
DECREP'ITUDE,* the feebleness of age.

DISCREP'ANCY, *literally*, disagreement of sound; inconsistency.

* The derivation of this word is doubtful. If derived from *crepo*, its signification has reference to the rattling or creaking of anything which is broken, or loosened from its place.

95. Cres'co, (cre'tum), to grow.

CRES'CENT, the shape of the new moon †
CON'CRETE, to coalesce into one mass; to coagulate.
EXCRES'CENCE, something growing out of another.

DECREASE', to grow less.
INCREASE', to grow larger.
RECRUIT', v. to raise new soldiers; to gain new strength.
RECRUIT', s. a newly enlisted soldier.

† So called from its change of size.

96. Cri'men, (crim'inis), an accusation; a crime.

CRIME, an offence; a great fault.
CRIM'INAL, partaking of crime.
CRIMINA'TION, an accusing.

RECRIMINA'TION, return of one accusation with another.
RECRIM'INATE, to retort a charge.

97. Cru'dus, raw, unripe.

CRUDE, raw; unripe; undigested.
CRU'DITY, unripeness; indigestion; crudeness.
CRU'EL, (Lat. crude'lis), hardhearted.
CRU'ELTY, inhumanity.

98. Crux, (cru'cis), a cross.

CROSS, s. one straight body laid across another.
CROSS, a. peevish.
CRUCIFIX'ION, (172), death on a cross.
CRU'CIFIX, a cross bearing an image of our Saviour.
CRU'CIAL, crosswise; transverse.
CRU'CIFY, (152), to put to death by nailing to a cross.
EXCRU'CIATE, to extort by suffering; to put to severe pain.
EXCRU'CIATING, extremely painful; torturing.

99. Cu'bo or cum'bo, to lie down.

ENCUM'BER, to oppress with a burden; to hinder.
ENCUM'BRANCE, a burden.
INCUBA'TION, the act of sitting upon eggs.
IN'CUBUS, (Lat.), the nightmare; a sense of weight.
INCUM'BENT, resting upon.
RECUM'BENT, lying; leaning.
PROCUM'BENT, lying down.
SUCCUMB', to yield; to sink under a difficulty.
SUPERINCUM'BENT, lying on the top of something.

100. Cul'pa, a fault.

CUL'PABLE, faulty; blamable.
CUL'PRIT, an accused person.
EXCUL'PATE, to clear from blame.
INCUL'PATE, to blame.

101. Cu'mulus, a heap.

CU'MULATIVE, piled up. | ACCU'MULATE, to heap up.

102. Cu'ra, care.

CURE, a healing.
CU'RABLE, admitting of a remedy.
CU'RATE, a clergyman hired to do the duties of another.
CU'RIOUS, inquisitive.
CU'RATOR, a superintendent.
CURIOS'ITY, inquisitiveness; a rarity.
AC'CURATE, exact; done with care.
PROCURE', to obtain.
PROCURE'MENT, the act of procuring; attainment.
PROX'Y, (contracted from procuracy), agency for another.
SECU'RITY, safety.
SI'NECURE, (Lat. si'ne, without), a station which gives income without employment.

103. Cur'ro, (cur'sum), to run.

Cur'rent, a. passing.
Cur'rent, s. a running stream.
Cur'rency, circulation; money.
Cur'ricle, an open chaise, with two horses abreast.
Cur'sory, hasty.
Career', course.
Cou'rier, (Fr.), a messenger sent in haste. [succession.
Course, race; passage; order of
Cours'er, a swift horse.
Concur', to agree.
Concur'rence, combination of circumstances; agreement.
Con'course, a confluence of persons or things.
Discourse', conversation; a sermon.
Discur'sive, roving; by gradation of argument.
Excur'sion, an expedition; a digression.
Incur'sion, inroad; invasion.
Incur', to become liable to.
Occur', to happen.
Occur'rence, an event.
Recur', to happen again; to go back.
Precur'sor, forerunner.
Recourse', application to for help.
Suc'cor, help in distress.

104. Cur'vus, crooked; winding.

Curve, a bent line.
Curv'ature, crookedness.
Cur'vated, bent; crooked.
Incur'vate, to bend.

105. Cus'tos, (custo'dis), a keeper.

Cus'tody, watch, imprisonment. | Custo'dial, relating to custody.

106. Cu'tis, the skin.

Cuta'neous, affecting the skin. | Cu'ticle, the thin outer skin.

107. Dam'num, harm, loss.

Dam'age, (3), injury.
Damna'tion, the word used in the New Testament to signify condemnation to everlasting punishment.
Condemn', to give sentence against; to denounce.
Indem'nify, (152,) to relieve from loss.

108. De'beo, (deb'itum), to owe.

Debt, that which is due.
Debt'less, free from debt.
Deb'it, v. to charge with debt.
Debt'or, one who is indebted.

109. De'cem, ten.

DEC'IMAL, numbered by tens.
DEC'IMATE, to tithe; to take the tenth; to destroy a large but indefinite part of any aggregate body.
DECIMA'TION, selection of every tenth; a heavy loss of life from any cause in an army or other large body of persons.
DEC'ADE, the sum or number of ten; (as, ten days, ten years, or ten parts).
DECEN'NIAL, (14), happening every ten years.
DECEM'VIRATE, (591), a body of ten magistrates.
DUODEC'IMAL, (Lat. *duod'ecim*, twelve), reckoned by twelves.
DUODEC'IMO, (Lat.), a sheet folded into twelve leaves.

110. De'cet, to be becoming or proper.

DE'CENT, becoming.
DE'CENCY, propriety of manner.
DECO'RUM, (Lat.), propriety of behavior.
DEC'ORATE, to adorn.
DEC'OROUS, observing propriety.
INDECO'RUM, (Lat.), impropriety.

111. Dens, (*den'tis*), a tooth.

DEN'TAL, belonging to the teeth; sounded by the aid of the teeth.
DEN'TIST, a dental surgeon.
DEN'TIFRICE, (Lat. *fri'co*, to rub or chafe), tooth powder.
DENTI'TION, cutting the teeth; teething.
INDENT', to make inequalities like teeth.
TRI'DENT, (549), Neptune's sceptre with three prongs.
INDENTA'TION, a notch.
INDENT'URE, a species of contract.*

* So called from a custom of cutting notches in the edge of the paper or parchment on which it is written.

112. Den'sus, thick, close.

DENSE, close, compact.
DENS'ITY, closeness, compactness.
CONDENSE', to compress.
CONDENSA'TION, a thickening or compression.

113. Dete'rior, worse.

DETE'RIORATE, to become worse.
DETERIORA'TION, becoming worse.

114. De'us, God. Di'vus, a god.

DE'ITY, the nature and essence of God.
DE'IST, one who believes in God, but denies revelation.

DIVINA'TION, foretelling
DIVINE', *a.* of the nature of God.
DIVINE', *s.* a theologian.

DIVINE', *v.* to presage.
DIVIN'ITY, the nature of God; theology.

115. *Dex'ter*, pertaining to the right hand.

DEX'TEROUS, expert; ready.
DEXTER'ITY, expertness; activity; readiness.

DEX'TER, right as opposed to left; (as, the *dexter* cheek).
DEX'TEROUSLY, with dexterity; expertly.

116. *Di'co*, (*dica'tum*), to devote; to show.

DED'ICATE, to devote; to inscribe to.
IN'DICATE, to point out; to show.

AB'DICATE, to give up right; to resign.
INDICA'TION, mark; token.

117. *Di'co*, (*dic'tum*), to say.

DIC'TION, language; style.
DIC'TIONARY, a book containing the words of a language.
DIC'TATE, to give directions authoritatively.
DICTA'TOR, (Lat.), a Roman magistrate.
DICTATO'RIAL, authoritative.
BENEDIC'TION, (38), a blessing.
CONTRADIC'TION, opposition; inconsistency.
CONTRADIC'TORY, implying contradiction or denial.
E'DICT, a proclamation.

INDICT', to charge by formal accusation.
INDITE', to draw up; to compose.
INTERDICT', to prohibit.
MALEDIC'TION, (279), a curse.
PREDICT', to foretell; to prophesy.
PRED'ICATE, to assert.
PRED'ICABLE, that may be asserted.
VER'DICT, (580), the decision of a jury.

118. *Di'es*, a day.

DI'ARY, a daily account.
DIUR'NAL, daily.
QUOTID'IAN, (Lat. *quot*, as many as), happening daily.
DI'AL, a plate with the hours of the day marked on it.

MERID'IAN, (287), noon; midday.
POST-MERID'IAN, relating to or being in the afternoon; P. M.
NOCTID'IAL, (336), comprising a night and a day.

119. *Dig'itus*, a finger; a finger's breadth.

DIG'IT, a numerical figure; three-fourths of an inch.

DIG'ITATED, branched like fingers.

WORDS DERIVED FROM THE LATIN.

120. *Dig'nus*, worthy.

Dig'nity, honor.
Dig'nify, (152), to advance to honor.
Deign, to think worthy; to condescend.
Indig'nity, unworthy treatment.
Indig'nant, angry and disgusted.
Indigna'tion, anger mixed with contempt.
Condign', suitable; merited.
Disdain', to think unworthy.

121. *Dimid'ium*, half.

Dem'i-god, one esteemed as half a god.
Dem'i-deify, (114), to half deify.

122. *Dis'co*, to learn. *Discip'ulus*, a learner.

Disci'ple, a learner; a follower.
Dis'cipline, instruction; education.

123. *Di'vido*, (586), (*divi'sum*), to divide.

Divide', to separate into parts.
Divis'ion, the act of separating.
Div'idend, the number to be divided.
Divi'sor, the number given to divide by.
Divis'ible, separable into parts.
Individ'ual, a single being or thing.

124. *Do*, (*da'tum*), to give.

Do'nor, a giver.
Dona'tion, a gift.
Donate', to give; to contribute.
Add, (Lat. *ad'do*), to join to.
Addi'tion, increase.
Condi'tion, (Lat. *con'do*, to bring together), state.
Ed'it, to give forth; to publish.
Ed'itor, one who prepares for publication.
Par'don, to forgive.
Perdi'tion, destruction; ruin.
Ren'der, (Lat. *red'do*), to yield; to furnish.
Rendi'tion, the act of yielding possession; surrender.

125. *Do'ceo*, (*doc'tum*), to teach.

Doc'tor, a man who has taken the highest degree in divinity, law, or physic, viz., D. D., LL. D, or M. D.
Doc'trine, whatever is taught.
Doc'ument, a paper containing evidence.
Do'cile, teachable.
Docil'ity, readiness to be taught.

6

126. *Do'leo*, to grieve; to be in pain.

Dole'ful, sorrowful.
Dol'orous, melancholy.
Condole', to sympathize with the grief of another.
In'dolence, laziness.*

* Literally, freedom from pain or trouble.

127. *Dom'inus*, a master or lord.

Domin'ion, supreme authority.
Domina'tion, power; tyranny.
Domain', (Lat *domin'ium*), property; empire; dominion.
Dom'inant, prevailing.
Domineer', to rule with insolence. [the rest.
Predom'inate, to prevail over

128. *Do'mo*, (*dom'itum*), to subdue; to tame.

Indom'itable, not to be subdued.
Dom'ify, (152), to tame; to domesticate.

129. *Do'mus*, a house; a home.

Dome, a house; a spherical roof.
Domes'tic, belonging to the house or family.
Domes'ticate, to accustom to the residence of man.
Dom'icil, (Lat. *domicil'ium*, an abode), a mansion or abode.
Do'mal, relating to a house.
Domicil'iate, to fix a residence.

130. *Dor'mio*, (*dormi'tum*), to sleep.

Dor'mant, sleeping; insensible. | Dor'mitory, a sleeping-room.

131. *Dor'sum*, the back.

Dor'sal, pertaining to the back.
Endorse', to write on the back of a paper.

132. *Du'bius*, doubtful.

Du'bious, uncertain.
Indu'bitable, not to be doubted.
Doubt, uncertainty of mind.

133. *Du'co*, (*duc'tum*), to lead.

Duct, a little channel or canal.
Duc'tile, capable of being drawn out into a thread or wire.
Abduc'tion, a leading away.
Adduce', to bring forward.
Aq'ueduct, (19), a channel or tube for conveying water.

Conduct', v. to lead or guide.
Con'duct, s. behavior; management.
Conduce', to lead or tend.
Con'duit, (Fr.), a water pipe or canal.
Deduce', to draw an inference.
Deduct', to subtract.
Deduc'tion, an inference.
Duke, a leader; a noble.
Educe', to draw out.
Ed'ucate, to lead by instruction and discipline.
Induce', to lead by motives; to bring on; (as, a disease).
Induce'ment, a motive.

Introduce', to bring or usher in
Introduc'tion, the act of introducing or ushering; exordium; preface.
Introduc'tory, serving to introduce; preliminary.
Produce', to bring forward; to bear.
Produc'tive, capable of producing.
Reduce', to bring down; to subject.
Seduce', to draw aside into error or crime.
Seduc'tive, fitted to entice.
Traduce', to calumniate.

134. *Du'o*, two.

Du'al, relating to two or a pair.
Du'el, a combat between two.
Duet', a piece of music in two parts.

Doub'le, consisting of two.
Du'plicate, (392), two-fold.
Duplic'ity, double dealing; deception.

135. *Du'rus*, hard.

Du'rable, lasting.
Du'rance, imprisonment.
Dura'tion, continuance.
Endure, to bear; to last.

Ob'duracy, hardness of heart; stubborn impenitence.
Ob'durate, stubborn; hard-hearted.

136. *Eb'rius*, drunken.

Ebri'ety, drunkenness.
Ine'briate, an habitual drunkard.

Sobri'ety, (Lat. *si'ne*), freedom from intoxication; dignity of deportment.

137. *Æ'des*, (*æ'dis*), a house or building.

Ed'ifice, (152), a building.

Ed'ify, to build up in knowledge or faith.

138. *E'do*, to eat.

Edac'ity, greediness.

Ed'ible, eatable.

139. E'go, I.

E'gotism, talking much of one's self.

Egotist'ical, self-conceited; opinionated.

140. E'mo, (emp'tum), to buy.

Exempt', (*literally*, bought off,) not liable.
Exemp'tion, freedom from a task or burden.
Per'emptory,* positive; abso-[lute.

Prompt,† ready; quick.
Redeem', to buy back; to ransom.
Redemp'tion, the act of redeeming.

* The Latin word *peri'mo*, signifies to take away wholly; to destroy; and *peremp'tor*, signifies a destroyer.

† From *pro'mo*, (*promp'tum*), which is compounded of *pro* and *emo*, and signifies to bring or put forward.

141. Æm'ulus, a rival.

Emula'tion, a desire to vie or compete with another.

Em'ulous, rivalling; competing.
Em'ulate, to strive to equal or to excel.

142. E'o, (i'tum), to go.

Am'bient, surrounding.
Ambi'tion,‡ a desire of honor.
Cir'cuit, (71), (Lat. *cir'cum*), extent round about.
Ex'it, (Lat.), a going out; a departure.
Ini'tial, placed at the entrance or beginning.
Ini'tiate, to give entrance to, (as to a custom or society); to admit to the knowledge of; to introduce. [sion.
Initia'tion, reception; admis-
Obit'uary, (Lat. *ob'itus*, decease), relating to the decease of a person.

Per'ish, to die.
Per'ishable, subject or liable to decay.
Sedi'tion, a going into a separate or rebellious party.
Trans'ient, soon past; momentary.
Trans'itory, passing quickly; not permanent.
Trans'it, a passing over.
Transi'tion, the act or state of passing from one condition to another.
Trans'itive, in *grammar*, passing over upon some object.

‡ The Latin word *ambi'tus*, signifies a going round or about; and was used to denote the canvassing for votes, and the soliciting of popular favor employed by those who sought office.

143. E'quus, a horse.

Eques'trian, pertaining to horsemanship.

Eq'uipage, the arms, &c., of a mounted soldier; any accoutrements.

WORDS DERIVED FROM THE LATIN. 83

144. Æ'quus, equal, just.

E'QUAL, of the same size or importance.
E'QUALIZE, to make even or equal.
E'QUABLE, not varying.
AD'EQUATE, equal to; sufficient.
EQUA'TION, a making equal.
EQUA'TOR, a line which divides the earth into two equal parts.
EQUILIB'RIUM, (259), equal weight.

E'QUINOX, (336), the time when the day and night are of equal length.
EQ'UITY, justice.
EQUIV'ALENT, (567), of equal value or force.
EQUIV'OCATE, (596), to use words in a doubtful and deceptive manner.
INIQ'UITY, injustice.

145. Er'ro, (erra'tum), to wander.

ERR, to mistake.
ERRA'TUM, (Lat.), (pl. erra'ta), an error in writing or printing.
ERRAT'IC, deviating from the usual way; wandering.

ERR'ING, irregular; vicious.
ERRO'NEOUS, wrong; incorrect.
ABERRA'TION, wandering from the right path.
UNER'RINGLY, without mistake.

146. Æ'stimo, to value.

ES'TIMATE, to judge concerning the value.
ESTIMA'TION, opinion respecting value.

ES'TIMABLE, worthy of esteem.
ESTEEM', high regard.
INES'TIMABLE, of value too great to be computed.

147. Æ'vum, an age.

COE'VAL, existing at the same period. [life.
LONGEV'ITY, (269), length of

PRIME'VAL, (412), of the first age; existing in the earliest times.

148. Exem'plum, an example.

EXAM'PLE, model, pattern; instance. [tated.
EXEM'PLAR, a pattern to be imitated.
EX'EMPLARY, worthy of imitation. [by example.
EXEM'PLIFY, (152), to illustrate

SAM'PLE, a specimen.
SAM'PLER, a pattern of needlework. [tion.
EXEMPLIFICA'TION, illustration.
UNEXAM'PLED, without precedent.

149. Ex'terus, outer; foreign.

EXTE'RIOR, the outside.
EXTER'NAL, pertaining to the outside.

EXTRA'NEOUS, not belonging to the subject; foreign to the subject.

Extreme', utmost.
Extrem'ity, the utmost point.

Extrin'sic, (Lat. *secus*, otherwise), from without.
Strange, foreign; unusual.

150. *Fa'ber*, an artificer.

Fab'ric, a structure.

Fab'ricate, to form; to devise falsely.

151. *Fa'cies*, a face.

Face, the countenance; appearance.
Deface', to disfigure.
Efface', to wipe out.

Sur'face, Superfic'ies, outside.
Superfi'cial, lying on the outside.

152. *Fa'cio*, (*fac'tum*), to do or make: and *Fi'o*, (*fac'tus*), to become.

Fact, a thing done; a reality.
Fac'tor, an agent or doer.
Fac'tion, a party counteracting the government.
Fac'tory, a building in which anything is manufactured; the residence of traders abroad.
Fac'ile, (Lat. *fa'cilis*, easy), easy to be done.
Facil'itate, to make easy.
Affect', to move the passions.
Affec'tion, love, kindness; any passion.
Affecta'tion, assumed feeling.
Confec'tionery, sweet-meats.
Coun'terfeit, a forgery.
Defeat', to undo; to overthrow.
Defect', want; a blemish.
Defec'tion, departure; revolt.
Defi'cient, Defec'tive, failing.
Dif'ficult, hard to be done.
Fi'at,* (Lat.), a command.
Effect', to bring to pass; the thing produced.

Effect'ive, Effic'ient, operative; active; producing.
Effect'ual, Effica'cious, not failing to accomplish the object in view.
Infect', to taint with disease.
Manufac'ture, (282), to make things by hand or machinery.
Of'fice, employment; station; place of business.
Offic'iate, to discharge an office.
Per'fect, (Lat. *perfic'io*, to accomplish), complete; pure.
Pon'tiff,† (Lat. *pons*, a bridge), a high priest; the pope.
Profic'iency, advancement or improvement in any study or business.
Refec'tory, an eating-room.
Sac'rifice, (453), to offer; to surrender; to devote.
Suffic'ient, competent; adequate.
Sur'feit, to feed to excess.

* The word signifies, *let it be done.*
† So called, because the first bridge over the Tiber was constructed and consecrated, it is said, by the chief priest.

WORDS DERIVED FROM THE LATIN. 85

153. *Fal'lo,* (*fal'sum*), to deceive.

FALSE, not true; not real; counterfeit.
FALS'ITY, the state of being false.
FALLA'CIOUS, fitted to deceive.
FAL'LACY, deceitful argument or appearance.
FAL'LIBLE, liable to error.
FALSE'HOOD, an untruth; a lie.
FAL'SIFY, (152), to make a false representation.

154. *Fa'ma,* a report.

FAME, celebrity; renown.
FA'MOUS, renowned.
DEFAME', to injure one's reputation maliciously.
DEFAMA'TION, calumny.
DEFAM'ATORY, slanderous.
IN'FAMOUS. openly censured.
IN'FAMY, public reproach.

155. *Fa'mes,* hunger.

FAM'INE, scarcity of food.
FAM'ISH, to suffer extreme hunger.

156. *Famil'ia,* a family.

FAM'ILY, the persons living in the house; a race; a class.
FAMIL'IAR, *a.* easy in conversation; affable; well known.
FAMILIAR'ITY, omission of ceremony; acquaintance.
FAMIL'IARIZE, to make easy by habit.

157. *Fa'num,* a temple.

FANE, a temple.
FANAT'IC, enthusiastic.
FANAT'ICISM, religious phrensy.
PROFANE', *v.* to pollute; to violate or abuse that which is consecrated.
PROFANE', *a.* irreverent to sacred things; secular.
PROFANA'TION, a violation of sacred things.
PROFANE'NESS, irreverence towards what is sacred.

158. *Fa'ri,* (*fa'tus*), to speak.

FATE, decree of destiny or a superior power.
FA'TAL, deadly; destructive.
AFFABIL'ITY, kindness of manner in conversation.
AF'FABLE, easy to be spoken to.
INEF'FABLE, unspeakable.
IN'FANT, (Lat. *in'fans,* not able to speak), a young child.
IN'FANCY, the first stage of life.
PREF'ACE, (Lat. *præfa'tio,* a speaking beforehand), an introductory speech or writing
PREF'ATORY, introductory.

159. *Fari'na*, meal, flour.

FARI'NA, the flour of any species of corn or starchy root.

FARINA'CEOUS, made of meal or flour.

160. *Fa'teor*, (*fas'sus*, or in composition *fes'sus*), to confess.

CONFESS', to own.

PROFESS', to declare; to avow.

161. *Fe'bris*, a fever.

FE'VER,* a disease.
FE'VERISH, affected with fever.
FE'BRILE, pertaining to fever.

FEBRIF'IC, (152), producing fever.
FEB'RIFUGE, (197), any medicine that mitigates fever.

* The Latin word *fe'bris* is supposed to be derived from *fer'veo*, to boil.

162. *Fœ'dus*, a league or covenant.

FED'ERAL, pertaining to a covenant or league.
CONFED'ERATE, one joined in a league.

FED'ERATIVE, securing union.
CONFED'ERACY, a number of persons or states united by a league.

163. *Fe'lix*, (*feli'cis*), happy.

FELIC'ITY, happiness.
FELIC'ITOUS, happy, fortunate.

FELIC'ITATE, to congratulate.
INFELIC'ITY, misfortune.

164. *Fem'ina*, a woman; a female.

FEM'ININE, of the female sex.
EFFEM'INATE, *a.* like woman; delicate.

EFFEM'INATE, *v* to grow or become womanish or weak.

165. *Fen'do*, (*fen'sum*),† to strike.

DEFENCE', guard, security; resistance.
FEN'CING, practice in using a sword for defence.
DEFEND', to protect.
DEFEND'ANT, one who makes his defence against a prosecutor or plaintiff.
FEND, to ward off.
FEND'ER, a utensil placed before the fire.

OFFEND', to displease; to transgress.
OFFENCE', crime; injury.
OFFEN'SIVE, making the first attack; aggressive.
INOFFEN'SIVE, harmless; innocent.
DEFEN'SIVE, resisting attack or aggression.
DEFENCE'LESS, without defence; destitute of protection.

† *Fendo* is used in Latin only in composition.

WORDS DERIVED FROM THE LATIN.

166. *Fe'ra*, a wild beast.

FERO'CIOUS, cruel, savage. | FIERCE, vehement; furious.

167 *Fe'ro, (la'tum),* to bear or carry.

FER'RY, a boat which carries passengers across a river.
FER'TILE, fruitful; producing abundantly.
CIRCUM'FERENCE, the measure around anything.
CONFER', to discourse or consult with another.
CON'FERENCE, a meeting for discussing a question.
COLLATE', to compare things of the same kind. [past.
COLLA'TION, a comparing; a re-
DEFER', to put off.
DEF'ERENCE, yielding to another's opinion.
DILATE', to enlarge; to extend.
DIL'ATORY, disposed to put off; tardy.
DIF'FER, to be unlike; to contend
DIF'FERENCE, distinction; dispute.
ELATE', to uplift; to render proud by success.
INFER, to draw a conclusion.
OF'FER, to present; to propose; to sacrifice.

OBLA'TION, a sacrifice; an offering.
PESTIF'EROUS, (Lat. *pes'tis*, a plague), producing the plague.
PREFER', to like better.
PREF'ERENCE, estimation of one thing before another.
PREL'ATE, a dignitary of the church.
PROF'FER, to bring forward; to offer.
REFER', to leave to the decision of another. [tell.
RELATE', to have respect to; to
RELA'TION, connection; narrative.
REL'ATIVE, a kinsman.
SUPER'LATIVE, surpassing.
SUF'FER, to bear, endure; to allow, permit.
SUF'FERANCE, pain; patience; permission.
TRANSFER', to convey; to remove.
TRANSLATE', to remove; to interpret into another language.
VOCIF'EROUS, (596), making loud vocal sounds.

168 *Fer'rum*, iron

FAR'RIER,* a horse doctor.
FAR'RIERY, the science of medicine for horses; the veterinary art.

FERRU'GINOUS, partaking of the quality of iron.
FER'RULE, an iron ring or band.

* A name applied originally to a shoer of horses.

169. *Fer'veo*, to boil; to be hot.

FER'VOR, heat; zeal.
FER'VENT, hot; zealous.

EFFERVESCE', to bubble up.
EFFERVES'CENCE, ebullition.

FERMENT', to be in intestine motion. | FERMENTA'TION, a state of intestine motion.

170. Fes'tus, joyful.

FES'TAL, belonging to a feast; joyful.
FES'TIVE, joyful. [joicing.
FES'TIVAL, an occasion of re-
FESTIV'ITY, gayety; joyfulness.
FEAST, a sumptuous entertainment.
INFEST', to harass; to disturb.

171. Fi'do, to trust.

FIDEL'ITY, honesty; faithful adherence.
CONFIDE', to trust; to rely.
CON'FIDENCE, trust; boldness.
CONFIDEN'TIAL, private.
DIF'FIDENCE, distrust.
IN'FIDEL, an unbeliever.
INFIDEL'ITY, unfaithfulness; disbelief.
PER'FIDY, treachery.
AFFI'ANCED, pledged for marriage.

172. Fi'go, (fix'um), to fix, to fasten.

FIX, to make fast; to settle.
FIX'EDLY, firmly; steadfastly.
AFFIX', to join to.
CRUCIFIX'ION, (98), fastening to a cross. [image.
CRU'CIFIX, a cross bearing an
FIX'TURE, furniture or apparatus not separate from the building.
PREFIX', to put before.
TRANSFIX', to pierce through.
SUFFIX', to add to the end of a word.

173. Fil'ius, a son; Fil'ia, a daughter.

FIL'IAL, pertaining to a son or daughter.
UNFIL'IAL, not becoming a child; undutiful.
AFFIL'IATED, adopted; received as a member of a family or association.

174. Fi'lum, a thread.

FIL'AMENT, a thread; a fibre.
FIL'LET, a little band for the hair.
FILE, a line of soldiers.
FIL'TER, a strainer.

175. Fin'go, (fic'tum), to form; to fashion.

FIC'TION, an invention; a falsehood.
FICTI'TIOUS, imaginary; not real.
EF'FIGY, image; likeness.
FEIGN, to pretend.
FEINT, a pretence.
FIG'URE, form; a statute; a character.
FIG'URATIVE, representing something else.
TRANSFIGURA'TION, change of form.

176. *Fi'nis*, an end or limit.

Fin'ish, to complete, to end.
Fi'nite, limited; having an end.
In'finite, unlimited; immense.
Infin'ity, infinite extent.
In'finitely, without limits.
Infin'itive, the name of a mode, in grammar, which is not limited by person or number.
Define', to limit; to explain.
Def'inite, certain; limited.
Defin'itive, conclusive.
Defini'tion, a short description.
Confine', v. to limit; to restrain.
Con'fines, s. boundaries.
Affin'ity, relation; resemblance.
Indef'inite, not limited; not precise.
Infinites'imal, indefinitely small.

177. *Fir'mus*, strong.

Firm, hard; steady.
Firm'ament, the sky.
Affirm', to declare positively.
Affirma'tion, assertion.
Affirm'ative, declaring; opposed to negative.
Confirm', to settle; to establish.
Confirma'tion, additional proof; a religious rite.
Infirm', weak; decrepit.
Infirm'ity, weakness; a failing.
Infirm'ary, a hospital.

178. *Fis'cus*, a money bag; the exchequer.

Fis'cal, pertaining to the revenue.
Confisca'tion, transfer of forfeited goods to public use.
Confis'cate, to transfer private property to the public, by way of penalty.
Confis'cable, liable to confisca-[tion.

179. *Fla'gro*, to burn; to be in flames.

Fla'grant, glaring; enormous.
Fla'grancy, burning heat; enormity.
Conflagra'tion, an extensive fire; a great burning.

180. *Flam'ma*, a flame.

Flame, burning vapor. [torch.
Flam'beau, (Fr.), a kind of
Inflame', to kindle; to irritate.
Inflam'mable, easily set on fire.
Inflamma'tion, the act of setting on fire; diseased heat of the body.
Inflam'matory, having the power of inflaming.

181. *Flec'to*, (*flex'um*), to bend.

Flex'ible, pliable; that may be easily bent; manageable.
Flex'ure, the act of bending; a bending.

INFLEX′IBLE, not to be bent; obstinate.
REFLECT′, to throw back; to consider attentively.
INFLECT′, to bend; to vary.
INFLEC′TION, variation of the form of words; a modulation of the voice.

182. *Fli′go*, (*flic′tum*), to beat; to dash.

AFFLICT′, to give pain; grieve.
AFFLIC′TION, calamity.
CON′FLICT, contest; struggle.
INFLICT′, to impose a punishment.
PROF′LIGATE, shameless; abandoned.

183. *Flo*, (*fla′tum*), to blow.

INFLATE′, to fill with air; to elate with notions of self-importance.
INFLA′TION, the act of inflating or swelling.

184. *Flos*, (*flo′ris*), a flower.

FLO′RA, (Lat.), the goddess of flowers; a list or account of flowers.
EFFLORES′CENCE, an appearance resembling flowers.
FLO′RAL, pertaining to flowers.
FLO′RIST, a cultivator of flowers.
FLOR′ID, bright in color; flushed.
FLORIF′EROUS, (167), producing flowers.
FLOW′ER, *s.* a blossom.
FLOW′ER, *v.* to blossom.
FLOUR′ISH, to be in vigor.
FLOUR, the edible part of wheat or other grain, bolted and sifted; meal.

185. *Flu′o*, (*flux′um*), to flow.

FLU′ENT, flowing; voluble; ready in the use of words.
FLU′ENCY, readiness of speech.
FLU′ID, anything that flows.
FLUC′TUATE, (Lat. *fluc′tus*, a wave), to move backwards and forwards.
FLUCTUA′TION, wavering.
EF′FLUX, a flowing out.
AF′FLUENCE, plenty; riches.
CIRCUM′FLUENT, flowing round.
CON′FLUENCE, a junction of streams.
CON′FLUENT, running into one another.
EFFLU′VIA, (Lat. plural of *efflu′vium*, a flowing or running over), those minute particles which are always flying off from bodies.
IN′FLUX, a flowing in.
IN′FLUENCE, power; tendency to produce change.
INFLUEN′TIAL, exerting power.
RE′FLUX, backward course; ebb
REF′LUENT, flowing back.
SUPER′FLUOUS, more than enough.
SUPERFLU′ITY, plenty beyond necessity.

WORDS DERIVED FROM THE LATIN. 91

186. *Fo′lium*, a leaf.

Fo′LIAGE, a growth of leaves.
FOLIA′CEOUS, consisting of leaves.
Fo′LIATE, to beat into leaves.
FOLIA′TION, beating a metal into foil or thin leaves.

FOIL, leaf metal.
Fo′LIO, (Lat.), a large book, in which the sheets of paper are only once folded.
PORTFO′LIO, (402), a case for loose leaves.

187. *For′ma*, form; beauty.

FORM, *s.* shape.
FORM, *v.* to make; to contrive.
FORM′AL, ceremonious; solemn.
FORMAL′ITY, ceremony.
FORMA′TION, the act of forming; manner or shape. [form.
FORM′ULA, (Lat.), a prescribed
CONFORM′, to make like; to comply with.
CONFORM′ITY, agreement.
CONFORMA′TION, the relative form of things.
CRU′CIFORM, (98), having the form of a cross.
DEFORM′, to disfigure.
DEFORM′ITY, unsightly shape.
INFORM′, to instruct; to acquaint.

INFORM′ANT, INFORM′ER, one who gives intelligence.
INFORMA′TION, intelligence.
INFORMAL′ITY, the absence of form.
MUL′TIFORM, (317), of various shapes.
PERFORM′, to do or act; to execute.
PERFORM′ANCE, action; work.
REFORM′, to grow better.
REFORMA′TION, change from worse to better.
TRANSFORM′, to change.
TRANSFORMA′TION, change of form.
UNIFORM′ITY, (563), agreement with one pattern.

188. *Fors*, (*for′tis*), chance.

FOR′TUNE, the good or ill that befalls man.
FOR′TUNATE, successful.

UNFOR′TUNATE, unlucky.
MISFOR′TUNE, calamity.
FORTU′ITOUS, accidental.

189. *For′tis*, brave; strong.

FOR′TITUDE, courage; bravery.
FOR′TIFY, (152), to strengthen.
FORT, a fortified place.
FORTIFICA′TION, military architecture for defence.

FOR′TRESS, a fortified place.
FORCE, strength.
COM′FORT, to strengthen; to cheer.
EF′FORT, exertion.

190. *Fos′sa*, a ditch or trench.

Fosse, (Fr.), a trench.   Fos′sil, a substance dug from the earth.

191. *Fran′go*, (*frac′tum*), to break.

Frac′tion, a part.
Frac′tious, breaking out into violence.
Frac′ture, a breaking; (as, of a bone); a breach.
Frag′ment, a broken part.
Frag′ile, frail; easily broken.
Fragil′ity, brittleness.
Frail′ty, weakness.

Infringe′, to break in upon; to transgress.
Infrac′tion, violation of a contract or law.
Irref′ragable, not capable of being broken or refuted.
Infringe′ment, a breach; a violation; a transgression.
Refrac′tory, obstinate; perverse.
Suf′frage,* a vote.

* Lat. *Suffra′gium*.—The name was derived from the custom of using potsherds in voting.

192. *Fra′ter*, a brother.

Frater′nal, brotherly.
Frater′nity, brotherhood.

Frat′ricide, (41), the murder or murderer of a brother.

193. *Fraus*, (*frau′dis*), deceit.

Fraud, deceit.
Fraud′ulent, deceitful.

Defraud′, to cheat, to impose upon.

194. *Fri′gus*, (*fri′goris*), cold.

Frig′id, cold; without warmth of affection.
Frigid′ity, coldness; want of liveliness or spirit.

Refrig′erant, a cooling medicine.
Refrig′erate, to cool.
Refrig′erator, a cooler.

195. *Frons*, (*fron′tis*), the forehead.

Front, the face; the forepart.
Front′let, a band worn upon the forehead.
Front′ispiece. (504), a picture opposite the title-page of a book.

Front′iers, the limits of a territory; borders.
Affront′, to offend.
Confront′, to meet face to face.
Effront′ery, impudence.

WORDS DERIVED FROM THE LATIN.

196. *Fru'or,* (*fru'itus*), to enjoy.

FRUI'TION, enjoyment.
FRUC'TIFY, (152), (Lat. *fruc'tus,* fruit), to render fruitful.

FRUIT, the produce of a tree or plant.

197. *Fu'gio,* (*fu'gitum*), to flee.

FUGA'CIOUS, volatile; fleeting.
FUGAC'ITY, instability.
FU'GITIVE, running away.
CENTRIF'UGAL, (G. 44), having a tendency to fly from the centre.

REF'UGE, a shelter; a hiding place.
REFUGEE', one who flies for protection.
SUB'TERFUGE, a trick; an evasion.

198. *Ful'geo,* to shine.

FUL'GENCY, brightness.
FUL'GENT, shining.
EFFUL'GENCE, REFUL'GENCE, great lustre.

FUL'MINATE, (Lat. *ful'mino*), to thunder; to send out; (as, a denunciation).
FULMINA'TION, denunciation.

199. *Fu'mus,* smoke.

FUME, smoke; vapor.
FU'MIGATE, to smoke.
FUMIGA'TION, application of medicines in vapor.

FUM'ING, smoking; raging.
PERFUME', *v.* to scent; to impregnate with odors.
PERFUM'ERY, perfumeries in general.

200. *Fun'do,* (*fu'sum*), to pour out.

FUSE, to melt.
FU'SION, the act of melting. [ed.
FU'SIBLE, capable of being melt-
CONFOUND', to mingle things; to perplex.
CONFU'SION, irregular mixture; tumult.
DIFFUSE', to spread; to scatter.

EFFU'SION, a pouring out.
INFUSE', to pour in; to instil.
PROFU'SION, abundance.
REFUND', to pour back; to restore.
SUFFUSE', to spread over.
TRANSFUSE', to pour from one into another.

201. *Fun'dus,* a foundation, or bottom.

FOUND, to establish.
FOUND'ER, one who establishes.
FOUNDA'TION, establishment; basis of an edifice.

FUNDAMENT'AL, lying at the foundation.
PROFOUND', deep; thorough.
PROFUND'ITY, depth.

202. *Gĕ'lu*, frost; ice.

GEL'ID, extremely cold.
GEL'ATINE, an animal substance resembling jelly.
GELAT'INOUS, like gelatine; stiff and cohesive.

CONGEAL'ABLE, susceptible of congelation.
CONGEAL', to turn by cold from a fluid to a solid; to freeze.
CONGELA'TION, a freezing.

203. *Gĕ'ro*, (*ges'tum*), to bear; to carry on.

GES'TURE, action intended to convey ideas.
GESTIC'ULATE, to accompany words with gestures
GESTICULA'TION, the act of making gestures.
BELLIG'ERENT, (35), carrying on war; engaged in war.
BELLICOSE', inclined to war.

CONGES'TION, an accumulation of blood in some part of the body.
DIGEST', to arrange; to soften or dissolve.
INDIGES'TION, the state of food undissolved in the stomach.
SUGGEST', to intimate.
VICEGE'RENT, (585), one who acts in the place of another.

204. *Gig'no*, (*gen'itum*), to generate; to produce.

GE'NIAL, causing production or growth.
GE'NIUS, (Lat.), natural disposition.
GENTIL'ITY, elegance in manners; refinement.
GEN'ERAL, comprehending many individuals.
GENER'IC, belonging to a genus.
GEN'DER, sex.
GE'NUS, (Lat.), a kind including many species.
GEN'UINE, natural; unadulterated.
GEN'TILE, (Lat. *gens*, a nation), one of a nation ignorant of God.
GEN'TLE, soft; mild; tame.
GENTEEL', elegant in manners.
CONGE'NIAL, of the same kind.
DEGEN'ERATE, to grow worse.
ENGEN'DER, to produce.

GEN'ERALIZE, to arrange particulars under heads.
GEN'ERATE, to produce.
GENERA'TION, the people living at one period.
GEN'EROUS, noble minded; liberal.
INDIG'ENOUS, (Lat. *in'de*, thence), native in a country.
INGE'NIOUS, having genius; inventive.
INGENU'ITY, acuteness; power to invent.
INGEN'UOUS, candid; open; fair.
INGEN'UOUSNESS, candor.
PRIMOGEN'ITURE, (412), the state of being a first-born.
PROGEN'ITOR, a forefather.
PROG'ENY, offspring; race.
REGEN'ERATE, to renew.
REGENERA'TION, new birth to the Christian life.

WORDS DERIVED FROM THE LATIN.

205. *Gla'dius,* a sword.

GLA'DIATOR, a sword-player.
GLADIATO'RIAL, pertaining to sword-playing.

206. *Glu'tio,* to swallow.

GLUT, to fill; to cloy.
GLUT'TON, an excessive eater.
GLUT'TONIZE, to eat to excess; to gormandize.

207. *Gra'dior, (gres'sus),* to take steps; to walk.

GRADA'TION, regular advance step by step.
GRAD'UAL, (Lat. *gra'dus,* a step), advancing by steps.
GRAD'UATE, to mark with degrees.
DEGREE', a step; a rank.
DEGRADE', to put into a lower rank.
DEGRADA'TION, a low condition.
AGGRES'SION, an attack.
AGGRESS'OR, one who makes an attack.
CON'GRESS, a coming together; an assembly of legislators.
DIGRESS', to wander.
DIGRESS'ION, a deviation.
E'GRESS, departure out of.
IN'GRESS, entrance.
PROG'RESS, advancement; motion forward.
RET'ROGRADE, going backwards.
TRANSGRESS', to pass over; to violate.
TRANSGRES'SION, offence; crime.

208. *Gran'dis,* great.

GRAND, great; noble; chief.
GRAND'EUR, magnificence.
GRANDEE', a man of high rank.
GRANDIL'OQUENCE, (270), loftiness of language. [exalt.
AG'GRANDIZE, to make great; to

209. *Gra'num,* a grain of corn.

GRAIN, a seed of corn; a minute particle.
GRAN'ARY, a storehouse for grain.
GRAN'ULAR, consisting of grains.
GRANIV'OROUS, (601), living upon grain; eating grain.
GRAN'ITE, a stone composed of crystalline grains of several different minerals.

210. *Gra'tus,* pleasing; agreeable; thankful.

GRATE'FUL, thankful; pleasing.
GRAT'ITUDE, desire to return benefits; thankfulness. [son.
IN'GRATE, *s.* an ungrateful per-
IN'GRATE, *a.* unthankful.
INGRAT'ITUDE, unthankfulness.
GRA'TIS, (Lat. *gra'tia,* a favor), for nothing.

GRATU'ITOUS, given without necessity or reward.
GRATU'ITY, a free gift. [delight.
GRAT'IFY, (152), to indulge; to
CONGRAT'ULATE, to rejoice with another.

GRACE, favor; pardon; elegance.
DISGRACE', to put out of favor; to dishonor.
GRA'CIOUS, merciful; favorable.
INGRA'TIATE, to bring into favor

211. *Gra'vis,* heavy; grievous.

GRAVE, serious; weighty.
GRAV'ITY, weight; seriousness.
GRAVITA'TION, tendency to the centre of the earth.
GRIEF, sorrow; regret.

GRIEV'OUS, mournful; sad.
GRIEVE, to mourn.
AGGRIEVE', to harass.
AG'GRAVATE, to make worse.
AGGRAVA'TION, increase of evil.

212. *Grex, (gre'gis),* a flock of sheep.

GREGA'RIOUS, going in flocks or herds.
CON'GREGATE, to assemble.
CONGREGA'TION, an assembly.
EGRE'GIOUS,* eminently bad.

AG'GREGATE, the result of the conjunction of many particulars.
SEG'REGATE, to separate from others.

* Compounded of *e* and *grex;* signifying, *literally,* chosen from the flock; distinguished.

213. *Guberna'tor,* a pilot; a director.

GOV'ERN, to direct; to control.

GUBERNATO'RIAL, belonging to a governor.

214. *Gus'to, (gusta'tum),* to taste.

GUST, taste; relish.†
GUST'FUL, well tasted.
DISGUST', aversion; disrelish.

DISGUST'ING, nauseous; exciting strong aversion.

† *Gust,* signifying a blast of wind, is not of Latin derivation.

215. *Ha'beo, (hab'itum),* to have.

HAVE, to possess.
HAB'IT, usual state of a thing; custom.
HABITA'TION, (Lat. *hab'ito,* to dwell), a place of abode.
HABIT'UAL, customary.
ABIL'ITY,‡ faculty; power.
HABIL'IMENT, a garment.

A'BLE, powerful; fit.
DEBIL'ITATE, to enfeeble.
DEBIL'ITY, feebleness; decay of strength; infirmity.
EXHIB'IT, to show.
INHAB'IT, to dwell in.
PROHIB'IT, to forbid; to hinder.

‡ Supposed to be from the Latin word *hab'ilis,* easily managed; suitable.

216. Hæ'reo, (hæ'sum), to stick to, to adhere.

ADHERE', to stick to.
HES'ITATE, to doubt; to delay.
COHE'SION, state of union; connection.

COHE'RENT, sticking together; consistent. [loose.
INCOHE'RENT, inconsistent;
INHE'RENT, existing in; innate.

217. Hæ'res, (hære'dis), an heir or heiress.

HER'ITAGE, property inherited.
INHER'IT, to possess by descent.
HEIR, one who inherits.
INHER'ITANCE, patrimony; possession by descent.
HEIR'SHIP, the state of an heir.

HERED'ITARY, descending from father to son.
CO-HEIR', an heir with another.
DISINHER'IT, to cut off from succession.
HEIR'LOOM, any movable owned by inheritance.

218. Ha'lo, to breathe.

EXHALE', to breathe out.
EXHALA'TION, vapor.
EXHA'LANT, sending forth vapor.

ANHELA'TION, shortness of breath; panting.
INHALE', to draw in with the breath.

219. Hau'rio, (haus'tum), to draw.

EXHAUST', to draw out until nothing is left.

INEXHAUST'IBLE, that cannot be exhausted; unfailing.

220. Ho'mo, man.

HU'MAN, belonging to mankind.
HUMANE', having the feelings proper to man.
INHU'MAN, barbarous; cruel.

HUMAN'ITY, the nature of man; kindness.
HU'MANIZE, to civilize.
HOM'ICIDE, (41), manslaughter

221. Ho'nor, honor.

HON'OR, dignity; respect.
HON'ORARY, done in honor.
HON'ORABLE, worthy of honor.
DISHON'OR, reproach; disgrace.

HON'EST, without fraud; upright
HON'ESTY, disposition to be honest.
DISHON'EST, unjust; iniquitous.

222. Hor'tus, a garden.

HOR'TICULTURE, (82), cultivation of a garden.

HORTICUL'TURAL, pertaining to the cultivation of gardens.

223. *Hos'pes*, a host or guest.

Hos'pitable, kind to visitors.
Hospital'ity, readiness to entertain strangers and friends.
Hos'pital, a building for the sick or infirm.
Host, the master of a feast; the landlord of an inn.
Hotel',* (Fr.), an inn.
Host'ler, one who takes care of horses at an inn.

* The word *Hotel* was once written *Hostel*.

224. *Hos'tis*, an enemy.

Host, an army; a multitude.
Hos'tile, adverse; opposite.
Hostil'ity, enmity.
Hostil'ities, hostile proceed-   [ings.

225. *Hu'mus*, the ground. *Hu'milis*, humble.

Inhume', Inhu'mate, to bury.
Exhume', to disinter.
Post'humous, published after the author's death.
Hu'mid, moist; damp.
Humid'ity, dampness.
Hum'ble, modest; submissive.
Humil'ity, freedom from pride.
Humilia'tion, abasement of pride.
Hu'mor, moisture; turn of mind; [wit.

226. *I'dem*, the same.

Iden'tity, sameness.
Iden'tical, the same.
Iden'tify, (152), to discover or prove sameness.

227. *Ig'nis*, fire.

Ignite', to set on fire.
Ig'neous, of the nature of fire.
Igni'tion, the state of red heat.

228. *Ima'go*, (*imag'inis*), an image.

Im'age, a representation; statue; picture.
Im'agery, figurative representa-   [tion.
Imag'ine, to fancy.
Imagina'tion, fancy; idea.
Imag'inary, fancied; visionary.

229. *Im'pero*, to command.

Imper'ative, commanding; authoritative; the name of a mode in grammar.
Impe'rious, overbearing; domineering.
Impe'rial, pertaining to an emperor.
Em'peror, a monarch.
Em'pire, the dominion of an emperor.

230. Ina'nis, empty.

INAN'ITY, emptiness; vacancy; vanity. | INANI'TION, emptiness; exhaustion.

231. In'dex, (in'dicis), a sign; a pointer.

IN'DEX, s. a pointer; a table of contents.
IN'DEX, v. to place in an index or table. | IN'DEX-HAND, a hand that points to something.
IN'DICES, (Lat. plural of in'dex), algebraic signs.

232. In'ferus, nether; subterranean.

INFE'RIOR, lower; less honorable. | INFER'NAL, hellish.

233. In'sula, an island.

IN'SULAR, belonging to an island.
ISL'AND, ISLE, a portion of land surrounded by water.
I'SOLATED, placed by itself. | IN'SULATE, to detach from surrounding objects.
PENIN'SULA, (375), land nearly surrounded by the sea.

234. In'teger, whole; entire.

IN'TEGRAL, entire; whole; unbroken.
IN'TEGER, a whole number. | INTEG'RITY, entireness; honesty; purity of mind.

235. In'tus and In'tra, within.

INTE'RIOR, and INTER'NAL, inner, pertaining to the inside.
IN'TIMATE, (Lat. in'timus, inmost), familiar; acquainted with the private feelings and views of another. | INTIMA'TION, (Fr.), a hint; an obscure or indirect suggestion.
INTRIN'SIC, (Lat. secus, otherwise), belonging to the nature of a thing; inherent.

236. I'ra, anger.

IRE, anger. | IRAS'CIBLE, easily made angry.

237. I'ter, (itin'eris), a journey. I'tero, to repeat.

ITIN'ERANT, wandering; unsettled.
ITIN'ERARY, travelling.
IT'ERATE, to go or do over again.
ITERA'TION, repetition. | REIT'ERATE, to repeat again and again.
ITIN'ERATE, to travel from place to place

238. *Ja'ceo,* to lie.

JA'CENT, lying at length.
ADJA'CENT, lying or situated next.
CIRCUMJA'CENT, lying round.
INTERJA'CENT, lying between.

239. *Ja'cio, (jac'tum),* to throw.

EJAC'ULATE, to utter suddenly; (as, a prayer).
EJACULA'TION, the uttering of a short prayer in the midst of other occupations.
AB'JECT, thrown away; worthless; mean.
AD'JECTIVE, a word added to a noun to qualify it.
CONJEC'TURE, to guess.
DEJECT', to cast down; to grieve.
DEJEC'TION, lowness of spirits.
EJECT', to cast out; to expel.
INJECT', to throw in.
INTERJEC'TION, an exclamation thrown in between the parts of a sentence.
OB'JECT, that to which any action or thought is directed.
OBJECT'IVE, belonging to the object; acted on.
OBJEC'TION, fault found.
PROJECT', *v.* to throw out; to scheme.
PROJ'ECT, *s.* a design; contrivance.
PROJEC'TILE, a body thrown forwards.
REJECT', to refuse.
SUBJECT', *v.* to put under; to subdue.
SUB'JECT, *s.* that which is acted upon; one who is under the dominion of another.

240. *Jo'cus,* a joke.

JOKE, a jest; a merry trick.
JOCOSE', JOC'ULAR, merry; waggish.
JOCULAR'ITY, merriment.
JOC'UND, gay; lively.

241. *Ju'dico, (judica'tum),** to judge.

JU'DICATORY, a tribunal.
JUDI'CIAL, pertaining to courts of justice.
JUDI'CIARY, the system of courts of justice. [mine.
ADJU'DICATE, to try and determine.
ADJUDGE', to decree judicially.
EXTRAJUDI'CIAL, out of the ordinary judicial course.
JUDGE, to decide. [ment.
JUDI'CIOUS, guided by judgment.
PREJ'UDICE, opinion formed without due examination.
PREJUDI'CIAL, hurtful.

* *Judico* is compounded of *jus* and *dico.*

242. *Jun'go, (junc'tum),* to join.

JUNC'TION, union.
JOIN, to unite.
JOINT, (Fr.), a joining; a connection allowing motion.

JOIN'ER, one who joins pieces of wood.
ADJOIN'ING, next; contiguous.
AD'JUNCT, something joined.
CONJOIN', to unite; to associate.
CON'JUGAL, relating to marriage.
CONJUNC'TION, a connecting word.
CONJUNCT'URE, concurrence of circumstances.
DISJOIN', to separate.
DISJUNC'TION, separation; disunion.
DISJUNC'TIVE, separating.
ENJOIN', to command.
INJUNC'TION, precept; order.
SUBJOIN', to add at the end.
SUB'JUGATE,* to conquer; to subdue.
SUBJUNCT'IVE, conditional.

* Lat. *sub*, under, and *ju'gum*, a yoke.

243. *Ju'ro*, to swear.

ABJURE', to renounce upon oath.
ADJURE', to put one upon oath.
CONJURE', to summon or call upon one in a solemn manner.
CON'JURE, to practise secret or magical arts.
JU'RY, a set of men sworn to give a true verdict.
JU'ROR, a member of a jury.
PER'JURE, to swear falsely; to take a false oath.
PER'JURY, false swearing.

244. *Jus*, (*ju'ris*), right; justice; law.

JUST, equitable; honest.
UNJUST', iniquitous; dishonest.
JUST'ICE, right; a magistrate.
INJUST'ICE, wrong.
JUST'IFY, (152), to clear from guilt.
JU'RIST, one versed in the law.
ADJUST', to set right.
IN'JURE, to treat unjustly; to wrong; to hurt.
INJU'RIOUS, hurtful.
JURISDIC'TION, (117), legal authority; extent of power.
JURISPRU'DENCE, (Lat. *prudentia*, knowledge), the science of law.

245. *Ju'venis*, young.

JU'VENILE, youthful; fit for children.
JUVENIL'ITY, youthfulness.
JU'NIOR, (Lat.), younger than another.

246. *La'bor*, labor.

LA'BOR, work, toil.
LABO'RIOUS, diligent in work; tiresome.
LAB'ORATORY, a chemist's workroom.
ELAB'ORATE, finished with care.

247. La'bor, (lap'sus), to slide.

LAPSE, fall; trifling error or fault.
COLLAPSE', to fall inward or together.
ELAPSE', to glide away.
RELAPSE', to fall back again.
LA'BENT, gliding.

248. La'pis, (lap'idis), a stone.

LAP'IDARY, a worker in precious stones.
DILAPIDA'TION,* ruin; demolition.

* *Primary meaning*, the falling down of the stones of a wall.

249. La'tus, broad.

LAT'ITUDE, breadth; extent; distance from the equator.
LATITUDINA'RIAN, a person who indulges freedom in thinking.

250. La'tus, (lat'eris), a side.

LAT'ERAL, pertaining to the side.
COLLAT'ERAL, placed by the side; classed with.
EQUILAT'ERAL, (144), of equal sides.
TRILAT'ERAL, (549), having three sides.

251. Laus, (lau'dis), praise.

LAUD, to praise; to extol.
LAUD'ABLE, praise-worthy.
LAUD'ATORY, containing praise.
LAUD'ANUM,† tincture of opium.

† This word is supposed to have been derived, in some humorous usage, from *laus*.

252. Le'go, (lega'tum), to send as an ambassador; to appoint.

LEG'ATE, a deputy; an ambassador.
LEGA'TION, a deputation; an embassy.
LEG'ACY, something left by will.
LEGATEE', one who receives a legacy.
ALLEGE', to adduce; to plead an excuse.
ALLEGA'TION, affirmation; plea.
COL'LEAGUE, a fellow ambassador or officer.
DEL'EGATE, *v.* to send on an embassy.
DEL'EGATE, *s.* a deputy, a commissioner.

253. Le'go, (lec'tum), to gather; to select; to read.

LECT'URE, a discourse designed to communicate formal instruction.
LEG'IBLE, that can be read.
LE'GEND, a narrative of fabulous character.

WORDS DERIVED FROM THE LATIN.

× LE'GION, a chosen body of men.
LES'SON, anything read or said to a teacher.
COLLECT', to gather together.
COLLECT'IVE, gathered into one mass.
DI'ALECT, peculiar mode of speech.
⊂ DIL'IGENT, industrious.
ELEC'TION, the act of choosing.
◯ EL'IGIBLE, fit to be chosen.

IN'TELLECT, understanding.
INTEL'LIGENT, able to understand. ◯
INTEL'LIGIBLE, that can be ◯ understood; clear; plain.
NEGLECT', (Lat. *nec*, not), to slight; to postpone.
NEG'LIGENCE, inattention. ◯
RECOLLECT', to call up in memory.
SELECT', to choose out.

254. *Le'nis*, mild; gentle.

LE'NIENT, mild; fitted to soothe.
LEN'ITIVE, that which softens or mitigates.

LEN'ITY, mildness of temper; tenderness; mercy.

255. *Le'vo*, to raise.

LEV'ITY, lightness; vanity; mirth.
EL'EVATE, to lift up.
ALLE'VIATE, to lighten.
LEV'IGATE, to grind to powder.

LEV'Y, to raise; to collect.
REL'EVANT, capable of aiding; applicable.
IRREL'EVANT, not applicable.
RELIEVE', to aid; to succor.

256. *Lex*, (*le'gis*), a law.

LE'GAL, lawful.
ILLE'GAL, unlawful.
LE'GALIZE, to make lawful.
LEGIT'IMATE, correctly derived.
LEG'ISLATURE, (167), the law-making power.

LEG'ISLATE, to enact laws.
PRIV'ILEGE,* (413), a special right or advantage.
LEGIT'IMACY, a political term, signifying lawful hereditary succession in the government.

* *Primary signification*, a law for the advantage of particular individuals.

257. *Li'ber*, free.

LIB'ERAL, bountiful; generous.
LIB'ERTY, freedom. [free.
LIB'ERATE, DELIV'ER, to set
LIB'ERALIZE, to remove narrow views.

LIB'ERTINE, one under no moral restraint.
ILLIB'ERAL, mean; suspicious.
ILLIBERAL'ITY, want of generosity.

258. *Li'ber*, (*li'bri*), a book.

LI'BRARY, a collection of books.
LI'BEL, (Lat. *libel'lus*, a small writing or document), a defamatory writing.

LIBRA'RIAN, one who has the care of books.
LI'BELLOUS, defamatory.

259. *Li'bro*, (*libra'tum*), to weigh in a balance.

DELIB'ERATE, to weigh mentally.

EQUILIB'RIUM, (144), equality of weights in a balance.

260. *Li'cet*, to be lawful, or allowable.

LI'CENSE, permission.
LICEN'TIOUS, wanton; unrestrained.

ILLIC'IT, unlawful; improper.
LICEN'TIATE, one who has received a license.

261. *Li'go*, (*liga'tum*), to bind.

LIG'AMENT, a band.
LIG'ATURE, anything that binds; a bandage.
ALLE'GIANCE, acknowledged obligation to obey.

OBLIGE', to compel; to place under bonds of duty.
OBLIGA'TION, a binding requirement. [man.
RELIG'ION, our duty to God and

262. *Li'men*, a threshold.

ELIM'INATE, to put out of doors; to cast out.

PRELIM'INARY, before the threshold; introductory.

263. *Lin'gua*, the tongue; a language.

LAN'GUAGE, human speech; style.

LIN'GUIST, one skilled in languages.

264. *Lin'quo*, (*lic'tum*), to leave.

DELIN'QUENT, failing in duty.
DERELIC'TION, a forsaking.
RELIN'QUISH, to abandon.

REL'IC, something left.
REL'ICT, *literally*, one left; a widow.

265. *Li'num*, flax.   *Lin'ea*, a line.

LIN'EN, cloth made of flax.
LIN'SEED, the seed of flax.

LIN'SEY-WOOLSEY, made of linen and wool.

LINT, down scraped from linen.
LINE, (*lin'ea*), a thread or cord.
LIN'EAR, consisting of lines.
LIN'EAL, in a line.
LIN'EAGE, descent; family line.
LIN'EAMENT, an outline of the face or of a portion of it.
CURVILIN'EAR, (104), having curved lines. [line.
DELIN'EATE, to draw an out-

266. *Lis*, (*li'tis*), strife.

LITIGA'TION, going to law.
LIT'IGANT, one engaged in a law-suit.

267. *Lit'era*, a letter.

LIT'ERATURE, learning.
LIT'ERARY, relating to learning.
LIT'ERAL, exact to the letter.
LITERA'TI, (Lat.), the learned.
ILLIT'ERATE, unlearned.
OBLIT'ERATE, to rub out.
LET'TER, a character representing some sound; an epistle.
LIT'ERALLY, exactly to the letter.
ALLITERA'TION, beginning several words in succession with the same letter.

268. *Lo'cus*, a place.

LO'CAL, relating to place.
LOCAL'ITY, situation; place.
LO'CATE, to place
LOCOMO'TION, (316), power of changing place.
LOCOMO'TIVE, having the power
of motion from one place to another.
ALLOCA'TION, putting one thing to another.
COLLOCA'TION, placing together.
DIS'LOCATE, to put out of joint.

269. *Lon'gus*, long.

LONG, *a*. not short.
LONG, *v*. to desire earnestly.
LON'GITUDE, length; distance east or west. [life.
LONGEV'ITY, (147), length of
PROLONG', to lengthen out.
OB'LONG, longer than broad.
ELON'GATE, to lengthen.
ELONGA'TION, the state of being lengthened.

270. *Lo'quor*, (*locu'tus*), to speak.

LOQUAC'ITY, talkativeness.
COL'LOQUY, a conference.
COLLO'QUIAL, relating to conversation. [expression.
CIRCUMLOCU'TION, a round about
ELOCU'TION, the art of oratorical delivery.
EL'OQUENT, having oratorical powers. [ing speech.
GRANDIL'OQUENCE, (208), swell-

EL'OQUENCE, the art of speaking well; oratory.
OB'LOQUY, censorious speech.
LOQUA'CIOUS, full of talk; garrulous.
SOLIL'OQUY, (496), a speech in solitude.
VENTRIL'OQUIST, (573), one who can speak as if from his stomach.

271. *Lu'crum*, gain.

LU'CRE, (Fr.), gain; profit. | LU'CRATIVE, profitable.

272. *Luc'tor*, (*lucta'tus*), to struggle.

RELUC'TANCE, unwillingness. | RELUC'TANT, unwilling.

273. *Lu'do*, (*lu'sum*), to play.

LU'DICROUS, exciting laughter.
ALLU'SION, a reference to something.
COLLU'SION, dishonest agreement or compact.
ELUDE', to escape by stratagem.
DELU'SION, deceptive appearance.
IN'TERLUDE, a play performed between the principal exhibitions.
PRE'LUDE, an introductory play.

274. *Lu'na*, the moon.

LU'NAR, relating to the moon.
LUNE, a figure in the form of a crescent; a crescent or half-moon.
LU'NACY, a sort of madness.*
LU'NATIC, an insane person.
SUB'LUNARY, beneath the moon; earthly.

* The name was derived from a superstitious notion that insanity was connected with the influence of the moon.

275. *Lu'o*, (*lu'tum*), to wash away.

ABLU'TION, a washing or cleansing.
ANTEDILU'VIAN, (Lat. *dilu'vium*, a deluge), existing before the deluge.
ALLU'VIAL, deposited by inundation.
DILU'VIAN, relating to the deluge.
DILUTE', to make thin or weak.
DILU'TION, a making thin or weak; a diluted liquid.
POLLUTE', (Lat. *pol'luo*, to defile), to defile; to make unclean.
POLLU'TION, defilement; impurity.

WORDS DERIVED FROM THE LATIN.

276. *Lux*, (*lu'cis*), and *Lu'men*, (*lu'minis*), light.

Lu'cid, Lu'cent, bright; shining; giving light.
Lu'cifer, (167), the morning star.
Lu'minous, emitting light; shining.
Lu'minary, anything that gives light.
Elu'cidate, to explain.
Illu'minate, to enlighten.
Illumina'tion, lighting up.
Translu'cent, clear; transparent.

277. *Magister*, a master.

Mag'istrate, one having civil authority.
Mag'istracy, the office or dignity of a magistrate.
Magiste'rial, having the air of authority.
Mas'ter, one having the direction or control.

278. *Mag'nus*, great; *Ma'jor*, greater.

Mag'nitude, greatness.
Mag'nify, (152), to make great; to extol.
Magnan'imous, (13), of noble mind.
Magnif'icence, (152), grandeur.
Main, *s.* the gross; the chief part.
Main, *a.* chief; principal.
Ma'jor, *a.* greater.
Ma'jor, *s.* a military officer.
Major'ity, the part of any number greater than the sum of all the other parts.
Maj'esty, grandeur; sovereignty; royal title.
Majes'tic, stately; grand.

279. *Ma'lus*, bad.

Maledic'tion, (117), a curse.
Malefac'tor, (152), a criminal.
Mal'ice, a disposition to injure without cause.
Malig'nity, extreme enmity.
Mali'cious, intending ill to others.
Malev'olent, (598), wishing ill to another.
Malig'nant, partaking of malice and envy.
Maladministra'tion, (299), bad use of power.
Malign', to slander; to defame.
Mal'content, (530), a dissatisfied, restless member of society.
Malprac'tice, (G. 191), evil or illegal practice or conduct.

280. *Man'do,** (*manda'tum*), to commit; to give a charge or command.

Man'date, an order.
Command', to govern; to order.
Recommend', to commend to another.

* Manda'mus, signifying *we command*, is the name of a command or writ issuing from the King's Bench in England, and in America from some of the higher courts, directed to any person, corporation, or inferior court, requiring them to do some act therein specified.—*Webster.*

COUNTERMAND', to revoke a former command.
DEMAND', to call for with autho-
REMAND', to send back. [rity.

281. *Ma'neo,* (*man'sum*), to stay.

MAN'SION, place of abode; house.
REMAIN'DER, the difference between two quantities.
PER'MANENT, durable; lasting.
REMAIN', to stay; to be left.
REM'NANT, that which is left; residue.

282. *Ma'nus,* the hand.

MAN'UAL, performed by hand; a book which may be held in the hand.
MANUFAC'TORY, (152), a working place.
MANUFAC'TURE, anything made by art.
MANUMIS'SION, (305), giving liberty to slaves.*
MAN'USCRIPT, (468), a writing.
MAN'ACLES, shackles, handcuffs.
MANIP'ULATE, to handle.
AMANUEN'SIS, (Lat.), a person employed to write what another dictates.
EMAN'CIPATE, (47), to set at liberty.
MAINTAIN',† (530). to support.
MAN'AGE, (3). to conduct.
MANŒU'VRE,‡ a dextrous movement.
MANURE'.§ to apply fertilizing matter.

* *Literally,* sending away from under the hand.

† From the French word *maintenir.*

‡ Derived, through the French, from *manus* and *opera* or *opus,* (349), and therefore signifying, *literally,* a work of the hand.

§ The word originally signified—to cultivate by hand.

283. *Ma're,* the sea.

MARINE', belonging to the sea.
MAR'INER, a seaman.
MAR'ITIME, bordering on the sea; relating to the sea; naval.
SUBMARINE', under the sea.
TRANSMARINE', across the sea
ULTRAMARINE', (Lat. *ul'tra,* beyond), across the sea; a blue dye-stuff.

284. *Ma'ter,* a mother.

MATER'NAL, pertaining to a mother.
MAT'RIMONY, marriage.
MATERN'ITY, the character or relation of a mother.
MA'TRON, a married woman; an elderly lady.
MATRIMO'NIAL, pertaining to marriage.

285. *Matu'rus*, ripe.

MATURE', ripe; well digested.
MATU'RITY, ripeness; completion.
IMMATURE', unripe.
PREMATURE', ripe too soon; too hasty.

286. *Me'deor*, to cure.

MED'ICINE, any substance used in curing disease.
MED'ICAL, relating to medicine.
MEDIC'INAL, having the power of healing.
MED'ICATED, mingled with something medicinal.
MEDICA'TION, the use of medicine. [edy.
REME'DIAL, intended for a remedy.
REM'EDY, a cure; reparation.
REME'DIABLE, curable.
IRREME'DIABLE, incurable.

287. *Me'dius*, middle.

ME'DIUM, (Lat.), the middle point; that which comes between.
ME'DIATE, v. to interpose between parties, for the purpose of effecting a reconciliation.
ME'DIATE, a. middle; intervening.
IMME'DIATE, instant; direct; acting without any intervening cause.
INTERME'DIATE, lying between.
MEDIOC'RITY, middle state, rate, or degree; moderate degree.

288. *Mel*, honey.

MELLIF'EROUS, (167), producing honey; (as, melliferous plants).
MELLIF'LUOUS, (185), sweetly flowing; smooth.

289. *Me'lior*, better.

AMEL'IORATE, to make better; to improve.
MELIORA'TION, improvement.

290. *Mem'ini*, to remember

MEM'ORY, the faculty by which we remember.
MEM'ORABLE, worthy to be remembered.
MEMORAN'DUM, (Lat.), a note to help the memory.
MEM'OIR, (Fr. *mémoire*), a short account.
MEMEN'TO, that which reminds.
MEMO'RIAL, a monument; a petition.
MEN'TION, to speak of.
COMMEM'ORATE, to preserve in memory by some public act.
IMMEMO'RIAL, beyond memory.
REMINIS'CENCE, recollection.
REMEM'BER, to bear in mind

291. Mens, (men'tis), the mind.

MENT'AL, pertaining to the mind.

DEMENTA'TION, making frantic.

292. Mer'go, (mer'sum), to dip; to sink.

MERGE, to sink, or cause to be swallowed up.
EMERGE', to rise out of.
EMER'GENCY, pressing necessity.*

IMMER'SION, the act of putting any thing below the surface of a fluid.
SUBMER'SION, the state of being wholly covered by a fluid.

* The word is derived from the idea of an event suddenly coming upon one, as if something had arisen unexpectedly from the water.

293. Merx, (mer'cis), merchandise.

COM'MERCE, traffic, exchange.
MER'CHANDISE, things bought and sold.
MER'CHANT, a trader.

MER'CANTILE, pertaining to the business of a merchant.
MER'CENARY, serving for pay.
MER'CER, one who deals in silks.

294. Me'tior,* (men'sus), to measure.

METE, to measure.
MEAS'URE, that by which any thing is reckoned.
MENSURA'TION, the art of measuring.
COMMEN'SURATE, of equal measure.
DIMEN'SION, the extent of a [body.

ADMEAS'UREMENT, the act or result of measuring according to rule.
IMMEAS'URABLE, that cannot be measured.
IMMENSE', immeasurably great.
IMMENS'ITY, unlimited extent; vastness.

* See Gr. 137.

295. Mi'gro, (migra'tum), to remove; to depart from a place of residence.

MIGRA'TION, departure to a distant place of residence.
MI'GRATORY, roving; unsettled.
EM'IGRATE, to remove from a place.
EM'IGRANT, one who removes.

IMMIGRA'TION, the coming of foreigners into a country.
IM'MIGRANT, one who comes into a country to reside.
TRANSMIGRA'TION, a passing from one state to another.

296. *Mi'les*, (*mil'itis*), a soldier.

Mili'tia, the enrolled soldiers. | Mil'itant, fighting, contending.
Mil'itary, pertaining to soldiery. | Mil'itate, to act against.

297. *Mil'le*, a thousand.

Millen'nium, (14), a thousand years. | Mil'leped, (380), an insect having many feet.

298. *Mi'neo*, to hang over.

Im'minent, impending; at hand. | Em'inent, high; distinguished.
Prom'inent, standing out. | Em'inence, elevation.

299. *Minis'ter*, a servant or attendant.

Min'ister, one who is appointed to transact business of state under the direction of the chief executive; a clergyman.*
Min'istry, the office of a minister.
Min'istrant, attendant upon.
Ministe'rial, pertaining to a minister.

Admin'ister, to perform duties in an official station; to dispense; to bring that which is needed.
Administra'tor, one who takes charge of the property of a person dying without a will.
Administra'tion, management; actual government.

* So called from his being appointed to *serve* the church in the sacerdotal office.

300. *Mi'nor*, less.

Mi'nor, *a.* smaller; *s.* one not of age.
Minor'ity, the smaller number. [trait.
Min'iature, (Fr.), a small portrait.
Minute', *a.* small.
Min'ute, *s.* a portion of time.
Min'imum, (Lat.), the least quantity possible in the case.
Min'ion, a mean, low dependant.

Min'uend, the number to be diminished.
Mi'nus, (Lat.), a mathematical term signifying subtraction.
Minu'tiæ, (Lat.), small particulars.
Dimin'ish, to make less.
Diminu'tion, a growing less.
Dimin'utive, little.
Dimin'utiveness, smallness; littleness.

8

301. *Mi'rus*, strange; wonderful.

Mir'acle, a supernatural event.
Mirac'ulous, performed supernaturally. [or high esteem.
Admire', to regard with wonder
Ad'mirable, of wonderful excellence.
Admira'tion, wonder mingled with affection or esteem.

302. *Mis'ceo*, (*mix'tum*), to mix.

Mix, to mingle.
Mix'ture, a compound formed by mingling.
Mis'cellany, a collection of various things.
Miscella'neous, mixed; of various kinds.
Mis'cible, that may be mixed.
Admix'ture, the substance which is mixed with another.
Intermix', to mingle together.
Promis'cuous, mingled indiscriminately.

303. *Mi'ser*, wretched.

Mis'ery, wretchedness, distress.
Mi'ser, one who makes himself miserable by his niggardliness.
Mi'serly, very covetous.
Mis'erable, unhappy.
Commis'erate, to pity; to compassionate.

304. *Mi'tis*, meek; mild.

Mit'igate, to assuage; to render more mild.
Unmit'igated, unassuaged; not softened in severity.

305. *Mit'to*, (*mis'sum*), to send.

Mis'sion, the state of being sent by authority.
Mis'sionary, one sent to propagate religion.
Mis'sile, something thrown by the hand.
Admit', to let in; to allow.
Admis'sion, Admit'tance, permission to enter.
Commit', to intrust; to perpetrate.
Commis'sion, a trust; authority given; the act of committing.
Commis'sioner, one bearing a commission.
Com'missary, a kind of military commissioner.
Commit'tee, one or more persons to whom a matter is referred by a legislative body or a society.
Com'promise, to adjust by concession.
Demise', departure from life.
Dismiss', to send away.
Em'issary, one sent out as a secret agent.
Emit', to send forth.
Intermis'sion, cessation for a time.

WORDS DERIVED FROM THE LATIN. 113

INTERMIT'TENT, ceasing at intervals.
MANUMIS'SION, (282), sending away from bondage.
MIS'SIVE, sent; a letter or message sent.
OMIT', to leave out.
PERMIS'SION, leave granted.
PREMISE', to state beforehand.
PREM'ISES, propositions previously proved or assumed.
PROM'ISE, to engage to do.
PROM'ISSORY, containing a promise.
REMIT', to relax; to forgive.
REMISS', slack; negligent.
SUBMIS'SIVE, humble; yielding.
SUBMIT', to yield to authority.
SURMISE', suspicion.
TRANSMIT', to send over; to suffer to pass through; to deliver to posterity.

306. *Mo'dus*, a manner.

MODE, manner.
MOOD, temper of mind.
MOD'EL, a copy to be imitated.
MOD'IFY, (152), to change the form or character of a thing.
MOD'ULATE, to vary the pitch of sounds.
MOD'ERATE, observing proper bounds; not excessive.
MOD'EST, restrained by a sense of propriety.
MOD'ICUM, (Lat.), a small quantity.
COMMO'DIOUS, convenient.
COMMOD'ITIES, wares; goods.
ACCOM'MODATE, to supply with conveniences.
INCOMMODE', to trouble.
MODERA'TOR, (Lat.), a presiding officer.

307. *Mo'lior*, (*moli'tus*), to rear or build.

DEMOL'ISH, to throw down.
DEMOL'ISHMENT, ruin; destruction.
DEMOLI'TION, the act of demolishing.

308. *Mol'lis*, soft.

MOL'LIFY, (152), to soften; to assuage.
EMOL'LIENT, fitted to soften or assuage.

309. *Mo'neo*, (*mon'itum*), to put in mind; to warn.

MON'ITOR, (Lat.), one who warns of duty.
MON'UMENT, a memorial.
MON'ITORY, calculated to give warning.
ADMON'ISH, to remind of a fault.
ADMONI'TION, warning; reproof.
PREMON'ITORY, giving warning beforehand.
SUMMON, (Lat. *submo'neo*), to call by authority.

310. *Mons, (mon'tis),* a mountain.

MOUNT, a hill.
MOUN'TAIN, a large hill.
MOUND, a heap or bank of earth.
AMOUNT', the sum.
DISMOUNT', to alight from a horse.

PAR'AMOUNT, superior; chief.
PROM'ONTORY, a high land projecting into the sea.
SURMOUNT', to rise above.
TANT'AMOUNT, (Lat. *tan'tus,* equivalent), of the same amount or force.

311. *Monstro, (monstra'tum),* to point out; to show.

MON'STER, something deformed or horrible.
MON'STROUS, unnatural; huge.
DEMON'STRATE, to prove rigorously.

DEMON'STRATIVE, proving by irresistible argument; pointing out.
REMON'STRATE, to present strong reasons against any measure.

312. *Mor'bus,* disease.

MOR'BID, diseased; not sound or healthful.

CHOLERA-MOR'BUS, (Gr. 50), the name of a disease.

313. *Mor'deo, (mor'sum),* to bite.

MOR'SEL, a piece bitten off.
REMORSE', sense of guilt.

REMORSE'LESS, unpitying; cruel.
REMORSE'LESSLY, without remorse.

314. *Mors, (mor'tis),* death.

MOR'TAL, subject to death; deadly.
MORTAL'ITY, death; human nature.
IMMOR'TAL, exempt from death.

IMMOR'TALIZE, to render immortal.
MOR'TIFY, (152), to lose vitality; to abase.
MORTIFICA'TION, vexation; loss of vitality.

315. *Mos, (mo'ris),* custom; practice.

MOR'AL, relating to the practice or conduct of men; conformed to law and rectitude.
MOR'ALIST, one who teaches the duties of life; one who practises moral duties.

MOR'ALIZE, to apply to moral subjects.
MORAL'ITY, correctness of life.
IMMOR'AL, not virtuous.
DEMOR'ALIZE, to render corrupt in morals.

316. Mo'veo, (mo'tum), to move.

MOVE, to put out of one place into another.
MOVE'MENT, change of place.
MOV'ABLES, goods; furniture.
MOBIL'ITY, capacity of being moved.
MOB, a disorderly multitude.
MOMEN'TUM, (Lat.), force of motion.
MO'TIVE, moving power; inducement.
MO'TION, the act of moving.
COMMO'TION, tumult; disturbance.
EMO'TION, disturbance of mind.
PROMO'TION, advancement to higher rank.
PROMOTE', to advance; to exalt.
PROMO'TIVE, tending to promote.
REMOVE', to put from its place.
REMOTE', at a distance.

317. Mul'tus, much.

MULTIFA'RIOUS, (Lat. va'rius, different), having great variety.
MUL'TIFORM, (187), having many forms.
MUL'TIPLE, (392), a number which exactly contains another several times.
MUL'TIPLY, to increase in numbers.
MULTIPLICA'TION, increase in number.
MULTIPLICAND', the number to be multiplied.
MUL'TITUDE, a great number.

318. Mun'dus, the earth; the world.

MUN'DANE, belonging to the world; earthly.
EXTRAMUN'DANE, beyond the material world.

319. Mu'nio, to fortify.

AMMUNI'TION, MUNI'TION, materials used in war.
MU'NIMENT, a strong hold; a fortress; support; defence.

320. Mu'nus, (mu'neris), an office; a gift.

MUNIC'IPAL, (47), pertaining to a corporation.
MUNIF'ICENCE, (152), liberality.
COMMUNE', (Lat. con), to converse together.
COMMU'NICATE, to impart.
COMMU'NICATIVE, liberal in imparting knowledge.
COMMU'NITY, common possession or enjoyment; society.
COMMUN'ION, fellowship; intercourse.

Com′mon, shared by all; general.*

Excommu′nicate, to cut off from church membership.

Immu′nity, exemption from duty.

Remunera′tion, recompense.

* A *common* inheritance is one which all the inheritors own and enjoy alike. A characteristic is said to be *common* to our race, which every human being possesses.

321. *Mu′rus*, a wall.

Mu′ral, pertaining to a wall.*

Immure′, to enclose within walls; to imprison.

* Among the ancient Romans, a golden crown was bestowed on him who first mounted the wall of a besieged place; this was called *coro′na mura′lis*, a mural crown.

322. *Mu′sa*, a Muse.

Muse, *s.* a heathen deity presiding over poetry, &c.
Muse, *v.* to ponder.
Amuse′, to divert.

Muse′um, (Lat.), a repository of curiosities.
Mu′sic, melody or harmony.
Music′ian, one skilled in music.

323. *Mu′to*, (*muta′tum*), to change.

Mu′table, changeable.
Muta′tion, change.
Mu′tual, reciprocal; interchanged.
Commute′, to exchange.

Immu′table, unchangeable.
Transmute′, to change to a different nature.
Transmuta′tion, change of substance; alteration.

324. *Nas′cor*, (*na′tus*), to be born.

Na′tal, relating to one's birth.
Na′tive, conferred by birth; original.
Nativ′ity, birth.
Na′tion, a distinct people.
Na′ture, original quality; the established course of things in creation; the visible creation.

Nat′uralist, a student of nature.
Nat′ural, produced by nature; unaffected.
Innate′, born with us; constitutional.
Preternat′ural, extraordinary, but not miraculous.
Supernat′ural, above nature.

325. *Na′to*, to swim.

Nata′tion, the act of swimming. | Superna′tant, floating above.

WORDS DERIVED FROM THE LATIN.

326. *Na'vis*, a ship or vessel.

NA'VY, the national establishment of war vessels.
NA'VAL, relating to vessels.
NAVIGA'TION, (3), travelling by ships; the art of navigating.
NAV'IGABLE, passable by ships.
NAU'TICAL, (Lat. *nau'ta*, a sailor), pertaining to seamen or navigation.
CIRCUMNAV'IGATE to sail round. [round.
CIRCUMNAVIGA'TION, sailing

327. *Nec'to*, (*nex'um*), to tie or bind.

CONNECT', to tie or join together.
CONNEC'TION, a joining; relation.
DISCONNECT', to sever.
ANNEX', to unite at the end.
ANNEXA'TION, the act of joining or annexing.

328. *Ne'go*, (*nega'tum*), to deny.

NEGA'TION, denial.
NEG'ATIVE, implying denial.
DENY', (Fr. *denier;* Lat. *de'ne-go*), to contradict; to refuse.

329. *Nego'tium*,* business.

NEGO'TIATE, to transact business.
NEGO'TIABLE, that may be transferred in business.

* Compounded of *nec*, not, and *o'tium*, leisure, ease.

330. *Neu'ter*, neither of the two.

NEU'TER, of neither gender.
NEU'TRAL, not engaged on either side.
NEU'TRALIZE, to render neutral; to destroy the peculiar properties.

331. *Ni'hil*, nothing.

NIHIL'ITY, nothingness.
ANNIHILA'TION, reducing to nothing or non-existence.

332. *No'ceo*, to hurt; to harm.

NOX'IOUS, hurtful.
INNOX'IOUS, harmless.
IN'NOCENT, not chargeable with mischief.
IN'NOCENCE, simplicity, purity.
NUI'SANCE, that which does injury.
OBNOX'IOUS, liable; exposed to penalty.

333. Nor'ma, a rule.

Nor'mal, according to a rule or precept; elementary.
Enor'mous, beyond the usual measure; huge; excessive.
Enor'mity, a wrong or irregular act; atrociousness.
Enor'mously, excessively; beyond measure.

334. Nos'co, (no'tum), to know. No'men, a name.

Note, a mark; a hint.
Nota'tion, (Lat. no'ta, a mark), mode of marking.
No'ted, Noto'rious, well known; remarkable.
No'tice, observation.
No'tify, (152), to make known.
No'tion, idea; opinion.
Annota'tion, a comment.
Cog'nisance, notice; perception.
Cogni'tion, certain knowledge.
Denote', to point out.
No'ble, (Lat. no'bilis), generous; famous.
Nobil'ity, dignity; high rank.
Enno'ble, to dignify; to elevate.
Igno'ble, mean; worthless.

Rec'ognise, to remember a thing as one previously known.
Reconnoi'tre, (Fr.), to survey.
Nom'inal, in name only.
No'menclature, (Lat. ca'lo, to call), a system of names; the terms or words of an art or science.
Nom'inate, to name for appointment.
Name, the term by which we distinguish things.
Noun, a part of speech.
Pro'noun, a word used instead of a noun.
Denomina'tion, a class of things or persons called by the same name.
Ig'nominy, disgrace, dishonor.
Misno'mer, a misnaming.

335. No'vus, new.

Nov'el, a. new; s. a tale.
Nov'elist, a writer of novels.
Nov'elty, newness.
Nov'ice, one new in the business.

In'novate, to introduce something new.
Innova'tion, introduction of something new.
Ren'ovate, to renew.

336. Nox, (noc'tis), night.

Noctur'nal, nightly.
E'quinox, (See 144).

Equinoc'tial, pertaining to the equinox.

337. Nu'bo, (nup'tum), to marry.

Connu'bial, pertaining to marriage.

Nup'tials, marriage ceremonies.

WORDS DERIVED FROM THE LATIN. 119

338. *Nu'dus*, naked.

Nu'dity, nakedness. | Denude', to make bare or naked

339. *Nul'lus*, no one.

Nul'lify, (152), to render of no force.
Nul'lity, nothingness.

Annul', to make void.
Disannul, to annul.

340. *Nu'merus*, a number.

Num'ber, multitude; more than one thing.
Nu'merous, containing many.
Numera'tion, the art of numbering.
Numer'ical, pertaining to numbers.

Enu'merate, to reckon up singly.
Innu'merable, too many to be counted.
Supernu'merary, a person or thing beyond the usual number.

341. *Nun'cio*, to announce.

Announce', to proclaim; to give notice.
Denounce', to declare against.
Denuncia'tion, public menace.
Enun'ciate, to declare; to proclaim; to utter.

Nun'cio, an ambassador from the Pope.
Pronuncia'tion, mode of utterance.
Renounce', to disown; to reject.

342. *Oc'ulus*, the eye.

Oc'ular, perceived by the eye.
Oc'ulist, one skilled in diseases of the eye; an eye-doctor.

Inoc'ulate, to transfer an eye or bud of a tree to another stock.

343. *O'di*, to hate.

O'dious, hateful; causing hatred. | O'dium, dislike; offensiveness.

344. *O'leo*, to emit odor.

Olfac'tory, (152), pertaining to the sense of smelling.

Red'olent, diffusing a sweet scent.

345. *Om'nis*, every; all.

Omnip'otent, (403), having all power. [where present.
Omnipres'ent, (520), every-

Omnis'cient, (467), having infinite knowledge.
Om'nibus, (Latin), for all.

346. *O'nus*, (*on'eris*), a burden.

EXON'ERATE, to disburden. | ON'EROUS, burdensome.

347. *Opi'nor*, to be of opinion; to think.

OPINE', to think.
OPIN'ION, belief; judgment.

OPIN'IONATED, obstinate in opinion.

348. *Op'to*, (*opta'tum*), to wish.

OP'TION, the power of choosing; choice; preference.

ADOPT', to assume; to choose or take to one's self.

349. *O'pus*, (*op'eris*), a work.

OP'ERATE, to act; to produce effects.
CO-OP'ERATE, to labor jointly with others.
CO-OPERA'TION, joint effort; aid.
INOP'ERATIVE, inefficient.
MANŒU'VRE,* (282), a skilful movement.

OP'ERATIVE, active.
OPERA'TION, action; effect.
OP'ERATOR, one who operates.
OP'ERA, (Lat.), a dramatic composition set to music; a musical drama.

* *Œuvre* is a French word, signifying a work, action, or performance.

350. *Or'bis*, a circle; a circular body.

ORB, a spherical body.
OR'BIT, the circular path of a planet.

ORBIC'ULAR, circular.
EXORB'ITANT,† extravagant; excessive.

† *Literally*, departing from an orbit or usual track.

351. *Or'do*, (*or'dinis*), order.

OR'DER, regularity.
OR'DINANCE, a public command or law.
OR'DINARY, in the usual order or manner.

INOR'DINATE, excessive.
EXTRAOR'DINARY, beyond the usual course.
SUBOR'DINATE, in a lower rank.
SUBORDINA'TION, subjection.

352. *O'rior*, to rise or spring from.

O'RIENT, rising, as the sun; eastern.
OR'IGIN, beginning; source.

ORIENT'AL, eastern; belonging to the east.
ORIG'INATE, to bring into exist- [ence.

ORIG'INAL, primitive, first; having new ideas.
ORIGINAL'ITY, the state of being
original.

ABOR'TIVE, produced in an imperfect state; ineffectual.
EXOR'DIUM, (Lat. or'dior, to
begin), a formal preface.

353. Or'no, (orna'tum), to embellish.

OR'NAMENT, an embellishment.
OR'NATE, decorated; beautiful.
ADORN', to beautify.

SUBORN',* to induce a person to
swear falsely.

* The Latin word *subor'no*, signifies *to fit out privately.*

354. O'ro, (ora'tum), to pray; to ask.

ORA'TION, a formal speech.
OR'ATOR, a public speaker.
OR'ATORY, eloquence.
OR'ISON, a prayer.
OR'ACLE, a place where heathen
deities or priests were con-
sulted.
ORAC'ULAR, positive; having an
affected air of wisdom.

O'RAL, (Lat. os, (o'ris), the
mouth), pertaining to speech.
ADORE', to worship.
ADORA'TION, worship.
EX'ORABLE, to be moved by
entreaty.
INEX'ORABLE, not to be moved.
PERORA'TION,† the conclusion
of an oration.

† *Literally,* the going over the oration; the peroration recapitulates the
main points, and presents the argument in a small compass.

355. Os, (os'sis), a bone.

OS'SIFY, (152), to change into
a bony substance.
OSSIFICA'TION, change into
bony substance.

OS'SIFRAGE, (191), the bone
breaker or sea eagle; a kind
of sea eagle.
OS'SEOUS, bony.

356. O'vum, an egg.

O'VAL, egg-shaped.

OVIP'AROUS, (363), producing
eggs.

357. Pa'gus, a village.

PA'GAN,‡ a heathen; an idol-
ater.

PA'GANISM, the worship of false
gods.

‡ When the Roman Emperor Constantine and his successors forbade the
worship of the heathen deities in the cities, its adherents retired to the vil-
lages, where they could practise their rites unmolested. Hence they obtained
the appellation *paga'ni*, pagans. The word is now applied to all nations
which are neither Christian, Jewish, nor Mohammedan.

358. *Pan'do, (pan'sum)*, to lay open.

Expand', to open; to spread.
Expan'sion, the act of expanding; enlargement.
Expanse', a wide extent.
Expans'ive, capable of being expanded.

359. *Pan'go, (pac'tum)*, to drive in; to fix.

Compact', close; dense; firmly united.
Com'pact, an agreement.
Compact'ly, closely.
Com'pacted, closely united; joined together.

360. *Pal'lium*, a cloak.

Pall, a covering for the dead.
Pal'liate, to cloak; to cover with excuse; to extenuate; to mitigate
Pallia'tion, mitigation.
Pal'liative, tending to mitigate or relieve.

361. *Par*, equal; like.

Pair, two things like each other; a couple.
Par'ity, equality; resemblance.
Dispar'ity, inequality.
Compare', to examine things with reference to their likeness or unlikeness.
Dispar'age, (3), to cause disgrace.
Dispar'agement, an undervaluing; detraction.
Peer, an equal; a nobleman.
Peer'less, unequalled; matchless.
Peer'age, the rank of a peer.

362. *Pa'reo, (par'itum)*, to be present.

Appa'rent, visible; evident.
Appear', to become visible; to seem.
Appari'tion, a spectre, a ghost.
Disappear', to vanish; to withdraw.
Transpa'rent, capable of being seen through.

363. *Pa'rio, (par'tum)*, to bring forth.

Pa'rent, a father or mother; that which produces.
Paren'tal, relating to parents; tender.
Pa'rentage, (3), birth, descent.
Paren'tally, in a parental manner; affectionately.

364. *Pa'ro, (para'tum)*, to prepare.

Appara'tus, furniture or utensils prepared for a particular business.
Sev'er,* to separate.
Prepare', to make ready.
Repair', to mend.

* This word was probably derived indirectly from the Latin word *separo*.

WORDS DERIVED FROM THE LATIN. 123

REPARA'TION, making good what was injured or lost.
IMPAIR', to injure.
SEP'ARATE, to disunite, to part.

365. *Pars*, (*par'tis*), a part.

PART, a share.
PAR'TICLE, a little part.
PARTIC'ULAR, having reference to individual things; attentive to minute matters.
PARTIC'IPATE, (47), to have part or share.
PARTI'TION, division.
PAR'TY, a set of persons engaged in one design.
PAR'TISAN, one devoted to the interests of a party.
POR'TION, a part; a share.
PAR'TIAL, inclined to favor one party or side.
PART'NER, a sharer.

PAR'CEL, a number of things taken together; a small package.
PARSE, to analyze grammatically.
APART'MENT, a room or separate enclosure.
COMPART'MENT, a portion of any surface marked off.
DEPART', to go away.
DEPART'MENT, a separate class of duties or of topics.
IMPART', to communicate; to give a share.
IMPAR'TIAL, not partial.
BIP'ARTITE, (37), having two parts.

366. *Pas'co*, (*pas'tum*), to feed.

PAS'TOR, (Lat. *pas'tor*, a shepherd), a minister of the gospel having the care of a congregation.
REPAST', a meal.

PAS'TORAL, relating to shepherds; rural; relating to a pastor.
PAS'TURE, a field or ground where cattle may graze.

367. *Pa'ter*, (*pa'tris*), a father

PATER'NAL, pertaining to a father.
PAT'RIMONY, an inherited estate.
PA'TRIOT, (Lat. *pa'tria*, one's country), a lover of his country.
PA'TRIARCH, (G. 18), the father and ruler of a family; (applied particularly to the heads of families in the early history of the human race, and especially to the ancestors of the people of Israel).

PA'TRON, a protector; one who affords support.
PA'TRONAGE, (3), special support.
PATRIC'IAN, a Roman nobleman.
COMPA'TRIOT, one of the same country.
EXPA'TRIATE, to banish from one's country.
JU'PITER, the father and king of the heathen gods.
PA'TER-NOS'TER, (Lat. *nos'ter*, our), the Lord's prayer.

368. *Pa'tior*, (*pas'sus*), to suffer; to endure.

PA'TIENCE, endurance.
PA'TIENT, *a.* enduring without complaint.
PA'TIENT, *s.* a sick person.
IMPA'TIENT, unable to bear pain.
PAS'SIVE, suffering; unresisting.
PAS'SION, emotion; the suffering of our Saviour on the cross.
PAS'SIONATE, influenced by passion.
COMPAS'SION, pity; sympathy.
COMPAS'SIONATE, to pity; to have compassion for.
DISPAS'SIONATE, calm.
IMPAS'SIONED, characterized by strong feeling.

369. *Pax*, (*pa'cis*), peace.

PEACE, quiet; rest.
PACIF'IC, (152), peacemaking; gentle.
PAC'IFY, APPEASE', to quiet.
PACIFICA'TION, an appeasing.

370. *Pec'co*, (*pecca'tum*), to err; to sin.*

PEC'CANCY, a bad quality; an offence.
PECCADIL'LO, (Sp.), a slight transgression or offence.

* *Pecca'vi*, is the perfect of the same verb, and signifies—*I have sinned.*

371. *Pec'tus*, (*pec'toris*), the breast.

PEC'TORAL, pertaining to the breast.
EXPEC'TORATE, to discharge from the trachea or the lungs.

372. *Pe'cus*, a herd or flock; cattle.

PEC'ULATE,† (167), to steal or embezzle public property.
PECUL'IAR,‡ belonging to; appropriate; special.
PECUN'IARY,§ relating to money.

† In early times, herds and flocks constituted the sole wealth; and hence words derived from *pe'cus*, &c., came to represent property in general.

‡ *Pecul'ium*, in Latin, signifies a treasure or stock of money laid up by an individual; every portion of this stock would therefore be *peculia'ris*, peculiar, i. e., his own.

§ Money was first coined at Rome under the reign of Servius Tullius; and the figure stamped upon the coin was that of the ox. Hence, money came to be called *pecun'ia* in the Latin language.

373. *Pel'lo*, (*pul'sum*), to drive.

PULSE, the throbbing of the arteries.
PULSA'TION, a beating or throbbing.

WORDS DERIVED FROM THE LATIN. 125

Compel′, to force; to constrain.
Compul′sion, act of compelling; force.
Compul′sory, driving by violence.
Dispel′, to drive away.
Expel′, to drive out.
Expul′sion, a driving out.
Impel′, to urge forward; to excite to any action.

Im′pulse, force given or communicated instantaneously.
Impuls′ive, having power to impel.
Propel′, to drive onward.
Repel′, to drive back.
Repul′sion, the act or power of driving back.
Repuls′ive, fitted to repel; forbidding.

374. *Pen′deo*, to hang; *Pen′do*, (*pen′sum*), to weigh; to pay out.

Pen′dent, hanging.
Pen′dulum, (Lat.), a vibrating body suspended from a fixed point.
Pen′sion, a stated allowance.
Append′, to hang to another thing; to annex.
Append′ix, something added at the end.
Compend′ium, an abridgment
Compend′ious, brief; comprehensive.
Compen′sate, to reward.
Compensa′tion, remuneration.
Depend′, to hang from; to trust to.
Dispense′, to distribute; *to dispense with*, to do without.

Expend′, to lay out
Expense′, cost; charges.
Impend′, to hang over.
Indispens′able, that cannot be omitted or spared.
Pend′ing, remaining undecided.
Perpendic′ular, directly downwards.
Pen′dent, hanging, projecting.
Propen′sity, inclination; tendency.
Rec′ompense, reward.
Sti′pend, (Lat. *stips*, a piece of money), wages; stated pay.
Suspend′, to hang; to delay.
Suspen′sion, a hanging; an interruption.
Suspense′, uncertainty; a stop.

375. *Pe′ne*, almost.

Penin′sula, (233), a portion of land almost surrounded by water.
Penin′sular, relating to a peninsula.

376. *Pœ′na*, punishment.

Pe′nal, enacting punishment.
Pen′alty, suffering or loss in consequence of crime.
Pen′ance, suffering voluntarily endured for the sake of obtaining pardon.

PEN'ITENCE, (Lat. *pœnit'eo*, to repent), repentance.
PENITEN'TIARY, a prison.
IMPEN'ITENT, not contrite.

REPENT', to feel sorrow or regret for what one has done.
SUBPŒ'NA,* a writ commanding one to appear in court.

* The word signifies *under penalty;* i. e., penalty to be suffered if the command is disobeyed.

377 Pen'itus, inwardly; deeply.

PEN'ETRATE, to pierce; to enter.
PENETRA'TION, the act of piercing; acuteness.

PEN'ETRATING, piercing; sharp; discerning.
IMPEN'ETRABLE, that cannot be pierced.

378. Pen'na, a feather; a wing.

PEN, a writing instrument. | PEN'NATE, winged.

379. Perso'na, the mask worn by players.†

PER'SON, an individual human being.
PER'SONATE, to represent by action or appearance.

PERSON'IFY, (152), to represent an inanimate thing as having intelligence.
PER'SONALLY, in person.

† *Perso'na* also signifies *character, person,* &c.

380. Pes, (pe'dis), a foot.

PED'AL, a key designed to be moved by the foot.
PED'ESTAL, the base on which a pillar or statue is placed.
PEDES'TRIAN, going on foot.
BI'PED, (37), a two-footed animal.
QUAD'RUPED, (426), a four-footed animal.
PED'LER, a travelling foot trader.
PED'DLE, to travel as a pedler.
PED'IGREE, genealogy.

EXPEDI'TION, haste; an enterprise on which one undertakes a journey.
EXPE'DIENT, tending to promote the object; advisable.
EXPE'DIENCY, fitness of measures to secure a desirable end.
IMPEDE', to hinder; to obstruct.
IMPED'IMENT, hindrance
EX'PEDITE, to hasten.

381. Pe'to, (peti'tum), to seek.

PET'ULANT, peevish; fretful in respect to what is wished for from others.

AP'PETITE, hunger; longing.
CENTRIP'ETAL, (Gr. 44), tending towards the centre.

COMPETE', to rival.
COM'PETENCE, a sufficiency.
COMPETI'TION, rivalry; contest.
IMPET'UOUS, headstrong; forcible.

IM'PETUS,(Lat.),force of motion.
REPEAT', to try again; to recite.
REPETI'TION, the act of doing or uttering a second time.

382. *Pi'lo*, to pillage; to rob.

COMPILE', to select and put together.
PIL'LAGE, (3), to plunder; to rob.

383. *Pin'go*, (*pic'tum*), to paint.

PICT'URE, a painting; a representation.
PICTURESQUE', like a picture.
PIG'MENT, paint; color.
DEPICT', to paint; to describe.

384. *Pi'o*, (*pia'tum*), to appease by sacrifice.

EX'PIATE, to atone for.
EXPIA'TION, atonement.
EX'PIATORY, having power to atone.

385. *Pis'cis*, a fish.

PIS'CATORY, relating to fishes. | PIS'CINE, of the fish kind.

386. *Pla'ceo*, to please.

PLAC'ID, quiet; mild.
COMPLA'CENCE, satisfaction.
IMPLA'CABLE, (Lat. *pla'co*, to appease), not to be appeased.
PLEAS'URE, (Fr. *plaisir*), satisfaction; enjoyment.
COM'PLAISANCE, civility.
DISPLEASE', to offend.

387. *Plan'ta*, a plant.

PLANT, a vegetable.
PLANTA'TION, a place planted.
PLAN'TAIN, an herb; a tree.
IMPLANT', to set; to insert.
IMPLANT'ED, deeply fixed.
SUPPLANT', to displace by taking the place of the person ejected.
TRANSPLANT', to remove and plant in another place.

388. *Pla'nus*, even; level; evident.

PLANE, to make smooth.
PLAIN, a level region; manifest.
EXPLAIN', to make plain or intelligible. [planation.
EXPLAN'ATORY, containing ex-

9

389. *Plau'do*, (*plau'sum*), to clap; to applaud.

PLAUD'IT, applause. [ance.
PLAUS'IBLE, right in appearAPPLAUD', to join in applause.
APPLAUSE', expression of approbation by clapping the hands, &c.

EXPLODE', to drive out in disgrace; to burst with a loud report.
EXPLO'SION, violent bursting.
EXPLO'SIVE, liable to cause explosion.

390. *Plebs*, (*ple'bis*), the common people.

PLEBE'IAN, *a.* pertaining to the common people.
PLEBE'IAN, *s.* one of the common people.

391. *Ple'o*, (*ple'tum*), to fill; *Ple'nus*, full.

PLE'NARY, full; complete.
PLENIPOTEN'TIARY, (403), invested with full powers.
PLEN'ITUDE, fulness.
PLEN'TEOUS, abundant.
PLE'ONASM, a redundancy of words.
PLEN'TY, abundance; exuberance.
ACCOM'PLISH, (Fr. *accomplir*), to finish entirely.

COMPLETE', full; perfect.
COM'PLEMENT, full quantity.
DEPLE'TION, an emptying.
EX'PLETIVE, something added to fill up.
IM'PLEMENT, a utensil; a tool.
REPLEN'ISH, to fill again.
REPLETE', filled.
SUPPLY', to fill up; to furnish.
SUP'PLEMENT, an addition to supply defects.

392. *Pli'co*, (*plica'tum*), to fold. *Plec'to*, (*plex'um*), to twine or weave.

ACCOM'PLICE, one united with another in a plot.
APPLY', to put one thing to another.
APPLICA'TION, the act of applying; the thing applied.
COM'PLICATED, entangled; interwoven with other things.
COMPLEX'ION, the hue of the skin and features; general appearance of a thing.
COMPLY', to yield.
DISPLAY', to unfold; to show; to exhibit.

DUPLIC'ITY, (134), doubleness of heart or speech.
DU'PLICATE, a second thing of the sort.
EXPLIC'IT, plain; clear.
INEX'PLICABLE, that cannot be explained or interpreted.
IM'PLICATE, to involve; to show a connection.
IMPLIC'IT, relying upon; trusting without reserve.
IMPLY', to express some opinion, although not in direct language.

INEX'PLICABLE, not to be explained.
MULTIPLICA'TION, (317), increase; repeated addition of a quantity to itself.
PERPLEX', to entangle; to involve.
PLI'ANT, easily bent.
REDUPLICA'TION, (134), doubling.
SIM'PLE, (Lat. *si'ne*, without), plain; artless; single.
SIMPLIC'ITY, innocence; plainness.
SIM'PLIFY, (152), to render less complex; to make easier.
SUP'PLICATE,* to entreat.
TRIP'LE, (549), three-fold.
TRIP'LET, three verses rhyming together.

* Lat. *sup'plex*, for *subplex*; literally, bending beneath; kneeling before one.

393. *Plo'ro*, (*plora'tum*), to cry; to bewail.

DEPLORE', to regret; to bewail.
DEPLOR'ABLE, lamentable; wretched.
EXPLORE', to search; to examine.
IMPLORE', to call upon; to beseech.

394. *Plum'bum*, lead.

PLUMB, PLUM'MET, a leaden weight at the end of a line.
PLUMB, *ad.* perpendicularly.
PLUMB'ER, one who works lead.
PLUMBA'GO, black lead; graphite.

395. *Plus*, (*plu'ris*), more.

PLU'RAL, containing more than one.
PLURAL'ITY,† greater number.
SUR'PLUS, what remains beyond the necessary quantity.
NON'PLUS,‡ to bring to a stand.

† A candidate is said to have a plurality of votes, when he has more than any other single candidate.

‡ *Literally*, no more.

396. *Po'lio*, (*poli'tum*), to polish.§

POL'ISH, to smooth; to brighten.
POLITE', elegant in manners; well-bred.

§ See Gr. 187.

397. *Po'mum*, an apple.

POM'ACE, the substance of apples or of similar fruit crushed by grinding.
POMEGRAN'ATE,‖ (209), a kind of fruit.
POM'MEL, a knob or ball.

‖ *Literally*, an apple having many grains or seeds.

398. *Pon'dus*, (*pon'deris*), a weight.

Pound, a weight.
Pon'derous, heavy.
Pon'der, to weigh mentally.

Prepon'derate, to outweigh.
Impon'derable, not having perceptible weight.

399. *Po'no*, (*pos'itum*), to put or place.

Posi'tion, place; situation.
Pos'itive, distinctly laid down.
Post, station.
Pos'ture, situation; attitude.
Postpone', to put off; to delay.
Ap'posite, proper; fit.
Compo'nent, forming part of a composition.
Compose', to put together.
Compos'itor, a setter of types.
Compo'sure, calmness; tranquillity.
Decompose', to separate into the constituent parts.
Depôt', (Fr.), a place of deposit.
Deposi'tion, that which is laid or thrown down; written testimony.
Depose', to put down.
Depos'itory, the place where anything is lodged.
Discompose', to disorder; to disturb.
Dispose', to place in order.

Expose', to lay open.
Expos'itor, an explainer.
Exposi'tion, explanation.
Impose', to put upon; to cheat.
Imposi'tion, a cheat.
Im'post, a tax laid on imported merchandise.
Impos'ture, fraud; imposition.
Interpose', to put between.
Oppose', to resist.
Op'posite, situated in front or over against.
Preposi'tion, a word placed before another.
Propose', to offer to consideration.
Pur'pose, intention; design.
Repose', to rest; to rely.
Repos'itory, a place for storing anything.
Suppose', to imagine or state something possible, but not known to be true.
Transpose', to put each into the place of the other.

400. *Pop'ulus*, the people; *Pub'lico*, to publish.

Peo'ple, persons; a nation.
Popula'tion, the whole number of people in a country or district.
Pop'ulace, the common people.
Pop'ular, suitable to people in general.
Pop'ulous, full of people.

Depop'ulate, to deprive of inhabitants.
Pub'lic, general; national.
Public'ity, general notoriety.
Pub'lish, to make known; to send out to the public.
Publica'tion, a publishing; a book.

WORDS DERIVED FROM THE LATIN.

401. *Por'ta*, a gate.

Por'tal, a gate; an entrance.
Por'tico, a covered walk; an entrance.
Por'ter, a doorkeeper.

Port'-hole, a gun hole in a ship's side.
Port, a harbor; a place where vessels may enter.

402. *Por'to*, to carry.

Por'ter, a carrier.
Port'able, easily carried.
Portman'teau, (282), a kind of valise.
Comport', to agree; to suit.
Deport'ment, conduct.
Export', to send abroad.
Import', to bring into a country.
Import'ant, weighty; momentous.
Importune', to tease; to molest.
Importu'nity, urgent solicitation.

Opportu'nity, fit time; occasion.
Opportune', well timed.
Inopportune', unseasonable.
Portfo'lio, (186), a case for carrying loose papers.
Pur'port, meaning.
Port'ly, corpulent.
Report', rumor; an account.
Support', to bear up; to prop.
Transport', to carry from place to place.

403. *Pos'sum*, (*pot'ui*), to be able.

Pos'sible, that can be done.
Po'tent, powerful.
Im'potent, powerless.
Omnip'otent, (345), having infinite power.

Plenipoten'tiary, (391), having full power.
Po'tentate, one having kingly power.
Poten'tial, relating to power.

404. *Pos'terus*, following; coming after.

Poste'rior, later; coming after.
Poster'ity, succeeding generations.

Pos'tern, *primarily*, a back door or gate; hence, any small door or gate.
Prepos'terous,* absurd.

* *Literally*, having that first which ought to be last; inverted in order.
Webster.

405. *Pos'tulo*, (*postula'tum*), to demand.

406. *Po'to,* (*pota'tum* or *po'tum*), to drink.

PO'TION, a draught; a dose.
POTA'TION, a drinking; a draught.
COMPOTA'TION, a drinking together. [with another.
COMPOTA'TOR, one who drinks

407. *Pre'cor,* (*preca'tus*), to entreat.

DEP'RECATE, to pray for deliverance from any evil; to dread or regret.
IM'PRECATE, to invoke calamity to rest upon any one.
PRECA'RIOUS,* uncertain; not sure to be retained.

* *Original signification,* asked for, and therefore dependent on the will of another.

408. *Præ'da,* prey; booty.

PREY, plunder.
PRED'ATORY, plundering.
DEPREDA'TION, a robbing; a spoiling.
DEP'REDATOR, a robber.

409. *Prehen'do,* (*prehen'sum*), to seize.

APPREHEND', to lay hold on; to suspect with fear.
APPREN'TICE, (Fr. *apprenti*), a learner of au art or trade.
APPRISE', to inform, to give notice.
COMPREHEND', to include.
EN'TERPRISE, that which is undertaken.
IMPREG'NABLE, (Fr. *imprenable*), not to be stormed or taken.
INCOMPREHEN'SIBLE, not to be understood.
PRIS'ON, (Fr.), a place of confinement.
PRIZE, that which is taken in contest.
REPRI'SAL, seizure of property in war.
REPREHEND', to blame; to chide.
REPREHEN'SIBLE, blame-worthy.
SURPRISE', astonishment at something unexpected.

410. *Pre'mo,* (*pres'sum*), to press.

PRESS, to squeeze; to urge.
IMPRESS', to imprint; to stamp.
IMPRES'SION, a print; a mark made by pressure.
COMPRESS', to force together.
COMPRESS'IBLE, yielding to pressure.
DEPRESS', to bear down.
EXPRESS', to squeeze out; to declare.
OPPRES'SION, cruelty; severity.
PRINT, (Fr. *imprimer*), to stamp with letters or figures.
REPRESS', to force back.
SUPPRESS', to subdue; to conceal.

WORDS DERIVED FROM THE LATIN.

411. *Pre'tium,* price, reward.

PRICE, value; rate; reward.
PRE'CIOUS, valuable; costly.

APPRE'CIATE, to estimate justly.
DEPRE'CIATE, to undervalue.

412. *Pri'mus,* first.

PRIME, *a.* first rate.
PRIME, *v.* to put on the first coat in painting.
PRIM'ER, a child's first book.
PRIME'VAL, (147), original; ancient.
PRINCE, (Lat. *prin'ceps*), a sovereign or his kinsman.
PRI'MARY, first; original.
PREM'IER, (Fr.), the first minister of state.
PRIM, nice; formal.

PRIM'ROSE, (Lat. *rosa,* a rose), a rose which opens very early in the spring.
PRIN'CIPLE, (47), element; original cause; ground of action.
PRIN'CIPAL, chief; capital.
PRI'OR, (Lat.), former; antecedent.
PRIOR'ITY. precedence.
PRIMOGEN'ITURE, (204), state of being first born.

413. *Pri'vus,* single; one's own.

PRI'VATE, secret; particular.
PRI'VACY, secrecy; retirement.
PRIV'ILEGE, (256), peculiar advantage.
PRIVA'TION, a taking away; absence of what is necessary for comfort.

PRIV'Y, secret; sharing in a secret.
PRIV'ILY, in a secret manner.
PRIVATEER', a vessel fitted out by private owners, to plunder the vessels of a hostile nation.
DEPRIVE', to take away from.

414. *Pro'bo, (proba'tum,)* to approve; to try. *Pro'bus,* honest.

PROB'ITY, honesty; integrity.
PROBE, to search into.
PROB'ABLE, likely.
PROBA'TION, trial.
PROVE, to try, to test. [with.
APPROVE', to like; to be pleased

APPROBA'TION, the act of approving.
DISPROVE', to confute.
IMPROVE', to make better.
REPROVE', to blame; to censure.
REP'ROBATE, lost to virtue.

415. *Pro'pe,* near. *Prox'imus,* nearest; next.

PROPIN'QUITY, (Lat. *propin'-quitas*), nearness.
PROX'IMATE, nearest; next.
PROXIM'ITY, immediate nearness.

APPROX'IMATE, APPROACH', (Fr. *approcher*), to come near.
REPROACH', (Fr. *reprocher*), to censure.

416. *Pro'prius*, belonging to; peculiar.

Appro'priate, *v.* to take for one's own use.
Appro'priate, *a.* suitable, fit.
Prop'er, fit; suitable: *also,* belonging to; peculiar.
Prop'erty, that which belongs to a person or thing.
Propri'etor, an owner of property. [ownership.
Propri'ety, suitableness: *also,*

417. *Pu'er*, a boy.

Pu'erile, boyish. | Pueril'ity, boyishness.

418. *Pug'nus*, the fist.

Pugna'cious, (Lat. *pug'na,* a battle), quarrelsome; disposed to fight. [fists.
Pu'gilist, a fighter with the
Impugn', to attack; to reproach.
Repug'nance, aversion; dislike.
Repug'nant, adverse; antagonistic.

419. *Pul'vis*, (*pul'veris*), dust.

Pul'verize, to reduce to powder.
Pulveriza'tion, the act of pulverizing.

420. *Pun'go*, (*punc'tum*), to sting.

Pun'gent, stinging; acute.
Punct'ure, a hole pierced.
Punctua'tion, (Lat. *punc'tum,* a point or dot), the art of pointing written language.
Punctil'ious, exact in behavior.
Punctual'ity, scrupulous exactness in regard to time.
Compunc'tion, the sting of conscience.
Expunge', to cross out or efface.

421. *Pu'nio*, (*puni'tum*), to punish.

Pun'ish, to inflict pain for evil conduct.
Pu'nitive, awarding or inflicting punishment.
Impu'nity, freedom from punishment; freedom or exemption from evil consequences.

422. *Pu'to*, (*puta'tum*), to think.

Account', (Fr. *compte*), a reckoning; a narrative.
Am'putate, to cut off.*
Compute', to count or reckon.

* The primary signification of the Latin word *puto* is *to lop off* or *prune;* it also signifies secondarily, *to adjust accounts; to reckon.*

COUNT, to enumerate.
DEPUTE', to send as a substitute.
DEP'UTY, one appointed to act for another.
DEPUTA'TION, the person or persons deputed.

DISPUTE', to contend in argument.
IMPUTE', to set to the account of; to ascribe.
REPUTA'TION, character; public estimation.

423. *Qua'lis*, such as; of what kind.

QUAL'ITY, character; nature; degree of excellence.
QUAL'IFY, (152), to render fit.

QUALIFICA'TION, fitness; modification.
DISQUAL'IFY, to render unfit.

424. *Quan'tus*, how great; as great as.

QUAN'TITY, that property of anything which may be increased or diminished.

QUAN'TUM SUFFI'CIT, (Lat.), a sufficient quantity or amount.

425. *Qua'tio*, (*quas'sum*), to shake.

QUASH, to crush; to annul.
CONCUS'SION,* a violent agitation; a shock.

DISCUSS',†to examine; to debate.
PERCUS'SION, a striking; a stroke.

* From *concu'tio*, which is compounded of *con* and *qua'tio*.
† From *discu'tio*, signifying to shake apart or in pieces.

426. *Quat'uor*, four; *Quad'ra*, a square.

QUAD'RANT, a quarter of a circle; an instrument.
QUADRAT'IC, pertaining to the square or second power of a quantity.
QUADRAN'GULAR, (12), having four angles.
QUAD'RATE, to suit; to correspond (followed by *with*).
QUADRILAT'ERAL, (250), four-sided.
QUAD'RUPED, (380), a four-footed animal.
QUAD'RUPLE, (392), fourfold.

QUAR'ANTINE,‡ the term during which a vessel suspected of infection is kept at a distance from the port or city.
QUART, the fourth part of a gallon.
QUART'AN, coming every fourth day (as, a *quartan* fever).
QUART'ER, to divide into four equal parts or quarters.
QUAR'TO, (Lat.), a book in which every sheet makes four leaves.
QUAR'TERLY, every quarter.

‡ *Literally*, the space of forty days.

SQUAD'RON,* a division of a fleet; a detachment of ships of war.

SQUARE, (Fr. *quarré*), having four equal sides and four right angles.

* *Primary signification,* a square or square form.

427. Que'ror, (ques'tus), to complain.

QUAR'REL, (Fr. *quereller*), to contend angrily; to find fault; to cavil.

QUER'ULOUS, disposed to murmur or complain.

428. Quæ'ro, (quæsi'tum,) to seek; to ask.

QUEST, search; inquiry.
QUE'RY, QUES'TION, an asking; a doubt.
ACQUIRE', to obtain.
ACQUISI'TION, the thing acquired; the act of acquiring.
CON'QUER, (Fr. *conquérir*), to subdue; to gain by force.
CON'QUEST, the act of conquering.
DISQUISI'TION, a systematic examination of a subject.
EX'QUISITE,† nice; excellent.
INQUIRE', to ask a question.

INQUIS'ITIVE, apt to ask questions; curious.
INQUISI'TION, an investigation or trial.
INQUISITO'RIAL, pertaining to the Catholic court of inquisition.
PER'QUISITE, a fee; an allowance beyond the stated wages.
REQUEST', to solicit; to entreat.
REQUIRE', to demand.
REQUISI'TION, a demand.
REQ'UISITE, required; necessary.

† *Literally,* sought out from among others; *whence,* choice; select.

429. Qui'es, (quid'tis), rest.

QUIET, tranquil; at rest.
QUIES'CENCE, a state of repose; quietude.
ACQUIESCE', to assent; to rest satisfied.

DISQUI'ET, to disturb.
RE'QUIEM,‡ (in the Romish church), a hymn or mass sung for the dead, for the rest of the soul.

‡ So called from the first word of the form used.

430. Quin'que, five.

QUINTES'SENCE, (520), the fifth essence; the essence highly refined.

QUINT'UPLE, (392), five-fold.
QUINTIL'LION, a million four times multiplied by a million.

WORDS DERIVED FROM THE LATIN.

431. *Quot*, how many; as many.

QUO'TA, (Lat.), a just part or share.
QUOTID'IAN, (118), daily; (as, a *quotidian* fever).
QUO'TIENT, the number which shows how often the divisor is contained in the dividend.

432. *Ra'bies*, madness.

RAB'ID, mad; (as, a dog). | RAVE, to be delirious or furious

433. *Ra'dius*, a rod; a spoke.

RA'DIUS, the semi-diameter of a circle.
RAY, a line of light.
RA'DIATE, to emit rays.
RA'DIANCE, effulgence.
IRRA'DIATE, to illuminate.

434. *Ra'dix*, (*rad'icis*), a root.

RAD'ICAL, pertaining to the root;* deep seated.
ERAD'ICATE, to root out.

* The word *radical*, when used in a political sense, denotes a disposition to *go to the root* in respect to the constitution of society, and to set out anew with first principles, rejecting artificial arrangements.

435. *Ra'do*, (*ra'sum*), to shave.

ABRADE', to rub or wear off.
ABRA'SION, the act of rubbing off.
ERASE', to rub out; to obliterate.
ERA'SURE, the act of erasing.
RAZE, to demolish; to destroy utterly.
RA'ZOR, an instrument for shaving.
RAZEE', to cut down or reduce to a lower class; (as, a ship).

436. *Ra'mus*, a bough or branch.

RAM'IFY, (152), to branch out; to be divided and subdivided.
RAMIFICA'TION, division into branches.

437. *Ra'pio*, (*rap'tum*), to snatch.

RAP'INE, plunder.
RAPA'CIOUS, plundering; greedy.
RAPT, carried away by feeling or enthusiasm.
RAPT'URE, ecstasy; transport.
RAPT'UROUS, ecstatic.
ENRAPT'URE, to put into ecstasy; to delight.
RAP'ID, swift.
RAV'AGE, (3), to lay waste.
RAV'ISH, to bear away with joy or transport. [stealth.
SURREPTI'TIOUS, done by

438. *Re'go,* (*rec'tum*), to direct; to rule. *Rec'tus,* straight.

RE'GAL, (Lat. *rex,* (*re'gis*), a king), kingly.
CORRECT', to make right.
CORREC'TION, a making right; taking away faults.
DIRECT', *v.* to guide; to order.
DIRECT', *a.* straight; not winding.
DIRECT'LY, immediately.
ERECT', upright; perpendicular.
INCOR'RIGIBLE, bad beyond correction.
INTERREG'NUM, (Lat. *reg'num,* a reign), the time in which a throne is vacant between two reigns.
REC'TIFY, (152), to set right.
RE'GENT, a governor.
REC'TOR, a director; a pastor.
RECTILIN'EAR, (265), consisting of right lines.
REC'TITUDE, virtue; uprightness.
REG'ICIDE, (41), the murderer of a king.
REG'IMEN, a system of regulations; a course of diet.
REG'ULAR, agreeable to rule.
REG'ULATE, to adjust methodically.
REIGN, to exercise royal authority.
RIGHT, fit; just; true.

439. *Re'or,* (*ra'tus*), to think; to judge.

RATE, *v.* to determine value according to a standard.
RATE, *s.* mode of estimating.
RAT'IFY, (152), to sanction; to confirm.
RATIFICA'TION, the act of ratifying; confirmation; agreement.
RATIONA'LE, (Lat.), a series of reasons assigned.
RA'TIONAL, agreeable to reason.
IRRA'TIONAL, not rational.
REAS'ON, (Fr. *raison*), the faculty of judging, which man possesses.
RA'TION, a fixed allowance

440. *Re'po,* (*rep'tum*), to creep.

REP'TILE, a creeping animal.
RE'PENT, creeping; (as, a reptile, or plant.)

441. *Res,* a thing.

RE'AL, actually existing.
REAL'ITY, actual existence.
RE'ALIZE, to bring into actual existence; to consider as real.

442. *Ri'deo,* (*ri'sum*), to laugh.

RID'ICULE, *s.* a laughable representation.
RID'ICULE, *v.* to make sport of.
RIDIC'ULOUS, worthy of ridicule.

DERIDE', to laugh at in a contemptuous manner.
DERIS'ION, contempt.

RIS'IBLE, pertaining to laughter; exciting laughter.

443. *Ri'geo*, to be stiff, as with cold.

RIG'ID, stiff; strict; exact.
RIGID'ITY, stiffness; harshness.

RIG'OR, austerity; severity.
RIG'OROUS, severe; exact.

444. *Ri'go*, (*riga'tum*), to water.

IR'RIGATE, to water, as a garden. | IRRIG'UOUS, watered; watery.

445. *Ri'vus*, a stream.

RIV'ULET, a little stream.
RIV'ER, a large stream.
ARRIVE',* to come to or reach.

DERIVE',† to deduce or draw from some source.
RI'VAL,‡ a competitor.

* *Literally*, to come to the shore or bank. *Webster.*

† This word signifies, *primarily*, to draw a rivulet from the main stream or reservoir.

‡ Among the Romans, those whose lands were separated by a brook were called *riva'les*; the word *rival* seems to have originated in the idea of contention as occurring between such proprietors.

446. *Ro'bur*, (*rob'oris*), an oak; strength.

CORROB'ORATE, to confirm; to make more certain.

CORROB'ORATIVE, tending to confirm.
ROBUST', strong; vigorous.

447. *Ro'go*, (*roga'tum*), to ask.

AB'ROGATE,§ to repeal; to annul.
AR'ROGATE, to claim.
AR'ROGANCE, claiming much for one's self; pride; conceitedness.
AR'ROGANT, haughty; conceited.
DER'OGATE, to detract; to disparage.
DEROG'ATORY, tending to detract from the estimation in which anything is held.

INTERROGA'TION, the act of questioning; a question.
INTERROG'ATIVE, containing a question.
PREROG'ATIVE,‖ an exclusive privilege.
PROROGUE',¶ to put off; to appoint at a future time.
REINTER'ROGATE, to interrogate or question again.
SUR'ROGATE, a deputy.

§ *Literally*, to propose or seek freedom *from*.

‖ A privilege sought or asked which places the person before others, or gives superiority.

¶ To ask or propose with respect to future time.

448. *Ro'ta*, a wheel.

Ro'tary, turning; (as, a wheel on its axis).
Rota'tion, rotary motion.
Rote, a round of words; repetition of mere words.
Rotund', round; spherical.

Rotund'ity, roundness; sphericity.
Rotund'o, (Lat.), a round building.
Routine', (Fr.), a round of business.

449. *Ru'dis*, unpolished; uncultivated.

Rude, rough; coarse; unfinished.
Er'udite,* learned.

Ru'diment, an elementary truth or principle.
Rudiment'al, initial; primary.

* Compounded of *e*, from, and *rudis*, and signifying, literally, brought out from ignorance or rudeness.

450. *Ru'ga*, a wrinkle.

Cor'rugate, to wrinkle. | Ru'gose, wrinkled.

451. *Rum'po*, (*rup'tum*), to break.

Rup'ture, a breaking.
Abrupt', broken off short; having a sudden termination; unconnected.
Bank'rupt, (It. *banc'o*, a bench), a trader who cannot pay his debts.
Corrupt', decomposed; debased; impure.

Corrupt'ible, capable of becoming corrupt.
Disrup'tion, the act of breaking asunder.
Erup'tion, a bursting out.
Interrupt', to break in upon the progress of anything.
Interrup'tion, a hindrance; stop.

452. *Rus*, (*ru'ris*), the country.

Ru'ral, belonging to the country.
Rus'tic, plain; unpolished.

Rustic'ity, the qualities of a countryman.
Rus'ticate, to reside for a time in the country.

453. *Sa'cer*, consecrated.

Sa'cred, holy; inviolable.
Con'secrate, to devote to sacred purposes.
Des'ecrate, to abuse or pervert a sacred thing.

Ex'ecrate, (Lat. *ex'secror*, to utter imprecations), to detest.
Sacerdo'tal, (Lat. *sacer'dos*, a priest), belonging to the priesthood.

SAC′RAMENT, a religious ceremony.
SAC′RILEGE, (253), a violation of what is sacred.

SAC′RIFICE, (152), a religious offering; a surrender of some good for the sake of an ulterior object.

454. *Sa′gus,* wise; discerning.

SAGE, wise; prudent.
SAGAC′ITY, discernment; acuteness.

SAGA′CIOUS, discerning.
PRE′SAGE, to forebode; to foreshow.

455. *Sal,* (*sa′lis*), salt.

SAL′AD, (Fr. *salade*), raw herbs dressed with salt, &c.
SAL′ARY,* a fixed annual compensation for services.

SALINE′, partaking of the qualities of salt.
SALT, a substance used for seasoning; the chloride of sodium.

* The Latin word *sala′rium,* signifies, properly, *money for salt;* hence, *allowance for expenses. Leverett.*

456. *Sa′lio,* (*sal′tum*), to leap; to spring.

ASSAIL′, to attack.
ASSAIL′ANT, one who makes an attack.
DES′ULTORY, leaping; passing immethodically from one subject to another.
EXULT′, to rejoice greatly.
INSULT′, to treat with contempt or abuse.

IN′SULT, an affront.
RESULT′, to fly back or rebound; to follow as an effect.
SAL′LY, to rush out suddenly.
SA′LIENT, leaping; shooting out.
SALM′ON, a leaping fish.
SAL′TATORY, adapted to leaping; skipping; dancing.

457. *Sa′lus,* (*salu′tis*), health; safety.

SAL′UTARY, healthful; advantageous.
SAFE, free from danger.
SALU′BRITY, tendency to promote health.   [or success.
SALUTE′, to greet; to wish health
SALUTA′TION, a greeting.
SALVA′TION, preservation from destruction.

SALU′TATORY, containing salutations; greeting; (applied to an oration which introduces the exercises of commencement in colleges).
SALVE, an ointment.
SAVE, to preserve; to rescue.
SAV′IOUR, one who rescues.

458. *San'cio, (sanc'tum),* to consecrate; to ordain or establish.

SAINT, a person sanctified.
SANC'TIFY, (152), to make holy.
SANCTIMO'NIOUS, having the appearance of sanctity; saintly; seeming holy.
SANC'TION, confirmation; approval.
SANC'TITY, (Lat. *sanc'tus,* holy), sacredness; holiness.
SANC'TUARY, a sacred place.

459. *San'guis, (san'guinis),* blood.

SAN'GUINARY, bloody.
SAN'GUINE, ardent in feeling; confident.
CONSANGUIN'ITY, relationship by blood.

460. *Sa'nus,* sound; healthy.

SANE, sound; having reason.
SAN'ITY, soundness; reason.
INSANE', disordered in mind.
INSAN'ITY, derangement; madness.
SAN'ATIVE, tending to heal.

461. *Sa'pio,* to have flavor or taste; to be wise.

SA'PIENT, wise; discerning.
SA'PIENCE, wisdom.
SAPORIF'IC, (152), producing taste.
INSIP'ID, tasteless.
SA'VOR, taste or odor.
SA'VORY, pleasing to the organs of taste or smell.

462. *Sapo, (sapo'nis),* soap.

SAPONA'CEOUS, soapy.
SAPON'IFY, (152), to convert into soap.

463. *Sa'tis,* enough.

SA'TIATE, to feed to the full; to fill beyond natural desire.
SATI'ETY, an excess of gratification; fulness producing disgust.
SAT'URATE, to add an ingredient until no more can be absorbed.
SAT'ISFY, (152), to gratify wants or demands to the full extent.
INSA'TIABLE, not to be satisfied.

464. *Sca'la,* a ladder.

SCALE, to climb; (as, by a ladder). | SCAL'ABLE, that may be scaled.

WORDS DERIVED FROM THE LATIN.

465. *Scan'do,* (*scan'sum*), to climb; to mount.

Ascend', to climb or go up.
Ascent', the way by which one ascends.
Descend', to go down.
Condescend', to stoop; to descend from the dignity of rank or character.

Condescen'sion, voluntary descent from rank, &c.
Transcend', to rise beyond; to surmount.
Scan, to examine with critical care; to examine a verse by counting the feet.

466. *Scin'do,* (*scis'sum*), to cut; to divide.

Scis'sors, small shears.
Exscind', to cut off.

Rescind', to abrogate; to revoke.

467. *Sci'o,* to know; *Scien'tia,* knowledge.

Sci'ence, knowledge.
Scientif'ic, (152), pertaining to science.
Sci'olist, a smatterer; one who knows many things superficially.
Con'science, the knowledge of right and wrong.

Con'sciousness, the knowledge of what passes in one's own mind.
Conscien'tious, obedient to the dictates of conscience.
Omnis'cience, (345), knowledge of all things.
Pre'science, foreknowledge.

468. *Scri'bo,* (*scrip'tum*), to write.

Scribe, a writer; a secretary.
Scrib'ble, to write carelessly.
Script'ure, a writing.*
Scriv'ener, one who draws contracts or other writings.
Scrip, a small writing or certificate.
Subscribe', to write underneath; to sign with one's own hand.
Describe',† to give an account of.
Ascribe', to attribute to.

Prescribe', to give a written direction; to give a rule of conduct.
Proscribe',‡ to censure and condemn as unworthy of reception.
Transcribe', to write a copy of anything.
Circumscribe', to limit; to enclose by a boundary.
Inscribe', to write upon; to dedicate in a short written address.

---

* Used only in reference to the Sacred Writings contained in the Bible.

† *Literally,* to write concerning.

‡ *Primitive signification,* to write the name of a person on the list of those who are placed out of the protection of the law.

Conscrip'tion, a compulsory enrolment of men for military or naval service.
Superscrip'tion, that which is written on the outside.
Man'uscript, (282), that which is written with the hand.
Post'script, something written after a letter has been concluded and signed.

469. *Scru'tor*, (*scruta'tus*), to examine.

Scru'tiny, close examination.
Scru'tinize, to examine closely.
Inscru'table, unsearchable; not to be understood.

470. *Se'co*, (*sec'tum*), to cut.

Se'cant, *in geometry*, a line which cuts another or divides it into two parts. [tion.
Sec'tion, a part; a distinct portion.
Sect, a party holding peculiar sentiments in philosophy or religion.
Seg'ment, a part cut off.
Bisect', (37), to separate into two equal parts.
Dissect', to cut in pieces in such a manner as to show the several constituent parts.
In'sect, a small animal.
Insec'tion, a cutting in.
Intersec'tion, the point where lines cut each other.
Venesec'tion, (Lat. *ve'na*, a vein), the act of opening a vein.

471. *Sec'ulum*, an age.

Sec'ular, pertaining to the present world.
Sec'ularize, to make worldly.

472. *Se'deo*, (*ses'sum*), to sit.

Sed'entary, accustomed to sitting.
Ses'sion, a sitting.
Sedate', settled; calm; sober.
Sed'iment, that which settles.
Assid'uous, diligent in application.*
Insid'ious, [*properly*, lying in wait], deceitful; treacherous.
Assess', to fix the value of property for the purpose of taxation.
Assess'or, one who assesses.
Possess', (403), to hold; to own.
Preside', to be set over; to direct.
Reside', to dwell. [rect.
Res'idue, the remaining part.
Subside', to sink away.
Subsid'iary, aiding; furnishing supplies.
Sub'sidize, to purchase the assistance of another.
Supersede',† to take the place of; to set aside by having superior influence.

* *Literally*, sitting close to work.
† *Literally*, to sit above.

473. *Se'men*, (*sem'inis*), seed.

SEM'INARY, a place of education.* | DISSEM'INATE, to scatter abroad; (as, seed).

* Because the *seeds* of knowledge are there planted.

474. *Sem'i*, (an inseparable particle), half.

SEM'I-AN'NUAL, (14), half yearly.
SEM'I-CIRCLE, (71), half of a circle.
SEM'I-DIAM'ETER, (Gr. 137), half the diameter.
SEM'I-TONE, (Gr. 218), half a tone.

475. *Se'nex*, aged—*Se'nior*, older.

SE'NIOR, one more advanced in years or in the course of appointment or station.
SE'NILE, pertaining to old age.
SEN'ATOR, a member of a senate.†
SEIGN'IOR, a nobleman; a title of honor.

† The Romans called their highest legislative body the Senate, from its having been composed at first of the older men.

476. *Sen'tio*, (*sen'sum*), to perceive; to think.

SEN'TIMENT, thought; opinion; notion.
SENTIMENT'AL, reflective.
SEN'TIENT, having the faculty of perception.
SEN'TENCE, a judgment pronounced upon a criminal; a complete expression in words.
SENSE, the faculty of perceiving by the senses or by the intellect; meaning.
SENS'UAL, pertaining to the senses.
SENS'ITIVE, easily affected.
SENS'IBLE, able to perceive; intelligent; perceptible by the senses.
ASSENT', to agree to.
CONSENT', to yield.
DISSENT', to differ in opinion; to refuse assent.
PRESENT'IMENT, apprehension of something future.
RESENT', to manifest anger in consequence of a supposed injury.

477. *Sepe'lio*, (*sepul'tum*), to bury.

SEP'ULCHRE, a tomb or place of burial.
SEP'ULTURE, burial; the act of interring.

478. *Sep'tem*, seven.

SEPTEM'BER, the seventh month.*
SEPTEN'NIAL, (14), of seven years.

SEP'TUAGINT,† (Lat. *septuagin'ta*, seventy), a Greek version or translation of the Old Testament.

* Reckoning from March, which was once accounted the first month in the year.
† So called because it was made by *seventy* (or more exactly *seventy-two*) interpreters. The date of its execution was about 280 B. C.

479. *Se'quor*, (*secu'tus*), to follow.

SE'QUEL, the succeeding part.
SE'QUENCE, a following; succession.
CON'SEQUENCE, that which follows from any act or event.
CONSEC'UTIVE, following in regular order.
EX'ECUTE, (Lat. *ex'sequor*), to carry into effect.
OBSE'QUIOUS, complying in a servile manner.

PER'SECUTE, to pursue with injuries and vexation.
PROS'ECUTE, to follow with a view to accomplish; to bring to trial.
OB'SEQUIES, funeral solemnities.
ENSUE', to follow as a consequence.
PURSUE', to follow; to chase.
SUB'SEQUENT, occurring at a later period.

480. *Se'ro*, (*ser'tum*), to knit together; to connect.

SE'RIES, (Lat.), a succession of things.
SER'MON, (Lat. *ser'mo*, speech), a discourse.
ASSERT', to declare; to affirm.
ASSERT'OR, a vindicator.

DESERT', to forsake.
DISSERTA'TION, a treatise.
EXERT', to put forth; to put into action.
INSERT', to set in or among.

481. *Ser'po*, to creep.

SER'PENT, a creeping animal. | SER'PENTINE, winding; spiral.

482. *Ser'ra*, a saw.

SER'RATED, notched like a saw; having the margin cut into teeth pointing forwards; (as, a leaf).

483. *Ser'vo*, (*serva'tum*), to watch; to preserve. *Ser'vus*, a slave or servant.

SERVE, to attend at command; to wait on.

SERV'ANT, one who serves.
SERF, a kind of slave.

Serv'ice, labor performed for another.
Ser'vile, slavish.
Ser'vitude, slavery.
Servil'ity, mean dependence.
Conserv'atory, a place where anything is preserved.
Deserve', to merit.
Observe', to watch; to have regard to.
Preserve', to save.
Reserve', to keep back; to keep in store.
Subser'vient, useful as an instrument in promoting some end.
Res'ervoir, (Fr.), a place for containing what is kept in store; particularly a cavity for holding a fluid.

484. *Seve'rus*, severe.

Severe', sharp; strict; exact.
Sever'ity, sharpness; strictness. [pursuit.
Perseve'rance, constancy in a
Persevere', to persist in an attempt.
Assevera'tion, a solemn affirmation.

485. *Sex*, six.

Sexagena'rian, (Lat. *sexagin'ta*, sixty), one at the age of sixty years.
Sex'tant, the sixth part of a circle; an instrument for measuring angles.

486. *Si'dus*, (*sid'eris*), a star.

Side'real, pertaining to stars.

487. *Sig'num*, a sign; a seal.

Sign, *s.* a token; a mark.
Sign, *v.* to write one's name under any form or document.
Sig'nal, that which gives notice.
Sig'nify, (152), to express; to mean.
Insignif'icant, wanting meaning; unimportant.
Assign', to allot; to appoint.
Consign', to deliver over; to commit.
Design', to purpose; to plan.
Des'ignate, to point out.
Designa'tion, a name.
En'sign, a standard; a badge.
Resign', to yield; to give up.
Sig'net, a seal.

488. *Sim'ilis*, like.

Sim'ilar, like; resembling.
Sim'ile, an illustrative comparison.
Similar'ity, Simil'itude,
Sem'blance, Resem'blance, likeness; comparison.
Assim'ilate, to make like; to cause to resemble.

Dissem'ble, to hide under a false appearance.
Dissimula'tion, hypocrisy.
Dissim'ilar, unlike.
Fac-sim'ile, (152), an exact imitation.

Resem'ble, (Fr. *ressembler*), to be like.
Simulta'neous, (Lat. *si'mul*, together), at the same time.
Simula'tion, pretence; disguise.

489. *Sinis'ter*, left.

Sin'ister, left handed; dishonest.
Sin'istrously, wrongly; perversely.

490. *Si'nus*, a fold; a bosom.

Sinuos'ity, a bending or curving in and out.
Insin'uate, to introduce by slow, gentle, or artful means.
Insinua'tion, a hint.

491. *Sis'to*, or *sto*, (*sta'tum*), to stand; to place; to set up.

State, condition.
Sta'tion, a standing place.
Sta'tionary, fixed; settled.
Stat'ure, the height of a person.
Stat'ue, an image set up.
Sta'ble, a house for beasts to stand in.
Stabil'ity, steadiness.
Ar'mistice, (25), a cessation from hostilities; a truce.
Arrest', to stop.
Assist', to stand by; to help.
Cir'cumstance,* something attending a fact or case.
Consist', to stand together; to be composed of.
Consist'ent, compatible; congruous. [tinual.
Con'stant, unchanged; conCon'stitute, to form or compose.
Constitu'tion, established system.

Con'stable,† an officer of the peace.
Desist', to stand off; to stop.
Des'titute, not possessing; needy.
Dis'tant, remote; far off.
Dis'tance, space between two objects.
Estab'lish, to settle firmly.
Exist', to be.
Ex'tant, now in being.
Insist', to stand upon; to urge.
In'stant, pressing; present; a point of time.
In'stance, urgency; example.
Instate', to set or place.
In'terstice, a narrow space between things. [the way.
Ob'stacle, that which stands in
Persist', to persevere.
Pros'titute, to devote to a base purpose.
Resist', to withstand.

* *Literally*, that which stands around or near.

† Lat. *co'mes stab'uli*, overseer of the stable; an office which existed under the Roman emperors.

RESTITU'TION, giving back.
SOL'STICE, (493), the tropical point.
STAT'ICS, that branch of *mechanics*, which treats of bodies at rest.
STA'MEN, (Lat.), the fixed, firm part of a body which gives it strength.
STAND, to be erect; to remain fixed.

SUB'STITUTE, that which is put in the place of something else.
SUBSIST', to be; to continue.
SUBSIST'ENCE, being; support.
SUB'STANCE, being; body.
SUBSTAN'TIAL, not imaginary; solid.
SUPERSTI'TION, false religion; belief in omens and prognostics.

492. *So'cius*, a companion.

SO'CIABLE, agreeable as a companion; familiar.
SOCI'ETY, a union of persons for any particular purpose.
SO'CIAL, pertaining to society.

ASSO'CIATE, CONSO'CIATE, to unite.
ASSOCIA'TION, CONSOCIA'TION, union; alliance.
DISSO'CIATE, to disjoin.

493. *Sol*, (*so'lis*), the sun.

SO'LAR, pertaining to the sun.

IN'SOLATE, to expose to the heat of the sun.

494. *Sol'idus*, solid.

SOL'ID, not fluid; strong; compact.
SOLID'ITY, firmness; hardness.
SOLID'IFY, (152), to make solid.
CONSOL'IDATE,* to form into a compact mass.

SOL'DER, to unite by a metallic cement.
SOLD'IER,† a man engaged in military service.
SOLD'IERY, the body of military men.

* *Con'sols*, in England, are stocks formed by the *consolidation* of different annuities.

† The Romans had a gold coin called the Sol'idus or Sol'dus; it is supposed that the word *soldier* was derived from the mode of military payment.

495. *So'lor*, (*sola'tus*), to comfort; to soothe.

CONSOLE', to comfort; to cheer.
DISCON'SOLATE, destitute of consolation; dejected; not expecting comfort.

INCONSOL'ABLE, not to be consoled.
SOL'ACE, alleviation; comfort.

496. *So'lus*, alone; only.

Sole, single; only.
Sol'itary, living alone.
Sol'itude, a state of being alone; a lonely place.
Des'olate, laid waste; cheer- [less.
Desola'tion, destitution; ruin.
Solil'oquy, (270), a speech to one's self alone.
So'lo, (It.), a passage of music for a single instrument or voice.

497. *Sol'vo*, (*solu'tum*), to loose.

Solve, to explain.
Solu'tion, the process of dissolving; explanation.
Sol'uble, capable of being dissolved.
Sol'vency, ability to pay.
Sol'vent, a fluid which dissolves a substance.
Absolve', to clear; to acquit of a crime.
Ab'solute, complete; unconditional. [sion.
Absolu'tion, acquittal; remis-
Dis'solute, loose in morals.
Dissolve', to melt; to break up.
Resolve', to determine.

498. *Som'nus*, sleep.

Somnam'bulist, (8), one who walks in sleep
Somnif'ic, (152), causing sleep.
Som'nolency, drowsiness.

499. *So'nus*, a sound.

Sound, a noise.
Sono'rous, giving sound.
Con'sonant, s, a letter that can be sounded only in connection with a vowel
Con'sonant, a. consistent.
Resound', to send back sound.
Res'onant, resounding.
U'nison, (563), agreement of sound.

500. *So'por*, drowsiness; lethargy.

Soporif'ic, (152), causing sleep.
Soporif'erous, (167), inducing sleep.

501. *Sors*, (*sor'tis*), a lot; chance; a share.

Assort', to separate into classes.
Con'sort, s. a companion; a wife or husband.
Consort', v. to associate.
Resort', to betake; to repair.
Sort, a kind; a species.
Sorti'tion, selection, choice, or determination by lot.

502. *Spar'go*, (*spar'sum*), to strew; to scatter.

SPARSE, thinly scattered.
ASPERSE', to bespatter with calumny.
ASPER'SION, calumny.

DISPERSE', to scatter; to dissipate.
INTERSPERSE', to scatter between.

503. *Spa'tium*, space.

SPACE, room; extension.
SPA'CIOUS, roomy; extensive.

EXPA'TIATE, to move at large; to enlarge in discourse.

504. *Spe'cio*, (*spec'tum*), to look; to see.

AS'PECT, appearance; view.
CIR'CUMSPECT, watchful; cautious.
CONSPIC'UOUS, easily seen; prominent.
DESPISE', to look down upon; to abhor.
DES'PICABLE, worthy of contempt.
EXPECT', to look or wait for.
INSPECT', to look on or into; to examine.
PERSPECT'IVE,* appearance represented on a plane surface.
PERSPICAC'ITY, acuteness of discernment.
PERSPICU'ITY, clearness; freedom from obscurity.
PROS'PECT, view of objects within the reach of the eye.
PROSPECT'IVE, regarding the future.
RESPECT', regard.
RESPECT'ABLE, worthy of regard.

RESPECT'IVE, particular.
RE'TROSPECT, a looking back on things past.
SPE'CIAL, ESPE'CIAL, particular; uncommon.
SPE'CIES, a sort or kind.
SPE'CIE, coin.
SPECIF'IC, (152), designating the peculiar properties.
SPEC'IFY, to mention particulars.
SPEC'IMEN, a sample.
SPE'CIOUS, apparently right; having a fair or plausible appearance.
SPEC'TACLE, a sight; a show.
SPEC'TACLES, glasses to assist the sight.
SPECTA'TOR, one who looks on.
SPEC'TRE, an apparition.
SPEC'ULATE, to contemplate; to theorize.
SUSPECT', to mistrust.

* *Primary signification*, a glass through which objects are viewed.

505. *Spe'ro*, to hope.

DESPAIR', hopelessness.
DES'PERATE, without hope; reckless.
DESPERA'DO, a desperate fellow.

PROS'PER, to be successful.
PROSPER'ITY, successful progress. [ful.
PROS'PEROUS, thriving; success-

506. *Spi'ro*, to breathe.

SPIR'IT, an immaterial, intelligent being; courage.
SPIR'ITUAL, immaterial; mental.
SPIR'ACLE, a breathing hole.
ASPIRE', to aim at something elevated.
ASPIRA'TION, a breathing after.
ASPI'RANT, one who aspires or aims at something elevated; an ambitious candidate.
CONSPIRE', to agree together.
CONSPIR'ACY, a plot; treason.
EXPIRE', to breathe out; to die.
INSPIRE', to breathe into; to infuse into the mind.
INSPIRA'TION, a drawing in of the breath; a supernatural infusion of ideas into the mind.
INSPIR'IT, to animate; to enliven.
PERSPIRE', to send out moisture from the skin.
RESPIRE', to breathe; to catch breath.
TRANSPIRE', to pass out in vapor; to escape from secrecy.
SUSPIRA'TION, a sigh; a deep breath.

507. *Splen'deo*, to shine.

SPLEN'DID, shining; magnificent; showy.
SPLEN'DOR, brilliancy; elegance.
RESPLEN'DENT, very bright.

508. *Spon'deo*, (*spon'sum*), to promise.

SPON'SOR, one who promises for another.
SPON'SAL, relating to marriage.
SPOUSE, a husband or wife.
ESPOUSE', to marry; to take to one's self.
CORRESPOND', to answer; to be congruous; to communicate by letters.
DESPOND', to be cast down; to lose courage.
RESPOND', to answer.
RESPONSE', a reply.
RESPONS'IBLE, accountable; answerable.
IRRESPONS'IBLE, not liable or able to answer for consequences.

509. *Stel'la*, a star.

CONSTELLA'TION, a cluster of fixed stars.
STEL'LAR, starry; pertaining to stars.

510. *Ster'no*, (*stra'tum*), to spread; to strew.

STRA'TUM, (Lat.), (*pl.* stra'ta), a layer, as of earth.
STRAT'IFIED, (152), placed in strata. [layer.
SUBSTRA'TUM, (Lat.), a lower
CONSTERNA'TION, great surprise and terror.
PROS'TRATE, lying flat.
PROSTRA'TION, loss of vigor.
—

511. *Stil'la*, a drop.

Instil', to pour in gradually; to teach slowly.
Distil', to fall by drops; to extract by heat and evaporation.
Distilla'tion, the act of distilling.
Distill'ery, a place where distilling in carried on.
Still, a vessel for distillation.

512. *Sti'po*, (*stipa'tum*), to fill up; to stuff.

Con'stipate, to stop, by filling a passage.
Constipa'tion, a crowding together; condensation.

513. *Stirps*, (*stir'pis*), a root or stock.

Extir'pate, to root out; to destroy totally.
Extirpa'tion, eradication; total destruction.

514. *Strin'go*, (*stric'tum*), to bind.

Strict, rigorously nice; exact; severe.
Strict'ure, a contraction; critical censure.
Astrin'gent, binding; contracting.
Constrain', to compel.
Constraint', confinement.
Dis'trict, circuit of authority.
Restrain', to withhold; to repress.
Restrict', to limit; to confine.
Restric'tion, limitation.
Straight, not crooked.
Strait, narrow; compressed.
Strain, to extend with force.

515. *Stru'o*, (*struc'tum*), to build; to construct.

Struct'ure, an edifice; a building.
Construct', to form; to build.
Construc'tion, structure; conformation.
Con'strue, to interpret; to explain. [by precept.
Instruct', to teach, to inform
In'strument, a tool; means employed.
Obstruct', to hinder; to block up.
Destroy', to lay waste; to put an end to.
Destruct'ive, that destroys, ruinous; mischievous.
Destruc'tion, waste; ruin.
Superstruc'ture, an erection upon something else.

516. *Sua'deo*, (*sua'sum*), to advise.

PERSUADE', to bring over to an opinion.
DISSUADE', to exhort or advise against any proposed course.
DISSUA'SIVE, tending to dissuade.
SUA'SION, the act of persuading.

517. *Sua'vis*, sweet; pleasant.

SUAV'ITY, softness; agreeableness.
INSUAV'ITY, unpleasantness.

518. *Su'do*, (*suda'tum*), to sweat.

EXUDE', to flow out in the manner of sweat.
SUDORIF'IC, (152), exciting perspiration.

519. *Su'i*, of one's self.

SU'ICIDE, (41), self-murder.
SUICI'DAL, destructive to one's self.

520. *Sum*, I am; *Es'se*,* to be; *Ens*, (*en'tis*), being; *Futu'rus*, about to be.

NONEN'TITY, anything not existing; nothing.
ES'SENCE, the peculiar nature or quality of anything.
ESSEN'TIAL, necessary to the existence of a thing; pertaining to elementary or constituent principles.
FU'TURE, to be hereafter.
FUTU'RITY, time to come.
AB'SENT, not present.
PRES'ENT, at hand; near; before the face.
REPRESENT', to exhibit; to describe.
IN'TEREST, concern; advantage.

* *Es'se*, is the present infinitive of the verb *Sum*, *Ens* the present participle, and *Futu'rus* the future participle.

521. *Su'mo*, (*sump'tum*), to take.

ASSUME', to take; to claim.
ASSUMP'TION, a taking; a supposition.
CONSUME', to waste; to destroy.
CONSUMP'TION, waste; a disease.
PRESUME' to suppose; to venture.
PRESUMP'TION, confidence; arrogance; strong probability.
RESUME', to take back; to begin again.
SUMP'TUOUS, expensive.
SUMP'TUOUSLY, expensively; splendidly.

522. Su'per, above; over.

SUPE'RIOR, higher in place or excellence.
SUPER'LATIVE, (167), highest in degree; most eminent.
SUPERB', (Lat. super'bus), grand; splendid.
SUPERABUN'DANCE,(Lat. abun'do, to abound), more than enough; excessive quantity.
INSU'PERABLE, not to be overcome or surmounted.
SUPERCIL'IOUS, (Lat. supercil'ium, the brow), haughty; overbearing.
SUPREME', highest in authority; greatest.
SUPREM'ACY, highest power.

523. Sur'go, (surrec'tum), to rise.

INSUR'GENT, rising in opposition to the government.
INSURREC'TION, a rising in rebellion.
RESURREC'TION, a rising again.
SURGE, a billow; a rolling swell of water.

524. Taber'na, a shed; a shop.

TAB'ERNACLE, a temporary habitation.
TAV'ERN, (Fr. taverne), an inn; a drinking place.

525. Ta'ceo, (tac'itum), to be silent.

TAC'IT, silent; implied but not expressed.
TAC'ITURN, habitually silent; not free to converse.

526. Tan'go, (tac'tum), to touch.

TAN'GENT, a line touching a curve.
TAN'GIBLE, that can be touched or taken hold of.
TACT, peculiar skill, faculty or aptness.
INTACT', (Lat. intac'tus, untouched), uninjured.
CONTA'GION, communication of disease from body to body.
CON'TACT, touch; close union.
CONTIG'UOUS, touching; having no intervening space.
CONTIGU'ITY, contact.
CONTIN'GENT, accidental; depending on an uncertainty.

527. Te'go, (tec'tum), to cover.

INTEG'UMENT, that which naturally invests or covers another thing.
PROTECT', to cover; to defend.
DETECT', to discover in spite of concealment.
DETEC'TION, discovery.

528. Tem'pus, (tem'poris), time.

TIME, measure of duration.
TEM'PORAL, relating to time; not eternal.
TEM'PORARY, lasting only a time.
CONTEM'PORARY,* living at the same time.
TENSE, (Fr. *temps*), an inflection of verbs by which time is denoted.
EXTEMPORA'NEOUS, produced at the time; not premeditated.
TEM'PER, v. to moderate.†
TEM'PER, s. disposition.
TEM'PEST, storm; commotion.
TEM'PORIZE, to comply with the time or occasion; to delay; to procrastinate.
TEM'PERANCE, moderation.
INTEM'PERANCE, excess.
DISTEM'PER, disease.
TEM'PERAMENT, native constitution.

* For the sake of easier pronunciation, this word is often changed to *cotemporary*, which Dr. Webster considers the preferable word.

† The primary signification seems to be, *to appoint a time or limit*.

529. Ten'do, (ten'sum or ten'tum), to stretch; to go towards; to aim at.

TEND, to move towards; to watch.
TEND'ENCY, direction towards any result; inclination.
ATTEND', to listen; to have regard to.
ATTEN'TION, regard.
CONTEND', to strive; to contest.
DISTEND', to fill out; to expand.
DISTEN'TION, expansion by filling.
EXTEND', to spread; to enlarge.
EXTENT', compass; size.
EXTENS'IVE, large; widespread.
INTEND', to purpose.
INTEN'TION, s. design.
INTENT', a. fixed on; eager in pursuing.
INTENSE', strained; vehement; ardent.
INTENS'ITY, vehemence.
OSTENS'IBLE, (Lat. *osten'do*, to show), seeming.
OSTENTA'TION, ambitious display.
PORTEND', to forebode; to foretoken.
PORTENT'OUS, ominous.
PRETEND', to hold out, as a false appearance.
PRETENCE', a feigning or pretending.
PRETEN'SION, a claim.
SUBTEND', to extend under.
SUPERINTEND', to have the direction of.
TEN'DON, a cord.
TENSE, stretched to stiffness.
TEN'SION, tightness.
TENT, a covering stretched on poles.

WORDS DERIVED FROM THE LATIN.

530. Té'neo, (ten'tum), to hold; to keep.

TEN'URE, a holding.
TEN'ABLE, that can be held or maintained.
TENA'CIOUS, holding fast.
TEN'ET, an opinion held.
ABSTAIN', to refrain from.
AB'STINENCE, the act of refraining.
CONTAIN', to hold; to comprehend.
CON'TENTS, s. that which is contained within any limits or boundaries.
CONTENT',* a. satisfied.
CONTIN'UE, to remain.
CONTIN'UAL, uninterrupted.
CONTINU'ITY, unbroken connection.
COUN'TENANCE,† the visage or look.
DETAIN', to keep back.
DETEN'TION, restraint; confinement.
ENTERTAIN', to receive with hospitality; to cherish.

LIEUTEN'ANT, (Fr. *lieu*, place), an officer who supplies the place of a superior in his absence.
MAINTAIN', (282), to uphold.
OBTAIN, to gain; to get.
PERTAIN', to belong to.
PER'TINENT, applicable.
IMPER'TINENT, inapplicable; ill-mannered.
PERTINA'CIOUS, adhering resolutely; obstinate. [stinacy.
PERTINAC'ITY, inflexibility; ob-
RETAIN', to hold; to keep.
RETEN'TIVE, having the power to retain.
SUSTAIN', to hold up; to support.
SUS'TENANCE, support.
TEN'ANT, one who holds or occupies a house and lands.
TEN'DRIL, the clasper of a vine.
TEN'EMENT, a dwelling or habitation.
TEN'ON, the end of a stick of timber fitted to a mortise.
TEN'OR, (Lat.), continued course.

* *Literally*, held, restrained.
† *Primary sig.*, the contents of a body.

531. Ten'to, (tenta'tum), to try.

ATTEMPT', v. to endeavor.
ATTEMPT', s. an endeavor.

TEMPT, to solicit or incite.
TEMPT'ING, attractive.

532. Ten'uis, slender.

ATTEN'UATE, to make slender.

EXTEN'UATE, to lessen; to palliate.

533. Ter'go, (ter'sum), to scour; to make clean.

TERSE, elegant in style without pompousness.

TERSE'NESS, neatness of style; elegance and conciseness.

534. Ter'minus, a bound or limit.

TERM, a limit; a limited time; a word or expression.
TERM'INATE, to bring to an end.
CONTERM'INOUS, having a common boundary.
DETERM'INE, to fix; to decide.
DETERM'INATE, limited; definite.
EXTERM'INATE, to drive away; to destroy utterly.
INDETER'MINATE, not definite.
INTERM'INABLE, boundless.

535. Te'ro, (tri'tum), to wear by rubbing.

TRITE, worn out.
CON'TRITE, broken-hearted for sin.
DET'RIMENT, damage; injury.
DETRIMENT'AL, causing detriment; injurious; hurtful.

536. Ter'ra, the earth.

INTER', to bury in the earth.
MEDITERRA'NEAN, (287), the sea between Europe and Africa.
SUBTERRA'NEAN, beneath the surface of the earth.
TER'RACE, a raised bank of earth; a flat roof.
TERRA'QUEOUS, (19), consisting of land and water.
TERRES'TRIAL, pertaining to the earth.
TER'RIER, a dog that hunts under ground.
TER'RITORY, a district; a tract of land.

537. Ter'reo, (ter'ritum), to affright.

DETER', to stop by fear.
TER'ROR, fear; dread.
TER'RIBLE, frightful; dreadful.
TER'RIFY, (152), to frighten.
TERRIF'IC, causing terror.

538. Tes'tis, a witness.

ATTEST', to bear witness; to certify.
ATTESTA'TION, solemn declaration.
CONTEST', to strive; to litigate.
DETEST', to abhor.
INTEST'ATE,* not having made a [will.
PROTEST', to make a formal declaration.
PROT'ESTANT,† one who joins in a protest.
TEST'AMENT, a will.
TESTA'TOR, one who makes a will.

* A will was called by the Latins *testamen'tum*.

† Martin Luther protested against a decree of Charles V., and the diet of Spires; his followers are therefore called Protestants.

WORDS DERIVED FROM THE LATIN. 159

Test′ify, (152), to bear witness. | Test′imony, that which is af-
Testimo′nial, a certificate. | firmed by a witness.

539. *Tex′o, (tex′tum)*, to weave.

Context′, knit or woven toge- | Text, a composition on which
ther. | a commentary is written; a
Con′text, the connected pas- | passage of Scripture.
sages. | Text-book, a book used in
Pre′text, a pretence; an osten- | teaching.
sible reason, assumed to con- | Text′ure, a web; that which
ceal the true one. | is woven, or the manner of
| weaving.

540. *Tim′eo*, to fear.

Tim′id, fearful. | Intim′idate, to render fearful;
Tim′orous, cowardly; full of fear. | to deter.

541. *Tin′go, (tinc′tum)*, to dip; to dye.

Tinge, to infuse or impregnate | Tinc′ture, a liquid containing
slightly. | the principal qualities of some
Taint, stain; infection. | substance; a slight quality
Tint, a slight coloring. | added to anything.

542. *Tol′lo*, to lift up; to bear away.

Extol′, to praise highly. | Tol′erate, (Lat. *tol′ero*), to en-
| dure.

543. *Tor′peo*, to be numb or stupid.

Tor′pid, inactive; stupid. | Torpe′do, (Lat.), a machine
Tor′por, sluggishness; want of | invented for blowing up ships
activity or feeling. | by submarine explosion.

544. *Tor′queo, (tor′tum)*, to twist.

Contor′tion, a twisting or | Retort′, to throw back a cen-
writhing. | sure or objection.
Distort′, to twist out of shape. | Tor′ment, extreme pain.
Extort′, to wrest or force from | Tort′ure, pain inflicted by an-
one. | other; agony.
Extor′tion, illegal exaction; | Tort′uous, crooked; winding
unreasonable demand. |

11

545. To'tus, whole; all.

To'tal, the whole.
Facto'tum, (152), one who can perform all kinds of service.

To'tally, wholly; entirely.
Surtout', (Fr. *sur tout*, over all), an overcoat.

546. Tra'do, (trad'itum), to deliver.

Tradi'tion, that which is handed down from age to age by oral communication.

Trai'tor, (Fr. *traitre*), one who delivers his country to its enemy.

547. Tra'ho, (trac'tum), to draw.

Ab'stract, *a.* separate; existing in the mind only.
Abstract', *v.* to draw from; to separate.
Attract', to draw to; to allure.
Attract'ive, engaging.
Contract', to draw together.
Detract', to take from the reputation or value of anything.
Detrac'tion, slander.
Distract', to draw apart; to separate; to throw into confusion.
Distrac'tion, confusion; derangement of reason.
Extract', to draw out.
Portray', to delineate.
Por'trait, a likeness.

Protract', to prolong.
Retract', to draw or take back.
Subtract', to deduct.
Sub'trahend, the number to be deducted.
Trace, a mark left by anything passing.
Track, a foot-print; a path.
Tract, a region; a small treatise.
Tract'able, that may be easily led, managed, or taught.
Trail, to draw along on the ground.
Trait, a feature; a line.
Treat, (Fr. *traiter*), to use; to discuss.
Treat'y, a contract or league.

Note.—The words *draw, drag, betray*, seem to be of the same family with *traho*.

548. Tre'mo, to shake.

Trem'ble, to quake; to totter.
Tremen'dous, fitted to excite trembling; terrible.

Tre'mor, a trembling.
Trem'ulous, shaking; quivering.

549. Tres, (tri'a), three.

Trip'le, (392), three-fold.
Tri'ad, the union of three.

Tri'angle, (12), a figure having three angles.

WORDS DERIVED FROM THE LATIN. 161

TRI'DENT, (111), an instrument having three prongs.
TRIN'ITY, (563), a union of three in one.
TRI'O, a passage in music for three performers. [stool.
TRI'POD, (380), a three legged
TRIV'IAL, (584), unimportant.

550. *Trib'uo, (tribu'tum),* to render or give.

TRIB'UTE, a tax paid to a conqueror.
TRIB'UTARY, paying tribute.
ATTRIB'UTE, to ascribe.
CONTRIB'UTE, to give in common with others.

DISTRIB'UTE, to divide; to dispense.
RETRIBU'TION, reward or punishment.
RETRIB'UTIVE, repaying; bringing reward or punishment.

551. *Tru'do, (tru'sum),* to thrust; to push.

ABSTRUSE', difficult to be comprehended or understood.
ABSTRUSE'NESS, quality of being abstruse.
INTRUDE', to thrust one's self in; to encroach.

INTRU'SIVE, entering without right.
OBTRUDE', to thrust in or on.
OBTRU'SIVE, bold; coming uninvited.
PROTRUDE', to thrust forward.

552. *Tu'ber,* a swelling; an excrescence.

PROTU'BERANCE, a prominence; a swelling.
TU'BERCLE, a small tumor.

553. *Tu'eor, (tui'tus),* to view; to guard.

INTUI'TION, immediate perception of truth.
TUI'TION, instruction; guardianship.

TU'TELAR, protecting.
TU'TOR, an instructor or guardian.

554. *Tu'meo,* to swell.

TU'MID, swollen; pompous.
TU'MOR, a swelling.
CON'TUMACY, stubbornness; contempt of authority.
CON'TUMELY, insolence; contemptuous language.
CONTUMA'CIOUS, obstinate; perverse.

TOMB, (Lat. *tu'mulus,* a mound); a grave; a place of burial.
ENTOMB', to put into a tomb; to bury.
ENTOMB'MENT, burial; sepulture.
TU'MULT, a commotion.

555. *Tun'do*, (*tu'sum*), to beat; to bruise.

CONTU'SION, a bruise. | OBTUSE', blunted; dull.

556. *Tur'ba*, a crowd; a bustle.

DISTURB', to disquiet.
DISTURB'ANCE, confusion.
PERTURBA'TION, disquiet or agitation of mind.
IMPERTURB'ABLE, not to be disquieted.

TROUB'LE, perplexity.
TUR'BID, muddy; not clean.
TUR'BULENCE, insubordination; violence.
TUR'BULENT, tumultuous.

557. *Tur'geo*, to be inflated.

TUR'GID, bloated; tumid; pompous. | TURGID'ITY, bombast; inflated style.

558. *Tur'ris*, a tower.

TUR'RET, a little tower. | TUR'RETED, furnished with turrets.

559. *Ul'timus*, last.

UL'TIMATE, furthest; final; last.
UL'TIMATELY, finally; in the end.

ULTIMA'TUM, a final proposition.
ULTE'RIOR, (Latin comparative), further.

560. *Um'bra*, a shade.

UMBRA'GEOUS, shady.
UM'BRAGE, suspicion of injury; offence.

UMBREL'LA, a shade or screen carried in the hand.

561. *Un'da*, a wave.

UN'DULATE, to have a motion like that of waves.
UN'DULATING, rising and falling.
ABOUND', (Lat. *abun'do*), to be in great plenty.

ABUND'ANCE, plenty.
INUN'DATE, to flow upon; to overflow.
REDUND'ANT, *literally*, flowing back; superfluous.

WORDS DERIVED FROM THE LATIN.

562. *Un'guo*, (*unc'tum*), to anoint.

UN'GUENT, ointment.
UNC'TION, an anointing.

UNC'TUOUS, oily; having an oily consistency.

563. *U'nus*, one.

U'NITY, oneness.
UNITE', to make one; to join.
DISUNITE', to separate.
REUNITE', to unite again.
UNANIM'ITY, (13), agreement in opinion.
UNIFORM'ITY, (187), sameness; regularity.
U'NION, conjunction; agreement.

UNIQUE', (Fr.), sole; without another of the kind.
U'NISON, (499), concord of sounds; perfect harmony.
U'NIT, a single thing.
U'NIVERSE,* (579), the whole system of created things.
UNIVERS'AL, all; whole; comprehending the whole.

* The Latin word *univer'sus* signifies literally—turned into one, collected into one whole.

564. *U'tor*, (*u'sus*), to use.

UTIL'ITY, profitableness; advantage.
USE, to employ.
ABUSE', to use improperly.
DISUSE', cessation of use or practice.
MISUSE', to treat ill.
PERUSE', to read.
U'SAGE, custom; treatment.

USE'FUL, beneficial; profitable.
U'SUAL, customary; ordinary.
U'SURY, illegal or exorbitant interest.
USURP', (Lat. *usur'po*), to seize without right.
UTEN'SIL, that which is used; an instrument.

565. *Va'do*, (*va'sum*), to go.

EVADE', to escape; to elude.
EVA'SION, an artifice to elude.
INVADE', to enter as an enemy.

PERVADE', to pass through; to permeate.
WADE, to walk in water.

566. *Va'gus*, wandering.

EXTRAV'AGANT, going beyond proper limits.
EXTRAV'AGANCE, excess.
VAG'ABOND, (Lat. *vagabun'dus*), a wanderer; an outcast.

VAGA'RY, a wandering of the thoughts.
VA'GRANT, wandering; having no home.
VAGUE, unsettled; indefinite.

567. *Va'leo*, to be strong; to have force or value.

AVAIL', to be of use; to have effect.
AVAIL'ABLE, that may be used with success or advantage.
CONVALES'CENT, recovering health and strength.
EQUIV'ALENT. (144), of equal force or value.
INVAL'ID, *a*. of no force.
IN'VALID, *s*. an infirm person.
INVAL'IDATE, to lessen the force of. [influence.
PREVAIL', to overcome; to gain
PREV'ALENT, victorious; having influence extensively.
VALEDIC'TORY,* (117), a farewell address.
VALETUDINA'RIAN, a person seeking health.
VAL'IANT, brave; strong.
VAL'ID, effectual; having force.
VAL'OR, bravery; prowess.
VAL'UE, worth; importance.
VALUA'TION, apprizement.
INVAL'UABLE, precious above estimation.

* From *va'le*, farewell, and *di'co*, to speak.

568. *Ve'ho*, (*vec'tum*), to carry.

VE'HICLE, a carriage.
CON'VEX, swelling; spherical.
CONVEY', to carry.
INVEIGH', to rail against; to reproach.
INVEC'TIVE, censure; reproach.

569. *Vel'lo*, (*vul'sum*), to pluck; to tear.

AVUL'SION, a rending; separation of parts from each other.
CONVUL'SION, violent muscular contraction.

570. *Ve'lo*, to cover; to conceal.

VEIL, a curtain; a covering.
DEVEL'OP, to unfold; to disclose.
ENVEL'OP, to wrap up.
REVEAL', to disclose; to make known.
REVELA'TION, a disclosing what was before hidden.

571. *Ven'do*, to sell.

VEND, to sell.
VEND'ER, a seller.
VENDUE', an auction.
VE'NAL, (Lat. *ve'neo*, to be sold), mercenary; that may be obtained for money.

572. *Ve'nio*, (*ven'tum*), to come.

AD'VENT, a coming; *appropriately*, the coming of our Saviour.
ADVENT'URE, an enterprise of hazard.

WORDS DERIVED FROM THE LATIN. 165

Av'enue, a passage.
Circumvent', to come round;
 to deceive by stratagem.
Contravene', to hinder; to
 oppose; to baffle.
Convene', to assemble.
Conven'tion, a coming together.
Con'vent, a household of
 monks or nuns.
Conven'ient, fit; suitable;
 commodious.
Conven'tional, agreed upon.
Cov'enant, a mutual agreement
 or stipulation.

Event', that which happens or
 takes place.
Event'ually, in the event or
 issue.
Intervene', to come between.
Invent', *literally*, to come
 upon; to devise.
Prevent',* to hinder, to obstruct.
Rev'enue, the income of the
 government.
Supervene', to come in addition.
Ven'ture, to run a hazard; to
 dare.

* *Literally*, to come before; it is used in this sense in the New Testament,
1 Thess. iv. 15.

573. *Ven'ter,* (*ven'tris*), the belly.

Ventril'oquist, (270), *literally*, one who speaks from
 the stomach or belly.

Ventril'oquism, a modifying
 of the voice so that it seems to
 come from different directions.

574. *Ven'tus,* the wind.

Vent, *s.* an air-hole.
Vent, *v.* to let out; to pour out.

Ven'tilate, to afford free circulation of air.

575. *Ver'bum,* a word.

Verb'al, spoken; expressed in
 words.
Verb, a part of speech.
Verbose', full of words.
Verb'iage, superabundance of
 words.

Ad'verb,* a part of speech.
Prov'erb, a maxim; a brief
 saying.
Verba'tim, (Latin), word for
 word.

* *Literally*, a word joined to another word.

576. *Ve'reor,* to fear.

Revere', to regard with fear
 and respect.
Rev'erent, impressed with
 reverence.

Reveren'tial, feeling or expressing reverence.
Rev'erend, worthy of reverence; a clerical title.

577. Ver'go, to turn or tend towards.

VERGE, to tend; to incline.
CONVERGE', to tend to one point.
DIVERGE', to separate or recede more and more.

578. Ver'mis, a worm.

VERMIC'ULAR, pertaining to or resembling a worm or the motion of a worm.
VER'MIFORM, (187), having the shape or form of a worm.
VER'MIFUGE, (197), a medicine which destroys worms in animal bodies.
VERM'IN, noxious animals, insects, &c.

579. Ver'to, (ver'sum), to turn.

ADVERT', to turn the attention to.
INADVERT'ENCE, heedlessness.
AD'VERSE, opposed; hostile.
ADVERS'ITY, calamity; affliction.
AD'VERSARY, an enemy.
ADVERTISE', to publish a notice.
ANIMADVER'SION, (13), a criticism; a censure.
AVERT', to turn away.
AVER'SION, disinclination; dislike.
CON'TROVERT, to oppose in argument.
CON'TROVERSY, disputation.
CONVERT', to change from one state to another.
CONVERSE', to discourse or associate with.
CON'VERSE, familiar intercourse; an opposite proposition.
DIVERT', to turn off; to amuse.
DIVER'SION, amusement.
DI'VERSE, different; various.
DIVERS'ITY, difference.
DIVERS'IFY, (152), to vary.
DIVORCE', a legal dissolution of the bonds of matrimony.
IRREVER'SIBLE, that cannot be revoked or changed.
INVERT', to turn into the contrary position.
INVERSE'LY, in an inverted order.
INVER'SION, change of order; change of place.
PERVERT', to turn to a wrong use.
PERVERSE', obstinately wrong.
PERVER'SION, a wrong use or interpretation.
REVERT', to turn back.
REVERSE', to change to an opposite direction.
SUBVERT', to overthrow from the foundation.
SUBVERS'IVE, tending to overthrow.
TRANSVERSE', lying across.
TRAV'ERSE, to cross; to pass over.
VERS'ATILE, easily turned from one employment to another.
VERSE,* a line of poetry; a short division of any composition.

* A furrow was anciently called *ver'sus*, because at the end of it the plough was turned round; hence, a line in writing, from its resemblance to a furrow, received the same name.

WORDS DERIVED FROM THE LATIN.

VER′SION,* a translation.
VERT′EBRA, (Lat. plural *vert′-ebræ*), a joint of the spine.

VER′TEX,† (Lat.), the top.
VERT′ICAL, over head.
VERT′IGO, (Lat.), giddiness
VOR′TEX, (Lat.), a whirlpool.

* *Literally*, a turning from one language into another.
† The turning point.

580. *Ve′rus*, true.

VER′ITY, truth.
VERAC′ITY, habitual observance of truth.
VERA′CIOUS, observant of truth.
VER′DICT, (117), the report of a jury.

VER′IFY, (152), to prove to be true.
VER′ITABLE, true; genuine.
VER′ILY, truly.

581. *Vestig′ium*, a foot-step.

VES′TIGE, a track; a trace.
INVES′TIGATE, to search into.

582. *Ves′tis*, a garment.

INVEST′, to clothe.
VEST, to put in possession of; to furnish with.

VEST′URE, a robe.
VEST′RY, a room in which the sacerdotal vestments are kept.

583. *Ve′tus*, (*vet′eris*), old; ancient.

VET′ERAN, an old soldier.

INVET′ERATE, fixed by long continuance.

584. *Vi′a*, a way.

DE′VIATE, to turn aside from the path.
DE′VIOUS, wandering.
OB′VIATE,‡ to remove.
OB′VIOUS,§ evident.
PER′VIOUS,‖ penetrable.

IMPER′VIOUS, not to be penetrated or passed through.
PRE′VIOUS, antecedent.
TRIV′IAL,¶ (549), unimportant.
VI′ADUCT, (133), a structure supporting a carriageway or railway.

‡ *Properly*, to meet in the way and oppose or conquer; hence to put out of the way an obstacle.
§ Meeting one in the way.
‖ Admitting a way or passage through.
¶ The Romans worshipped some of their minor deities at places where *three roads* met; which deities were thence called *Di′i Triv′ii*. Thus the word *trivial* derived the signification *secondary*, *unimportant*.

585. *Vi'cis*, change; succession.

Vic'ar, a substitute.
Vica'rious, acting for another.
Vicege'rent, (203), a deputy.

Vice-pres'ident, (472), one who takes the place of the president.

586. *Vid'eo*, (*vi'sum*), to see.

Vis'ion, sight.
Vis'ible, that can be seen.
Vis'ionary, imaginary.
Vis'it, to go to see.
Vis'ual, pertaining to sight.
Vi'sor, a mask.
Vis'age, the countenance.
Vis'ta, (Lat.), a view or prospect.
View, (Fr. *vue*), to look at.
Vi'de, (Latin), see.
Ev'ident, apparent; clear.
Invis'ible, not to be seen.

Provide',* to prepare.
Prov'idence, forethought; prudence.
Provis'ion, that which is procured or prepared beforehand.
Provi'so, (Lat.), an exception provided for.
Pru'dent, cautious; wise.
Purvey'or, a provider.
Revise', to examine again.
Supervis'ion, oversight.
Survey', to look over carefully.

* *Literally*, to look out beforehand.

587. *Vi'geo*, to flourish; to thrive.

Vig'or, strength; energy. | Invig'orate, to strengthen.

588. *Vin'co*, (*vic'tum*), to conquer.

Convince', to persuade.
Convic'tion, the state of being convinced; belief.
Convict', to prove one to be guilty.
Con'vict, a person found guilty.
Evince', to make evident.
Invin'cible, unconquerable.

Prov'ince, a country subject to a foreign power; a district or division of a country.
Van'quish, to conquer.
Vic'tor, a conqueror.
Vic'tory, success over an enemy.
Vic'tim, a living being sacrificed.

589. *Vin'dex*, (*vin'dicis*), a defender or avenger.

Vin'dicate, to defend; to sustain.
Vindic'tive, revengeful.

Revenge', to return an injury.
Ven'geance, (Fr.), recompense of evil.

590. *Vi'num*, wine.

VINE, the plant which produces grapes.
VIN'EGAR, vegetable acid.
VINE'YARD, a plantation of grape-vines.
VI'NOUS, having the qualities of wine.
VINT'AGE, the gathering of the crop of grapes.

591. *Vir*, a man.

VI'RILE, masculine.
VIRA'GO, (Lat.), (3), a bold wo- [man.
VIR'TUE, (Lat. *vir'tus*), efficiency; excellence.

592. *Vi'rus*, poison; venom.

VIR'ULENCE, malignancy.
VIR'ULENT, malignant; venomous.

593. *Vi'to*, to shun; to avoid.

INEV'ITABLE, unavoidable.
INEV'ITABLY, certainly.

594. *Vi'trum*, glass.

VIT'REOUS, resembling glass.
VIT'RIFY, (152), to convert into [glass.

595. *Vi'vo*, (*vic'tum*), to live.

CONVIV'IAL, festal; social.
REVIVE', to live again; to arouse.
SURVIVE', to outlive. [of food.
VI'AND, (Fr. *viande*), an article
VICT'UALS, food; provisions.
VI'TAL, (Lat. *vi'ta*, life), pertaining to life.
VIVAC'ITY, liveliness.
VIV'ID, lively; bright. [life.
VIV'IFY, (152), to endue with

596. *Vo'co*, (*voca'tum*), to call.

AD'VOCATE, a pleader.
AVOCA'TION, a calling or employment.
CONVOCA'TION, an assembly.
EQUIV'OCAL, (144), ambiguous.
EQUIV'OCATE, to use ambiguous expressions.
INVOKE', to pray to.
INVOCA'TION, a solemn address or prayer.
PROVOCA'TION, a calling out; an incitement.
REVOKE', to call back; to repeal.
IRREV'OCABLE, that cannot be repealed.
VO'CAL, (Lat. *vox*, (*vo'cis*), the voice), pertaining to the voice; uttered by the voice.
VOCAB'ULARY, (Fr. *vocabulaire*), a list of words.
VOCAB'ULIST, the writer of a vocabulary; a lexicographer.

VOCA'TION, a business or profession.
VOCIF'ERATE, (167), to cry out loudly.
VOICE, (Fr. *voix*), sound uttered by the mouth.
VOUCH, to attest; to affirm.
VOW'EL, a simple sound.

597. *Vo'lo*, (*vola'tum*), to fly.

VOL'ATILE, easily evaporated; gay; fickle.
VOL'LEY, a flight of shot; a burst or emission of many things at once.

598. *Vo'lo*, to will; to wish.

BENEV'OLENCE, (38), good will.
MALEV'OLENCE, (279), ill will.
VOL'UNTARY, acting from choice.
VOLUNTEER', s. a voluntary soldier.

599. *Volup'tas*, pleasure.

VOLUP'TUOUS, given to luxury and pleasure.
VOLUP'TUARY, a person devoted to pleasure.

600. *Vol'vo*, (*volu'tum*), to roll.

DEVOLVE', *literally*, to roll down; to deliver over; to pass from one to another.
EVOLVE', to unroll; to unfold.
INVOLVE', to envelop; to infold.
REVOLT', to renounce allegiance.
REVOLVE', to roll in a circle.
REVOLU'TION, rotation; an entire change.
VOL'UBLE, rolling; fluent.
VOL'UME, *primarily*, a roll; a book.

601. *Vo'ro*, to devour.

DEVOUR', to eat up greedily.
VORAC'ITY, greediness of appetite.
VORA'CIOUS, ravenous.
CARNIV'OROUS, (50), feeding on flesh.

602. *Vo'veo*, (*vo'tum*), to vow.

AVOW', to declare openly.
DEVOTE', to dedicate; to set apart. [devoted.
DEVOTEE', one who is wholly
DEVOUT', earnest in worship.
VO'TARY, one devoted or addicted.
VOTE, suffrage; a ballot.
VOT'IVE, given by vow.

WORDS DERIVED FROM THE GREEK. 171

603. *Vul'gus*, the common people.

VUL'GAR, common; unrefined.
VULGAR'ITY, grossness or clownishness.

VUL'GARISM, a vulgar phrase or expression.
DIVULGE', to make public.

604. *Vul'nus*, (*vul'neris*), a wound.

VUL'NERABLE, that may be wounded.

INVUL'NERABLE, that cannot be wounded.

CHAPTER III.

WORDS DERIVED FROM THE GREEK.

Greek Alphabet.

Letter.		Sound.	Name.
A	α	a	Alpha.
B	β ϐ	b	Beta.
Γ	γ	g	Gamma.
Δ	δ	d	Delta.
E	ε	e as in *met*	Epsilon.
Z	ζ	z	Zeta.
H	η	e as in *me*	Eta.
Θ	θ ϑ	th	Theta.
I	ι	i	Iota.
K	κ	k	Kappa.
Λ	λ	l	Lambda.
M	μ	m	Mu.
N	ν	n	Nu.
Ξ	ξ	x	Xi.
O	ο	o as in *not*	Omicron.
Π	π ϖ	p	Pi.
P	ρ	r	Rho.
Σ	σ, ς final	s	Sigma.
T	τ	t	Tau.
Υ	υ	u or y	Upsilon.
Φ	φ	ph	Phi.
X	χ	ch	Chi.
Ψ	ψ	ps	Psi.
Ω	ω	o as in *no*	Omega.

Gamma has always the hard sound of *g*, as in *give*.
Kappa is represented by *c* in English words, although in Greek it has but one sound, that of our *k*.
Upsilon is represented by *y* in English words; in Greek it has always the sound of *u* in *mute*.
Chi is represented in English by *ch* having the sound of *k*; as in *chronic*.
In Greek words, as in Latin, there are always as many syllables as there are vowels and diphthongs.
The accents placed over the Greek letters need not be regarded in pronunciation.
An inverted comma placed over a letter denotes that the sound of our *h* precedes that letter. Thus, the word ἐξ is pronounced *hex*. A comma not inverted does not affect the sound of the vowel over which it is placed. For information respecting accentual marks, &c., see the Greek grammars.

1. *Acade'mia*, (ἀκαδημία), a place near Athens, where Plato taught philosophy.

ACAD'EMY, a high school. | ACADEM'IC, belonging to a school or college.

2. *Ach'os*, (ἄχος), pain.

ACHE, to suffer pain. | ACH'ING, painful.

3. *Ak'me*, (ἀκμή), the summit.

4. *Akou'o*, (ἀκούω), to hear.

ACOUS'TICS, the science of sounds. | OTACOUS'TIC, (Gr. ὦτα, the ears), fitted to aid the hearing.

5. *Ak'ron*, (ἄκρον), the extremity.

ACROP'OLIS, (187), the height or citadel. | ACROS'TIC, (208), a kind of poetical composition.

6. *Adel'phos*, (ἀδελφος), a brother.

This word is used in forming botanical terms.

7. *A'er*, (ἀήρ), the air.

AE'RIAL, consisting of air.
A'EROLITE, (127), a meteoric stone.
A'ERONAUT, (145), one who sails in the air.
| AEROSTA'TION, (204), aerial navigation.
AEROL'OGY, that branch of philosophy which treats of the air.

WORDS DERIVED FROM THE GREEK. 173

8. A'go, (ἄγω), to lead.

DEM'AGOGUE, (67), a leader of the people. | PED'AGOGUE, (163), a schoolmaster.

9. A'gon, (ἀγών), a contest.

AG'ONY, anguish. | AG'ONIZE, to writhe with pain.

10. Al'gos, (ἄλγος), pain.

CEPH'ALALGY, (45), the headache. | ODONTAL'GIA, (153), the toothache.

11. Allax'is, (ἄλλαξις), a change.

PAR'ALLAX, an astronomical term. | PARALLAC'TIC, pertaining to the parallax.

12. Al'pha, (ἄλφα), the first letter in the Greek alphabet.

AL'PHABET, (34), a list of the letters of a language. | ALPHABET'ICAL, pertaining to the alphabet.

13. An'emos, (ἄνεμος), the wind.

ANEMOM'ETER, (137), a wind-gauge. | ANEM'ONE, the wind-flower.

14. An'er, (ἄνηρ, ἄνδρος), a man.

AN'DROID, (122), a machine in human form. | ANDROPH'AGUS, (170), a man-eater.

15. Anggel'lo, (ἀγγέλλω*), to bring tidings.

AN'GEL, a spirit; a spiritual messenger. | EVAN'GELIST, (89), a preacher of the gospel.

* The first *gamma* has the sound of *ng* when the letter is doubled.

16. An'thos, (ἄνθος), a flower.

ANTHOL'OGY, (128), a discourse on flowers. | HELIAN'THUS, (105), the sun-flower.

17. *Anthro'pos*, (ἄνθρωπος), man.

MIS'ANTHROPE, (139), a hater of mankind. | PHILAN'THROPIST, (175), a friend of the human race.

18. *Ar'che*, (ἀρχή), the beginning; government.

AN'ARCHY, want of government.
AR'CHAISM, an ancient phrase.
ARCHAN'GEL, the highest angel.
ARCHEOL'OGY, (128), a discourse on antiquity.
AR'CHETYPE, (222), the original or model.

AR'CHITECT, (Gr. τέκτων, a builder), one skilled in building.
AR'CHIVES, records.
PA'TRIARCH, (Gr. πατήρ, a father), the father and ruler of a family.

19. *Ark'tos*, (ἄρκτος), a bear.

ARC'TIC,* northern. | ANTARC'TIC,† southern.

* *Literally*, pertaining to the constellation called the Bear.
† Opposite to the north or north pole.

20. *Ar'gos*, (ἀργός), inactive.

LETH'ARGY, (125), drowsiness; stupidity. | LETHAR'GIC, inactive.

21. *Aris'tos*, (ἄριστός), best.

ARISTOC'RACY, (60), the rule or government of the nobility. | AR'ISTOCRAT, one who favors an aristocracy.

22. *Arith'mos*, (ἀριθμός), number.

ARITH'METIC, the science of numbers. | LOG'ARITHM, a mathematical term.

23. *Aro'ma*, (ἄρωμα), spicy flavor.

AROMAT'IC, fragrant; spicy. | AR'OMATIZE, to give a spicy taste.

24. *As'keo*, (ἀσκέω), to exercise; to train.

ASCET'IC, *a.* self mortifying; austere; retired from the world. | ASCET'IC, *s.* one who retires from the world and devotes himself to religious discipline.

WORDS DERIVED FROM THE GREEK. 175

25. *As'tron*, (ἄστρον), a star.

As'terisk, a mark like a star. | As'tral, star-like.
Astrol'ogy, divination by the | Astron'omy, (149), the science
stars | of the stars.

26. *Ath'los*, (ἆθλος), a combat.

Athlet'ic, pertaining to active | Ath'lete, a contender for vic-
sports; vigorous. | tory.

27. *At'mos*, (ἀτμὸς), vapor; steam.

At'mosphere, (Gr. σφαῖρα, a | Atmospher'ic, pertaining to
sphere), the air, &c., above us. | the atmosphere.

28. *Au'los*, (αὐλὸς), a pipe.

Hydrau'lic, (119), transmit- | Hydrau'lics, the science of the
ting water through pipes. | motion and force of fluids.

29. *Au'tos*, (αὐτὸς), one's self.

Au'tocrat, (60), a despotic | Autom'aton, a self moving
ruler. | machine.
Au'tograph, (99), one's hand | Auton'omy, (149), the right
writing. | of self-government.

30. *Bal'lo*, (βάλλω), to cast or throw.

Em'blem,* a representation. | Prob'lem,‡ a question pro-
Hyper'bole,† an exaggeration. | posed.
Par'able, a similitude. | Sym'bol, a sign.

* The Greek word ἔμβλημα signifies *anything inserted;* hence, *mosaic work,* or *a picture.*
† A casting over or beyond.
‡ Something cast or placed before one.

31. *Bapti'zo*, (βαπτίζω), to baptize.

Bap'tism, a Christian sacra- | Pe'dobaptist, (Gr. παῖς, a
ment. [tism. | child), one who holds to infant
Baptis'mal, pertaining to bap- | baptism.

32. *Ba'sis*, (βάσις), a foundation.

Base, *s.* the foundation; *a.* mean. | Debase', to render mean or vile.

12

33. *Ba'ros*, (βάρος), weight.

BAROM'ETER, (137), an instrument for measuring the pressure of the atmosphere. | BAR'YTONE, having a grave deep sound.

34. *Be'ta*, (βῆτα), the second letter of the Greek alphabet. (see 12.)

35. *Bib'los*, (βίβλος), a book.

BI'BLE, the Holy Scriptures.
BIB'LICAL, pertaining to the Bible. | BIBLIOG'RAPHY, (99), a history or description of books.

36. *Bi'os*, (βίος), life.

AMPHIB'IOUS,* having the power of living in two elements. | BIOG'RAPHY, (99), the history of a person's life.

* *Literally*, having double life.

37. *Bot'ane*, (βοτάνη), an herb or plant.

BOT'ANY, the science of vegetables. | BOT'ANIST, one skilled in botany.

38. *Bou'colos*, (βουκόλος), a herdsman.

BUCOL'IC, *a.* pastoral. | BUCOL'IC, *s.* a pastoral poem.

39. *Ka'kos*, (κακὸς), bad.

CACHEX'Y, (Gr. ἕξις, condition), a deranged state of the body. | CACOPH'ONY, (176), harshness of sound.

40. *Kalup'to*, (καλύπτω), to cover; to veil.

APOC'ALYPSE, a revelation. | APOCALYP'TIC, pertaining to a revelation.

41. *Kan'on*, (κανὼν), a rule.

CAN'ON, a rule or law; a catalogue of saints. | CAN'ONIZE, to declare one a saint.

42. *Kai'o*, (καίω, καύσω), to burn.

CAUS'TIC, burning; corroding. | CAU'TERY, a burning or searing.

WORDS DERIVED FROM THE GREEK. 177

43. *Kar'dia*, (καρδία), the heart.

CAR'DIAC, pertaining to the heart. | PERICAR'DIUM, a membrane enclosing the heart.

44. *Ken'tron*, (κέντρον), a central point.

CEN'TRE, the middle point.
CONCEN'TRATE, to bring together; to bring into a smaller compass.
| CENTRIF'UGAL, (197), tending from the centre.
ECCEN'TRIC, deviating from the centre; irregular; anomalous.

45. *Keph'ale*, (κεφαλή), the head.

CEPHAL'IC, pertaining to the head. | HYDROCEPH'ALUS, (119), dropsy of the head.

46. *Ke'ras*, (κέρας), a horn.

MONOC'EROS, (141), an animal having but one horn. | RHINOC'EROS, (Gr. ῥίν, the nose), an animal having a horn upon the nose.

47. *Cha'os*, (χάος), a chasm or abyss.

CHA'OS, confusion; disorder. | CHAOT'IC, without order.

48. *Cha'ris*, (χάρις, χάριτος), favor; grace.

CHAR'ITY, kindness; good will. | EU'CHARIST, (89), the Lord's supper.

49. *Cheir*, (χείρ), the hand.

CHIROG'RAPHY, (99), handwriting. | CHIRUR'GEON, (83), a surgeon.

50. *Cho'le*, (χολή), bile; anger.

CHOL'ERA, a disease.
CHOL'ER, anger; wrath.
CHOL'ERIC, irascible.
| COL'IC, pain in the bowels.
MEL'ANCHOLY,* gloom; dejection.

* Gr. μέλας, black; *literally*, black bile.

51. *Chore'o*, (χωρέω), to go.

AN'CHORET, or AN'CHORITE, a hermit; one who retires from society to avoid the temptations of the world.

52. *Chris'tos*, (Χριστὸς), the Anointed.

CHRIST, the Messiah.
CHRISTIAN'ITY, the religion of Christ.
CHRIST'MAS, a Christian festival.
CHRISM, consecrated oil.

53. *Chro'ma*, (χρῶμα) color.

CHROMAT'ICS, the science of colors.
ACHROMAT'IC, destitute of color.

54. *Chron'os*, (χρόνος), time.

CHRON'IC, of long duration.
CHRON'ICLE, a record or history.
CHRONOL'OGY, (128), the science of time or eras.
CHRONOM'ETER, (137), a timepiece.
ANACH'RONISM, an error in dates.
ISOCH'RONOUS, (123), performed in equal times.

55. *Chru'sos*, (χρυσὸς), gold.

CHRYS'ALIS, the caterpillar in its dormant state.*
CHRYS'OLITE, a mineral of a yellowish color.

* The name is derived from the golden color.

56. *Konch'e*, (κόγχη),† a shell.

CONCH, a marine shell.
CONCHOID'AL, (122), shaped like a shell.
CONCHOL'OGY, (158), the science of shells.

† Gamma here has the sound of *ng*.

57. *Kop'to*, (κόπτω), to cut.

APOC'OPATE, to cut off from the end of a word.
SYN'COPATE, to remove letters from the middle of a word.

58. *Kos'mos*, (κόσμος), the world.

COSMOG'ONY, (94), an account of the origin or creation of the world.
COSMOP'OLITE, (187), a citizen of the world.

WORDS DERIVED FROM THE GREEK. 179

Mic'rocosm, (138), a little world.
Cosmet'ic, a preparation de-signed to beautify the complexion.*

* A primary signification of the word κόσμος, is—*order; beautiful arrangement.*

59. Kra'nion, (κρανίον), the skull.

Cra'nium, the skull.
Pericra'nium, (Gr. περὶ, around), the membrane which covers the skull.

Craniol'ogy, the science of skulls.
Cranios'copy, (197), the examination of the skull.

60. Kra'tos, (κράτος), might; power.

The terminations *cracy, cratic,* &c., are from this word. See 21.

61. Kri'tes, (κριτής), a judge.

Crit'ic, a judge in literature or art.
Crite'rion, a standard of judg-[ing.
Hypercrit'ical, critical beyond reason.
Cri'sis, the deciding point.

62. Krup'to, (κρύπτω), to conceal.

Apoc'ryphal, of doubtful origin.
Cryptog'amy, (91), concealed union.

63. Kuk'los, (κύκλος), a circle.

Cy'cle, a period of time.
Cy'cloid, (122), a curve.
Cyclope'dia, Encyclope'dia, (163), the circle of sciences.

64. Ku'on, (κύων), a dog.

Cyn'ical,† surly; austere.
Cyn'osure,‡ a constellation.

† The Cynics were philosophers who valued themselves on their contempt of riches and amusements, and laughed at the errors and follies of mankind.

‡ *Literally,* the dog's tail. That which attracts general notice, is sometimes called, figuratively, a *cynosure.*

65. Kus'tis, (κύστις), a bladder; a bag.

Cyst, a bag; a vesicle.
Encyst'ed, enclosed in a bag.

66. Dek'a, (δέκα), ten.

Dec'alogue, (128), the ten commandments.
Dec'agon, (98), a figure having ten angles.

67. *De'mos*, (δῆμος), the people.

DEM'AGOGUE, (8), a popular leader.
DEM'OCRAT, one who favors democracy.
DEMOC'RACY, (60), a popular government.
EPIDEM'IC, (ἐπί, upon), a prevailing disease.

68. *Despo'tes*, (δεσπότης), a master or lord.

DES'POT, a monarch; a tyrant; an absolute ruler.
DES'POTISM, unlimited monarchy.

69. *Didas'ko*, (διδάσκω), to teach.

DIDAC'TIC, adapted to teach; preceptive.
DIDAC'TICALLY, in a didatic manner.

70. *Dox'a*, (δόξα), an opinion.

HET'ERODOX, (111), holding erroneous opinions.
PAR'ADOX, a proposition seemingly absurd.
OR'THODOX, (160), correct in opinion.
DOXOL'OGY,* (128), an ascription of praise.

* The word δόξα signifies also, *glory; renown.*

71. *Dra'ma*, (δρᾶμα†), an action; a drama.

DRAMAT'IC, pertaining to the drama.
DRAM'ATIST, a writer of plays.

† From δράω, to do or perform.

72. *Drom'os*, (δρόμος), a race.

DROM'EDARY, a species of camel.
OR'THODROMY, sailing in a straight course.

73. *Du'namis*, (δύναμις), power.

DYNAM'ICS, the science of forces.
DY'NASTY, a race of kings.

74. *Dus*, (δυς), an inseparable particle, denoting *difficulty, pain, &c.*

DYS'ENTERY, (Gr. ἔντερα, the bowels), a disease of the bowels.
DYSPEP'SY, (Gr. πέψις, digestion), difficulty of digestion.
DYS'PHONY, (176), difficulty of speaking.
DYSPNŒ'A, (Gr. πνέω, to breathe), difficult breathing.

WORDS DERIVED FROM THE GREEK. 181

75. *Oi'kos,* (οἶκος), a house.

DI'OCESE,* the jurisdiction of a bishop.
PAR'ISH,‡ an ecclesiastical district.
ECON'OMY,† a system of management; frugality.
PARO'CHIAL, pertaining to a parish.

* From διοίκησις, which signifies, primarily, *the management of a household.*

† Sometimes written *œconomy.* The Greek diphthong οι is usually represented in English by œ or e. Οἰκονομία is compounded of οἶκος and νόμος, (149), *a regulation* or *rule;* and therefore signifies *the regulation of a house, or family.* Economy is the corresponding English word.

‡ From παροίκησις, which signifies *the state of dwelling near; a neighborhood.*

76. *Hed'ra,* (ἕδρα), a seat.

CATHE'DRAL, (Gr. καθέδρα), the see or seat of a bishop; the principal church in a diocese.
SAN'HEDRIM, (Gr. συνέδριον), the chief council of the Jews.
TETRAHE'DRON, (213), a solid having four faces or sides.

77. *Hege'sis,* (ἥγησις), a leading; an explanation.

EXEGE'SIS, (ἐξήγησις), exposition.
EXEGET'ICAL, pertaining to exegesis.

78. *E'meo,* (ἐμέω), to vomit.

EMET'IC, a medicine that causes vomiting.
EM'ETIN, a substance obtained from the ipecacuana.

79. *En'tera,* (ἔντερα), the bowels.

DYS'ENTERY, (74), a disease of the bowels. [intestines.
ENTERI'TIS, inflammation of the
MES'ENTERY, (Gr. μέσος, middle), a membrane supporting the intestines.

80. *En'tomos,* (ἔντομος), cut into. See 217.

ENTOMOL'OGY, (128), the science which treats of insects.§
ENTOMOL'OGIST, one versed in the science of insects.

§ The words *insec'tum* in Latin and ἔντομον in Greek correspond to each other precisely. The former is compounded of *in,* into, and *se'co,* to cut; and the latter of ἐν and τέμνω, which have the same significations as the Latin words above mentioned. The names were undoubtedly suggested by the form which many insects have, i. e., the appearance of being almost cut in two.

81. *Ep'os*, (ἔπος), a speech; a poem.

Ep'ic, containing narration of an elevated character. | Or'thoepy, (160), correct pronunciation.

82. *Er'emos*, (ἐρῆμος), lonely.

Er'emite, one who lives in a wilderness. | Her'mit, (same signification).

83. *Er'gon*, (ἔργον), a work.

En'ergy, (ἐνέργεια), vigor of operation.
Lit'urgy, (Gr. λιτή, prayer), a formulary of public prayer. | Metal'lurgy, (Gr. μέταλλον, a metal), the art of working metals and obtaining them from the ore.

84. *Es'o*, (ἔσω), within.

Esot'ery, (little used), mystery. | Esoter'ic, private; secret.

85. *Ai'ther*, (αἰθήρ), the air.

E'ther, a light fluid. | Ethe'real, immaterial; subtile.

86. *Eth'os*, (ἔθος), a custom.

Eth'ics, the science of morals; moral philosophy. | Eth'ical, relating to morals or duty.

87. *Eth'nos*, (ἔθνος), a nation.

Eth'nical, relating to the races of mankind. | Ethnol'ogy, (128), a classification and description of races.

88. *Et'umon*, (ἔτυμον),* the true derivation.

Et'ymon, a root or primitive word. | Etymol'ogy, the study of derivation and inflection.

* The adjective ἔτυμος signifies *true, genuine.*

WORDS DERIVED FROM THE GREEK. 183

89. *Eu,* (εὖ), well; rightly.

Eu'logy, (128), praise; pane-gyric.
Eu'phony, (176), pleasantness of sound.

Evan'gelist,* (15), a preacher of the gospel.
Evan'gelize, to instruct in the gospel.

* The Greek υ had, in certain words, the sound of the English v. The word εὐαγγέλιον signifies, primarily, *good tidings.*

90. *Ga'lax,* (γάλαξ), milk.

Gal'axy, the milky way; a splendid assemblage.

91. *Ga'meo,* (γαμέω), to marry.

Big'amy, (Lat. 37), the crime of having two wives at once.
Polyg'amy, (188), the having a plurality of wives.

92. *Gas'ter,* (γαστήρ), the belly.

Gas'tric, belonging to the stomach.
Gastril'oquist, a ventriloquist, (see Lat. 270).

93. *Ge,* (γῆ), the earth.

Geog'raphy, (99), a description of the earth's surface.
Geol'ogy, (128), the science of the structure of the earth.
Geom'etry,† the science of magnitude.

Geopon'ics (Gr. πόνος, labor), agriculture.
Ap'ogee, greatest distance from the earth.
Per'igee, nearest approach to the earth.

† *Primarily,* the art of measuring the earth or globe.

94. *Genna'o,* (γεννάω), to produce. *Ge'nea,* (γενεά), birth; origin.

Geneal'ogy, (128), lineage; an account of one's descent.
Gen'esis, (Gr. γένεσις), origin; creation.

95. *Glo'tta* or *Glossa,* (γλῶττα or γλῶσσα), the tongue; language.

Glot'tis and Epiglot'tis, parts of the throat, lying near the root of the tongue.
Pol'yglot, (188), in many languages.
Gloss'ary, a limited dictionary.

96. *Glu'pho,* (γλύφω), to carve or engrave.

Glyph, a kind of ornament in sculpture.
Hi'eroglyph, (114), a mystical character or symbol.

97. *Gno'me*, (γνώμη), reason; judgment. *Gno'sis*, (γνῶσις), knowledge.

DIAGNO'SIS, judgment respecting the character of a disease.
IG'NORANT, destitute of knowledge.
GNOS'TICS, an ancient sect of philosophers.

PHYSIOG'NOMY, (180), the art of discerning the character of the mind from the countenance.
PROGNOS'TIC, a sign by which a future event may be known.

98. *Go'nia*, (γωνία), an angle or corner.

DIAG'ONAL, passing through the opposite angles.
GONIOM'ETER, (137), an instrument for measuring angles.

POL'YGON, (188), a figure having many angles.
TRIGONOM'ETRY, (137), the measuring of triangles.

99. *Graph'o*, (γράφω), to write: *Gramma*, (γράμμα), a writing.

AN'AGRAM, a transposition of the letters of a word.
AU'TOGRAPH, (see 29).
DI'AGRAM, a delineation; a figure.
EP'IGRAM, a short, pointed poem.
GRAM'MAR, the science which treats of the laws of language.
GRAPH'IC, well delineated; giving vivid description.

GRAPH'ITE, a substance used for pencils.
PAR'AGRAPH, a distinct part of a composition.
PARALLEL'OGRAM, a figure whose opposite sides are parallel.
STENOG'RAPHY,* (206), shorthand.
TEL'EGRAPH, (Gr. τῆλε, afar), a machine for communicating intelligence by signals.

* The termination *graphy*, which is found in a large class of words, denotes a *writing or treatise*.

100. *Gum'nos*, (γυμνὸς), naked.

GYMNA'SIUM,† a place for athletic exercises.

GYMNAS'TIC, belonging to a gymnasium.

† In the ancient games the combatants were naked, or nearly so, and hence their exercise was called γυμνασία.

101. *Gu'ne*, (γυνή),‡ a woman.

GYN'ARCHY, (18), government by a female.
GYNÆ'CIAN, relating to women.

GYNÆOC'RACY, (60), government over which a woman may preside.

‡ The word γυνή enters into a number of botanical terms.

WORDS DERIVED FROM THE GREEK. 185

102. *Gu'ros*, (γῦρος), a circle.

GYRA'TION, a whirling round. | GY'RAL, whirling.

103. *Heb'domos*, (ἕβδομος), the seventh.

HEB'DOMAD, (obsolete), a week. | HEBDOM'ADAL, weekly.

104. *Hek'aton*, (ἕκατον), a hundred.

HEC'ATOMB, (Gr. βοῦς, an ox), an ancient heathen sacrifice | of a hundred oxen or other animals at once.

105. *He'lios*, (ἥλιος), the sun.

APHE'LION, greatest distance from the sun.
HELI'ACAL, emerging from the light of the sun or passing into it.
HE'LIOTROPE, (221), a plant that turns to the sun.
PERIHE'LION,* nearest approach of a planet to the sun.

* The word ἥλιος enters into various astronomical terms.

106. *Hel'len*, (Ἕλλην), a Greek.

HELLEN'IC, pertaining to Greece.
HEL'LENIST, one skilled in the Greek language.

107. *Hai'ma*, (αἷμα), blood.

HEM'ORRHAGE, (195), a flow of blood.
HEM'ORRHOIDS, bleeding tumors.

108. *He'mera*, (ἡμερα), a day.

EPHEM'ERAL, lasting but a day. | EPHEM'ERIS, a kind of almanac.

109. *He'mi*, (ἡμι), a prefix signifying *half*.

HEM'ISPHERE, (Gr. σφαῖρα, a ball), a half sphere.
HEM'ISTICH, (208), half a line in poetry.

110. *Hep'ta*, (ἑπτά), seven.

HEP'TAGON, (98), a figure having seven angles.
HEP'TARCHY, (18), a government by seven persons.

111. *Het'eros,* (ἕτερος), other; another.

HET'ERODOX, (70), heretical; holding erroneous sentiments.

HETEROGE'NEOUS, (94), of different nature or kind.

112. *Hex,* (ἕξ), six.

HEX'AGON, (98), a figure having six angles.

HEXAM'ETER, (137), having six metrical feet.

113. *Hip'pos,* (ἵππος), a horse.

HIPPOPOT'AMUS, (189), the river horse.

HIP'PODROME, (71), *anciently,* a circus.

114. *Hi'eros,* (ἱερὸς), sacred.

HI'ERARCHY, (18), ecclesiastical government.

HIEROGLYPH'IC, (96), a sacred character or symbol.

115. *Hom'ilos,* (ὅμιλος), an assembly or company.

HOM'ILY, a discourse pronounced to an audience.

HOMILET'IC, pertaining to pulpit discourse.

116. *Hom'os,* (ὁμὸς), united; like.

HOMOGE'NEOUS, (94), of the same kind or nature.

HOMOL'OGOUS, (128), proportionate to each other.

117. *Ho'ra,* (ὥρα), an hour.

HO'RAL, relating to an hour.

HOROL'OGY, the art of making time-pieces.

118. *Hori'zo* (ὁρίζω), to fix a limit.

HORI'ZON, the limit which bounds the sight.

HORIZON'TAL, parallel to the horizon.

119. *Hu'dor,* (ὕδωρ), water.

HY'DRA, a water serpent.
HY'DRANT, a pipe for discharging water.

HYDRAUL'IC, (28), relating to the conveyance of water through pipes.

WORDS DERIVED FROM THE GREEK. 187

Hy'drogen, (94), one of the elements of water.

Hydropho'bia, (Gr. φόβος, fear), dread of water.

Hydrostat'ic, (204), relating to the weight and equilibrium of fluids.

Drop'sy, (Gr. ὕδρωψ), a disease.

120. *Ich'thus,* (ἰχθὺς), a fish.

Ichthyol'ogy, the science of fishes.

Ich'thyolite, (127), fossil fish.

121. *Id'ios,* (ἴδιος), belonging to one; peculiar.

Id'iom, peculiarity of expression or phraseology.

Id'iot,* a fool.

Idiosyn'crasy, (Gr. σύγκρασις, constitution), peculiar liability to some form of disease.

* The Greek word ἰδιώτης signifies *a private individual;* it was used also to signify *a very ignorant person.*

122. *I'dos,* (εἶδος), appearance; figure.

Cy'cloid,† (63), a geometrical curve.

Spheroid', a solid resembling a sphere.

† *Literally,* the likeness or resemblance of a circle. The termination *oid* is found in a number of words not here given, and has the same signification, viz.: *resemblance.*

123. *I'sos,* (ἴσος), equal.

Isoch'ronous, (54), performed in equal times, (as the vibration of a pendulum).

Isos'celes, (Gr. σκέλος, the leg), having two legs or sides which are equal.

124. *La'os,* (λαὸς), the people.

La'ity, the people, as distinguished from the clergy.

Lay, not clerical.

Lay'man, one who is not a clergyman.

125. *Le'the,* (λήθη), forgetfulness; oblivion.

Lethe'an, inducing forgetfulness.

Leth'argy, (20), morbid drowsiness.

126. *Lex'is,* (λέξις), a word or expression.

Lex'icon, a dictionary, (*Anglicè,* a word-book).

Lexicog'raphy, (99), the compilation of a dictionary.

127. *Li'thos*, (λίθος), a stone.

LITHOG'RAPHY, (99), writing or drawing on stone. | CHRYS'OLITE,* (55), a precious stone.

* The termination *lite*, from λίθος, is found in many names of minerals.

128. *Log'os*, (λόγος), a speech, account, or description.

ANAL'OGY, correspondence.
APOL'OGY, an excuse; a plea.
CAT'ALOGUE, (Gr. κατάλογος), a list.
DI'ALOGUE, a conversation.
| LOG'IC, the art of reasoning.
LOGOM'ACHY, (130), a war of words.
PHILOL'OGY,†(175), the science of language.

† The termination or suffix *logy*, which is found in a large number of words, is from λόγος, and denotes *art, science, description, account*, &c.

129. *Lu'sis*, (λύσις), a loosing or dissolving.

ANAL'YSIS, the separation of a compound into its constituent parts. | PARAL'YSIS, palsy.
PARALYT'IC, affected with palsy.

130. *Mach'omai*, (μάχομαι), to fight.

MONOM'ACHY, (141), single combat. | NAU'MACHY, (145), a sea-fight.

131. *Mantei'a*, (μαντεία), soothsaying; divination.

The suffix *mancy*, as in *nec'romancy*, is from this word. *Necromancy*, (Gr. νεκρός, dead), signifies *the revealing of future events by pretended communication with the dead*.

132. *Mar'tur*, (μάρτυρ), a witness; a martyr.

MAR'TYR, one who is put to death for adherence to any cause. | MAR'TYRDOM, the death of a martyr. [martyr.
PRO'TO-MARTYR, (192), the first

133. *Mathe'ma*, (μάθημα), knowledge; that which is learned.

MATHEMAT'ICS, the science of quantity. [knowledge.
POLYM'ATHY, (188), various | CHRESTOM'ATHY, (Gr. χρηστός, easily used), a series of easy lessons.

WORDS DERIVED FROM THE GREEK. 189

134. *Mechana'o*, (μηχανάω), to contrive or invent.

MECH'ANISM, the construction of a machine, engine, or instrument.

MECHAN'ICS, the science which treats of forces, the laws of motion, &c.

135. *Mel'os*, (μέλος), a song.

MEL'ODY, an agreeable succession of sounds.

MELO'DIOUS, musical; agreeable to the ear.

136. *Meteo'ros*, (μετέωρος), floating in the air.

ME'TEOR, a shooting star.
METEOROL'OGY, that science which treats of the atmosphere and its phenomena.

137. *Met'ron*, (μέτρον), a measure.

ME'TRE, arrangement of poetical feet.
MET'RICAL, pertaining to metre.
DIAM'ETER, measure through anything.

SYM'METRY, due proportion of parts.
THERMOM'ETER, (Gr. θέρμη, heat), an instrument for measuring heat.

NOTE.—The suffixes *meter* and *metry*, in such words as *barometer, geometry*, &c., are derived from μέτρον. Many words having these suffixes will be found in this book, and a reference to this paragraph usually accompanies them.

138. *Mik'ros*, (μικρός), small.

MI'CROCOSM, (58), a little world; (*man* is often so called).

MI'CROSCOPE, (200), a glass for viewing minute objects.

139. *Mi'sos*, (μῖσος), hatred.

MISAN'THROPY, (17), hatred of mankind.

MISOG'AMIST, (91), a hater of marriage.

140. *Mne'me*, (μνήμη), memory.

MNEMON'ICS, the art of memory.
AM'NESTY, (Gr. ἀμνηστεία), an act of oblivion; a general pardon.

141. *Mon'os*, (μόνος), sole; only.

MON'AD, an indivisible thing.
MONK, (Gr. μοναχός), a religious recluse.

MON'ACHISM, the condition of monks; a monastic life.

MON'ASTERY, a house of religious retirement.
MONAS'TIC, pertaining to the life of a monk.
MON'ARCH, (18), a sole ruler; a king.
MON'OGRAM, (99), a character combining several letters.

MONOP'OLIZE, (186), to become the only dealer in any commodity; to engross the whole.
MONOSYL'LABLE,* a word of one syllable.
MONOT'ONY, sameness of sound; want of variety.

* The prefix *mono* or *mon*, which is found in a number of words, is from μόνος.

142. Mor'phe, (μορφή), form; shape.

AMORPH'OUS, of irregular shape. | METAMORPH'OSE, to transform.

143. Mu'thos, (μῦθος), a fable.

MYTH'IC, fabulous.
MYTHOL'OGY, (128), the system of fables respecting heathen deities.

144. Nar'ke, (νάρκη), numbness; stupor.

NARCO'SIS, stupefaction. | NARCOT'IC, causing stupor.

145. Naus, (ναῦς), a ship.

NAU'SEA, *properly*, sea-sickness; disposition to vomit.
NAU'SEOUS, sickening; disgusting; loathsome.

NAUT'ICAL, pertaining to navigation.
NAU'TILUS, the shell-fish which sails.

146. Ne'os, (νέος), new.

NEOL'OGY, (128), a new system of doctrines.
NE'OPHYTE, (Gr. φυτὸν, a plant or shoot), a novice.

147. Ne'sos, (νῆσος), an island.

PELOPONNE'SUS, the island of Pelops, now called the Mo-re'a.
POLYNE'SIA, (188), a part of the Pacific Ocean, containing many islands.

148. Neu'ron, (νεῦρον), a cord; a nerve.

NEUROL'OGY, (128), a description of the nerves, (a department of anatomy).
NEURAL'GIA, (10), a diseased state of the nerves.
ENER'VATE, to weaken.

WORDS DERIVED FROM THE GREEK. 191

149. *No'mos,* (νόμος), a law or rule.

Anom'aly, a deviation from the general course or law.
Antino'mian, against law; undervaluing good works.

Deuteron'omy, (Gr. δεύτερος, second), the second book of the law.
Econ'omy,* see 75.

* The suffix *nomy,* which is found in many words, as in *astronomy,* (25), is from νόμος.

150. *No'sos,* (νόσος), disease.

Nosol'ogy, the description of diseases.
Nosol'ogist, one who classifies and describes diseases.

151. *O'de,* (ὠδή), an ode; a song.

Ode, a short poem or song.
Mel'ody, (135), sweetness of sound.
Pal'inode, (Gr. πάλιν, back again), a recantation.
Par'ody, a humorous imitation.
Pros'ody, the study of versification.
Psal'mody,† the singing of sacred songs.
Rhap'sody, an unconnected effusion.

† The Greek word ψάλλω signifies *to play on a stringed instrument.*

152. *O'dos,* (ὁδός), a road or way.

Ex'odus,‡ a departure.
Meth'od,§ arrangement; manner.
Pe'riod,‖ a circuit.
Syn'od,¶ an ecclesiastical convention.

‡ *Particularly,* the departure of the Israelites from Egypt.
§ Compounded of μετὰ, *according to,* and ὁδός; signifying, therefore, *the following of a way or mode.*
‖ From περὶ, *around, about,* and ὁδός.
¶ From σὺν, *together,* and ὁδός; and signifies a journeying or coming to meet one another.

153. *Od'ous,* (ὀδοὺς, ὀδόντος), a tooth.

Odontal'gia or Odontal'gy, (10), toothache.
Odontal'gic, pertaining to the toothache.

154. For the suffix *oid,* see 122.

155. *Ol'igos,* (ὀλίγος), few; small.

Ol'igarchy, (18), a government in which a few persons hold the supreme power.

13

156. On'oma, (ὄνομα), a name.

ANON'YMOUS, without name.
METON'YMY, a change of names.
PARON'YMOUS, resembling another word.

SYNON'YMOUS, conveying the same idea.
SYN'ONYM, a word conveying the same idea as another.

157. Op'tomai, (ὄπτομαι), to see.

OP'TICS, the science of light and vision.
OP'TICAL, pertaining to sight.

OPHTHAL'MIA, (Gr. ὀφθαλμός, the eye), a disease of the eyes.
SYNOP'SIS, a general view.

158. Ora'ma, (ὅραμα), a sight; a spectacle.

DIORA'MA, (Gr. διά, through), an optical machine.

PANORA'MA, (164), a complete or entire view.

159. Or'nis, (ὄρνις, ὄρνιθος), a bird.

ORNITHOL'OGY, (128), the science of birds.

ORNITH'OLITE, (127), a petrified bird.

160. Or'thos, (ὀρθός), erect; right.

OR'THODOX, (70), correct in opinion or belief.
OR'THOEPY, (81), correct pronunciation.

OR'THOEPIST, one skilled in pronunciation.
ORTHOG'RAPHY, (99), correct spelling.

161. Os'teon, (ὀστέον), a bone.

OSTEOL'OGY, (128), that part of anatomy which treats of the bones.

PERIOS'TEUM, a vascular membrane investing the bones of animals.

162. Ox'us, (ὀξύς), sharp; acid.

OXAL'IC, (Gr. ὀξαλίς, sorrel), pertaining to sorrel.
OX'YGEN, (94), the gas which generates acids.

OX'YD, a substance combined with oxygen.
PAR'OXYSM, an exacerbation or temporary violence of disease.

163. *Paidei'a*, (παιδεία*), education.

PED'AGOGUE, (8), a teacher of children.
PED'ANT, one who makes a vain display of learning.
PEDANT'IC, ostentatious of learning.
CYCLOPE'DIA, ENCYCLOPE'DIA, see 63.

* From παῖς, παιδός, a child.

164. *Pan*, (πᾶν, παντός), every; all.

PANACE'A, a universal medicine.
PANEGYR'IC,† a public eulogy.
PAN'OPLY, (Gr. ὅπλον, a weapon), complete armor.
PANORA'MA, see 158.
PAN'THEISM, (216), the doctrine that the *universe* is God.
PANTHE'ON, (216), a temple dedicated to all the gods.
PAN'TOMIME, (Gr. μιμος, a mimic), an imitation of all kinds of action, &c., without speaking. [instrument.
PAN'TOGRAPH, (99), a copying

† Compounded of πᾶν and ἀγορά, an *assembly*.

165. *Pa'thos*, (πάθος), suffering; affection; emotion.

ANTIP'ATHY, aversion.
AP'ATHY, want of feeling.
PATHET'IC, exciting emotion.
PATHOL'OGY, the science of diseases.
SYM'PATHY, fellow-feeling.

166. *Pen'te*, (πέντε), five.

PEN'TAGON, (98), a figure having five angles.
PEN'TATEUCH, (τεῦχος, a book), the five books of Moses.

167. *Pep'to*, (πέπτω), to boil; to concoct.

DYSPEP'SY, (74), difficulty of digestion.
PEP'TIC, promoting digestion.

168. *Pet'alon*, (πέταλον), a leaf.

PE'TAL, a flower-leaf.
PET'ALLED, having petals.
MONOPET'ALOUS, (141), having only one petal.

169. *Pe'tra*, (πέτρα),‡ a rock.

PET'RIFY, to convert into stone.
PETRO'LEUM, rock oil.

‡ *Peter*, (Πέτρος), the name given to one of the apostles, is from πέτρα. See Matt. xvi. 18.

170. Pha'go, (φάγω), to eat.

Esoph'agus, or Œsoph'agus,* the gullet. | Sarcoph'agus,† (196), a stone coffin.

* Compounded of οἴω, (οἴσω), *to carry*, and φίγω, and signifying, literally, *that which carries or conducts the food to the stomach*.

† The word is derived from the name of a calcareous stone anciently used by the Greeks, (λίθος σαρκοφάγος), which rapidly decomposed bodies deposited in it.

171. Phai'no, (φαίνω), to appear; to show.

Diaph'anous, transparent.
Em'phasis,‡ special stress upon some word or sentence.
Epiph'any,§ the manifestation.
Phan'tasm, Phan'tom, a fancied appearance.

Phase, or Pha'sis, (*pl.* Phases), an appearance, as of the moon.
Phenom'enon, (*pl.* Phenom'ena), an appearance; a change; an event.

‡ *Literally*, the making anything distinct or manifest.
§ The manifestation of Christ to the Gentiles.

172. Phar'makon, (φάρμακον), a drug; a medicine.

Phar'macy, the art of preparing medicine.
Pharmaceut'ic, pertaining to the art of pharmacy.

Pharmacopœ'ia, (Gr. ποιέω, to make), a dispensatory; a book describing the preparation of the several kinds of medicine.

173. Phe'mi, (φημί), to say or tell.

Blaspheme', to speak impiously.
Proph'esy, to foretell.

Proph'et, (Gr. προφήτης), one who foretells.   [phecy.
Prophet'ic, containing pro-

174. Phe'ro, (φέρω), to bear or carry.

Diaphoret'ic,‖ causing perspiration.
Met'aphor,¶ a short similitude.

Periph'ery,** circumference.
Phos'phorus,††a luminous substance.

‖ *Literally*, carrying through; i. e., causing moisture to pass through the pores of the skin.

¶ From μεταφέρω, which signifies to transfer.

** The words *periphery* and *circumference* are formed of corresponding words in the Latin and Greek. The former has a more limited signification than the latter.

†† Compounded of φῶς, light, and φέρω, and signifying, literally, *lightbearing*.

WORDS DERIVED FROM THE GREEK. 195

175. Phi'los, (φίλος), a friend or lover.

PHILADEL'PHIA,* (6), the name of a city.
PHILAN'THROPY, (17), love for mankind.
PHILOL'OGIST, (128), a student of language.
PHILOS'OPHY,† (202), the study of general laws.

* *Literally*, brotherly love; the Greek word is φιλαδελφία.
† *Literally*, love of wisdom.

176. Pho'ne, (φωνή), a sound.

PHONOL'OGY, the science which treats of the sounds uttered in human speech. [sound.
EUPHON'IC, (89), agreeable in
SYM'PHONY, *properly*, a harmony of sounds; an instrumental passage in music, designed to relieve the vocalist.

177. Phos, (φῶς), light.

PHOSPHORES'CENCE, faint luminousness. See 174.
PHOS'PHATE, a chemical salt.
PHOTOM'ETER, an instrument for measuring the intensity of light

178. Phra'zo, (φράζω), to say or relate.

PHRASE, an expression or short sentence.
PER'IPHRASE, (Gr. περί, around), circumlocution.
PAR'APHRASE, a fuller expression of the meaning of an author.
PERIPHRAS'TIC, circumlocutory.

179. Phren, (φρήν), the mind.

PHRENOL'OGY, (128), the science of the mind as connected with the brain.
PHREN'SY, madness; delirium.
FRAN'TIC or PHRENET'IC, violently delirious.

180. Phu'sis, (φύσις),‡ nature.

PHYS'ICS,§ the study or science of nature.
PHYS'ICAL, pertaining to nature.
PHYSIOL'OGY, the science of the properties and functions of animals and plants.

‡ The Latin verb *nas'cor* and the Greek verb φύω have nearly the same signification, viz.: *to come into being*. The former gives rise to the substantive *natu'ra*, and the latter to the substantive φύσις.

§ *Metaphysics* signifies, literally, *after* or *next to physics*. It is the science which treats of the relations between abstract ideas.

181. *Peira'o*, (πειράω), to try.

EMPIR'ICAL, derived from experiment. | EM'PIRIC, one who makes experiments; a quack.

182. *Pla'ne*, (πλάνη), a wandering.

PLAN'ET, a wandering or moving star. | PLAN'ETARY, pertaining to the planets.

183. *Plas'so*, (πλάσσω), to mould or shape.

PLAS'TIC, giving shape. | CAT'APLASM,* a poultice.

* The word πλάσσω signifies, primarily, to smear with any soft mixture, as wet clay.

184. *Pne'o*, (πνέω), to blow; to breathe: *Pneu'ma*, (πνεῦμα), a breath; a blast.

DYSPNŒ'A, (74), difficulty of breathing.
PNEUMAT'IC, pertaining to air. | PNEUMAT'ICS, the science which treats of the air. [lungs.
PNEUMON'IC, pertaining to the

185. *Pol'emos*, (πόλεμος), war.

POLEM'IC, *a.* controversial. | POLEM'IC, *s.* a disputant.

186. *Po'leo*, (πωλέω), to sell.

BIBLIOP'OLIST, (35), a bookseller. | MONOP'OLY, (141), exclusive sale.

187. *Po'lis*, (πόλις), a city.

METROP'OLIS, (Gr. μήτηρ, a mother), the chief city.
POLICE', the government of a city or town.
POL'ITY,† civil constitution.
POL'ITIC, prudent; sagacious.
POL'ITICS, the science of government.

† *Pol'icy* is sometimes used to denote *a course of political measures.*

188. *Po'lus*, (πολὺς), much; many.

POLYANTH'OS, (16), a plant which produces many flowers. | POL'YGON, (98), a figure having many angles.

WORDS DERIVED FROM THE GREEK. 197

Pol'ypus, (190), an insect having many feet. | Pol'ytheism, (216), the doctrine of a plurality of gods.

NOTE.—The signification of the prefix *poly* will be seen from the above examples, and it is therefore unnecessary to adduce more.

189. Pot'amos, (ποταμός), a river. See 113.

190. Pous, (πούς, ποδός), a foot.

An'tipode, one who lives on the opposite side of the globe, | and whose feet are directly opposite to ours.

191. Pras'so, (πράσσω), to do; Prak'tos, (πρακτός), done: Prag'ma, (πράγμα), a deed.

Prac'tice, frequent performance. | Pragmat'ical, officious; meddling.
Prac'ticable, that may be done. | Prax'is, a form to teach practice.

192. Pro'tos, (πρώτος), first.

Pro'tocol,* a record or registry. | Pro'totype, (222), an original or model.
Prothon'otary,† a register or clerk. | Protox'yd, the first oxyd.

* Compounded of πρώτος and κόλλα, *glue.* The word was originally used to denote the upper part of a leaf or writing, and was probably derived from the practice of gluing or pasting pieces of paper or parchment together, as in forming a long sheet for an extended document; the *protocol* was, therefore, *the first of the pasted sheets.*

† *Literally*, the chief register or clerk.

193. Psu'che, (ψυχή), the soul.

Metempsycho'sis, the transmigration of souls. | Psychol'ogy, (128), a discourse on the human soul.

194. Pur, (πύρ), fire.

Empyr'eal, formed of pure fire or light. | Pyre, a funeral pile.
Pyrolig'neous,‡ produced from [smoke. | Pyrotech'nics, (212), the art of making fire-works.

‡ Lat. *lig'num*, wood; *pyroligneous*, produced by wood and fire.

195. Rhe'o, (ῥέω), to flow.

Catarrh', a defluxion of mucus. | Diarrhe'a, purging or flux.
Hem'orrhage, (107), a flow of blood. | Rheu'matism,§ a painful disease of the limbs.

§ So called because the ancients supposed it to arise from a defluxion of humors.

196. *Sarx,* (σάρξ, σαρxός), flesh.

SAR'CASM,* a satirical remark; a taunt. | HYPERSARCO'SIS, the growth of fungous or proud flesh.

* *Literally,* a cutting or tearing of the flesh.

197. *Skep'tomai,* (σχέπτομαι), to examine or consider.

SKEP'TIC, one who doubts.
SKEP'TICAL, doubting. | SKEP'TICISM, a state or habit of doubting.

198. *Schis'ma,* (σχίσμα), a splitting; a division.

SCHISM, division or separation in a church. | SCHISMAT'IC, promoting schism.

199. *Scho'le,* (σχολή), leisure.

SCHOOL, a place of instruction.
SCHOL'AR, one who learns; a person of learning. | SCHOLAS'TIC, pertaining to a school, or to *the schools.*
SCHO'LIAST, a commentator.

200. *Sko'peo,* (σxοπέω), to observe; to watch.

EPIS'COPAL, governed by bishops.†
EPIS'COPATE, a bishopric.
SCOPE,‡ design; view; sufficient space. | STETH'ESCOPE, (Gr. στῆθος, the breast), a surgical instrument.§
TEL'ESCOPE, (Gr. τῆλε, afar), a glass for viewing distant objects.

† The Greek word, corresponding to our word *bishop,* is ἐπίσxοπος, which signifies, in general, *an overseer.*

‡ *Literally,* the object looked at or aimed at; *also,* space in which to look about.

§ The instrument is pressed against the chest or stomach, and the ear of the surgeon is then applied to it, for the purpose of distinguishing the internal disease by the sounds communicated.

NOTE.—The suffixes *scope, scopy, scopic,* are found in many terms of science and art.

201. *Si'tos,* (σίτος), food.

PAR'ASITE, ‖ a flatterer; a hanger on | PARASIT'ICAL, fawning for bread or favors.

‖ *Literally,* one who feeds beside, or at the table of another. A parasitic plant is one which grows on the stem or branch of another plant, as the mistletoe.

202. *So'phia*, (σοφία), wisdom.

PHILOS'OPHY, (175), literally, the love of wisdom.
SOPH'ISM, a specious but fallacious argument.
SOPH'ISTRY, fallacious reasoning.
UNSOPHIS'TICATED, not instructed in evil; pure.

203. *Spa'o*, (σπάω), to draw.

EPISPAS'TIC, drawing, as a blister.
SPASMOD'IC, consisting in spasm.
SPASM, an involuntary contraction of the muscles; a convulsion.

204. *Sta'sis*, (στάσις), a standing or position; a placing.

APOS'TASY, a departure from original profession.
EC'STASY,* excessive joy or delight.
HYDROSTAT'IC, (119), pertaining to the pressure of fluids.
SYS'TEM, (σύστημα),† regular method.

* *Literally*, a sudden removal from the ordinary condition; a distraction in consequence of joy.
† A *standing together*; *consistency*.

205. *Stel'lo*, (στέλλω), to send.

APOS'TLE, (ἀπό, from), one sent or commissioned.
EPIS'TLE, a writing or letter sent.

206. *Sten'os*, (στενός), narrow.

STENOG'RAPHY, (99), the art of writing in *short-hand*, i. e. in a narrow compass.
STENOG'RAPHER, a short-hand writer. [hand.
STENOGRAPH'IC, written in short-

207. *Ster'eos*, (στερεός), standing firm.

STEREOM'ETRY, (137), the art of measuring solid bodies.
STER'EOTYPE, (222), to make fixed metallic types, or plates of fixed types.

208. *Sti'chos*, (στίχος), a line; a row.

ACROS'TIC,‡ (5), a kind of poem.
DIS'TICH, a couple of poetic lines.

‡ Compounded of ἄκρον, *an extremity*, and στίχος, and signifying a poem in which the first letters of the lines form a name, when taken in order.

209. *Stro'phe*, (στροφή), a turning round.

APOS'TROPHE, a turning aside from the course of a speech, to address some absent person, as if present.

CATAS'TROPHE, a turn or issue of a course of events; *generally used to denote* a disastrous issue.

210. *Ta'phos*, (τάφος), a tomb.

CEN'OTAPH, (Gr. κενὸς, empty), a tomb or monument erected to one who is buried elsewhere.

EP'ITAPH, (ἐπὶ, upon), an inscription on a tomb; a record in honor of the dead.

211. *Tax'is*, (τάξις), arrangement; *Tak'tos*, (τακτὸς), arranged.

SYN'TAX, the construction of sentences according to established usage.

TAC'TICS, the art of directing military and naval movements.

212. *Tech'ne*, (τέχνη), art; skill.

TECH'NICAL, pertaining to an art or profession.

TECHNOL'OGY, (128), a treatise on the arts.

213. *Tes'sares*, (τέσσαρες, τέτρα), four.

TET'RACHORD, a series of four sounds.

TES'SELATED, formed in little squares.

214. *Thea'omai*, (θεάομαι), to behold.

THE'ATRE, a place of exhibition; a conspicuous place of action.

THEAT'RICAL, resembling the manner of dramatic performers.

215. *The'sis*, (θέσις), a putting or placing; *The'ma*, (θέμα), something placed.

ANATH'EMA, excommunication with curses.
EP'ITHET,* an adjective.

ANTITH'ESIS, an opposition of words or sentiments.
HYPOTH'ESIS,† a supposition.

* *Literally*, something placed upon; a descriptive word applied to anything in representing it.

† *A placing under;* which is the literal signification of the word *supposition.* See Lat. 399. A position assumed as the *basis* of an argument.

WORDS DERIVED FROM THE GREEK. 201

Paren'thesis,* a clause or sentence within another.
Syn'thesis, a putting together; a combining.
Synthet'ical, proceeding by synthesis.
Theme, a topic. [synthesis.
The'sis, a position; a proposition advanced.

* Compounded of the prepositions παρά and ἐν, signifying *in* or *beside*, and θέσις.

216. *The'os*, (θεὸς), God.

A'theism, the disbelief of the existence of a God.
The'ism, the belief of the existence of a God. [one God.
Mon'otheism, the doctrine of
Theoc'racy, (60), government by the immediate direction of God.
Theology, (128), the science of God and divine things.

217. *To'me*, (τομή), the act of cutting.

Anat'omy,† the art of dissecting.
At'om,‡ an indivisible particle.
Epit'ome,§ a compendium or summary.
Tome,‖ a volume.

† *Literally*, a cutting up.
‡ The *A* in this word is the A *privative* or *negative*. Atom therefore signifies, a thing which cannot be cut or divided.
§ The Greek word ἐπιτομή signifies *a lopping or curtailing*.
‖ *Literally*, a section, or part cut off; a portion of a work.

218. *To'nos*, (τόνος), tension; tone.

At'ony, relaxation; want of vigor.
Det'onate, to explode.
Intona'tion, manner of sounding.
Tone, tension; vigor; sound; a musical interval.
Ton'ic, increasing tension or vigor; giving tone to the system.

219. *To'pos*, (τόπος), a place.

Top'ic, a subject of discourse.
Top'ical, local.
Topog'raphy, (99), the description of a particular place.

220. *Treis*, (τρεῖς), three. See Lat. (549).

221. *Trop'os*, (τρόπος), a turning.

Trope, a figurative turning of a word from its ordinary signification.
Trop'ic, the point at which the sun appears to turn again towards the equator.

222. *Tu'pos*, (τύπος), a shape, figure, or model.

TYPE, an emblem; a model or form of a letter, used in printing.
TYP'ICAL, symbolical.

TYP'IFY, to represent by figure or symbol.
TYPOG'RAPHY, (99), the art or operation of printing.

223. *Xu'lon*, (ξύλον), wood.

XYLOG'RAPHY, (99), the art of engraving on wood.

224. *Zo'on*, (ζῶον), an animal.

ZOOL'OGY, (128), the science or description of animals.
ZOON'OMY, (149), the *science* which treats of animal life.

ZO'OPHYTE, (φυτὸν, a plant), a body partaking of the properties both of an animal and a vegetable.

CHAPTER IV.

MISCELLANEOUS TABLES.

I. CORRESPONDING DERIVATIVES.

The first column contains the word derived from the Greek, the second that derived from the Latin, and the third the corresponding word or phrase of English or Saxon origin.

N. B.—This table may be studied with advantage; but the pupil must not suppose that the corresponding words in the three columns are *synonymous*. In a few cases they are nearly so. Some of the words in the third column may be remotely derived from the Latin.

Amnesty,	oblivion,	forgetfulness.
Amorphous,	informal,	shapeless.
Analogy,	correspondence,	likeness.
Anatomy,	dissection,	a cutting up.
Anomalous,	irregular,	lawless.
Apathetic,	insensible,	unfeeling.
Apology,	excuse,	plea.
Apostle,	missionary,	messenger.
Bishop,	supervisor,	overseer.
Catalogue,	inventory,	list.
Cataract,	cascade,	waterfall.
Chronical,	enduring,	lasting.

GREEK AND LATIN PLURALS.

Chrysalis,	aurelia,	grub.
Democracy,	republic,	commonwealth.
Diaphanous,	transparent,	clear.
Dialogue,	conversation,	talk.
Didactic,	preceptive,	teaching.
Doxology,	glorification,	praise.
Dynasty,	dominion,	power.
Epitome,	abstract,	abridgment.
Elliptical,	oval,	egg-shaped.
Esophagus,	gullet,	throat.
Eucharist,	sacrament,	Lord's supper.
Eulogize,	commend,	praise.
Gnomon,	index,	pointer.
Graphite,	plumbago,	black-lead.
Lexicon,	dictionary,	word-book.
Metamorphose,	transform,	change.
Monarchical,	regal,	kingly.
Parable,	similitude,	likeness.
Pathetic,	affecting,	feeling.
Phenomenon,	appearance,	sight.
Physical,	medicinal,	healing.
Prophesy,	predict,	foretell.
Rhetoric,	oratory,	speaking.
Sphere,	globe,	ball.
Sympathy,	compassion,	fellow-feeling.
Tautology,	repetition,	a saying again.
Tetragon,	quadrangle,	a square.
Theology,	divinity,	godliness.
Tone,	sound,	noise.

II. PLURALS OF GREEK AND LATIN NOUNS WHICH ARE USED AS ENGLISH WORDS.

N. B. The pupil must not forget that in Latin and Greek words, a syllable must be given to every vowel and diphthong. He must pronounce *Apsides*, for instance, in *three* syllables. In the following table, the letter *e* with a horizontal mark over it is to be sounded as *e* in *me*.

GREEK.

Singular.		Plural.
Analysis,	The solution of any compound,	*Anal'ysēs.*
Antithesis,	Opposition or contrast,	*Antith'esēs.*
Aphis,	A minute insect on plants,	*Aph'idēs.*

Singular.		Plural.
Apsis,	A point in a planet's orbit,	*Ap'sidēs.*
Automaton,	A self-moving machine,	*Autom'ata.*
Basis,	A foundation or base,	*Ba'sēs.*
Chrysalis,	The second state of an insect,	*Chrysal'idēs.*
Crisis,	The decisive point,	*Cri'sēs.*
Criterion,	A standard of judging,	*Crite'ria.*
Diæresis,	The disjunction of vowels,	*Diær'esēs.*
Dogma,	An opinion propounded,	*Dog'mata.*
Ellipsis,	A figure of syntax,	*Ellip'sēs.*
Emphasis,	Particular stress upon a word,	*Em'phasēs.*
Ephemeris,	A kind of almanac,	*Ephemer'idēs.*
Ephemeron,	A worm that lives but one day,	*Ephem'era.*
Hypothesis,	A supposition or theory,	*Hypoth'esēs.*
Metamorphosis,	A transformation,	*Metamor'phosēs.*
Miasma,	A pernicious exhalation,	*Mias'mata.*
Oäsis,	A fertile spot in a desert,	*Oä'sēs.*
Phasis,	Form or appearance,	*Pha'sēs.*
Phenomenon,	An appearance,	*Phenom'ena.*
Thesis,	A proposition or theme,	*The'sēs.*

LATIN.

Singular.		Plural.
Addendum,	Something to be added,	*Adden'da.*
Amanuensis,	A private secretary,	*Amanuen'sēs.*
Animalcula,	A minute insect,	*Animal'culæ.*
Apex,	A tip or point,	*Ap'icēs.*
Appendix,	Something added,	*Appen'dicēs.*
Arcanum,	A secret,	*Arca'na.*
Aurora Borealis,	The northern light,	*Auro'ræ Borea'lēs*
Axis,	An axle,	*Ax'ēs.*
Calx,	A cinder,	*Cal'cēs.*
Corrigendum,	Something to be corrected,	*Corrigen'da.*
Datum,	Something given,	*Da'ta.*
Desideratum,	A thing wanted,	*Desidera'ta.*
Effluvium,	Odor; exhalation,	*Efflu'via.*
Encomium.	Praise; commendation,	*Enco'mia.*
Erratum,	A mistake,	*Erra'ta.*
Fascis,	A bundle of rods,	*Fas'cēs.*
Focus,	The point where rays meet,	*Fo'ci.*
Formula,	A prescribed form,	*For'mulæ.*
Fungus,	An excrescence,	*Fun'gi.*

LATIN WORDS AND PHRASES.

Singular.		Plural.
Genius,	A spirit,	*Ge'nii.*
Genus,	A kind or sort,	*Gen'era.*
Ignis Fatuus,	Will-with-the-wisp,	*Ignēs fat'ui.*
Index,	A pointer,	*In'dicēs.*
Lamina,	A thin plate or coat,	*Lam'inæ.*
Magus,	A wise man,	*Ma'gi.*
Medium,	Something intervening,	*Me'dia.*
Memorandum,	Something to be remembered,	*Memoran'da.*
Minutia,	A minute particular,	*Minu'tiæ.*
Momentum,	Force of motion,	*Momen'ta.*
Nebula,	A cloudy appearance,	*Neb'ulæ.*
Nucleus,	A kernel,	*Nu'clei.*
Radius,	The semi-diameter of a circle,	*Ra'dii.*
Radix,	A root,	*Rad'icēs.*
Speculum,	A mirror or looking-glass,	*Spec'ula.*
Stamen,	A fine thread in a flower,	*Stam'ina.*
Stimulus,	A goad or incitement,	*Stim'uli.*
Stratum,	A layer or bed,	*Stra'ta.*
Vertex,	The top of anything,	*Ver'ticēs*
Viscus,	An intestine or entrail,	*Vis'cera.*
Vortex,	A whirlpool,	*Vor'ticēs.*

III. LATIN WORDS AND PHRASES, WHICH ARE FREQUENTLY EMPLOYED BY ENGLISH WRITERS.

LATIN WORDS.

Aborig'inēs, the original inhabitants of a country.
A'lias, otherwise.
Al'ibi, elsewhere.
An'glicè,* in English.
Ca'veat, let him be cautious.
Con'tra, on the other hand.
Dēlē, expunge.
Detri'tus, matter worn off.
Equilib'rium, equality of weight.
Er'go, therefore.
Excerp'ta, extracts.
Exu'viæ, cast skins of animals.
Ex'it,† departure.
Ex-tem'pore, at the time; i. e., without previous writing.
Facē'tiæ, witty sayings.
Fi'at, let it be done.
Fi'nis, the end.
Gra'tis, for nothing.
Hia'tus, an opening or gap.

* See the remark at the beginning of Table II.
† A verb, signifying, *he* (*she or it*) *goes out.*

Im'petus, tendency to motion.
Imprima'tur, let it be printed.
Impri'mis, in the first place.
Impromp'tu, with promptness; off hand.
In'terim, in the mean time.
Interreg'num, the time between two reigns.
I'tem, also.
Ma'nēs, departed spirits.
Max'imum, the greatest quantity.
Min'imum, the least quantity.
Memorabil'ia, (*pl.*), memorable events.
Om'nēs, all.
Om'nibus, for all.
O'nus, a burden.

Pas'sim, everywhere.
Quon'dam, formerly; once.
Recipē, See Lat. 47.
Resur'gam, I shall rise again.
Seria'tim, in regular order.
Sim'ile, a comparison.
Syl'labus, (Gr. σύν, together, and λάβω, to take), a compendium.
Vac'uum, an empty space.
Vale! farewell!
Verba'tim, word for word.
Ver'sus, against.
Veto, I forbid it.
Vi'a, by the way of.
Videl'icet, to wit.
Vi'ce, in the place of.
Vul'go, commonly.

LATIN PHRASES.

Ab ini'tio,* from the beginning.
An'nus mirab'ilis, a year of wonders.
Ab o'vo, from the egg; i. e., from the birth or origin.
Ad captan'dum, for the purpose of taking, i. e., pleasing.
Ad infini'tum, to an unlimited extent.
Ad lib'itum, at pleasure.
Ad valo'rem, according to value.
Al'ma ma'ter, gentle mother.
A'mor pa'triæ, love of country.
Absente re'o, the accused person being absent.
A fortio'ri,* with stronger reason.
A prio'ri, beforehand; from previous knowledge.   [trial.
A posterio'ri, afterwards; from

Argumen'tum ad hom'inem, an argument particularly applicable to the person to whom it is offered.
Au'di al'teram par'tem, hear the other side; i. e., hear both sides.
Bo'na fide, in good faith.
Cacoë'thes scriben'di, a ridiculous fondness for writing.
Ca'put mor'tuum, the lifeless head.
Cat'eris par'ibus, other things being the same.
Com'pos men'tis, of sound mind.
Con'tra bo'nos mo'res, contrary to good manners.
Co'pia verbo'rum, abundance of words.

* *T* is here sounded like *sh*.

LATIN PHRASES.

Cui* bo'no? for what good? i. e. of what advantage? or, of advantage to whom?
Cum mul'tis a'liis, with many others.
Cum privile'gio, with privilege.
De fac'to, in fact.
De ju're, by right.
De gus'tibus non disputan'dum, about matters of taste it is idle to dispute.
De'i gra'tia, by the grace of God.
De no'vo, anew.
De'o volen'te, God willing.
De'sunt cœt'era, the rest are wanting.
Dram'atis perso'næ, the characters represented in a play.
Duran'te placi'to, during pleasure.
Ec'ce† ho'mo, behold the man! See N. T. John xix. 5.
Ex an'imo, from the mind; i. e. sincerely.
Ex cathe'dra, from the chair of authority.
Ex conces'sis, from points conceded.
Ex'eunt om'nes, they all go out or off.
Ex offi'cio, by virtue of the office.
Ex par'te, on one side only.
Ex post fac'to (bad Latin), after the deed.
Fac sim'ile, an exact copy.
Ge'nius lo'ci, the genius of the place.
Id ge'nus om'ne, all that class or sort.
In for'mâ pau'peris, as a pauper.
In fo'ro conscien'tiæ, at the bar of conscience.

In lim'ine, on the threshold; at the outset.
In o'tio, at ease.
In pro'pria perso'na, in his own person.
In sta'tu quo, in the state in which it was.
In terro'rem, as a warning.
In to'to, entirely.
In tran'situ, on the way or passage.
Ip'se dix'it, literally, he himself said so; mere assertion.
Ip'so fac'to, by the fact itself.
Ju're divi'no, by a divine right.
Ju're huma'no, by human law.
Jus gen'tium, the law of nations.
Lap'sus lin'guæ, a slip of the tongue.
Lex talio'nis, the law of retaliation.
Licen'tia va'tum, poetic license.
Lo'cum te'nens, literally, holding the place; a substitute.
Lu'sus natu'ræ, a sport or freak of nature.
Mag'na char'ta (karta), the great charter.
Ma'lum in se, an evil in itself.
Memen'to mo'ri, remember that thou must die.
Me'um et tu'um, mine and thine.
Mirab'ile dic'tu, strange to tell.
Mo'dus operan'di, the manner of operating.
Mul'tum in par'vo, a great deal in a small space.
Ne plus ul'tra, the greatest extent attainable; *literally,* nothing beyond.
Ne quid ni'mis, not too much of one thing.

* Pronounced *ky.*   † Pronounced *ek'se.*

14

Nil desperan'dum, nothing to be despaired of.
No'lens vo'lens, willing or not.
No'li me tan'gere, do not touch me.
Non com'pos men'tis, not in right mind.
Non est inven'tus, it is not found.
O'tium cum dignita'te, ease with dignity.
Par nob'ile fra'trum, a noble pair of brothers.
Pa'ri pas'su, with equal pace.
Par'ticeps crim'inis, a partaker of the crime.
Per se, by itself.
Pos'se comita'tus (bad Latin), the civil force.
Pri'ma fa'ciĕ, at first view.
Pri'mum mob'ile, the first mover.
Pro a'ris et fo'cis, for our altars and homes.
Pro bono pub'lico, for the public good.
Pro et con, for and against.
Pro for'ma, for form's sake.
Pro ra'ta, in proportion.
Pro tem'pore (*abbreviated*, pro tem.), for the time.
Quan'tum suffi'cit, as much as is sufficient.
Quid pro quo, an equivalent.
Quo'ad hoc, with respect to this.
Quo an'imo, with what temper or intention.
Res pub'lica, the common weal.
Rex et regi'na, the king and queen.

Secun'dum ar'tem, according to art or professional rule.
Si'ne di'e, without fixing the day.
Si'ne qua non (*literally*, without which it cannot be done), an indispensable condition.
Sub pœ'na, under fear of penalty.
Su'i gen'eris (*literally*, of its own kind), unique.
Sum'mum bo'num, the chief good.
Su'um cui'que (ky'quy), to every one his due.
Tem'pus fu'git, time flies.
To'ties quo'ties,* as often as.
To'to cœ'lo, by the breadth of the sky.
Tri'a junc'ta in u'no, three joined in one.
U'na vo'ce, with one voice.
U'tile cum dul'ci, the useful with the agreeable.
Ut su'pra, as above.
Ut in'fra, as below.
Va'de me'cum, (*literally*, come with me), a guide-book.
Ve'ni, vi'di, vi'ci, I came, saw, conquered.
Ver'bum sapien'ti, a word is enough to the wise.
Vi'ce ver'sa, the order being reversed.
Vi et ar'mis, with force and arms.
Vi'va vo'ce, with the living voice.
Vox et prete'rea ni'hil, voice, and nothing else.

---

* In these words *t* is sounded like *sh*.

IV. FRENCH WORDS AND PHRASES.

As French words and phrases are very frequently introduced into English conversation and writing, it is desirable that every person should have some idea of the pronunciation and signification of those, at least, which are most common. The following account of some of the French sounds will perhaps be sufficient for the purposes of this chapter.

a, short, sounds like   *a*   in the English word *fat*.
â, long,   "   *a*   "   *arm*.
e, at the end of monosyllables, sounds like *u* in *tub;* and is mute at the end of other words.
é, sounds like   *a*   in *able*.
è,   "   *e*   in *met*.
ê,   "   *e*   in *there*.
i, short,   "   *i*   in *idiot*.
î, long,   "   *ee* in *eel*.
o, short, "   *o*   in *ornithology*.
ô, long,   "   *o*   in *old*.
u   no similar sound in English.*
ou, sounds like *oo* in *cool*.
an,   "   *an* in *want*.
in,   "   *an* in *pang*.
on,   "   *on* in *long*.
eur,   "   *ur* in *fur*.
oi,   "   *wa* in *water*.
oir,   "   *war* in *warfare*.
oin,   "   *oo* in *cool,* and *an* in *pang*.
ail,   "   *a*   in *fat*, and *lli* in *billiard*.
eil,   "   *e*   in *there*, and *lli* in *billiard*.
euil, "   *u*   in *tub*, and *lli* in *billiard*.
gn,   "   *ni* in *union*.
j,   "   *s*   in *pleasure*.
ch,   "   *sh* in *shark*.

* Although the sound of the French *u* cannot be represented by English letters, the following rule will enable the pupil to form some idea of it. Place your lips as if about to pronounce *ou* as in *soup,* and bring the extremity of your tongue against your lower teeth. With your organs in this position, you will be likely to produce the sound of the French *u.*

FRENCH WORDS.

N. B.—In the following list of words and phrases, the representation of the French sound, which is given in parenthesis, is figured in accordance with the above table of sounds. A letter having *no mark* over it is to be sounded as that which has no mark in the table; the pupil must not suppose that he is to give it the English sound. The accents are only *marks indicating sound*, according to the above table. When the letter *n* is italicised in the parenthesis, it is to have the English sound of *n*, and not the French nasal sound.

Amateur, (a ma teur), an admirer.
Amour, (a mour), a love affair.
Bagatelle, (ba ga tèl), a trifle.
Beau, (bô), a fashionable man.
Belle, (bèll), a fashionable woman.
Bijou, (bi jou), a jewel or gem.
Bonhommie, (bon om î), good nature.
Boudoir, (bou doir), a private room.
Bulletin, (bul tin), a daily report.
Bureau, (bu rô), an office; a writing desk.
Caisson, (kê son), a chest or case.
Canaille, (ka nail), the rabble.
Champêtre, (shan pêtr'), rural.
Château, (shâ tô), a country seat.
Ci-devant, (sid van), formerly.
Clique, (clik), a party or faction.
Connoisseur, (kon nê seur), a skilful judge.
Contour, (kon tour), outline of a figure.
Corps, (kor), a body of men.
Cortége, (kor téj), a train of attendants.
Coterie, (kot rî), a company.
Coup, (kou), a stroke or blow.
Débris, (dé brî), broken remains.

Début, (dé bu), first appearance.
Dénouement, (dé nou man), the unravelling of a plot.
Devoir, (dvoir), duty.
Dépôt, (dé pô), a store or magazine.
Deshabillé, (dé za bi li é), an undress.
Domicile, (do mi sil), abode.
Douceur, (dou seur), a bribe or present.
Éclaircissement, (é clèr sisman), explanation.
Éclat, (é clâ), splendor.
Elève, (élèv), a pupil.
Élite, (é lit), the choice part; the flower.
Embonpoint, (an bon poin), jolly, plump.
Embouchure, (an bou shur), the mouth of a river.
Encore, (an cor), again.
Ennui, (an nu î), wearisomeness.
Entrée, (an tré: é is *long*), entrance.
Enveloppe, (en vlop), a cover.
Épaulette, (é pô lèt), a shoulder-knot.
Estafette, (ès ta fèt), an express.
Etiquette, (é ti kèt), ceremony.
Façade, (fa sad), front.
Fête, (fêt), a feast or festival.
Fracas, (fra câ), a squabble.
Gendarmes, (jan darm), soldiers of the police.

FRENCH PHRASES.

Goût, (gou), taste.
Hauteur, (hô teur), haughtiness.
Lever, (levé), a morning assembly at court.
Liqueur, (li keur), a cordial.
Manœuvre, (ma neuvr), a trick.
Mêlée, (mê lé), a conflict; a fray.
Messieurs, (mè si eû), gentlemen; used as the plural of Mr.
Mignonette, (mi gno nèt), a sweet smelling flower.
Morceau, (mor sô), a morsel.
Naïveté, (na iv té), ingenuousness.
Nonchalance, (non sha lans), indifference.
Nonpareil, (non pa reil), matchless.
Outré, (ou tré), preposterous.
Parole, (pa rol), word of promise.
Parterre, (par tair), a flowerbed.
Patois, (pa toi), provincialism.
Penchant, (pan shan), inclination.
Prairie, (prè rî), meadow land.
Protégé, (pro té jé), one that is patronized. [soned dish.
Ragoût, (ra gou), a highly seasoned dish.
Recherché, (re shèr shé), sought out; exquisite.

Rencontre, (ran kontr'), an unexpected meeting.
Rendez-vous, (ran dé vou), place of meeting.
Réservoir, (ré zair voir), a reserve of water, &c.
Restaurateur, (rès to ra teur), a tavern-keeper.
Rouge, (rouj), red paint.
Ruse, (ruz), a stratagem.
Sans, (san), without.
Savant, (sa van), a learned man.
Sobriquet, (so bri kè), a nickname.
Soi-disant, (soi di zan), pretended, self-styled.
Soirée, (soi ré, é *is long*), an evening party.
Souvenir, (souv nir), remembrance.
Suite, (su it), retinue, series.
Surtout, (sur tou), an outer coat.
Tapis, (ta pi), the carpet.
Tirade, (ti rad), a long train of harsh language.
Toilette, (toi lèt), a dressing table.
Tour, a journey.
Trait, (trè), a feature.
Unique, (u nik), singular.

FRENCH PHRASES.

Aide-de-Camp, (aid de kan), assistant to a general.
A la mode, (a la mod), in the fashion.
A propos, (a pro pô), seasonably; by-the-bye.
Au fait, (ô fè), to the point or business.
Beau monde, (bô mond), the gay world.
Belles lettres, (bèl lètr), polite literature.
Billet doux, (bi liè dou), a love letter.

Bon gré, mal gré, with good or ill will.
Bon mot, (bon mô), a witticism.
Bon ton, high fashion.
Bon vivant, (bon vivan), a high liver.
Carte blanche, (cart blansh : *art* is short), blank paper.
Chef-d'œuvre, (shè deuvr'), a master-piece.
Chevaux de frise, (shvôd'friz), a sort of spiked fence.
Comme il faut, (kom il fô), as it should be.
Congé d'élire, (kon jé dé lir), permission to elect.
Coup d'état, (kou dé tâ), a stroke of policy.
Coup de grâce, (koud grâss), the finishing stroke.
Coup de main, (koud min), a bold stroke.
Coup d'œil, (kou deuil), a glance of the eye.
Dejeûner à la fourchette, (dé jeu né a la fourshèt), a breakfast with meat, fowls, &c.
De pied en cap, (de pié tan kap), from head to foot.
Dernier ressort, (dair niè 'rsort), a last resort.
Dieu et mon droit, (dieu é mon droi : *eu* as *u* in *tub*), God and my right.
Double entendre, (doubl an tandr'), double meaning.
En masse, (an mas), in a body.
Entre nous, (an tr'nou), between ourselves.
Esprit de corps, (ès pri de kor), the spirit of the corps or body; mutual animation.
Faux pas, (fô pâ), a fault; misconduct.
Feu de joie, (feud joi), a discharge of fire-arms at a rejoicing.
Femme de chambre, (fam de shambr), a chambermaid.
Fête champêtre, (fêt shan pêtr), a feast out of doors.
Haut ton, (hô ton), the highest style or fashion.
Honi soit qui mal y pense, (oni soi ki mal i pans), evil be to him that evil thinks.
Hors de combat, (or de kom bâ), disabled.
Je ne sais quoi, (jeun sé koi), I know not what.
Jet d'eau, (jè dô), a water-spout; a fountain.
Jeu d'esprit, (je dès pri), a witticism.
Jeu de mots, (jeud mô), a play upon words.
Maître d'hôtel, (mêtr' dô tel), a tavern-keeper.
Mauvaise honte, (mô vèz hont), false modesty, bashfulness.
N'importe, (nan port), it is no matter.
Nom de guerre, (nond gair), an assumed name.
Nous verrons, (nou vèrron), we shall see.
On dit, (on di), *literally,* they say; a flying report.
Petit maître, (pti mêtr'), a fop.
Qui vive, (ki viv), look out.
Ruse de guerre, (ruz de gair), a stratagem of war.

ITALIAN PHRASES.

Sang froid, (san froi), coolness; indifference.
Tête à tête, (tait a tait), a private conversation.
Tout ensemble, (tout an sambl'), the whole.
Valet de chambre, (valèd chambr'), a gentleman's servant.
Vis à vis, (vi za vi), face to face.
Vive le roi, (viv le roi), long live the king.

ITALIAN PHRASES.

Che sarà, sarà, (kè sahrah', sahrah'), whatever will be, will be.
Chi tace confessa, (kee ta'tshe confeh'sa), silence is consent.
Cicerone, (tshee tsheh rone), he who accompanies a stranger to view the curiosities of a city, &c.
Con amore, (con ahmo're), with love; with earnestness and zeal.
Erba mala presto cresce, (erba mah'la pres'to cresh'), ill weeds grow apace.
In petto, (in peh'to), within the breast; held in reserve.
Majordomo, (mayordoh'mo), a steward or chief servant.
Mezzo termine, (may'dzo ter'me-neh), a middle course.
Pian piano, si va lontano, (pean' peah'no, se vah' lontah'no), he who goes slowly goes far; little strokes fell great oaks.
Se non é vero, é ben trovato, (se non eh veh'ro, eh ben trovah'to), if it be not true, it is well imagined or feigned.

V. ABBREVIATIONS.

A. B. or B. A. *ar'tium bacca-lau'reus,* bachelor of arts.
Abp. archbishop.
A. C. *an'te Chris'tum,* before Christ.
Acct. account.
A. D. *an'no dom'ini,* in the year of our Lord.
Admr. administrator.
Ala. Alabama.
A. M. *an'te merid'iem,* before noon; or, *an'no mun'di,* in the year of the world; or, *ar'tium magis'ter,* master of arts.
Anon. anonymous.
Apr. April.
Ark. Arkansas.
Att'y. Attorney.
A. U. C. *an'no ur'bis con'ditæ,* in the year of the city, i. e. Rome.
Bart. baronet.
Bbl. barrel.

B. C. before Christ.
B. D. *baccalau'reus divinita'tis,* bachelor of divinity.
Cap. *ca'put,* chapter or head.
Capt. captain.
C. A. S. *Connecticuten'sis Academiæ Socius,* fellow of the Connecticut Academy.
Chron. Chronicles.
Co. company.
Col. colonel.
Coll. college.
Com. commodore.
Cor. Corinthians.
C. P. Common Pleas.
Cr. Creditor.
Cts. cents.
Cwt. hundred weight.
D. C. District of Columbia.
D. D. *divinita'tis doc'tor,* doctor of divinity.
Dec. December.
Del. Delaware.
Deg. degree.
Dept. deputy.
Deut. Deuteronomy.
Do. or Ditto, the same.
Dr. doctor, or debtor.
D. V. *Dé'o volen'te,* God willing.
Dwt. pennyweight.
Eccl. Ecclesiastes.
Ed. editor or edition.
E. g. *exem'pli gra'tia,* for example.
Eng. English.
Ep. epistle.
Eph. Ephesians.
Esq. esquire.
Ex. Exodus; example.
Exr. executor.
Feb. February.
Fig. figure.
Fla. Florida.
Fol. folio.

Fr. French.
F. R. S. fellow of the Royal Society.
Ga. Georgia.
Gal. Galatians.
Gall. gallon.
Gen. general; Genesis.
Gent. gentleman.
Geo. George.
Gov. governor.
Gr. grain.
G. R. *Geor'gius Rex,* King George.
Heb. Hebrews.
Hhd. hogshead.
H. M. his or her majesty.
H. B. M. his or her Britannic majesty.
Hon. honorable.
Hund. hundred.
Ia. or Ind. Indiana.
Ib. *ibi'dem,* in the same place.
Id. *i'dem,* the same.
I. e. *id est,* that is.
I. H. S. *Ie'sus hom'inum Sal'va'tor,* Jesus, the Saviour of men.
Ill. Illinois.
Incog. *incog'nito,* unknown.
Inst. instant, i. e. present, at hand.
Isa. Isaiah.
Jac. Jacob.
Jan. January.
Jas. James.
Jno. John.
Jon. Jonathan.
Jos. Joseph.
Josh. Joshua.
Jun. *jun'ior,* younger.
K. B. knight of the bath.
Kt. knight.
Ky. Kentucky.
La. Louisiana.
Lam. Lamentations.

ABBREVIATIONS.

Lat. latitude.
L. C. Lower Canada.
Ldp. Lordship.
Lev. Leviticus.
Lieut. lieutenant.
LL. D. *le'gum doc'tor*, doctor of laws.
Lon. longitude.
L. S. *lo'cus sigil'li*, the place of the seal.
M. *mil'le*, a thousand.
Maj. major.
Mal. Malachi.
Mar. March.
Mass. or Ms. Massachusetts.
Matt. Matthew.
M. C. member of Congress.
Md. Maryland.
M. D. *medici'næ doc'tor*, doctor of medicine.
Me. Maine.
Messrs. Messieurs.
Mi. Mississippi.
Mich. Michigan.
Mo. Missouri.
M. P. member of parliament.
Mr. Mister.
Mrs. Mistress.
MS. manuscript.
MSS. manuscripts.
N. B. *no'ta be'ne*, mark well; i. e. take particular notice.
N. C. North Carolina.
N. E. New England; north east.
Nem. con. *nem'ine contradicen'te*, no one expressing dissent.
N. H. New Hampshire.
N. J. New Jersey.
No. number.
Nov. November.
N. S. Nova Scotia.
Numb. Numbers.
N. Y. New York.

O. Ohio.
Obj. objection.
Obs. obsolete.
Obt. obedient.
Oct. October.
O. S. old style.
Oxon. *Oxo'nia*, Oxford.
Oz. ounces.
Pa. or Penn. Pennsylvania.
Part. participle.
Pet. Peter.
P. M. post-master; or, *post merid'iem*, after noon.
P. M. G. post-master general.
P. O. post-office.
Pres. president.
Prof. professor.
Ps. psalm.
P. S. *post scrip'tum*, (written afterwards), postscript.
Q. or Qu. question.
q. d. *qua'si dic'tum*, as much as to say.
Q. E. D. *quod e'rat demonstran'dum*, which was to be demonstrated.
q. l. *quan'tum li'bet*, as much as you please.
q. s. *quantum suffi'cit*, as much as is necessary.
q. v. *quod vi'de*, which see.
Recd. received.
Rep. representative.
Rev. reverend; Revelation.
R. I. Rhode Island.
R. N. royal navy.
Rom. Romans.
Rt. Hon. right honorable.
S. A. South America.
S. C. South Carolina.
Sec. secretary; second.
Sen. senior; senator.
Sept. September.
Sol. Solomon.
Sq. square.

ss. *scil'icet*, to wit; namely.
St. street; saint.
S. T. D. *sand'tæ theolo'giæ doc'-tor*, doctor of theology.
Tenn. Tennessee.
Thess. Thessalonians.
Thos. Thomas.
Tim. Timothy.
Tit. Titus.
Tr. translator; treasurer.
U. C. Upper Canada.
Ult. *ul'timo (men'se)*, the last (month).
U. S. A. United States of America.
V. or vid. *vide*, see.
Va. Virginia.
Viz. *videl'icet*, to wit.
vs. *ver'sus*, against.

Vt. Vermont.
W. I. West Indies.
Wm. William.
Wp. worship.
Wt. weight.
Xmas, Christmas.
Yd. yard.
Yͤ ancient mode of writing *the*.
Yͬ your.
& *et*, and.
&c. *et cet'era*, and the other things, i. e. and so forth.
4to. quarto.
8vo. octavo.
12mo. duodecimo.
18mo. *duodeviges'imo*, eighteenth.
24to. *vices'imo quar'to*, twenty-fourth.

VI. WORDS DERIVED CHIEFLY FROM CLASSICAL PROPER NAMES.

Æo'LIAN, *a.* pertaining to Æ'olus, the fabled god of the winds.
ALEXAN'DRIAN, *a.* of or pertaining to Alexandria, a city of Egypt.
ANACREON'TIC, *a.* resembling the style of Anac'reon, a Grecian poet, who wrote amorous and Bacchanalian odes.
AO'NIAN, *a.* belonging to Ao'nia, a district of Greece in which was situated Mount Helicon, sacred to the Muses.
ARCA'DIAN, *a.* belonging to Arca'dia, a mountainous part of Greece, where dwelt herdsmen who cultivated pastoral music in a high degree.

AR'GIVE, *s.* a native of Argos.
ARISTOTE'LIAN, *a.* relating to the doctrines of Ar'istotle.
ARMOR'IC, *a.* pertaining to Brittany, in France.
AT'TIC, *a.* pertaining to At'tica, a district of Greece, in which Athens was situated.
AT'TICISM, *s.* an imitation of the Attic style; an elegant expression.
AUGE'AN, *a.* relating to Auge'as, king of Elis in Greece, whose stables, containing vast numbers of cattle, and not having been cleansed for many years, Hercules is fabled to have cleansed in one day, by turning a river through them.

Augus'tan, *a.* pertaining to Augustus the Roman emperor.

Bodlei'an, *a. library*, a library in Oxford, (Eng.) named after its founder, Sir Thomas Bodley.

Cadme'an, relating to Cadmus, who, it is supposed, brought the letters of the Greek alphabet from Phœnicia, about 1500 years before Christ.

Cap'itoline, *a.* pertaining to the temple of Jupiter Capitoli'nus at Rome.

Carte'sian, *a.* relating to the philosophy of Des Cartes.

Casta'lian, *a.* pertaining to Casta'lia, a fountain on Mount Parnassus, sacred to the Muses.

Cel'tic, *a.* pertaining to the Cel'tæ, a people who came from Asia and spread themselves over a great part of Europe.

Chalda'ic, *s.* the language of the ancient Chaldæ'ans.

Cimme'rian, *a.* relating to the ancient Cimme'rii, a people living near the Pa'lus Mæo'tis, now called the Sea of Azof. Their country was fabled to be shrouded in darkness and gloom.

Circe'an, *a.* pertaining to Cir'ce, a fabulous magician.

Coper'nican, *a.* relating to Coper'nicus, the celebrated European astronomer.

Cyclo'pean, *a.* relating to the Cyclops, fabulous giants who had but one eye, situated in the centre of the forehead. Certain massive remains of architecture are called Cyclopean in allusion to the superstitious notion that they were the work of an ancient race of giants.

Del'phic, *a.* pertaining to the city of Delphi, in Greece.

Elys'ian, *a.* pertaining to Elys'ium, the place represented in the classic mythology as the abode of the blessed in another world.

Epicu'rean, *a.* relating to Epicu'rus, an ancient philosopher who taught that men should seek pleasure as the supreme good and the object of existence.

Er'in, Ireland.

Erse, *s.* the language of the Highlands of Scotland; *a.* pertaining to the ancient Scotch.

Gae'lic, *s.* the language of the Highlands of Scotland.

Gor'dian, *a.* intricate, difficult; from Gordius, a Phrygian husbandman, who, on being made king by the oracle of Apollo, tied the yoke of his chariot to the pole, in a knot so intricate, that no one could find out where it began or ended. It was pretended, that whoever should loose this knot should be king of all Asia. Alexander cut it with his sword.

Goth'ic, *a.* respecting the country or language of the Goths; rude, uncivilized; denoting a style of architecture, whose principal characteristic is the pointed arch.

GREGO'RIAN, a. denoting the style of Pope Gregory XIII.
HELVE'TIAN, a. of or pertaining to Switzerland.
HESPE'RIAN, a. pertaining to the Hesperides; or to Hesperia, an ancient name of Italy.
HORA'TIAN, a. imitating Horace.
HYBLE'AN, pertaining to Hy'bla, a town in Sicily, famous in ancient times for its honey.
ION'IC Order, an order of architecture, invented by the people of Ionia.
JU'LIAN, a. denoting the computation of time by the Julian calendar, so called from Julius Cæsar.
LACEDÆMO'NIAN, a. of or pertaining to Lacedæmon or Sparta, a city of Greece :—s. a native of Lacedæmon.
LETHE'AN, a. of or pertaining to the fabulous river Lethe; causing oblivion.
LES'BIAN, a. of or pertaining to the island of Lesbos, the residence of Sappho the ancient poetess.
LYD'IAN, a. soft and slow; an epithet given by the Greeks to one of their kinds or modes of music.
MACCHIAVEL'LIAN, belonging to the political school of Macchiavelli, the celebrated Florentine politician, whose doctrines have been regarded as highly pernicious.
MOS'LEM, s. a Mussulman or Mohammedan believer; the plural of Mussulman is Mussulmans; the syllable *man* is not from the English word *man*.

NICENE', a. of or pertaining to Nice, in Asia Minor.
NOM'ADES, s. persons who are continually changing their place of residence; erratic hordes.
OLYM'PIAD, s. the time which elapsed between the celebrations of the Olympic Games, namely, four complete years; a noted era among the Greeks, who by it computed their time.
OLYM'PIAN, OLYM'PIC, a. of Olympia, a town of Elis in Peloponnesus, where famous games dedicated to Jupiter Olympius, were performed.
PA'RIAN, a. of or pertaining to Paros, an island of the Grecian archipelago, famous for its marble. In this island, 264 years before Christ, was engraved in capital letters, on marble, a chronicle of the city of Athens. It was presented by the Earl of Arundel to the University of Oxford, and from him takes the name of the Arunde'lian marbles.
PARMESAN', a. of or pertaining to, or made at Parma, in Italy.
PARNAS'SIAN, a. of or pertaining to Mount Parnassus, which was sacred to the Muses.
PELAS'GI, PELAS'GIANS, s. a people of Greece, so named from Pelasgus, their founder and first king.
PELOPONNE'SIAN, a. of or pertaining to Peloponnesus, in Greece; now the Morea.
PERSEPOL'ITAN, a. of or pertaining to Persepolis.
PIE'RIAN, a. of or pertaining to

Pieria, the fabled birthplace of the Muses.

PROME'THEAN, *a.* resembling Prometheus, who surpassed all mankind in cunning, and who is fabled to have stolen fire from heaven and given it to man, for which act he was punished by being chained to a rock where a vulture preyed upon his liver which was constantly renewed.

PROTE'AN, *a.* resembling Proteus, a seagod who could assume various forms.

PTOLEMA'IC, *a.* pertaining to the astronomical system of Claudius Ptolemy, an Egyptian philosopher; in which it is supposed the earth is fixed in the centre of the universe.

PU'NIC, *a.* of or pertaining to Carthage.

PYR'RHONISM, *s.* skepticism; from Pyr'rho, a Grecian philosopher, who doubted of everything.

PYTHAGO'REAN, *a.* denoting the discipline of Pythagoras:—*s.* a follower of Pythagoras.

PYTH'IAN *Games*, games instituted by Apollo, in commemoration of his victory over the serpent Python.

PY'THONESS, *s.* a witch.

ROMA'IC, *s.* the modern Greek language; so called in reference to the extension of Roman power over Greece.

SARACEN'IC, *a.* denoting the architecture of the Saracens, or the modern Gothic; of or pertaining to the Saracens, a celebrated people that came, some centuries ago, from the desert of Arabia:—they were the first disciples of Mohammed.

SARDON'IC *Grin*, an involuntary show of laughter, occasioned by a convulsive distortion of the muscles of the mouth; so called from the herb *sardonia*, which, it is said, produces it.

SATURNA'LIAN, *a.* sportive, loose, like the feasts of Saturn.

STA'GIRITE, *s.* a native of Stagira, a town of Macedonia, famed as the birthplace of Aristotle, who is hence called *the Stagirite.*

STENTO'RIAN, *a.* exceedingly loud or strong; from Stentor, a Grecian, whose voice, Homer tells us, was as loud as the united voices of fifty men.

STENTOROPHON'IC, *a.* loudly speaking or sounding:—*stentorophonic tube*, a speaking trumpet.

STY'GIAN, *a.* pertaining to the Styx, a fabulous river in the infernal regions.

SYB'ARITE, *s.* an inhabitant of Sybaris, once a powerful city of Calabria, whose inhabitants were proverbially effeminate and luxurious; one of whom, it is said, was unable to sleep, because one of the rose leaves which composed his bed was doubled under him.

TARTA'REAN, *a.* of or pertaining to Tartarus; the name given, in ancient mythology, to the place of punishment in another world.

TARPE'IAN ROCK, a name given to the height on which stood the capitol in ancient Rome.

THE'BAN, a. of or pertaining to Thebes; s. a native of Thebes.

TUS'CAN *Order*, an order in architecture, which had its origin in Tuscany.

TYR'IAN, a. of or pertaining to the city of Tyre, an ancient city of Phœnicia.

GEOGRAPHICAL DERIVATIVES, &c.

AF'GHAN, s. a native of Afghanistan.

ALGERINE', s. a native of Algiers; a. of or pertaining to Algiers.

AL'PINE, a. of or pertaining to, or resembling the Alps.

AN'GLICAN, a. English.

AN'GLO-DA'NISH, a. pertaining to the English Danes.

AN'GLO-NOR'MAN, a. pertaining to the English Normans.

AN'GLO-SAX'ON, a. pertaining to the English Saxons.

AR'ABS, s. tribes inhabiting the whole African coast of the Mediterranean, Egypt, Abyssynia, and the eastern side of Africa as far as the Cape of Good Hope, as well as the peninsula of Arabia in Asia.

AR'ABIC, a. of Arabia; s. the language of Arabia.

AR'NAUT, s. an Albanian.

ARRAGONESE', s. the natives of Arragon, in Spain. [Asia.

ASIAT'IC, a. of or pertaining to

ASSAMESE', s. the natives of Assam. [Babylon.

BABYLO'NISH, a. pertaining to

BEL'GIC, a. of or pertaining to Belgium. [Bengal.

BENGALESE', s. the natives of

BRAZIL'IAN, a. of or pertaining to Brazil.

BRIT'ON, s. a native of Britain.

BURMESE', a. of or pertaining to Ava, or the Birman empire; s. the natives of Ava.

BYZAN'TINE, a. of or pertaining to Byzantium, now Constantinople.

CAF'FRE, s. a native of Caffraria in Africa.

CALABRESE', CALA'BRIAN, a. of or pertaining to Calabria; s. a native of Calabria.

CALEDO'NIAN, a. of or pertaining to Scotland; s. a native of Scotland.

CAM'BRIAN, a. of or pertaining to Wales; s. a Welshman.

CAM'BRO-BRIT'ON, s. a Welshman.

CANA'DIAN, a. of or pertaining to Canada; s. a native of Canada.

CAN'DIOTE, a. of or pertaining to Candia; s. a native of Candia.

CARIBBE'AN, a. pertaining to the Caribbee islands.

CAUCA'SIAN, a. pertaining to Mount Caucasus.

CEPHALO'NIOTE, a. of or pertaining to Cephalonia; s. a native of Cephalonia.

CES'TRIAN, a. of or pertaining to Cheshire.

GEOGRAPHICAL DERIVATIVES, ETC.

CEYLONESE', *s.* the natives of Ceylon; *a.* of or pertaining to Ceylon.

CHIL'IAN, *a.* pertaining to Chili.

CHINESE', of or pertaining to China; *s.* the natives of China.

CISAL'PINE, *a.* an epithet applied to the countries on that side of the Alps next to France.

COP'TIC, *a.* pertaining to the Copts or ancient Egyptians.

COR'FUTE, or COR'FIOTE, *s.* a native of Corfu.

COR'NISH, *a.* of or pertaining to Cornwall.

COR'TES, *s.* the states, or assembly of the states, of Spain and of Portugal.

CRE'OLE, *s.* one born in the West Indies of Spanish parents.

DAMASCE'NE, *a.* of or pertaining to Damascus.

DANE, *s.* a native of Denmark.

EGYP'TIAN, *a.* of or pertaining to Egypt; *s.* a native of Egypt.

EN'GLISH, *a.* of or pertaining to England.

E'THIOP, *s.* a native of Ethiopia.

EUROPE'AN, *a.* of or pertaining to Europe;—*s.* a native of Europe.

FIN'NISH, *a.* of or pertaining to Finland.

FLEM'ISH, *a.* pertaining to Flanders.

FLOR'ENTINE, *a.* of or pertaining to Florence:—*s.* a native of Florence

FRANK, *s.* any European who is not a Greek, a Jew, or a Turk.

GAL'LICAN, *a.* French.

GENEVESE', *a.* of or pertaining to Geneva:—*s.* the natives of Geneva.

GENOESE', *a.* of or pertaining to Genoa.

GRE'CIAN, *a.* of or pertaining to Greece.

GREEK, *s.* a native of Greece; *a.* of or pertaining to Greece.

HANSE, *s.* a company of merchants; applied to certain towns in Germany, confederated for the mutual protection of their commerce.

HANSEAT'IC, *a.* pertaining to the Hanse Towns.

HES'SIAN, *a.* of or pertaining to Hesse in Germany.

HIBER'NIAN, *a.* of or pertaining to Ireland:—*s.* a native of Ireland.

HINDOO', *s.* a native of Hindoostan.

HINDOSTANEE', *a.* of or pertaining to Hindoostan.

HYD'RIOTE, *a.* pertaining to Hydra, a small island in the Grecian archipelago:—*s.* a native of Hydra.

ICELAN'DIC, *a.* of or pertaining to Iceland.

I'RISH, *a.* of or pertaining to Ireland.

ITAL'IAN, *a.* of or pertaining to Italy:—*s.* a native of Italy.

JAPANESE', *s.* the natives of Japan.

JA'VAN, *s.* a native of Java.

JAVANESE', *s.* the natives of Java.

LEVAN'TINE, *a.* pertaining to the Levant, a name given to the eastern part of the Mediterranean Sea and the countries bordering on it.

MADEGAS'SES, s. natives of Madagascar.
MAHARAT'TAS, s. natives of Maharatta.
MALTESE', s. the natives of Malta:—a. belonging to Malta.
MANK, s. a native of the Isle of Man.
MANX, a. of or pertaining to the Isle of Man.
MILANESE', s. the natives of Milan.
MO'REOTE, a. of or pertaining to the Morea.
NEPAULESE', a. of or pertaining to Nepaul.
NOR'MAN, a. of or pertaining to Normandy.
NORWE'GIAN, a. of or pertaining to Norway.
NORTHUM'BRIAN, a. of or pertaining to Northumberland.
OT'TOMAN, a. pertaining to the Turkish empire.
PARIS'IAN, a. of or pertaining to Paris.
PARSEE', s. a fire-worshipper of the East Indies.
PERU'VIAN, a. of or pertaining to Peru.
PIEDMONTESE', s. the natives of Piedmont.
POLE, s. a native of Poland.
PO'LISH, a. of or pertaining to Poland.
POLONESE', a. Polish.
PORTUGUESE', a. of or pertaining to Portugal.
PYRENE'AN, a. pertaining to the Pyrenees, mountains separating France and Spain.
RHÆ'TIAN, a. an epithet applied to a portion of the Alps, situated between the Grisons country and Milan.
SAVOY'ARD, s. a native of Savoy.

SAX'ON, a. of or pertaining to Saxony.
SCOTCH, SCOT'TISH, a. of or pertaining to Scotland.
SIAMESE', s. the natives of Siam.
SMYR'NIOTE, s. a native of Smyrna.
SPAN'IARD, s. a native of Spain.
SPAN'ISH, a. of or pertaining to Spain.
SU'LIOTE, a. of or pertaining to Suli:—s. a native of Suli.
SUMA'TRAN, s. a native of Sumatra.
SWEDE, s. a native of Sweden.
SWISS, a. of or pertaining to Switzerland.
SYR'IAC, a. of or pertaining to Syria.
TAR'TAR, s. a native of Tartary.
THIBE'TIAN, s. a native of Thibet.
TRANSAL'PINE, a. an epithet applied to the countries on that side of the Alps furthest from France.
TRANSATLAN'TIC, a. an epithet applied to the countries beyond the Atlantic Ocean.
TRIPOL'ITAN, s. a native of Tripoli:—a. pertaining to Tripoli.
TUNIS'IAN, TUNISINE', a. of or pertaining to Tunis.
TURK, a native of Turkey.
TYROLESE', a. of or pertaining to the Tyrol.
VENE'TIAN, a. of or pertaining to Venice.
WALDEN'SES, s. the natives of Vaudois in Piedmont.
WELSH, a. of or pertaining to Wales. [koutsk.
YAKOUTE', s. a native of Yazan'tiote, s. a native of Zante.

PART III.
ENGLISH SYNONYMS.

WORDS which are strictly *synonymous*, i. e., which are used to convey precisely the same idea, and might be substituted for each other in any possible connection, are almost, if not entirely unknown. But the term *synonymous* is applied, in common usage, to words which represent a given idea under different limitations or modifications, while the words belong to the same part of speech. As the degree of resemblance between the signification of such words may vary indefinitely, a larger or smaller number of words would, on different occasions, be classed together as synonyms, according to the different purposes for which the classification should be made.

In attempting to express ideas, either orally or in writing, it is often difficult to recall the word which most nearly meets the case. Young writers, especially, are much embarrassed in this way; and without some aid, they will not rapidly improve in pertinency and variety of expression. It is the object of the following collection of synonyms to furnish the aid which the difficulty above mentioned renders necessary.* When the student is in doubt respecting the distinction between the significations of words here classed together, he will of course resort, either to a large English dictionary, or to a proper dictionary of synonyms, like that of Crabbe. In consulting the following pages, he may not only have the appropriate word suggested, when the memory alone is at fault, but may become acquainted with new words, and be led to investigate their meaning.

In arranging the words in paragraphs in this Part, the aim has been to place those of a more general or comprehensive signification first, and those more limited afterwards; a transition to words of a distinct class is marked by a semicolon. Words are occasionally introduced which may seem too remote; but if it is borne in mind by the pupil that the words classed together are not to be considered as defining each other, no error will be occasioned by thus extending the classification.

This Part may be used, with great advantage, as the basis of exercises in which the pupil shall be required to discriminate carefully between the significations of words more or less nearly synonymous. These exercises may, of course, be much varied They will be found admirably adapted to cultivate habits of accuracy in thought and expression.

* This collection did not form a part of Butter's Expositor, but is derived from a work by William Carpenter.

ENGLISH SYNONYMS.

ABO   ACC

To ABASE, depress, degrade, bring low, humble, disgrace, cast down.

To ABBREVIATE, contract, curtail, shorten, abridge, compress, condense, reduce, epitomize.

To ABET, aid, assist.

ABETTOR, assistant, accessary, ally, accomplice.

To ABANDON, forsake, desert, renounce, relinquish, resign, give up, abdicate, quit, forego.

ABANDONED, profligate, corrupt, vitiated, depraved, reprobate, vicious, wicked.

To ABASH, confuse, confound, disconcert, shame.

To ABATE, diminish, reduce, decrease, lessen, liquidate, lower, subside.

To ABDICATE, abandon, relinquish, forsake, resign, renounce, give up, quit.

To ABHOR, detest, abominate, loathe.

To ABIDE, stay, remain, tarry.

ABILITY, capacity, faculty, talent, capability, aptness, aptitude, skill, efficiency.

ABLE, competent, capable, efficient, clever, skilful, fitted, qualified; strong, powerful, effective.

ABJECT, low, mean, base, despicable, worthless, servile, vile.

To ABJURE, forswear, recant, recall, revoke, retract.

ABODE, residence, dwelling, habitation, domicile.

ABOLISH, abrogate, annul, repeal, cancel, revoke; destroy, annihilate.

ABNEGATION, denial, renunciation.

To ABRIDGE, abbreviate, curtail, shorten, reduce, compress, contract, condense, epitomize.

ABNEGATE. See ABNEGATION and ABOLISH.

To ABOMINATE, abhor, detest, loathe.

ABRUPT, rugged, rough; sudden, unexpected.

ABSOLUTE, positive, peremptory; arbitrary, despotic.

ABSOLUTELY, completely, unrestrictedly, unconditionally.

To ABSOLVE, clear, acquit, set free; remit; pardon, forgive.

To ABSORB, swallow up, imbibe, engulf, engross, consume.

To ABSTAIN, refrain, forbear, withhold.

ABSTEMIOUS, abstinent, temperate, sober.

ABSTERGENT, cleansing, purgative, abstersive.

ABSTINENT, abstemious, temperate, sober.

ABSURD, foolish, irrational, ridiculous, preposterous.

ABUNDANT, ample, copious, exuberant, plentiful, plenteous.

To ABUSE, reproach, vilify, revile, deceive.

ABUSIVE, reproachful, scurrilous, opprobrious, insolent, insulting, offensive.

To ACCEDE, assent, consent, comply, agree, acquiesce.

To ACCELERATE, hasten, quicken, expedite.

To ACCEPT, take, receive.

ACCEPTABLE, agreeable, grateful, welcome.

Access, approach, admittance, admission.
Accessary, accomplice, assistant, abettor, ally.
Accession, addition, augmentation, increase.
Accident, casualty, contingency, incident, adventure, occurrence.
Accidental, casual, fortuitous, contingent, incident.
Acclamation, applause, plaudit, exultation, shouting.
To Accommodate, adapt, adjust, suit, fit, serve.
Accomplice, abettor, accessary, assistant, ally.
To Accomplish, fulfil, realize, effect, achieve, complete, execute.
Accomplishment, achievement, feat, deed; acquirement, qualification.
Accordance, agreement, harmony, unison, melody.
Accordant, consonant, consistent.
Account, narrative, description, relation, recital, detail, explanation, narration.
Accountable, amenable, answerable, responsible.
To Accumulate, amass, collect, gather, heap up.
Accurate, correct, exact, precise, nice.
To Accuse, charge, impeach, censure; arraign.
To Accuse falsely, asperse, calumniate, defame, detract, scandalize, slander, vilify.
To Achieve, accomplish, fulfil, realize, effect, complete, execute.
Achievement, feat, exploit, deed, accomplishment, acquirement.
Acid, sour, tart, sharp, acrimonious, acetous, acetose.
To Acknowledge, avow, confess, own, recognise.
To Acquaint, apprise, inform, make known; disclose, communicate.
Acquaintance, familiarity, intimacy; fellowship.
To Acquiesce, accede, assent, consent, comply, agree, yield.
To Acquire, obtain, attain, gain, procure; win, earn.
Acquirement, acquisition; qualification.
To Acquit, set free, clear, absolve; pardon, forgive.
Acrimony, asperity, harshness, smartness, tartness.
Active, agile, assiduous, alert, brisk, vigorous, nimble, lively, quick, sprightly; prompt; industrious, laborious.
Actual, real, positive, certain, genuine.
To Actuate, move, impel, induce, instigate.
Acute, keen, shrewd, penetrating, piercing; sharp, pointed.
Adage, maxim, aphorism, apophthegm, proverb, saying.
To Adapt, accommodate, adjust, suit, fit.
Adequate, equal, proportionate, commensurate.
Addicted, devoted, attached.
Addition, accession, augmentation, increase.
Address, ability, dexterity.
To Adduce, bring forward, advance, allege, assign, cite, quote.
To Adhere, attach, stick, hold, cleave, fix.
Adherence, adhesion, attachment.
Adherent, follower, disciple, partisan.
Adhesion, adherence, attachment.
Adjacent, near to, adjoining, contiguous, approximating.
Adjoining, adjacent, contiguous, approximating.
To Adjourn, prorogue; postpone, delay, defer.

To ADJUST, accommodate, adapt, set right, suit, fit.
To ADMINISTER, minister, contribute, supply; serve, manage.
ADMIRATION, amazement, astonishment, wonder, surprise.
ADMISSION, admittance, access, approach.
To ADMIT, allow, concede, permit, suffer, tolerate, grant.
ADMITTANCE, admission, access, approach.
To ADORN, decorate, embellish, beautify.
ADROIT, clever, skilful, dextrous, expert.
To ADULATE, flatter, compliment.
To ADULTERATE, corrupt, contaminate, defile, vitiate, sophisticate.
To ADVANCE, bring forward, assign, adduce, allege; proceed, go forward.
ADVANCEMENT, progress, progression; improvement, proficiency.
ADVANTAGE, good, benefit, profit.
ADVENTURE, occurrence, incident, contingency, casualty, event, accident.
ADVENTUROUS, enterprising; rash, foolhardy.
ADVERSARY, antagonist, opponent, enemy, foe.
ADVERSE, averse, contrary, opposite; inimical, repugnant, hostile.
To ADVERTISE, announce, proclaim, publish, promulgate.
ADVICE, counsel, instruction, information; notice, intelligence; deliberation, consultation.
To ADVISE with, seek counsel, deliberate, consult.
AFFABILITY, courteousness, urbanity, courtesy, complaisance.
AFFABLE, courteous, conciliating, gentle, urbane.
AFFAIR, business, concern, matter.

To AFFECT, influence, act upon, concern; assume, pretend to arrogate.
AFFECTING, pathetic, touching, moving.
AFFECTION, attachment, kindness, fondness, love.
AFFINITY, alliance; kindred, relationship.
To AFFIRM, assert, declare, assure, asseverate, aver, protest, pronounce.
To AFFIX, attach, subjoin, connect, annex.
To AFFLICT, distress, trouble, pain.
AFFLUENCE, wealth, riches, opulence.
To AFFORD, give, impart, yield, produce; spare.
AFFRAY, fray, quarrel, brawl, feud, altercation.
To AFFRIGHT, frighten, terrify, appall, dismay, shock.
AFFRONT, insult, offence, outrage.
AFRAID, fearful, timid, timorous.
AGE, time, period, generation, date, era, epoch, century.
AGED, elderly, old, senile.
AGENCY, action, operation; management.
To AGGRAVATE, provoke, irritate, exasperate, tantalize; heighten, raise, make worse.
AGGRESSION, assault, injury, offence.
AGILE, active, assiduous, alert, brisk, vigorous, nimble, lively, quick, sprightly, prompt; industrious, laborious.
To AGITATE, shake, disturb, toss, move.
AGITATION, disturbance, emotion, trepidation, tremor.
AGONY, anguish, pain, distress, pang, suffering.
To AGREE, accede, assent, consent, comply, acquiesce, concur.
AGREEABLE, pleasant, pleasing,

grateful, welcome, conformable, suitable, acceptable.

AGREEMENT, concurrence, compact, contract, bargain, covenant; accordance, harmony, unison; melody.

To AID, assist, help, relieve, succor.

To AIM, point, level; endeavor, aspire.

AIM, end, object, purpose, drift, scope, design, tendency.

AIR, look, manner, mien, aspect, appearance.

ALARM, terror, fright, affright, consternation, disquietude.

ALERT, active, agile, assiduous, brisk, vigorous, nimble, lively, quick, prompt, sprightly; industrious, laborious.

ALIEN, stranger, foreigner.

To ALIENATE, estrange, withdraw, transfer.

To ALLAY, appease, assuage, soothe, compose, calm, tranquillize.

To ALLEGE, adduce, advance, assign.

To ALLEVIATE, mitigate, relieve, abate, diminish.

ALLIANCE, affinity, connection; confederacy, league, combination, coalition.

To ALLOT, assign, apportion, appoint, distribute.

To ALLOW, admit, concede; permit, suffer, tolerate; grant, give.

ALLOWANCE, grant, stipend, pay, wages, salary; permission, concession.

To ALLUDE, hint, refer, glance at, suggest, intimate.

To ALLURE, attract, decoy, entice, tempt, seduce.

ALLY, associate, accomplice, accessary, assistant.

To ALTER, change, vary.

ALSO, likewise, too.

ALTERCATION, dispute, affray, quarrel, feud.

ALWAYS, constantly, continually, incessantly, perpetually, ever.

To AMASS, accumulate, collect, gather, pile up, heap up.

AMAZEMENT, wonder, surprise, astonishment, admiration.

AMBIGUOUS, equivocal, indistinct, doubtful.

AMENABLE, accountable, answerable, responsible.

To AMEND, correct, emend, better, mend, improve, reform, rectify.

AMENDS, restoration, restitution, reparation.

AMIABLE, lovely, charming, delightful.

AMOROUS, loving, fond.

AMPLE, spacious, capacious; abundant, copious, plenteous.

AMUSE, entertain, divert; beguile.

AMUSEMENT, diversion, entertainment, sport, recreation, pastime.

ANCESTOR, progenitor, forefather, predecessor.

ANCIENT, old, antique, antiquated, old-fashioned, obsolete.

ANECDOTE, story, tale, memoir, incident.

To ANGER, irritate, increase, aggravate, enrage, incite, stimulate, exasperate, inflame.

ANGRY, irascible, passionate, hasty, hot.

ANGUISH, pain, agony, distress, suffering.

ANIMADVERSION, criticism, stricture, censure.

To ANIMATE, inspire, exhilarate, enliven, incite, impel, instigate, urge; cheer.

ANIMATION, life, vivacity, spirits, buoyancy.

ANIMOSITY, enmity, hostility, malignity.

ANNALS, chronicles, memoirs, archives, records, registers.

To ANNEX, affix, attach, subjoin.

ANNOTATION, comment, note, observation, remark, elucidation.

To ANNOUNCE, advertise, proclaim, publish.
To ANNOY, molest, incommode, vex, tease.
ANNUL, abolish, abrogate, repeal, cancel, revoke, destroy, annihilate.
To ANSWER for, guaranty, warrant, secure.
ANSWER, reply, rejoinder, response, replication.
ANSWERABLE, responsible, accountable, amenable; suitable, correspondent.
ANTAGONIST, adversary, opponent, enemy, foe.
ANTECEDENT, anterior, previous, prior, preceding, foregoing, former.
ANTERIOR, antecedent, previous, prior, preceding, foregoing, former.
To ANTICIPATE, prepossess, precede, prejudge; forestall.
ANTIPATHY, aversion, dislike, hatred, repugnance, contrariety, opposition.
ANTIQUE, old, ancient, antiquated, old-fashioned, obsolete.
ANXIETY, care, solicitude, perplexity; caution, attention.
APATHY, indifference, insensibility, unfeelingness.
To APE, imitate, mimic, mock.
APERTURE, opening, cavity.
APHORISM, apophthegm, adage, maxim, proverb, saying.
To APPALL, dismay, terrify, daunt.
APPARENT, visible, obvious, clear, plain, evident, manifest, distinct.
To APPEAL, refer, call upon, invoke.
To APPEAR, look, seem.
APPEARANCE, air, look, manner, mien, aspect, semblance
APPEARANCE of truth, verisimilitude, probability, speciousness.
To APPEASE, pacify, allay, assuage, soothe, compose, calm, tranquillize, propitiate.

APPELLATION, name, denomination, title, cognomen.
To APPLAUD, commend, praise, extol, approve.
APPLAUSE, acclamation, plaudit, exultation, shouting.
To APPLY, devote, addict, address.
To APPOINT, allot, ordain, depute, order, prescribe, constitute, fix, provide.
To APPRECIATE, estimate, note, value; esteem.
To APPREHEND, take, seize, catch, hold; conceive, imagine; anticipate, fear, dread.
To APPRISE, acquaint, inform, make known, disclose, communicate.
APPROACH, access, admittance, admission.
APPROBATION, approval, concurrence, consent.
To APPROPRIATE, assume, arrogate, usurp; allot, assign.
APPROPRIATE, peculiar, particular, exclusive.
To APPROXIMATE, approach, come near.
APT, ready, fit, meet, prompt, suitable, dextrous.
ARBITER, arbitrator, judge, umpire.
ARBITRARY, absolute, despotic, peremptory, imperious, tyrannical; optional.
ARBITRATOR, arbiter, judge, umpire.
ARCHIVES, annals, chronicles, registers, records.
ARDENT, vehement, hot, eager, passionate, violent, fiery, fervent.
ARDUOUS, hard, difficult.
To ARGUE, dispute, debate, evince; expostulate, remonstrate.
ARGUMENT, reason, proof, dispute.
ARIDITY, dryness; sterility, barrenness, unfaithfulness.

To Arise, rise, mount, ascend; scale.
To Arraign, accuse, charge, impeach, censure.
To Arrange, place, class, range, dispose.
Array, apparel, attire; show, exhibition.
Arrogance, assumption, haughtiness, presumption, usurpation.
Art, cunning, deceit, duplicity; skill, aptitude, contrivance, expertness.
To Articulate, speak, utter, pronounce.
Artifice, trick, finesse, stratagem, deception, cheat, imposture, delusion, fraud, deceit, guile, imposition.
Artless, ingenuous, candid, open, frank.
To Ascend, arise, rise, mount, soar, scale, climb.
Ascendency, influence, authority, sway, domination.
To Ascribe, attribute, impute.
To Ask, request, solicit, entreat, beg, claim, demand; inquire, question.
Aspect, appearance, air, look, mien.
Asperity, acrimony, harshness, smartness, tartness.
To Asperse, accuse falsely, calumniate, defame, detract, scandalize, slander, vilify.
To Assail, attack, assault, encounter.
To Assassinate, kill, murder, slay.
To Assault, assail, attack, encounter.
Assemblage, assembly, collection, group.
To Assemble, collect, muster, convene, convoke.
Assailant, aggressor.
Assembly, assemblage, collection, group; company, congregation, congress, convention, diet, meeting, convocation, council.
Assent, consent, concurrence, approbation.
To Assert, affirm, declare, asseverate, aver, protest, pronounce; maintain, vindicate.
Assessment, tax, rate, impost.
To Asseverate, assert, affirm, aver, declare, assure, protest, pronounce, vouch.
Assiduous, active, agile, alert, brisk.
To Assign, adduce, allege, advance; allot, apportion.
To Assist, aid, help, relieve, succor.
Assistant, helper.
Associate, companion, ally, coadjutor, partner.
Association, combination, company, society, partnership.
To Assuage, allay, soothe, appease, calm, tranquillize, mitigate.
To Assume, arrogate, usurp, appropriate, affect.
Assurance, confidence, persuasion; impudence.
To Assure, affirm, assert, asseverate, aver, protest, vouch.
Astonishment, amazement, wonder, surprise, admiration.
Astringent, binding, styptic, astrictive, restringent, costive.
Astute, arch, cunning, penetrating, wily, crafty, artful.
Asylum, refuge, retreat, shelter.
Atrocious, flagrant, flagitious, heinous.
To Attach, affix, subjoin, connect, annex; adhere, stick, hold, cleave.
Attachment, affection, inclination, fondness, love.
To Attain, reach, acquire, obtain, gain, procure, get.
To Attack, assail, assault, encounter; impugn.
Attempt, effort, endeavor; es-

say, trial; enterprise, undertaking.
To ATTEND, accompany, escort, wait on; hearken, listen.
To ATTEND to, mind, heed, regard.
NOT ATTENDING to, absent, inattentive, abstracted.
ATTENTION, heed, care; application, study.
ATTENTIVE, careful, mindful.
ATTITUDE, posture, gesture, action, gesticulation.
To ATTRACT, draw, allure, entice.
ATTRACTIONS, charms, allurements.
To ATTRIBUTE, ascribe, impute.
ATTRIBUTE, quality, property.
AUDACITY, boldness, effrontery, hardihood.
AUGMENTATION, accession, addition, increase.
AUGUR, forebode, betoken, presage, portend.
AUGUST, majestic, magisterial, dignified, stately, pompous.
AUSPICIOUS, favorable, propitious.
AUSTERE, rigid, severe, stern, rigorous.
AUTHORITATIVE, commanding, imperative, imperious.
AUTHORITY, ascendency, sway, influence, power, dominion, force.
AVAIL, advantage, use, benefit, utility, service.
AVARICE, covetousness, cupidity.
To AVER, affirm, assert, declare, assure, asseverate, protest.
AVERSE, adverse, backward, loth, reluctant, unwilling.
To AVENGE, revenge, vindicate.
AVERSION, antipathy, dislike, repugnance, hatred.
AVIDITY, eagerness, greediness.
AVOCATION, calling, business, employment, engagement, office, trade, profession, occupation.

To AVOID, shun, elude, eschew.
AVOIDED (not to be), inevitable, unavoidable.
To AVOW, acknowledge, own, confess, recognise.
To AWAKEN, arouse, stir up, excite; provoke.
AWARE, apprised, on one's guard, cautious.
AWE, reverence, dread, fear.
AWKWARD, clumsy, uncouth, untoward, unhandy, unpolite.
AWRY, crooked, bent, curved, oblique.

B

To BABBLE, clatter, prate, prattle.
BABBLING, garrulity, loquacity, talkativeness.
BACKWARD, averse, unwilling, loth, reluctant.
To go BACKWARD, retrograde, retrocede, recede, retreat, retire, withdraw.
BAD, evil, unsound, wicked.
BADGE, mark, sign, stigma.
To BAFFLE, confuse, disconcert, confound, defeat.
To BALANCE, poise, equipoise, equiponderate, counterpoise; weigh.
BAND, shackle, fetter, chain; company, crew, gang.
BANE, pest, ruin; poison.
BANISHMENT, exile, outlawry, expulsion, proscription.
BANQUET, feast, entertainment, carousal, treat.
To BANTER, deride, ridicule, mock, rally.
BARBAROUS, savage, cruel, inhuman, brutal.
BARE, naked, uncovered, destitute; scanty, mere.
BAREFACED, glaring, impudent.
To BARGAIN, cheapen, buy, purchase.
BARGAIN, agreement, compact, contract, covenant.

BARRENNESS, unfruitfulness, sterility, aridity.
BARTER, exchange, interchange, dealing, trade, traffic, truck.
BASE, low, mean, dishonorable, vile.
BASHFUL, modest; diffident.
BASIS, foundation, ground; pedestal.
BASTARD, illegitimate, spurious, not genuine.
BATTLE, combat, engagement.
To BE, exist, subsist.
BEAM, ray, gleam.
To BEAR, support, endure, sustain, carry; suffer, undergo.
To BEAR down, oppress, overbear, overpower, subdue, overwhelm.
BEARING, endurance, suffering, patience; tolerance, toleration, sufferance.
BEAST, animal, brute.
BEASTLY, bestial, brutish, brutal; irrational, sensual.
To BEAT, strike, hit; overthrow, defeat, overpower.
BEATITUDE, happiness, bliss, felicity, blessedness.
BEAU, gallant, spark, sweetheart.
BEAUTIFUL, handsome, fine, pretty.
To BEAUTIFY, adorn, embellish, decorate, deck, ornament.
BECOMING, fit, meet, suitable, befitting, comely, decent, graceful.
BEFITTING, becoming, suitable, meet, fit, decent.
To BEG, ask, entreat, crave, solicit, beseech, implore, supplicate.
To BEGIN, enter upon, commence; originate.
To BEGUILE, amuse; deceive, impose upon.
BEHAVIOR, conduct, deportment, carriage, demeanor, manner, address.

To BEHEAD, decapitate, decollate.
BEHEST, command, injunction, mandate, precept, order, charge.
To BEHOLD, see, look, eye, view, observe.
BEHOLDER, observer, spectator, looker-on.
BELIEF, credence, credit, trust, faith, confidence.
BELOW, beneath, under.
To BEMOAN, bewail, lament.
To BEND, lean, incline, distort.
To BEND backward, recline.
BENEATH, under, low.
BENEFACTION, gift, donation, present.
BENEFICENT, benevolent, bountiful, bounteous, munificent, liberal, generous.
BENEFIT, advantage, good; service, avail, use.
BENEVOLENCE, beneficence, benignity, kindness, generosity, humanity, tenderness, goodness.
BENIGNITY. See BENEVOLENCE.
BENT, crooked, curved, awry; bias, inclination, prepossession, turn.
BENUMBED, numbed, torpid, senseless.
To BEQUEATH, give, devise.
To BEREAVE, deprive, strip.
To BESEECH, beg, entreat, crave, solicit, implore, supplicate.
BESIDES, moreover, more than that, over and above.
BESTIAL, beastly, brutish, brutal.
To BESTOW, give, confer, grant.
BETIMES, early, soon.
To BETOKEN, augur, presage, forebode, portend, signify.
To BETTER, improve, amend, emend, ameliorate, meliorate; reform; rectify.
To BEWAIL, bemoan, lament.
BEYOND, over, above.
BIAS, bent, inclination, prepossession, prejudice.

To BID, offer, tender, propose; call, invite, summon.
BIG, great, large.
BILLOW, wave, surge, breaker.
To BIND, tie; engage, oblige, lay under obligation.
BINDING, astringent, styptic, astrictive, restringent, costive.
To BLAME, censure, reproach, reprove, condemn, upbraid, reprehend.
BLAMABLE, culpable, censurable, reprehensible, reprovable.
BLAMELESS, inculpable, irreprehensible, irreprovable, irreproachable, guiltless; unblemished, spotless.
To BLAST, strike, desolate, wither up; destroy, annihilate.
BLAST, gust, gale, breeze, storm.
BLAZE, flare, glare, flame.
BLEEDING, phlebotomy, venesection.
BLEMISH, flaw, speck, spot, defect, fault.
To BLEND, mix, mingle, confound.
BLESSEDNESS, bliss, happiness, felicity, beatitude.
BLISS. See BLESSEDNESS.
BLOODY, bloodthirsty, sanguinary.
To BLOT out, expunge, erase, obliterate, cancel, efface.
BLUNDER, mistake, error.
BLUNT, pointless, obtuse.
To BOAST, glory, vaunt.
BOASTER, braggadocio, braggart, braggard, bravado.
BOASTING, vaunting, ostentation, vain-glory, parade, rodomontade.
BODILY, corporal, corporeal.
BODY, carcass, corpse.
BODYLESS, incorporeal; immaterial, spiritual.
BOISTEROUS, violent, furious, impetuous, vehement.
BOLD, fearless, undaunted, daring, intrepid, audacious; insolent, impudent, contumacious.
BOMBASTIC, tumid, turgid, inflated.
BONDAGE, slavery, servitude, imprisonment.
BOOTY, spoil, prey.
BORDER, edge, brim, rim, verge, brink, margin.
To BORE, pierce, penetrate, perforate.
To BOUND, limit, circumscribe, restrict, confine, terminate.
BOUNDLESS, illimitable, unlimited, unbounded, infinite.
To BOUND back, recoil, rebound, reverberate.
BOUNTY, munificence, liberality, generosity, benevolence, beneficence, benignity.
BOUNTEOUS, generous, beneficent, bountiful, liberal, munificent, kind.
BRACE, pair, couple.
BRAVE, courageous, gallant, daring, valorous, valiant, bold, heroic, intrepid, magnanimous, fearless.
BREACH, chasm, opening, gap, break.
To BREAK, rend, rack; violate, infringe; demolish, destroy.
BREAKER, wave, billow, surge.
BREEDING, education, instruction.
BREEZE, gale, gust, blast.
BREVITY, conciseness. See next word.
BRIEF, short, concise, compendious, summary, succinct, laconic.
BRIGHT, clear, lucid, limpid, splendid, translucent, resplendent.
To BRIGHTEN, polish, burnish.
BRILLIANCY, splendor, lustre, brightness, radiance.
BRIM, border, edge, rim, brink, margin, verge.
BRINK, brim, border, edge, rim, margin, verge.

To BRING forward, adduce, advance, assign, allege.
BRISK, active, agile, assiduous, alert, vigorous, nimble, lively, quick, sprightly, prompt.
BRITTLE, fragile, frail, frangible.
BROAD, wide, large, ample, extensive.
BROIL, affray, fray, quarrel, feud, altercation.
BROTHERHOOD, fraternity.
BRUTE, animal, beast.
BRUTISH, cruel, inhuman, barbarous, savage; irrational, sensual.
To BRUISE, break, crush, contuse, squeeze, pound.
To BUD, sprout, germinate, shoot forth.
To BUILD, erect, construct; found.
BULK, size, magnitude, greatness, extent, largeness.
BUOYANCY, lightness; animation, vivacity.
BURDEN, load, weight, freight, cargo.
BURDENSOME, heavy, weighty, ponderous.
BURIAL, interment, sepulchre, inhumation.
BURYING-PLACE, grave, tomb, sepulchre, cemetery.
BURLESQUE, satire, irony, humor, wit.
BURNING, ardent, fiery, hot.
To BURST, break, crack, split.
BURSTING forth, eruption, explosion.
BUSINESS, affair, concern, matter; avocation, calling, employment, engagement, occupation, trade, profession; office, duty.
BUSTLE, tumult, hurry.
BUTCHERY, carnage, slaughter, massacre.
To BUY, cheapen, bargain, purchase.
BY-WORD, adage, saying, reproach.

C

CABAL, combination, conspiracy, plot.
To CAJOLE, coax, wheedle, fawn, flatter.
CALAMITY, disaster, misfortune, mishap, mischance.
To CALCULATE, reckon, compute, number, count.
To CALL, cry, exclaim; name, bid, invite, summon.
To CALL back, retract, recant, recall.
To CALL together, convene, convoke.
CALLING, avocation, business, employment, engagement, occupation, trade, profession, office.
To CALL out, exclaim, ejaculate; evoke.
CALLOUS, hard, obdurate, unfeeling, insensible, unsusceptible.
To CALM, pacify, allay, appease, assuage, soothe, compose, tranquillize.
CALM, serene, placid, composed, unruffled, undisturbed, quiet.
To CALUMNIATE, accuse falsely, defame, detract, scandalize, slander, vilify.
To CANCEL, abolish, annul, repeal, revoke, abrogate, destroy, annihilate.
CANDID, open, artless, ingenuous, frank, plain.
CAPABLE, able, competent, efficient, qualified, fitted, clever, skilful, effective.
CAPACIOUS, ample, spacious.
CAPACITY, ability, faculty, talent, capability, skill, efficiency.
CAPRICE, humor, fancy, freak.
CAPRICIOUS, fantastical, whimsical.
CAPTIOUS, cross, petulant, fretful, peevish.
To CAPTIVATE, charm, enchant, fascinate; enslave, take prisoner.

Captivity, confinement, imprisonment, bondage.
Capture, seizure, prize.
Carcass, body, corpse.
Care, anxiety, solicitude, attention, concern, regard; management.
Careful, cautious, attentive, provident, circumspect, heedful, solicitous.
Careless, negligent, heedless, inattentive, incautious, thoughtless, remiss, indolent, supine, listless.
To Caress, fondle, endear.
Cargo, freight, lading, load.
Carnage, butchery, massacre, slaughter.
Carousal, feast, entertainment, banquet, treat.
To Carp, censure, cavil.
Carriage, gait, manner, walk, behavior, deportment, demeanor.
To Carry, bear, sustain; convey, transport.
To Carry on, conduct, manage, regulate, direct.
Case, situation, condition, state, plight, predicament.
Cast down, depressed, discouraged, dejected.
To Cast, hurl, throw.
To Cast off, reject, forsake, abandon.
To Cast back, retort, repel, rebuff.
Casual, accidental, fortuitous, contingent, incidental.
Casualty, accident, contingency, incident, adventure, occurrence, event.
Catalogue, list, register, roll, record.
To Catch, seize, lay hold on, grasp, gripe, snatch, capture.
A Catching, caption, capture; arrest, apprehension, seizure.
Catching, infectious, contagious, pestilential.

To Cavil, carp, censure.
Cavity, aperture, opening.
Cause, motive, reason, inducement, incitement.
To Cause, occasion, induce, give rise to.
Caution, admonition, warning, notice, advice; circumspection, care, solicitude.
Cautious, careful, wary, circumspect, prudent, watchful.
To Cease, leave off, desist, discontinue.
A Ceasing, cessation, discontinuance, pause, intermission.
Without Ceasing, incessant, continual, unintermitting.
To Cede, give up, concede, yield, surrender, deliver.
Celebrated, famous, renowned, illustrious.
Celerity, quickness, speed, swiftness, fleetness, rapidity, velocity.
Celestial, heavenly.
To Censure, blame, reprove, reproach, condemn, upbraid; carp, cavil, accuse.
Censure, blame, reproach, condemnation; animadversion, stricture.
Ceremony, form, observance, rite.
Certain, sure, doubtless, secure; real, actual, positive.
Cessation, intermission, rest, discontinuance.
To Chafe, rub, gall, fret, vex.
Chagrin, vexation, fretfulness, mortification.
Chance, fortune, hazard, accident, (happening by.)
Chance (to happen by), accidental, casual, fortuitous, contingent, incidental.
To Change, alter, vary; exchange, barter.
Change, variety, variation; alteration, mutation; vicissitude, revolution.

CHANGEABLE, mutable, fickle, variable, inconstant, unstable, uncertain, wavering, versatile, unsteady, irresolute.
CHARACTER, cast, turn, description; reputation.
To CHARACTERIZE, name, denominate, describe, designate, style, entitle.
To CHARGE, accuse, impeach, arraign.
CHARGE, care, custody, trust, management; cost, price, expense; assault, attack, encounter, onset.
To CHARM, enchant, fascinate, enrapture, captivate, transport, bewitch, allure.
CHARMING, delightful, pleasurable, graceful, fascinating, captivating, enchanting.
A CHARM, spell, incantation, enchantment.
CHASE, race, hunt.
To CHASTEN, chastise, correct, punish.
CHASTENESS, chastity, continence, purity; simplicity.
CHASTITY, continence, purity; chasteness, modesty.
To CHASTISE, chasten, correct, punish.
To CHAT, chatter, prattle, prate, babble.
CHATTELS, goods, furniture, effects, movables.
To CHEAPEN, bargain, buy, purchase.
To CHEAT, defraud, trick, beguile.
CHEAT, deception, imposture, fraud, delusion, artifice, deceit, trick, imposition, guile, finesse; stratagem.
CHRONICLES, annals, memoirs, archives, records, registers.
To CHECK, curb, restrain, repress, control, inhibit; chide, reprove, rebuke.
To CHEER, exhilarate, animate, enliven, encourage, comfort.

CHEERFULNESS, gayety, sprightliness, merriment, mirth, liveliness, blithesomeness, vivacity, jocundity, jollity.
To CHERISH, nurture, nourish, foster, indulge.
To CHIDE, check, reprimand, reprove, rebuke.
CHIEF, principal, main; leader, head, chieftain.
To CHEW, masticate.
CHILD (with) pregnant, enceinte, large.
CHIEFLY, principally, mainly, particularly, especially.
CHILDISH, infantine, puerile.
CHILDHOOD, infancy, minority.
CHILDREN, offspring, issue, progeny.
A CHINK, fissure, cranny.
CHILL, cold.
To CHOKE, stifle, suffocate, smother.
CHOICE, option; select.
CHOLER, anger, rage, fury.
To CHOOSE, prefer, select, elect, pick.
CIRCLE, orb, sphere, globe.
To CIRCULATE, spread, diffuse, disseminate, propagate.
To CIRCUMSCRIBE, bound, limit, restrict, confine, enclose.
CIRCUMSTANCE, situation, position; incident, fact.
CIRCUMSPECT, cautious, wary, particular.
CIRCUMSPECTION, caution, deliberation, thoughtfulness, wariness.
CIRCUMSTANTIAL, particular, minute.
To CITE, quote, summon, call.
CIVIL, polite, complaisant, obliging.
CIVILITY, courteousness, urbanity, courtesy, affability, complaisance, politeness.
CIVILIZATION, culture, cultivation, refinement.
To CLAIM, ask, demand.

CLAIM, pretension, right.
CLAMOR, cry, outcry, noise, uproar.
CLANDESTINE, secret, hidden, private.
To CLASP, embrace, hug.
CLASS, order, rank, degree, grade.
To CLASS, arrange, rank, distribute, classify.
CLEANSING, purgative, abstergent, abstersive.
To CLEAR, absolve, acquit, set free, remit; pardon, forgive, discharge.
CLEAR, apparent, visible, obvious, plain, evident, manifest, distinct; fair, lucid, bright.
CLEARLY, distinctly, plainly, obviously, explicitly.
To CLEAR from, extricate, disengage, disentangle, disembarrass, evolve.
To CLEAR of a fault, exonerate, exculpate; justify.
To CLEAVE, adhere, attach, stick, hold.
CLEMENCY, lenity, mercy, mildness.
CLERGYMAN, parson, priest, minister.
CLEVER, expert, dextrous, skilful, adroit.
To CLIMB, scale, mount, get up.
To CLOAK, mask, veil, cover, blind.
To CLOG, load, encumber; hinder, obstruct, embarrass.
CLOSE, compact, solid, dense, firm; near, nigh.
To CLOSE, shut; conclude, end, terminate.
To CLOY, glut, satiate.
CLOTHES, garments, dress, apparel, attire, array, vesture, raiment.
CLUMSY, awkward, unhandy, uncouth, untoward.
COADJUTOR, colleague, partner, assistant, ally.
COALITION, alliance, connection, union, confederacy, league, combination, conspiracy.
COALESCE, join, unite.
COARSE, rough, rude.
To COAX, wheedle, fawn, cajole.
To COERCE, restrain, check.
COEVAL, contemporary, contemporaneous.
COGENT, forcible, strong, resistless.
COGNOMEN, title, name, denomination, appellation.
COINCIDE, agree, concur.
COLD, frigid, chill.
COLDNESS, frigidity, algidity, algor.
COLLEAGUE, partner, coadjutor, assistant, ally.
To COLLECT, gather, assemble, muster.
COLLECTED, composed, calm, placid.
COLLECTION, assemblage, group.
COLLOQUY, convocation, conference, dialogue.
COLOR, hue, tint, tinge.
COLORABLE, specious, plausible, feasible.
COMBAT, battle, engagement, conflict, contest.
COMBINATION, alliance, union, confederacy, league, coalition, conspiracy, cabal.
COMELY, becoming, seemly, decent, agreeable, graceful.
To COMFORT, solace, console, encourage, revive.
COMFORTLESS, forlorn, disconsolate, desolate, wretched.
COMIC, droll, ludicrous, ridiculous, laughable.
A COMING forth, egress, egression.
COMING between, intervening, intermediate, intermedial, interposing, interfering.
COMMAND, order, injunction, mandate, precept, behest.
COMMANDING, authoritative, imperative, imperious.

To COMMENCE, begin, enter upon.
To COMMEND, applause, extol, praise, recommend, laud.
COMMENSURATE, proportionate, equal, adequate.
COMMENT, annotation, note, observation, remark, elucidation.
COMMERCE, dealing, trade, traffic; intercourse, communication.
COMMERCIAL, mercantile, trading.
COMMISERATION, sympathy, compassion, condolence.
To COMMISSION, authorize, empower.
To COMMIT, perpetuate; intrust, consign.
COMMODIOUS, suitable, useful.
COMMODITY, advantage, profit; wares, goods, merchandise.
COMMON, ordinary, vulgar, usual, frequent, low, mean; general.
COMMONWEALTH, state, realm; democracy, republic.
COMMOTION, disturbance, tumult.
To COMMUNICATE, impart, make known, disclose.
COMMUNICATION, commerce, intercourse.
COMMUNICATIVE, free, open, liberal.
COMMUNION, fellowship, converse.
COMMUNITY, society, commonwealth.
To COMMUTE, exchange, barter, truck.
COMPACT, agreement, contract, covenant, close.
COMPANION, coadjutor, partner, ally, associate, comrade, confederate, accomplice.
COMPANY, association, assembly, society, assemblage, corporation; troop, crew, gang.
COMPARISON, simile, similitude.
To COMPASS, encircle, environ, invest, enclose; grasp, obtain, attain, procure; bring about, consummate.

COMPASSION, pity, sympathy, commiseration.
COMPATIBLE, consistent, suitable, agreeable.
To COMPEL, force, oblige, necessitate.
COMPENDIOUS, summary, laconic, succinct, short, brief, concise.
To COMPENSATE. See COMPENSE.
COMPENSATION, amends, satisfaction, remuneration, reward, requital, recompense.
To COMPENSE, make amends, compensate, recompense, remunerate, requite.
COMPETENT, capable, efficient, able, qualified, fitted, clever, skilful, effective.
COMPETITION, rivalry, emulation, contest.
To COMPLAIN, murmur, lament, regret, repine.
COMPLAINING, querulous, querimonious.
COMPLAISANCE, condescension, civility, courtesy, urbanity, suavity.
COMPLAISANT, courteous, affable; civil, obliging.
To COMPLETE, accomplish, fulfil, realize, effect, execute, achieve; consummate, finish, fill up, terminate.
COMPLETE, finished, perfect; whole, entire, total.
COMPLEX, compound, complicate, composite, intricate.
COMPLIANT, yielding, submissive, complaisant.
To COMPLIMENT, praise, flatter.
To COMPLY, yield, accede, consent, assent, acquiesce.
To COMPOSE, form compound, put together, constitute; soothe, calm, settle.
COMPOUND, complex, complicate, intricate.
To COMPREHEND, comprise, embrace, include; conceive, understand.

COMPREHENSIVE, extensive; compendious.
COMPREHENSION, capacity, knowledge.
To COMPRESS, condense, press, squeeze.
COMPULSION, constraint, force.
COMPUNCTION, repentance, contrition, remorse, penitence.
To COMPUTE, calculate, count, number, reckon, estimate, rate.
To CONCEDE, give up, deliver, surrender, yield, cede, admit, allow, grant.
To CONCEAL, hide, secrete; disguise, dissemble.
CONCEIT, fancy, imagination; pride, vanity.
CONCEITED, proud, opinionated, egotistical, vain.
To CONCEIVE, apprehend, imagine, suppose, comprehend, understand.
CONCEPTION, notion, idea; perception.
CONCERN, care, regard, interest; affair, business, matter.
To CONCERT, contrive, manage.
To CONCILIATE, propitiate, reconcile.
CONCISE, brief, short, compendious, summary, succinct, laconic.
To CONCLUDE, close, finish, terminate.
CONCLUSION, inference, deduction.
CONCLUSIVE, decisive, convincing.
CONCOMITANT, accompaniment, comparison.
CONCORD, harmony, unity.
To CONCUR, agree, coincide, approve, acquiesce.
CONCUSSION, shock.
To CONDEMN, blame, reprove, reproach, upbraid, censure, reprobate; doom, sentence.
To CONDENSE, compress, contract.
CONDESCENSION, preference, complaisance.

CONDITION, situation, state, plight, case, predicament; article, term.
CONDOLENCE, sympathy, commiseration, compassion.
To CONDUCE, contribute, tend, lead, conduct.
CONDUCT, carriage, deportment, behavior, demeanor.
To CONDUCT, guide, lead; manage, direct.
CONFEDERACY, alliance, league, combination, coalition.
CONFEDERATE, accomplice, ally.
To CONFER, bestow, give; discourse.
CONFERENCE, conversation, dialogue, colloquy.
To CONFESS, acknowledge, avow, own, recognise.
To CONFIDE, trust, repose, defend, rely.
CONFIDENCE, assurance, hope, expectation, trust, reliance.
CONFIDENT, dogmatical, positive, absolute.
To CONFINE, limit, bound, circumscribe, restrict, restrain.
CONFINED, narrow, contracted, restrained.
To CONFIRM, corroborate, establish.
CONFLICT, combat, contest.
To CONFORM, submit, yield, comply.
CONFORMABLE, agreeable, suitable.
CONFORMATION, form, figure.
To CONFOUND. See CONFUSE.
CONFUSION, disorder, distraction.
To CONFUSE, abash, confound, disconcert.
CONFUSED, indiscriminate, indistinct; deranged, disordered; intricate, involved.
To CONFUTE, refute, disprove, oppugn.
To CONGRATULATE, felicitate.
CONJECTURE, surmise, supposition, guess.
CONJUNCTURE, crisis.

To Connect, unite, combine.
Connected, joined, united, related.
Connection, union; intercourse, commerce, communication; family.
To Conquer, vanquish, subdue, overcome, subjugate, surmount.
Consanguinity, kindred, relationship, affinity.
Conscientious, scrupulous.
Conscious, aware, apprised, sensible.
To Consecrate, dedicate, devote, hallow.
Consent, assent, acquiescence, concurrence, approval.
To Consent, assent, accede, comply, acquiesce, agree.
Consequence, effect, result, issue.
Of Consequence, avail, weight, importance, moment.
Consequently, accordingly, therefore.
To Consider, reflect, regard, ponder, deliberate.
Considerate, thoughtful, deliberate.
To Consign, commit, intrust.
Consistent, accordant, consonant.
To Console, solace, comfort, soothe.
Consonant, accordant, consistent.
Conspicuous, distinguished, noted, eminent, prominent, illustrious.
Conspiracy, combination, cabal, plot.
Constancy, firmness, stability, steadiness.
Constantly, continually, incessantly, perpetually, ever; unchangeably.
Consternation, alarm, fright, terror.
To Constitute, form, compose; appoint, depute.

Constitution, frame, temper, temperament.
Constraint, compulsion; confinement.
To Construct, build, erect; compile, constitute.
To Consult, advise with, deliberate; debate.
Consultation, deliberation.
To Consume, waste, destroy, swallow up, imbibe, engulf, absorb.
Consummation, completion, finish, perfection.
Consumption, decay, decline, waste.
Contact, touch.
Contagious, infectious, pestilential.
To Contain, comprise, comprehend, embrace, include, hold.
To Contaminate, pollute, defile, corrupt, taint.
To Contemn, despise, disdain, scorn.
To Contemplate, meditate, muse.
Contemporary, contemporaneous, coeval.
Contemptible, despicable, contemptuous, paltry, pitiful, disdainful, mean, vile.
To Contend, contest, debate, argue, dispute; strive, vie.
Contention, strife, discord, dissension, dispute.
Contentment, acquiescence, satisfaction, gratification.
To Contest, debate, argue, dispute, contend.
Contiguous, adjacent, adjoining, approximating to.
Continence, chastity.
Contingency, accident, casualty, incident, adventure, occurrence, event.
Contingent, accidental, casual, fortuitous, incidental.
Continual, perpetual, constant.
Continually, always, constantly,

16

incessantly, perpetually, unchangeably.
CONTINUATION, continuance, continuity, duration.
To CONTINUE in an attempt, persevere, persist, prosecute, pursue.
To CONTRACT, abbreviate, shorten, condense, abridge, reduce.
CONTRACT, agreement, compact, bargain, covenant.
To CONTRADICT, oppose, deny.
CONTRARY, adverse, opposite, inimical, repugnant.
CONTRAST, opposition.
To CONTRIBUTE, administer, minister, conduce.
CONTRITION, compunction, repentance, penitence, remorse.
CONTRIVANCE, device, plan, scheme, invention.
To CONTROL, check, curb, restrain, govern.
CONTROVERSY, debate, disputation, contest.
CONTUMACIOUS, obstinate, stubborn, headstrong.
CONTUMELY, obloquy, reproach, ignominy.
To CONVENE, convoke, assemble.
CONVENIENT, commodious, suitable, adapted.
CONVENTION, assembly, meeting, convocation, company.
CONVERSATION, dialogue, conference, colloquy.
CONVERSE, communion, discourse, conversation.
To CONVERSE, speak, talk, discourse, commune.
To CONVEY, carry, transport, bear.
CONVICT, malefactor, culprit, felon.
CONVIVIAL, social, sociable.
CONVOCATION, assembly, congregation, company, congress, meeting, diet, convention, synod, council.
To CONVOKE, assemble, convene, call together.

COOL, cold, frigid, dispassionate.
COPIOUS, ample, abundant, exuberant, plentiful, plenteous, full.
COPY, model, transcription, imitation, counterfeit.
COQUET, jilt, affected woman.
CORDIAL, warm, hearty, sincere.
CORNER, angle, extremity.
CORPORAL, corporeal, bodily, material.
CORPSE, body, carcass, corse.
CORPULENT, stout, lusty, robust.
To CORRECT, amend, emend, mend, better, rectify, reform, improve.
CORRECT, accurate, exact, precise, faultless; punctual, strict.
CORRECTION, discipline, punishment, chastisement.
CORRECTNESS, propriety, justness, exactness, exactitude, accuracy, precision, faultlessness.
CORRESPONDENT, answerable, suitable.
To CORROBORATE, confirm, establish, strengthen.
To CORRUPT, contaminate, defile, taint, pollute, infect, vitiate, adulterate, sophisticate.
CORRUPTION, defilement, contamination, pollution, infection, adulteration; depravity.
To CORUSCATE, shine, radiate, glisten, sparkle, gleam.
COST, price, charge, expense.
COSTIVE, close, bound, styptic.
COSTLY, valuable, precious.
COUNCIL, assembly, company, meeting, congress, diet, convention, convocation.
COUNSEL, advice, instruction, notice, intelligence; deliberation, consultation.
To COUNT, calculate, compute, estimate, reckon, number, rate.
To COUNTENANCE, encourage, sanction, support.
COUNTERFEIT, spurious, supposititious, false.

COUNTRYMAN, peasant, swain, rustic, hind, boor.
COUNTRIFIED, rural, rustic.
COUPLE, brace, pair.
COURAGE, resolution, fortitude, firmness, fearlessness, bravery, boldness.
COURAGEOUS, brave, gallant, daring, valorous, valiant, bold, heroic, intrepid, fearless.
COURSE, way, road, route, passage, race; series, succession; way, manner, method, mode.
COURTEOUS, affable, conciliating, complaisant.
COURTEOUSNESS, urbanity, civility, courtesy, affability, complaisance, politeness.
COVENANT, agreement, compact, contract, bargain.
To COVER, shelter, screen, hide, overspread.
COVERING, tegument.
To COVET, desire, long for, hanker after.
COVETOUSNESS, avarice, cupidity, inordinate desire.
COWARD, poltroon, dastard.
COWARDICE, timidity, pusillanimity, fear.
To CRACK, split, burst, break.
CRAFTY, cunning, artful, deceitful, sly, subtil, wily.
CRAPULOUS, drunken, inebriated, intoxicated.
CRITICISM, animadversion, stricture, censure.
To CRAVE, beg, entreat, solicit, beseech, implore.
To CREATE, cause, produce, make, form, occasion.
CREDIT, belief, trust, confidence; favor, influence; name, reputation, character.
CREW, company, band, gang.
CRIME, vice, sin, wickedness.
CRIMINAL, culprit, convict, malefactor, felon.
CRISIS, juncture, conjuncture.
CRITERION, standard, measure.
CROOKED, curved, incurvated, bent, bowed, awry, oblique; deformed, disfigured.

CROSS, perverse, intractable, vexatious, froward, peevish, petulant, untoward, fretful, splenetic, ill-tempered.
To CROSS, thwart, obstruct, embarrass, hinder, impede, perplex, retard.
CROWD, multitude, throng, swarm.
CRUEL, inhuman, barbarous, merciless, pitiless, savage, ferocious, brutal, unmerciful, inexorable.
To CRUSH, break, bruise; overwhelm.
To CRY out, exclaim, shout, ejaculate; call.
CULPABLE, faulty, blamable, censurable.
CULPRIT. See CRIMINAL.
CULTIVATION, culture, civilization, refinement.
CUNNING, art; deceit, duplicity; crafty, sly, subtil, wily.
CUPIDITY, avarice, covetousness, inordinate desire.
To CURB, check, control, restrain.
To CURE, heal, remedy, restore.
CURIOUS, inquisitive, prying.
CURRENT, stream, tide.
CURSE, malediction, execration, imprecation, anathema.
CURSORY, slight, superficial, hasty, desultory, careless.
To CURTAIL, abbreviate, contract, abridge, shorten.
CURVED, crooked, incurvated, bent, awry.
CUSTODY, keeping guard.
CUSTOM, habit, manner, usage, practice, fashion; prescription.
CUSTOM, tax, duty, impost, toll, tribute.
To CUT off, amputate, sever, separate.
CYNICAL, snarling, snappish, waspish.

D

Daily, diurnal, quotidian.
Dainty, nice, delicate, squeamish, scrupulous.
Damage, detriment, loss, hurt, injury.
Dampness, humidity, moistness.
Danger, peril, hazard, risk, venture.
To Dare, brave, challenge, defy; venture, presume.
Daring, bold, brave, courageous, valorous, fearless, intrepid, heroic.
Dark, opaque, obscure, dim, dismal, gloomy, mysterious.
Date, time, period, age, era, epoch.
To Daunt, dismay, appall, terrify, frighten.
Dead, inanimate, lifeless.
Deadly, mortal, fatal; implacable.
Dealing, commerce, trade, traffic.
Dearth, scarcity, famine.
Death, decease, demise, departure.
To Debar, deprive, hinder, exclude.
To Debase, abase, humble, degrade, disgrace.
To Debate, argue, dispute, contest.
To Debilitate, weaken, enervate, enfeeble.
Debility, weakness, infirmity, imbecility.
Debt, due, obligation.
To Decapitate, behead, decollate.
Decay, decline, consumption.
Decease, death, demise, departure.
Deceit, duplicity, guile, art, cunning, deception, fraud, double-dealing.
Deceitful, fallacious, delusive, illusive, fraudulent, subtil.
Decency, decorum, propriety.

Decent, becoming, comely, seemly, fit.
Deception, duplicity, artifice, guile, deception; fraud, trick, imposition, double-dealing.
To Decide, determine, conclude upon, resolve.
Decision, judgment, sentence.
Decisive, decided, conclusive, convincing.
To Declaim, inveigh, harangue.
To Declare, state, affirm, assert, aver, asseverate, assure, pronounce, protest, testify, utter, manifest, reveal, discover; proclaim.
To Decline, droop, sink, deviate; decay; refuse, repel, reject.
To Decollate, behead, decapitate.
To Decorate, adorn, embellish, ornament, beautify.
Decorum, decency, propriety.
To Decoy, allure, entice, inveigle, tempt, seduce, abduct.
To Decrease, lessen, diminish, abate, liquidate, lower, subside.
Decree, edict, proclamation, ordinance.
To Decry, disparage, detract, cry down, depreciate, traduce, degrade.
To Dedicate, devote, consecrate, hallow.
To Deduce, derive, draw from, trace, infer.
To Deduct, subtract, separate, dispart.
Deduction, conclusion, inference.
Deed, achievement, feat, exploit, accomplishment.
To Deem, think, suppose, imagine, believe.
Deepness, depth, profundity.
To Deface, disfigure, deform.
To Defame, calumniate, accuse falsely, asperse, detract, scandalize, vilify, slander.

To Defeat, overpower, overcome, beat, rout; baffle, disconcert, foil, frustrate.
Defect, fault, blemish, flaw, imperfection.
Defective, deficient, imperfect.
To Defend, vindicate, justify; plead; exculpate; guard, protect.
Defender, advocate, pleader, vindicator.
Defensible, justifiable.
Defence, apology, plea, excuse; vindication, justification.
To Defer, postpone, delay, protract, prolong, procrastinate, retard.
Deference, condescension, complaisance; respect, submission.
Deficient, defective, imperfect.
To Defile, corrupt, contaminate, taint, pollute, infect, vitiate.
Definite, positive, certain, exact, precise.
Definition, explanation, explication, description.
To Deform. See Deface.
To Defraud, cheat, trick, deceive.
To Defy, brave, dare, challenge.
To Degrade, abuse, depress, disgrace, humble, disparage, traduce, depreciate, decry.
Degree, class, rank, order.
Dejection, melancholy, depression.
To Delay. See Defer.
Delegate, deputy, substitute, representative.
Deliberate, thoughtful, considerate, wary.
To Deliberate, consult, seek, counsel, debate.
Deliberation, thoughtfulness, circumspection, wariness, caution.
Delicate, nice, fine, tender.
Delight, pleasure, joy, rapture, charm.
Delightful, charming, lovely, beautiful.

To Delineate, depict, sketch, paint.
Delinquent, offender, criminal, misdoer.
To Deliver, give up, surrender, yield, cede, concede; rescue, save.
To Delude, deceive, impose upon, cheat, lead away.
Deluge, overflow, inundation.
Delusion, fallacy, illusion, cheat, guile.
To Demand, ask for, claim, require.
Demeanor, behavior, deportment, carriage, conduct.
Demise, death, decease, departure.
To Demolish, destroy, dismantle, raze.
To Demonstrate, prove, evince, manifest.
To Demur, pause, doubt, hesitate, object.
To Denominate, name, entitle, style, designate.
Denomination, name, title, appellation.
To Denote, signify, imply, mark, betoken.
Dense, close, compact, heavy, thick.
To Deny, oppose, contradict, refuse, disown, disclaim, disavow.
Departure, exit, forsaking, abandoning.
Dependence, reliance; trust, confidence.
To Depict, delineate, paint, sketch, represent.
To Deplore, bewail, bemoan, lament, mourn.
Deponent, evidence, witness.
Deportment. See Demeanor.
Deposit, pledge, security, pawn.
Depraved, abandoned, profligate, corrupt, vitiated, vicious.
Depravity, corruption, vitiation; vice, wickedness.

To Depreciate, disparage, detract, traduce, degrade, decry, lower.

To Depress, abase, degrade, humble, bring low, disgrace.

Depression, dejection, melancholy.

To Deprive, bereave, hinder, debar, abridge.

Depth, profundity, deepness.

To Depute, constitute, appoint.

Deputy, delegate, substitute, envoy, representative.

To Derange, disorder, disconcert, discompose.

Derangement, insanity, madness, lunacy, mania.

To Deride, mock, ridicule, rally, banter.

To Derive, trace, deduce, infer.

To Derogate, despise, degrade.

To Describe, relate, recount, narrate, represent.

Description, account, narrative, relation, recital, detail, explanation, narration.

To Descry, discover, find out, espy.

Desert, merit, worth.

To Design, purpose, intend, propose, mean, project, scheme.

To Designate. See Denominate.

To Desire, wish, long for, hanker after, covet, beg, solicit.

To Desist, leave off, cease, discontinue.

Desolate, solitary, desert, devastated.

Despair, desperation, despondency, hopelessness.

To Despatch, hasten, accelerate, expedite, speed.

Desperate, despairing, hopeless, desponding.

Despicable, contemptible, pitiful, mean, vile, worthless.

To Despise, contemn, scorn, disdain.

Despondency. See Despair.

Despotic, arbitrary, absolute, self-willed.

Destination, destiny, purpose, appointment, fate, lot, doom.

Destitute, bare, scanty; forsaken, forlorn.

To Destroy, demolish, consume, waste, annihilate, raze, dismantle, ruin.

Desultory, loose, immethodical, cursory, hasty, slight, roving, wavering.

To Detach, separate, sever, disjoin.

Detail, account, narrative, description, relation, recital, explanation, narration.

To Detain, hold, keep, retain.

To Detect, discover, convict.

To Deter, discourage, dishearten.

To Determine, resolve, decide, conclude upon, fix, settle; limit, put an end to.

Determined, decided, fixed, resolute, firm.

To Detest, abhor, loathe, abominate.

To Detract, asperse, calumniate; defame, scandalize, vilify, slander.

Detriment, disadvantage, hurt, injury, prejudice, loss, damage.

Devastation, ravage, desolation, havoc, waste.

To Develop, unfold, unravel, exhibit.

To Deviate, swerve, stray, wander, err, digress.

Detestable, abominable, execrable, hateful.

Device, contrivance, invention, scheme, design.

To Devise, contrive, invent, design; bequeath.

Devoid, vacant, empty, void.

To Devote, addict, apply, dedicate; consecrate.

Devout, religious, holy, pious.

Dexterity, ability, skilfulness, adroitness, address.

Dextrous, clever, skilful, apt, ready, adroit, expert.
Dialect, tongue, language, speech, idiom.
Dialogue, conversation, conference, colloquy.
To Dictate, prescribe, suggest.
Diction, style, phrase, phraseology, expression.
Dictionary, vocabulary, lexicon, nomenclature.
To Die, expire, perish, depart.
Diet, food, regimen.
To Differ, vary, disagree, dissent.
Difference, variety, contrariety, variance, dissimilitude, inequality.
Different, distinct, separate, diverse, various; unlike.
Difficult, hard, arduous.
Difficulty, obstacle, impediment, obstruction, trouble, trial, embarrassment.
Diffident, distrustful, suspicious; modest, bashful.
Diffuse, prolix, expansive, spread out.
To Digest, dispose, arrange.
Dignified, magisterial, stately, august, pompous, lofty.
To Digress, deviate, wander.
To Dilate, enlarge, extend, expand; expatiate.
Dilatory, slow, tardy, tedious.
Diligent, active, assiduous, expeditious, sedulous, persevering, laborious.
Dim, obscure, dark, mysterious.
To Diminish, liquidate, abate, decrease, lessen, subside.
Diminutive, small, little.
To Direct, regulate, dispose, conduct, manage.
Direction, address, superscription.
Directly, immediately, promptly, instantly, instantaneously.
Disability, inability, weakness, incompetency.
Disadvantage, detriment, injury, hurt, prejudice.

To Disagree, differ, vary, dissent.
Disagreement, dissension, division, discord.
To Disappear, vanish.
To Disappoint, frustrate, foil, defeat.
Disapprobation, displeasure, censure.
Disaster, calamity, misfortune, mishap, mischance.
To Disavow, disown, disclaim, deny.
Disbelief, unbelief, skepticism.
To Discard, dismiss, discharge.
To Discern, distinguish, discover, penetrate, discriminate.
Discernible, perceptible, ascertainable, apparent, visible, evident, manifest.
Disciple, follower, scholar, adherent, partisan.
Discipline, education, government; correction, punishment, chastisement.
To Disclaim, disown, disavow, deny.
To Disclose, discover, reveal, make known, divulge.
To Discompose, disorder, disconcert, derange.
To Disconcert, unsettle, ruffle, discompose, derange, disorder, displace, confuse.
To Discontinue, cease, leave off, desist.
Discord, disagreement, contention, strife, dissension.
To Discourage, deter, dishearten; dissuade.
To Discover, uncover, disclose, make known, communicate, impart, reveal; detect, find out.
Discredit, disgrace, reproach, scandal, disrepute, ignominy, dishonor; opprobrium, obloquy, shame.
Discretion, judgment, prudence.
Discrimination, discernment, judgment, acuteness, penetration.

DISDAIN, arrogance, haughtiness, scorn, contempt.
DISEASE, disorder, distemper, malady.
To DISENTANGLE, disengage, extricate.
To DISFIGURE, deface, deform.
DISGRACE. See DISCREDIT.
To DISGRACE, degrade, abase, debase, dishonor.
To DISGUISE, dissemble, conceal.
DISGUST, aversion, dislike, distaste; loathing, nausea.
To DISHEARTEN, discourage, depress.
DISHONOR, disgrace, shame, opprobrium.
DISINCLINATION, dislike, aversion.
To DISJOIN, separate, sever, dissever, detach.
DISLIKE, aversion, antipathy, repugnance.
DISMAL, dull, gloomy, sad.
To DISMAY, appall, daunt, terrify.
To DISMEMBER, disjoint, dislocate.
DISMISS, discharge, discard.
DISORDER, derangement, confusion; disease, distemper, malady.
DISORDERLY, irregular, inordinate, intemperate.
To DISOWN, disavow, disclaim, deny, renounce.
To DISPARAGE, depreciate, derogate, detract, decry, degrade.
DISPARITY, inequality, dissimilitude, unlikeness.
DISPASSIONATE, cool, calm.
To DISPEL, dissipate, disperse.
To DISPERSE, distribute, deal out; scatter, spread.
To DISPLAY, exhibit, show, parade.
To DISPLEASE, offend, vex, anger.
DISPLEASURE, dislike, dissatisfaction, distaste, disapprobation.

DISPOSAL, disposition, arrangement.
To DISPOSE, arrange, place, regulate, order.
DISPOSITION, temper, inclination.
To DISPROVE, refute, confute, oppugn.
To DISPUTE, argue, debate, contest, contend, controvert.
DISPUTE, altercation, quarrel, contest, difference.
To DISREGARD, slight, neglect, contemn.
DISSATISFACTION. See DISPLEASURE.
To DISSEMBLE, disguise, conceal.
To DISSEMINATE, spread, propagate, circulate, diffuse.
DISSENSION, discord, contention.
To DISSENT, differ, disagree, vary.
DISSERTATION, essay, treatise, tract.
DISSIMULATION, simulation, deceit, hypocrisy.
To DISSIPATE, disperse, dispel, expend, squander, waste.
DISSOLUTE, loose, lax, vague, licentious.
DISTANT, far, remote.
DISTASTE, dislike, dissatisfaction, disgust.
DISTEMPER, disorder, disease, malady.
DISTINCT, separate, different; plain, visible, obvious.
DISTINCTION, difference; superiority, rank.
DISTINCTLY, clearly, plainly, obviously.
To DISTINGUISH, perceive, discern; discriminate; signalize, mark out.
DISTINGUISHED, conspicuous, noted, eminent, illustrious.
To DISTORT, turn, twist, bend, wrest, pervert.
DISTRACTED, discomposed, disturbed, perplexed.
To DISTRESS, afflict, trouble, pain, harass, perplex.

DISTRESS, anguish, agony, pain, suffering; adversity.
To DISTRIBUTE, apportion, assign, allot, share.
DISTRICT, region, division, tract, quarter, portion.
DISTRUSTFUL, suspicious; diffident.
To DISTURB, interrupt, trouble, molest, disquiet, tumultuate.
DISTURBANCE, derangement, commotion.
To DIVE, plunge.
To DIVE into, pry, scrutinize.
DIVERS, different, several, sundry, various.
DIVERSION, amusement, entertainment, recreation, sport, pastime.
To DIVERT, amuse, entertain.
To DIVIDE, separate, part; distribute, share.
DIVINE, heavenly, godlike, holy, sacred.
To DIVINE, guess, conjecture.
DIVISION, part, share, portion, section.
To DIVULGE, disclose, make known, communicate, reveal, discover, impart.
DIURNAL, daily, quotidian.
To DO, make, act; effect, effectuate, accomplish, perform, execute, achieve.
DOCILE, tractable, ductile, pliant, yielding.
DOCTRINE, dogma, tenet.
DOGMATICAL, positive, confident, authoritative, magisterial.
DOLEFUL, piteous, woful, rueful.
DOMESTIC, servant, menial, drudge.
DOMINEERING, imperious, lordly, overbearing.
DOMINION, rule, empire, authority; reign, strength, force.
DONATION, gift, present, alms.
DOOM, fate, destiny, lot, sentence.
DOUBLE-DEALING, deceit, duplicity, deception, fraud, dishonesty.

DOUBT, hesitation, uncertainty. suspense.
To DOUBT, question, hesitate, demur, scruple, waver.
DOUBTFUL, dubious, uncertain, equivocal, ambiguous, questionable, precarious.
To DOZE, sleep, slumber, drowse, nap.
To DRAG, draw, pull, haul, tug.
To DRAIN, exhaust, expend.
To DRAW. See DRAG.
To DRAW from, exact, extort, extract.
To DRAW back, withdraw, retreat, recede, retire.
To DREAD, fear, stand in awe; apprehend.
DREADFUL, fearful, frightful, terrific, awful, horrid, horrible, tremendous.
DREGS, sediment, refuse, dross, scum, recrement.
To DRENCH, steep, soak.
DRIFT, scope, aim, tendency.
DRESS, apparel, array, attire, garments, vestments.
DRINK, beverage, potion.
DROLL, laughable, ludicrous, ridiculous, comic, comical.
To DROOP, languish, pine, sink, fade.
DROSS. See DREGS.
To DROWSE. See DOZE.
DRUDGE, servant, domestic, menial.
DRUDGERY, labor, toil, work.
DRUNKENNESS, intoxication, inebriety, crapulousness.
DUBIOUS, doubtful, questionable, equivocal, ambiguous; precarious, uncertain.
DUCTILE, tractable, docile.
DRYNESS, drought, aridity.
DUE, debt, right.
DULL, stupid, heavy, drowsy, gloomy, sad, dismal.
DUMB, silent, mute, speechless.
DUPLICITY, deceit, deception, double-dealing, guile.

DURABLE, lasting, permanent, constant, continuing.
DUTIFUL, obedient, submissive, respectful.
DUTY, business, office; obedience, respect, obligation.
DWELLING, abode, residence, domicile, habitation.
To DWELL, abide, stay, rest, sojourn; reside, inhabit.

E

EAGER, hot, ardent, vehement, impetuous; forward.
EAGERNESS, avidity, greediness.
EARLY, soon, betimes.
To EARN, acquire, obtain, gain, win.
EARNEST, eager, serious; pledge.
EASE, quiet, rest, repose; lightness, facility.
To EASE, or calm, assuage, alleviate, allay, mitigate, appease, pacify.
EBULLITION, effervescence, fermentation, a boiling over.
ECCENTRIC, irregular, anomalous; singular, odd, particular, strange.
ECCLESIASTIC, divine, theologian.
ECONOMICAL, sparing, saving, thrifty, careful, frugal, parsimonious, niggardly, penurious.
ECSTASY, delight, rapture, transport.
EDGE, border, rim, margin, brink, brim, verge.
EDICT, decree, proclamation.
EDIFICE, structure, fabric.
EDUCATION, instruction, tuition, breeding.
To EFFACE, blot out, expunge, rase, erase, obliterate, cancel.
To EFFECT, accomplish, fulfil, realize, achieve, complete, execute.
EFFECT, consequence, result, issue, event.

EFFECTS, goods, chattels, furniture, movables, property.
EFFECTIVE, efficient, efficacious, effectual, operative.
EFFEMINATE, feminine, female, womanish, tender.
EFFETE, barren; worn out.
EFFICIENT, competent, able, capable, fitted, effectual, effective.
EFFIGY, image, picture, likeness.
EFFORT, endeavor, exertion, essay, trial, attempt.
EFFRONTERY, boldness, audacity, assurance, hardihood, impudence.
EFFUSION, dispersion; waste.
EGOTISTICAL, conceited, vain, opinionated.
ELDER, senior, older.
To ELECT, choose, select, appoint.
ELEGANT, graceful, beautiful.
To ELEVATE, raise, lift, exalt, erect.
ELIGIBLE, fit, worthy, preferable.
ELOCUTION, eloquence, oratory, rhetoric.
To ELUCIDATE, explain, illustrate, clear up.
ELUCIDATION, explanation, exposition, annotation, comment.
To ELUDE, evade, escape, avoid, shun.
To EMANATE, arise, proceed, issue, spring, flow.
To EMBARRASS, entangle, perplex, distress, trouble.
To EMBELLISH, adorn, decorate, beautify, deck, illustrate.
EMBLEM, figure, type, symbol, adumbration, allusion.
To EMBRACE, clasp, hug; comprise, comprehend, contain, include.
EMBRYO, fœtus, germ; unfinished, imperfect.
To EMEND, amend, correct, better, mend, reform, rectify; improve.
To EMERGE, rise, issue, emanate, come forth.

EMERGENCY, exigency, necessity.
EMINENT, distinguished, conspicuous, noted, prominent; elevated, illustrious
EMISSARY, spy, secret agent.
To EMIT, send forth, evaporate, exhale.
EMOLUMENT, gain, profit, lucre, advantage.
EMOTION, agitation, trepidation, tremor.
EMPHASIS, stress, accent.
EMPIRE, dominion, power, reign; kingdom, state.
EMPLOYMENT, business, avocation, engagement, office, trade, profession, occupation.
To EMPOWER, authorize, commission; enable.
EMPTY, void, devoid, vacant, vacuous, unfilled.
EMULATION, rivalry, competition.
To ENCHANT, charm, fascinate, captivate, enrapture.
To ENCIRCLE, enclose, embrace; surround, environ, circumscribe.
ENCOMIUM, eulogy, panegyric, praise.
To ENCOMPASS. See ENCIRCLE.
ENCOUNTER, attack, combat, assault.
To ENCOURAGE, countenance, sanction, support, foster, cherish; animate, embolden, cheer; incite, urge, impel, stimulate, instigate.
To ENCROACH, intrude, intrench, infringe, invade.
To ENCUMBER, load, clog; impede, hinder.
END, aim, object, purpose; close, termination, extremity, sequel, finish.
To ENDEAVOR, attempt, try, aim, essay, strive.
ENDEAVOR, aim, effort, exertion, attempt.

ENDLESS, eternal, everlasting, interminable, perpetual, infinite.
To ENDOW, endue, invest.
ENDOWMENT, gift, talent.
ENDURANCE, fortitude, patience, resignation.
To ENDURE, support, bear, suffer, sustain.
ENEMY, foe, opponent, antagonist, adversary.
ENERGY, force, vigor, strength, potency, efficacy.
To ENERVATE, enfeeble, weaken, unnerve, debilitate.
To ENGAGE, attract, invite, allure, entertain.
ENGAGEMENT, avocation, business, employment, occupation, office, profession; word, promise; battle, combat.
To ENGENDER, breed, generate, produce.
ENGRAVING, picture, print.
To ENGROSS, absorb, swallow up, imbibe; monopolize.
To ENGULF, swallow up, absorb, engross.
ENJOYMENT, pleasure, fruition, gratification.
To ENLARGE, increase, extend, lengthen.
To ENLIGHTEN, illumine, illuminate.
To ENLIST, enroll, register, record.
To ENLIVEN, animate, inspire, exhilarate, cheer.
ENMITY, animosity, hostility, hatred, ill-will, malignity.
ENORMOUS, huge, vast, immense, prodigious.
ENOUGH, sufficiency, plenty, abundance.
To ENRAGE, irritate, incense, aggravate, incite, stimulate, exasperate, inflame.
To ENRAPTURE. See ENCHANT.
To ENROLL. See ENLIST.
ENSAMPLE, example, pattern.
To ENSLAVE, captivate.

To ENSUE, follow, succeed.
To ENTANGLE, perplex, embarrass, inveigle, insnare, implicate, infold, involve, entrap.
ENTERPRISE, undertaking, adventure, attempt.
ENTERPRISING, adventurous.
To ENTER upon, begin, commence.
To ENTERTAIN, amuse, divert.
ENTERTAINMENT, amusement, diversion, recreation, pastime, sport; feast, banquet, carousal, treat.
ENTHUSIAST, visionary, fanatic.
To ENTICE, allure, attract, decoy, tempt, seduce, abduct.
ENTIRE, whole, complete, perfect, integral, total.
To ENTITLE, name, designate, denominate, style, characterize.
To ENTRAP. See ENTANGLE.
To ENTREAT, beg, crave, solicit, beseech, implore, supplicate.
ENTREATY, petition, prayer, request, suit.
To ENVEIGLE. See ENTANGLE.
To ENVIRON. See ENCIRCLE.
ENVY, jealousy, suspicion, grudging.
EPICURE, voluptuary, sensualist.
To EPITOMIZE, abridge, reduce, condense.
EPOCH, time, period, era, age, date.
To EQUIP, fit out, prepare, qualify.
EQUAL, equable, uniform; adequate, proportionate, commensurate; equivalent.
EQUAL to, adequate, commensurate, proportionate.
EQUITABLE, just, fair, honest, reasonable.
EQUIVOCAL, ambiguous, doubtful.
To EQUIVOCATE, evade, prevaricate.
ERA, time, point, period, date, epoch, age.

To ERADICATE, extirpate, root out, exterminate.
To ERASE, blot out, expunge, rase, efface, obliterate, cancel.
To ERECT, set up, raise, elevate, construct; institute, establish, found.
ERRAND, mission, message.
ERROR, mistake, blunder, fault.
ERUDITION, learning, knowledge, science.
ERUPTION, explosion, breaking out.
To ESCAPE, elude, evade.
To ESCHEW, avoid, shun, elude.
To ESCORT, attend, accompany, wait on.
ESPECIALLY, particularly, specially, principally, chiefly.
To ESPY, discern, discover, find out, descry.
ESSAY, attempt, trial, endeavor, effort; tract, treatise, dissertation.
ESSENTIAL, necessary, indispensable, requisite.
To ESTABLISH, confirm, settle, fix, institute, found.
To ESTEEM, prize, value, appreciate; respect.
ESTEEM, regard, respect, prize, value, revere.
To ESTIMATE, count, calculate, compute, reckon, number, rate, appraise; appreciate, esteem, value.
ETERNAL, everlasting, boundless, interminable, endless, infinite.
EULOGY, encomium, panegyric.
To EVADE, escape, elude; equivocate, prevaricate.
To EVAPORATE, exhale, emit.
EVASION, shift, subterfuge; prevarication, equivocation.
EVEN, equal, equable, uniform; smooth, plain, level.
EVENT, incident, occurrence, adventure, issue, consequence, result, accident.

Ever, always, perpetually, continually, incessantly, unceasingly, constantly.
Everlasting. See Eternal.
Evidence, testimony, deposition, proof; deponent, witness.
Evil, bad, wicked; misfortune, harm, mischief, ill.
To Evince, argue, prove, manifest, demonstrate.
To Exact, extort, draw from.
Exact, accurate, correct, precise, nice.
To Exalt, raise, elevate, erect, lift up.
Examination, search, inquiry, research, scrutiny, investigation; discussion.
Example, pattern, ensample, precedent.
To Exasperate, aggravate, provoke, excite, irritate.
To Exceed, excel, surpass, transcend, outdo.
Excellence, superiority, perfection.
Except, unless, besides.
Exception, objection, difficulty.
Excess, superfluity, redundance; intemperance.
To Exchange, change, barter, truck, commute.
Exchange, interchange, reciprocity; barter, dealing, trade, traffic.
To Excite, incite, awaken, arouse, stimulate, provoke, irritate.
To Exclaim, call, shout, cry.
To Exculpate, exonerate, absolve, acquit, justify.
Excursion, ramble, tour, trip, jaunt.
To Excuse, exculpate, absolve, acquit.
Excuse, pretence, pretension, pretext.
Execrable, abominable, detestable, hateful, accursed.
Execration, curse, malediction, imprecation.

To Execute, accomplish, fulfil, realize, effect, achieve, consummate, complete, finish.
Exemption, freedom, immunity, privilege.
To Exercise, exert, practise, carry on.
To Exhale, emit, evaporate.
To Exhaust, spend, drain, empty.
To Exhibit, show, display.
Exhibition, show, sight, spectacle, representation.
To Exhilarate, animate, inspire, enliven, cheer.
To Exhort, persuade, incite.
To Exhume, unbury, disinter.
Exigency, emergency, necessity.
Exile, banishment, expulsion, proscription.
To Exonerate, exculpate, relieve, absolve, clear, acquit, discharge, justify.
To Expand, spread, diffuse, dilate.
To Expect, look for, await.
Expectation, hope, anticipation, confidence, trust.
Expedient, fit, necessary, essential, requisite.
To Expedite, accelerate, quicken, hasten.
Expeditious, prompt, diligent, speedy, quick.
To Expel, cast out, banish, exile.
To Expend, spend, dissipate, waste.
Expense, cost, price, charge.
Expensive, costly, dear, sumptuous, valuable.
Experience, experiment, trial, proof, test,
Expert, clever, dextrous, adroit, skilful.
To Expiate, atone for, blot out.
To Explain, expound, interpret, elucidate.
Explanation, explication, reci-

tal, account, description, detail, relation.
EXPLICIT, express, plain, definite.
EXPLOIT, achievement, feat, deed, accomplishment.
To EXPLORE, search, pry into.
EXPOSED, subject, liable, obnoxious.
EXPOSTULATE, remonstrate, altercate, discuss.
To EXPOUND, explain, interpret, unfold.
EXPRESS, explicit, plain, definite.
To EXPRESS, declare, utter, signify, testify, intimate.
EXPRESSIVE, significant.
To EXPUNGE, blot out, erase, efface, obliterate.
To EXTEND, enlarge, increase, stretch out.
EXTENSIVE, comprehensive, wide, large.
EXTENUATE, palliate, lessen, diminish.
EXTERIOR, outward, external.
To EXTERMINATE, extirpate, eradicate, root out, destroy.
EXTERNAL, exterior, outward.
To EXTOL, praise, laud, applaud, commend.
To EXTORT, exact, draw from.
EXTRAORDINARY, remarkable, uncommon, eminent.
EXTRAVAGANT, prodigal, lavish, profuse, excessive.
EXTREME, extremity, end, termination.
To EXTRICATE, disengage, disentangle, disembarrass.
EXTRINSIC, extraneous, foreign.
EXUBERANT, plenteous, luxuriant, plentiful, abundant.
EXULTATION, transport, joy.

F

FABRIC, edifice, structure.
To FABRICATE, invent, frame, feign, forge.

FABRICATION, fiction, falsehood, invention.
To FACE, confront.
FACE, countenance, visage.
FACETIOUS, pleasant, jocular, jocose.
FACILITY, ease, lightness.
FACT, incident, circumstance.
FACTION, party, junta, junto.
FACULTY, ability, talent, gift, endowment.
FAILING, failure, imperfection, weakness, frailty, foible; miscarriage, misfortune.
FAINT, languid, weak, low.
FAIR, clear; honest, equitable, reasonable.
FAITH, belief, trust, credit, fidelity.
FAITHFUL, trusty.
FAITHLESS, perfidious, unfaithful, treacherous.
To FALL, drop, sink, tremble, droop.
To FALL short, fail, be deficient.
FALLACIOUS, deceitful, fraudulent, delusive, illusive.
FALSEHOOD, untruth, fiction, fabrication, falsity.
To FALTER, hesitate, waver.
FAME, reputation, renown, celebrity, credit, honor; report, rumor.
FAMILIAR, free, affable; intimate.
FAMILIARITY, acquaintance, intimacy, affability, fellowship.
FAMILY, house, lineage, race.
FAMOUS, celebrated, renowned, illustrious, eminent, distinguished, transcendent, excellent.
FANATIC, enthusiast, visionary.
FANCIFUL, fantastical, whimsical, capricious, ideal.
FANCY, imagination, conceit, ideality.
FAR, distant, remote.
FARE, provision; journey, passage.

FAREWELL, taking leave, valediction.
To FASCINATE, charm, enrapture, enchant.
FASHION, custom, manner, practice, mode.
To FASHION, form, mould, shape.
To FASTEN, fix, stick, hold; affix, attach, annex.
FASTIDIOUS, squeamish, over-nice.
FATAL, deadly, mortal.
FATE, destiny, lot, doom; chance, fortune.
FATIGUE, weariness, lassitude.
FAVOR, benefit, kindness, civility, grace.
FAVORABLE, auspicious, propitious.
FAULT, blemish, defect, imperfection, vice, error, failing.
To FAWN, coax, wheedle, cajole.
To FEAR, apprehend, dread.
FEAR, fright, apprehension, terror, alarm, consternation, trepidation, dread.
FEARFUL, afraid, timid, timorous; dreadful, frightful, horrible, distressing.
FEARLESS, brave, bold, courageous, undaunted, daring, valorous, heroic, intrepid, magnanimous.
FEASIBLE, specious, colorable, plausible.
FEAST, banquet, carousal, treat, entertainment, festival.
FEAT, achievement, exploit, deed, accomplishment.
FEEBLE, weak, infirm.
FEELING, sensibility, sensation, consciousness, susceptibility; kindness, generosity.
To FEIGN, pretend, dissemble; invent, forge.
To FELICITATE, make joyful, delight; congratulate.
FELICITY, happiness, bliss, blessedness, beatitude.
FELLOWSHIP, society; acquaintance, intimacy, familiarity.

FELON, criminal, culprit, malefactor.
FENCE, guard, security.
FEROCIOUS, fierce, savage, ravenous.
FERTILE, fruitful, prolific, productive.
FERTILITY, fruitfulness, fecundity, productiveness.
FERVOR, ardor, warmth, vehemence.
FEUD, affray, fray, quarrel, broil, dispute.
FICKLE, changeable, variable, inconstant, unstable, wavering, versatile.
FICTION, falsehood, fabrication, invention.
FIDELITY, faith, honesty, integrity.
FIERCE, ferocious, savage.
FIERY, hot, ardent, passionate, fervent, impetuous.
FIGHT, conflict, combat, contest, encounter, contention, battle, engagement, struggle.
FIGURE, form, semblance, shape; metaphor, allegory, emblem.
FILTHY, nasty, foul, unclean, dirty, gross.
FINAL, ultimate, last, latest, conclusive; decisive.
To FIND out, discover, descry, detect; ascertain.
FINE, delicate, pure, nice; handsome, pretty, beautiful, elegant, showy.
A FINE, mulct, penalty, forfeiture, amercement.
FINESSE, artifice, trick, stratagem, delusion, deceit, guile.
To FINISH, perfect, complete, conclude, terminate, close.
FINITE, limited, bounded, terminable.
FIRM, stable, solid, robust, strong, sturdy.
FIRST, primary, primitive, pristine, original.
To FIT, suit, adapt, adjust; equip, prepare, qualify.

Fit, apt, suitable, meet; becoming, decent; expedient.
Fitted, competent, adapted, qualified, suited.
To Fix, fasten, attach, stick; settle, establish, limit, determine; institute, appoint.
To Flag, decline, droop, languish, pine.
Flagitious, flagrant, heinous, atrocious.
Flat, level; insipid, dull, spiritless, tasteless, vapid, inanimate, lifeless.
Flattery, false compliment, adulation, obsequiousness, sycophancy, parasitism.
Flavor, taste, relish, savor.
Flaw, blemish, spot, speck, crack, defect.
Fleeting, temporary, transient, transitory.
Fleetness, quickness, celerity, swiftness, rapidity, velocity.
Flexible, pliant, supple.
Flightiness, levity, lightness, giddiness, volatility.
Flimsy, light, weak, superficial, shallow.
To Flirt, jeer, gibe, scoff, taunt.
To Flourish, thrive, prosper.
To Fluctuate, waver, hesitate, vacillate, scruple.
To Flutter, palpitate, undulate, vibrate, pant.
Foe, enemy, opponent, antagonist, adversary.
Foible, imperfection, failing, frailty, weakness.
To Foil, defeat, frustrate, disappoint.
Folks, persons, people, individuals.
To Follow, succeed, ensue; imitate, copy; pursue.
A Follower, adherent, disciple, partisan; pursuer, successor.
Folly, weakness, irrationality; foolery.
To Fondle, caress.

Fondness, affection, attachment, kindness, love.
To Forsake, abandon, desert, renounce, abdicate, relinquish, quit, give up, forego.
Food, diet, regimen.
Fool, idiot, buffoon.
Foolery, folly, absurdity.
Foolhardy, adventurous, rash, incautious, venturesome, venturous, hasty, precipitate.
Foolish, simple, silly, irrational; ridiculous, preposterous.
Footstep, trace, track, mark.
Foppish, finical, spruce, dandyish.
To Forbear, abstain, refrain, withhold.
To Forbid, interdict, prohibit.
Forecast, forethought, foresight, premeditation.
Force, strength, vigor, might, energy, power, violence.
To Force, compel, constrain, oblige, necessitate.
Forcible, strong, cogent, irresistible.
To Forebode, augur, presage, portend, betoken.
Forefather, progenitor, ancestor.
Foregoing, antecedent, anterior, previous, prior, former, preceding.
Foreign, extraneous, exotic, extrinsic.
Forerunner, precursor, harbinger, messenger.
Foresight. See Forecast.
To Foretell, predict, prophesy, prognosticate, presage, betoken, augur, portend.
Forethought, foresight, forecast, premeditation.
Forfeiture, fine, mulct, penalty, amercement.
To Forge, invent, frame, feign, fabricate, counterfeit.
Forgetfulness, oblivion.
To Forgive, pardon, absolve, remit, acquit, excuse.

FORLORN, forsaken, destitute.
FORM, figure, shape, conformation, fashion, appearance, representation, semblance; ceremony, observance, rite.
To FORM, make, create, produce, constitute; fashion, mould, shape.
FORMAL, ceremonious, precise, exact, stiff, methodical.
FORMER, antecedent, anterior, previous, prior, preceding, foregoing.
FORMERLY, anciently, in times past, in days of yore.
FORMIDABLE, terrible, tremendous, shocking.
To FORSAKE, abandon, desert, renounce; abdicate.
FORSAKEN, abandoned, forlorn, destitute.
To FORSWEAR, perjure.
To FORTIFY, strengthen, invigorate.
FORTITUDE, resolution, courage, bravery.
FORTUITOUS, accidental, casual, contingent, incidental.
FORTUNATE, lucky, prosperous, successful.
FORTUNE, chance, fate.
FORWARD, onward, progressive; confident, presumptuous, immodest.
To FORWARD, advance, promote, prefer.
To FOSTER, cherish, indulge, harbor.
FOUL, nasty, filthy, defiled.
To FOUND, ground, rest, build; institute, establish.
FOUNDATION, ground, basis; establishment, settlement.
FOUNTAIN, spring, source.
FRACTION, part, piece.
FRACTURE, rupture, breach.
FRAGILE, brittle, weak, frail.
FRAILTY, weakness, imperfection, failing, foible.
FRAME, temper, temperament, constitution.

To FRAME, invent, fabricate, forge, feign.
FRANK, artless, candid, free, open, ingenuous, plain.
FRATERNITY, brotherhood.
FRAUD, deceit, guile, cheat, imposition.
FRAY, affray; quarrel, broil, feud, altercation.
FREAK, whim, caprice.
FREE, liberal, generous, bountiful, munificent, unconstrained, unconfined, unreserved; familiar, easy, frank, candid, ingenuous; exempt, clear.
To FREE, set free, deliver, liberate, affranchise.
FREEDOM, liberty, independence, unrestraint; familiarity; exemption, privilege.
FREIGHT, cargo, lading, load, burden.
To FREQUENT, resort to, haunt.
FREQUENTLY, often, commonly, usually, generally.
FRESH, new, novel, recent, modern.
To FRET, gall, rub, chafe; agitate, vex.
FRETFUL, splenetic, peevish, petulant, captious.
FRIENDLY, amicable; social, sociable.
FRIGID, cool, cold.
FRIGHT, alarm, terror, consternation.
To FRIGHTEN, affright, intimidate.
FRIGHTFUL, fearing, dreadful, terrific, horrid, horrible.
FRIVOLOUS, trifling, trivial, petty.
FROLIC, gambol, prank, spree.
FROWARD, awkward, cross, untoward, perverse.
FRUGAL, economical, saving, parsimonious.
FRUITFUL, fertile, prolific, pregnant, productive, abundant, plentiful.
FRUITION, enjoyment, gratification.

17

FRUITLESS, ineffectual, vain, abortive.
FRUSTRATE, defeat, foil, disappoint.
To FULFIL, accomplish, realize, effect, complete.
FULLY, largely, copiously, abundantly, completely.
FULNESS, plenitude, completeness, satiety, copiousness, abundance.
FUNCTION, office, place, charge.
FURIOUS, violent, boisterous, vehement, impetuous, angry.
To FURNISH, provide, procure, supply.
FURNITURE, goods, chattels, movables, effects.
FURY, madness, frenzy, rage, anger.
FUTILE, trifling, trivial, frivolous, useless.

G

To GAIN, get, acquire, obtain, attain, procure; win.
GAIN, profit, emolument, advantage, lucre, benefit.
GAIT, carriage, walk.
GALE, breeze, blast, gust; hurricane, tempest, storm.
To GALL, rub, chafe, fret, vex.
GALLANT, brave, courageous, daring, valorous, valiant, bold, heroic, intrepid, fearless.
GAMBOL, frolic, prank, spree.
GAME, play, sport, amusement, pastime.
GANG, band, company, crew.
GAP, chasm, cleft, breach, break.
To GAPE, gaze, stare.
GARRULITY, loquacity, babbling, talkativeness.
To GATHER, assemble, muster, collect.
GAUDY, showy, gay, glittering.
GAY, cheerful, merry, sprightly, debonnair.
To GAZE, gape, stare.

GENERALLY, commonly, frequently, usually.
GENERATION, race, breed.
GENEROUS, beneficent, bountiful, munificent, liberal, bounteous.
GENIUS, intellect, invention, talent, taste.
GENTEEL, refined, polished, polite.
GENTLE, mild, meek, tame.
GENUINE, real, unalloyed, unadulterated, not spurious.
Not GENUINE, spurious, supposititious, adulterated.
To GERMINATE, bud, sprout, grow.
GESTURE, gesticulation, action, posture, attitude.
To GET, acquire, obtain, attain, gain, procure, realize.
GHASTLY, hideous, grim, grisly.
GHOST, spectre, apparition, phantom, vision.
To GIBE, scoff, sneer, jeer, mock, taunt.
GIDDINESS, lightness; flightiness, levity, volatility.
GIFT, donation, benefaction, gratuity, present; endowment, talent.
To GIVE, grant, bestow, confer, yield.
To GIVE up, abandon, forsake, renounce, dedicate, relinquish, quit.
GLAD, pleased, cheerful, joyful, exhilarated, delighted, gratified.
GLANCE, glimpse, look.
GLARE, flare, blaze, glitter, radiation.
To GLEAM, glimmer.
To GLIDE, slip, slide.
To GLITTER, shine, sparkle, glare, radiate.
GLOBE, circle, sphere, ball, orb.
GLOOM, heaviness, sadness, dullness, sullenness, moroseness, spleen.
To GLORY, boast, vaunt.
To GLOSS, varnish, palliate, cover, hide.

GLOSSARY, lexicon, dictionary, vocabulary.
To GLUT, satisfy, satiate, cloy.
GODLIKE, divine, heavenly, superhuman.
GODLY, righteous, holy, pious.
To GO before, precede.
GOOD, benefit, advantage, profit.
GOOD office, service, benefit.
GOODS, furniture, chattels, effects, movables; commodities, wares, merchandise.
GOVERNMENT, rule, administration, regulation, constitution.
GRACE, face, kindness, beneficence.
GRACEFUL, becoming, comely, elegant.
GRACIOUS, merciful, kind, benignant.
GRAND, majestic, stately, pompous, august, dignified, lofty, elevated, exalted, splendid, magnificent, sublime, noble.
To GRANT, give, yield, concede, cede, allow; bestow, confer.
GRANT, allowance, stipend; concession.
To GRASP, lay hold on, catch, seize, gripe.
GRATEFUL, agreeable, pleasing, welcome; thankful.
GRATIFICATION, enjoyment, fruition, pleasure.
GRATITUDE, thankfulness.
GRATUITOUS, voluntary.
GRATUITY, gift, recompense.
GRAVE, serious, sedate, thoughtful, solemn, sober; important, weighty.
GRAVE, tomb, sepulchre.
GREAT, big, large. See also GRAND.
GREATNESS, magnitude, bulk, size.
GREEDINESS, avidity, eagerness, voracity.
GREETING, salutation.
GRIEF, affliction, sorrow.

GRIEVANCE, hardship, uneasiness.
To GRIEVE, mourn, lament, sorrow, bewail.
GRIM, hideous, grisly, ghastly.
To GRIPE, lay hold on, catch, seize, grasp; press, squeeze, pinch.
To GROAN, moan.
GROSS, coarse; unseemly, shameful.
To GROUND, found, rest, base.
GROUP, assembly, assemblage, collection.
To GROW, increase.
GRUDGE, malice, rancor, spite, pique.
To GUARANTY, answer for, warrant, secure.
GUARD, fence, security, shield, defence.
To GUESS, conjecture, divine, surmise, suppose.
GUEST, visitant, visitor.
To GUIDE, lead, conduct, direct, regulate.
GUILE, deceit, fraud.
GUILTLESS, innocent, harmless.
GUISE, manner, mien, habit.
GULF, abyss.
To GUSH, stream, flow.
GUST, breeze, blast, gale.

H

HABIT. See GUISE.
HABITATION, dwelling, residence, abode.
To HALE, draw, drag, haul, pull, tug.
To HALLOW, consecrate, dedicate, sanctify.
HANDSOME, pretty, beautiful, fine.
To HANKER after, desire, long for, covet.
HANGING over, impending, imminent.
HAPPINESS, felicity, bliss, beatitude.
HARANGUE, address, speech, oration.
To HARASS, distress, perplex,

weary, tire, jade; molest, disturb.
HARBINGER, forerunner, precursor, messenger.
HARBOR, port, haven.
To HARBOR, lodge, shelter; indulge, cherish, foster.
HARD, firm, solid; hardy, unfeeling, insensible; difficult, arduous.
HARD-HEARTED, insensible, unfeeling, cruel, unmerciful, merciless.
HARDENED, hard, callous, obdurate, unfeeling, insensible, impenetrable.
HARDIHOOD, audacity, effrontery, boldness.
HARDLY, scarcely, with difficulty.
HARDSHIP, grievance.
HARM, evil, ill, misfortune, mishap; injury, damage, hurt.
HARMLESS, unconscious, innocent; inoffensive, unoffending.
HARMONY, agreement, accordance, unison; melody.
HARSH, rough, severe, rigorous.
HARSHNESS, acrimony, asperity, smartness, tartness.
To HASTEN, accelerate, quicken, expedite.
HASTINESS, precipitancy, rashness, temerity.
HASTY, quick; irascible, passionate, angry, hot; cursory, slight.
To HATE, detest, abhor, loathe, abominate.
HATEFUL, odious, detestable, execrable, abominable, loathsome.
HATRED, aversion, antipathy, repugnance, enmity, ill-will, rancour.
HAVEN, harbor, port.
HAUGHTINESS, arrogance, disdain, pride, loftiness, highmindedness.
To HAUL, draw, drag, hale, pull, tug.

HAZARD, danger, peril, chance, risk, venture.
HEAD, chieftain, leader, chief.
HEADSTRONG, heady, obstinate, stubborn, forward, venturesome.
To HEAL, cure, remedy.
HEALTHY, sound, sane; salubrious, wholesome, salutary, salutiferous.
To HEAP, pile, amass, accumulate.
To HEAR, hearken, overhear.
To HEARKEN, attend, listen.
HEARSAY, rumor, report.
HEARTY, warm, cordial, sincere.
HEATING, calorific, calefactory.
To HEAVE, hoist, lift, swell.
HEAVENLY, celestial, divine, godlike, angelic.
HEAVINESS, weight, gravity, gloom.
HEAVY, burdensome, ponderous, weighty, dull, drowsy, sluggish.
To HEED, attend to, mind, regard, notice.
HEEDLESS, inattentive, negligent, remiss, careless, thoughtless.
HEIGHT, crisis, acme.
To HEIGHTEN, raise, aggravate.
HEINOUS, flagrant, flagitious, atrocious.
To HELP, aid, assist, succor, relieve; serve.
HERESY, heterodoxy, schism.
HEROIC, brave, courageous, gallant, valiant, bold, intrepid, fearless.
To HESITATE, falter, pause; demur,-scruple.
HIDDEN, secret, latent, occult, mysterious.
To HIDE, conceal, disguise, secrete, cover; shelter, screen; dissemble.
HIDEOUS, ghastly, grim, grisly, frightful.
HIGH, tall, lofty, elevated.
HILARITY, mirth, merriment, joviality, jollity.

Hind, countryman, peasant, swain, rustic.
To Hinder, prevent, impede, obstruct, oppose, thwart, retard, stop, embarrass.
To Hint, allude, refer, glance at, intimate, suggest.
Hire, allowance, stipend, salary, wages, pay.
Hireling, mercenary, venal.
To Hit, strike, beat.
To Hoard, treasure, heap up.
To Hoist, lift, heave.
To Hold, keep, detain, retain; support, maintain, possess, occupy.
Holiness, sanctity, piety, devotion.
Hollow, vacant, empty, void.
Holy, pious, devout, religious; sacred, divine.
Holyday, feast, festival.
Honesty, integrity, purity, probity, sincerity, veracity, virtue, justice, equity, uprightness, rectitude, honor.
To Honor, reverence, venerate, respect, revere; dignify, exalt.
Hope, expectation, anticipation, trust, confidence.
Hopeless, desperate, desponding, despairing.
Horrible, fearful, dreadful, frightful, terrible, terrific, horrid.
Hostile, inimical, repugnant, adverse, opposite, contrary.
Hostility, animosity, enmity, opposition.
Hot, ardent, burning, fiery.
House, family, lineage, race; habitation, dwelling.
However, yet, nevertheless, notwithstanding.
Hue, color, tint.
To Hug, clasp, embrace, squeeze.
Huge, large, vast, enormous, immense.
Humanity, kindness, benevolence, benignity, tenderness.

To Humble, debase, abase, degrade, disgrace, humiliate.
Humble, lowly, modest, submissive, unpretending, unpresuming, unassuming.
Humidity, moisture, dampness.
Humor, temper, mood, frame; caprice, disposition; wit, burlesque, satire.
To Hurl, cast, throw.
Hurricane, tempest, storm, blast.
To Hurry, hasten; expedite; precipitate.
Hurt, harm, injury, damage, detriment, disadvantage, mischief, bane; sorry, grieved.
Hurtful, pernicious, baneful, nocent, noxious, mischievous, detrimental, injurious, prejudicial.
Husbandry, cultivation, tillage, farming.
Hypocrisy, simulation, dissimulation, deceit.

I

Idea, imagination, thought, conception, notion, perception.
Ideal, imaginary, intellectual.
Idiom, dialect.
Idiot, fool, natural.
Idle, lazy, indolent, sluggish; unemployed, vacant, at leisure.
Ignominy, opprobrium, infamy, shame, disgrace.
Ignorant, uninformed, uninstructed, unenlightened, unlearned, untaught, illiterate, unlettered.
Ill, bad, evil.
Illimitable, boundless, immense, unlimited, infinite.
Illiterate. See Ignorant.
Illness, sickness, indisposition, disease, distemper, disorder, malady.
Ill-tempered, morose, crabbed, sour.
To Illumine, illuminate, enlighten, illume.

ILLUSION, fallacy, chimera, deception.
To ILLUSTRATE, explain, elucidate, clear.
ILLUSTRIOUS, distinguished, conspicuous, noted, eminent, famous, celebrated, renowned.
ILL-WILL, enmity, hatred, rancor.
IMAGE, likeness, picture, representation, effigy.
IMAGINARY, ideal, fanciful.
To IMAGINE, think, conceive, apprehend; deem, suppose.
IMBECILITY, weakness, debility, infirmity.
To IMBIBE, absorb, swallow up, take in; ingulf, engross, consume.
To IMITATE, ape, mimic, mock; copy, counterfeit, follow.
IMMATERIAL, uncorporeal, unsubstantial, unbodied, spiritual; unimportant, insignificant, inconsiderable.
IMMEDIATELY, directly, instantly, instantaneously.
IMMENSE, enormous, huge, vast, prodigious, monstrous, illimitable.
IMMINENT, impending, threatening.
IMMODERATE, intemperate, excessive.
IMMODEST, indecent, indelicate, impudent, shameless.
IMMUNITY, privilege, prerogative, exemption.
To IMPAIR, injure; diminish, decrease.
To IMPART, communicate, make known, reveal, divulge, disclose, discover; give, yield.
IMPASSABLE, inaccessible, impervious.
To IMPEACH, accuse, charge, arraign, censure.
To IMPEDE, hinder, retard, obstruct, prevent.
To IMPEL, animate, actuate, induce, move, incite, instigate, encourage.
IMPENDING, imminent, threatening.
IMPERATIVE, commanding, authoritative, imperious, despotic.
IMPERFECTION, fault, defect, vice; weakness, frailty, failing, foible.
IMPERIOUS, commanding, imperative, authoritative; lordly, overbearing, domineering.
IMPERTINENT, irrelevant, inapplicable; rude, saucy, impudent, insolent.
IMPERVIOUS, unpassable, impassable, inaccessible, unapproachable.
IMPETUOUS, violent, boisterous, furious, vehement, rapid.
To IMPINGE, strike against, touch, clash with.
IMPIOUS, profane, irreligious.
IMPLACABLE, unrelenting, relentless, inexorable.
To IMPLANT, ingraft, instill, infuse, inculcate.
To IMPLICATE, involve, entangle, embarrass.
To IMPLORE, beg, solicit, beseech, entreat, crave, supplicate.
To IMPLY, infold, involve; denote, signify.
To IMPORT, imply, denote, mean, signify.
IMPORTANCE, signification, avail, consequence, weight, moment.
IMPORTANT, momentous, significant, weighty, consequential.
IMPORTUNATE, pressing, urgent.
IMPORTUNITY, solicitation.
To IMPOSE upon, deceive, delude.
IMPOST, tax, duty, custom, tribute.
IMPOSTOR, deceiver, cheat.
IMPOSTURE, cheat, deception, fraud, delusion, artifice, trick, imposition, stratagem.

IMPRECATION, curse, malediction, execration, anathema.
To IMPRESS, imprint, stamp, fix.
IMPRISONMENT, captivity, confinement.
To IMPROVE, amend, correct, emend, better, mend, reform, rectify.
IMPROVEMENT, progress, proficiency; amendment, &c.
IMPUDENCE, assurance, confidence, insolence.
IMPUDENT, impertinent, rude, saucy, insolent; immodest, shameless.
To IMPUGN, attack, assault, invade.
To IMPUTE, ascribe, attribute.
INABILITY, disability, impuissance, impotence.
INACCESSIBLE, unapproachable, impervious.
INACTIVE, inert, lazy, slothful, sluggish, idle.
INADEQUATE, incapable, insufficient, incompetent.
INADVERTENCY, inattention, oversight.
INANIMATE, lifeless, dead, inert.
INATTENTIVE, inadvertent, negligent, careless, remiss, thoughtless, heedless.
INBRED, inborn, inherent, innate.
INCAPABLE. See INADEQUATE.
INCESSANTLY, unremittingly, unceasingly, always, continually, perpetually.
INCIDENT, circumstance, fact, event, occurrence, adventure; accident, casualty, contingency.
INCIDENTAL, accidental, casual, fortuitous, contingent.
To INCITE, excite, provoke, stimulate, aggravate, move; encourage, animate, urge.
INCLINATION, disposition, tendency, bent, bias, prepossession, predilection, propensity, proneness; affection, attachment.
To INCLINE, lean, bend.

To INCLOSE, include, circumscribe.
To INCLUDE, comprise, comprehend, contain, embrace.
INCOHERENT, incongruous, inconsistent.
INCOMMODE, annoy, molest, disturb, inconvenience.
INCOMPETENT, inadequate, incapable, insufficient.
INCONSIDERABLE, unimportant, insignificant, immaterial.
INCONSISTENT, incongruous, incoherent.
INCONSTANT, changeable, fickle, variable, versatile.
INCONTROVERTIBLE, indubitable, unquestionable, indisputable, undeniable, irrefragable.
INCONVENIENCE, annoyance, molestation, disturbance, incommodiousness.
INCORPOREAL, unsubstantial, immaterial, spiritual.
IN COURSE, naturally, consequently.
INCREASE, augmentation, accession, addition.
INCREDULITY, unbelief, infidelity, skepticism.
To INCULCATE, infuse, instil, implant.
INCULPABLE, blameless.
INCURSION, invasion, irruption, inroad.
INDECENT, indelicate, immodest.
To INDICATE, point out, show, mark.
INDICATION, mark, sign, note, symptom, token.
INDIFFERENCE, apathy, carelessness, insensibility.
INDIFFERENT, unconcerned, regardless.
INDIGENCE, want, need, penury, poverty.
INDIGENOUS, natal, native.
INDIGNATION, anger, ire, wrath, resentment.
INDIGNITY, insult, affront; outrage.

INDISCRIMINATE, promiscuous, undistinguishing.
INDISPOSITION, illness, sickness; aversion, dislike.
INDISPUTABLE, indubitable, undeniable, incontrovertible, irrefragable, unquestionable.
INDISTINCT, confused; ambiguous, doubtful.
INDIVIDUAL, particular, identical.
INDOLENT, supine, listless, careless, idle, lazy.
INDUBITABLE. See INDISPUTABLE.
INDUCE, move, actuate, impel, instigate, urge.
INDUCEMENT, motive, reason, cause, incitement.
To INDULGE, foster, cherish, fondle, harbor.
INDUSTRIOUS, active, diligent, assiduous, laborious.
INEFFABLE, unspeakable, unutterable, inexpressible.
INEFFECTUAL, vain, fruitless, ineffective.
INEQUALITY, disparity, unevenness.
INERT, inactive, lazy, slothful, sluggish.
INEVITABLE, not to be avoided, unavoidable.
INEXORABLE, implacable, unrelenting, relentless.
INEXPRESSIBLE, unspeakable, ineffable, unutterable.
INFAMOUS, scandalous, shameful, ignominious, opprobrious.
INFATUATION, intoxication, stupefaction.
To INFECT, contaminate, taint, defile, pollute, vitiate.
INFECTION, contagion, taint, poison.
INFERENCE, conclusion, deduction.
INFERIOR, secondary; subordinate, subservient.
INFIDELITY, unbelief, incredulity, skepticism.
INFINITE, boundless, unbounded, unlimited, illimitable, immense.

INFIRM, weak, feeble, imbecile, debilitated.
To INFLAME, anger, irritate, incense, aggravate, exasperate.
INFLUENCE, credit, favor; authority, sway.
To INFORM, acquaint, apprise, make known; disclose, communicate.
INFORMANT, informer, accuser.
INFORMATION, advice, counsel, intelligence, notice.
INFRACTION, infringement, intrusion, encroachment.
To INFRINGE, encroach, infract, invade, intrude; transgress, violate.
To INFUSE, instil, ingraft, implant.
INGENIOUS, inventive, witty.
INGENUOUS, artless, candid, open, frank, plain.
To INGRAFT, implant.
To INGRATIATE, insinuate, recommend.
To INGULF, absorb, swallow up, engross.
To INHABIT, sojourn, reside; occupy, dwell.
INHERENT, innate, inbred, inborn.
INHUMAN, cruel, brutal, savage, barbarous.
INIMICAL, adverse, contrary, opposite, repugnant, hostile.
INIQUITOUS, wicked, nefarious, unjust.
INJUNCTION, command, order, mandate, precept.
INJURY, hurt, detriment, disadvantage; wrong.
To INJURE, impair, damage, deteriorate, hurt, wrong, harm.
INNATE. See INHERENT.
INNOCENT, guiltless, harmless, inoffensive.
INOFFENSIVE, unoffending, harmless.
INORDINATE, intemperate, irregular, disorderly, excessive.
INQUIRY, investigation, examination, research, scrutiny.

INQUISITIVE, prying, curious.
INROAD, incursion, invasion, irruption.
INSANITY, madness, derangement, lunacy, mania.
INSENSIBILITY, apathy, indifference, unfeelingness.
INSENSIBLE, hard, unfeeling, unsusceptible, callous.
INSIDE, interior.
INSIDIOUS, treacherous, sly, circumventive.
INSIGHT, inspection, introspection.
INSIGNIFICANT, unimportant, inconsiderable, trivial, immaterial.
To INSINUATE, hint, intimate, suggest; ingratiate.
INSIPID, dull, flat, spiritless.
To INSNARE, entrap, envigle.
INSOLENT, rude, saucy, impertinent, abusive, reproachful, scurrilous, opprobrious, insulting, offensive.
INSPECTION, insight, introspection; oversight, superintendence.
To INSPIRE, animate, exhilarate, enliven, cheer.
INSTANTANEOUSLY, directly, immediately, instantly.
To INSTIGATE, animate, incite, urge, impel, move, stimulate, encourage.
To INSTIL, infuse, insinuate.
To INSTITUTE, establish, found, erect; prescribe.
To INSTRUCT, inform, teach.
INSTRUCTION, advice, counsel, information.
INSTRUMENT, tool.
INSUFFICIENT, inadequate, incompetent, incapable.
INSULT, affront, offence, outrage, indignity.
INSULTING, insolent, rude, saucy, impertinent, abusive, reproachful, scurrilous, opprobrious, offensive.

INSUFFERABLE, insurmountable, unconquerable, invincible.
INSURRECTION, rebellion, revolt.
INTEGRAL, whole, entire, complete, total.
INTEGRITY, uprightness, honesty, probity.
INTELLECT, genius, talent.
INTELLECTUAL, mental, ideal.
INTELLIGENCE, advice, information, instruction, notice; understanding, intellect.
INTEMPERATE, immoderate, excessive, inordinate.
To INTEND, design, mean, purpose.
INTENSE, ardent.
INTENT, design, purpose, intention, view, drift, aim.
To INTERCEDE, interpose, interfere, mediate.
INTERCHANGE, exchange, reciprocity.
INTERCOURSE, communion, commerce, connexion.
To INTERDICT, forbid, proscribe, prohibit.
INTEREST, concern; advantage, good.
To INTERFERE. See INTERCEDE.
INTERIOR, inside.
INTERLOPER, intruder.
To INTERMEDDLE. See INTERCEDE.
INTERMEDIATE, intervening.
INTERMENT, burial, sepulture, inhumation.
INTERMISSION, cessation, rest, stop, interruption.
To INTERMIT, subside, abate.
To INTERPOSE, interfere, intermeddle; intercede, mediate.
To INTERPRET, explain, expound, elucidate.
To INTERPRET wrongly, misinterpret, misconstrue.
To INTERROGATE, question, ask, inquire of.
To INTERRUPT, disturb, hinder.
INTERVAL, interstice, vacancy; space.

Intervening, intermediate.
Intervention, interposition.
Interview, meeting, conference.
Intimacy, acquaintance, familiarity; fellowship.
To Intimate, hint, suggest, insinuate.
To Intimidate, frighten, dastardize.
Intoxication, drunkenness, inebriety, infatuation.
Intractable, stubborn, unmanageable, ungovernable; cross, obstinate, untoward.
To Intrench, encroach, infringe, invade, intrude.
Intrepid, bold, fearless, undaunted, courageous, valiant.
Intricacy, complexity, complication, involution, perplexity.
Intrinsic, real, genuine, native.
To Introduce, present.
Introductory, preliminary, previous, prefatory.
To Intrude, obtrude; encroach, intrench, infringe, invade.
Intruder, interloper.
To Intrust, commit, confide.
To Invade. See Intrude.
Invalid, weak, feeble, infirm, sick.
To Invalidate, weaken, enfeeble.
Invasion, incursion, irruption, inroad.
Invective, abuse, censure, reproach.
To Inveigh, declaim, censure.
To Invent, devise, contrive, frame, fabricate; find out, discover.
To Invert, overturn, overthrow, subvert, reverse.
To Invest, endue, endow.
Investigation, examination, search, inquiry, research, scrutiny.
Invidious, envious, malignant.
To Invigorate, strengthen, fortify.
Invincible, unconquerable, insuperable.

To Invite, ask, call, bid, summon; allure, attract.
To Inundate, overflow, deluge.
To Involve, implicate, entangle, enwrap.
Inward, interior, internal, intrinsic.
Irascible, angry, passionate, hasty, hot, fiery.
Ire, anger, wrath, resentment, indignation, passion.
Irksome, troublesome, vexatious, wearisome, tedious.
Irony, ridicule, sarcasm, satire, burlesque.
Irrational, foolish, silly.
Irrefragable, indubitable, unquestionable, indisputable, incontrovertible, undeniable.
Irregular, eccentric, disorderly; inordinate, intemperate.
Irreligious, profane, impious.
Irreprehensible. See next word.
Irreproachable, blameless, unblemished, spotless.
Irreprovable. See Irreproachable.
To Irritate, aggravate, provoke, exasperate, incite, excite.
Irruption, invasion, incursion, inroad.
Issue, effect, consequence, event, result; progeny, offspring.
To Issue, arise, proceed, flow, spring, emanate.

J

To Jade, harass, dispirit, weary, tire.
To Jangle, wrangle, jar.
Jaunt, ramble, excursion, trip, tour.
Jealousy, suspicion, envy.
To Jeer, gibe, sneer, scoff.
To Jest, joke, sport, make game.
Jest (given to), jocose, jocular, facetious.
Jilt, coquet.

JOCOSE, jocular, facetious, witty, pleasant.
JOCUND, lively, sprightly, vivacious, sportive, merry, lighthearted, mirthful.
To JOIN, add, unite, combine, coalesce, confederate, league.
To JOKE, jest, sport, make game.
JOLLITY, joviality, mirth, merriment, hilarity.
JOURNEY, travel, tour, voyage.
JOY, delight, gladness, charm, pleasure, ecstasy, rapture, transport.
JUDGMENT, discernment, penetration, discrimination; sagacity, intelligence; decision, sentence.
JUST, right, proper.
JUSTICE, right, equity, retribution.
To JUSTIFY, clear, exculpate, defend, excuse, absolve.
JUSTNESS, correctness, accuracy, exactness, propriety.
JUVENILE, youthful, puerile.

K

KEEN, shrewd, acute, penetrating, piercing, cutting.
To KEEP, detain, retain, hold, reserve, preserve; maintain, sustain, support; observe.
To KEEP back, retain, reserve, withhold.
To KEEP from, abstain, refrain; forbear, desist from.
KIND, bland, mild, tender, indulgent, compassionate, clement, gentle, meek, benevolent, benignant, generous, good, courteous, affable, gracious, lenient.
KIND, species, sort, class, genus.
KINDNESS, favor, civility; benignity, beneficence, benevolence, humanity, tenderness.
KINDRED, relationship, affinity, consanguinity.
KINGLY, royal, regal.
KINSMAN, relation, relative, kindred.

KNAVISH, dishonest, trickish.
KNOWLEDGE, learning, erudition, science.
To make KNOWN, acquaint, disclose, communicate, divulge, apprise, inform, reveal.

L

LABOR, work, toil, drudgery, task.
To LABOR, toil, drudge, work, strive, exert.
LABORIOUS, active, industrious, diligent, assiduous.
LABYRINTH, maze.
To LACK, want, need.
LACONIC, short, brief, concise, succinct.
LADING, freight, cargo, load, burden.
To LAG, linger, tarry, loiter, saunter.
To LAMENT, complain, bewail, deplore, bemoan, grieve, mourn, regret.
LANDSCAPE, view, prospect.
LANGUAGE, tongue, speech, idiom, dialect.
LANGUID, faint, exhausted, drooping, pining.
LARGE, extensive, big, capacious, comprehensive, huge, great.
LARGER (to make), enlarge, augment, magnify, extend, increase.
LASSITUDE, fatigue, weariness, enervation.
LAST, latest, final, ultimate.
LASTING, durable, permanent.
LATENT, secret, hidden, occult.
LAUDABLE, praiseworthy, commendable.
To LAUGH at, ridicule, banter, deride, mock.
LAUGHABLE, risible, ludicrous, ridiculous, comical, droll, mirthful.
LAVISH, extravagant, profuse, prodigal.
LAWFUL, legal, legitimate, licit.

Lax, loose, vague; dissolute, licentious.
To Lay open, dilate, expand, extend.
To Lay up, hoard, deposit, treasure, store.
Lazy, idle, indolent, slothful, sluggish, inactive, inert.
To Lead, conduct, guide, direct; induce, persuade, influence, bias, incline.
Leader, chief, chieftain, head, guide.
League, alliance, confederacy, combination, coalition.
To Lean, incline, bend, propend.
Learning, knowledge, erudition, science, literature.
Leave, liberty, license, permission.
To Leave, quit, relinquish, abandon, desert.
To Leave off, cease, desert, discontinue, stop.
Leaving off, ceasing, discontinuance, cessation, discontinuation.
Taking Leave, valediction, farewell.
Leavings, remains, relics, remnants, refuse.
Legal, legitimate, lawful, licit.
Leisure, idle, vacant, free.
Lenity, clemency, mercy, mildness, tenderness.
To Lessen, abate, diminish, decrease, liquidate, subside.
To Let, leave; permit, allow, suffer.
Lethargic, sleepy, drowsy.
Letter, epistle, note.
Level, even, plain, smooth, flat.
To Level, aim, point.
Levity, lightness, volatility, flightiness, giddiness.
Lexicon, dictionary, glossary, vocabulary.
Liable, exposed, subject, obnoxious.
Liberal, beneficent, bountiful, bounteous, munificent, generous.
To Liberate, free, set free, deliver, set at large.
Liberty, freedom; leave, license, permission.
License. See preceding word.
Licentious, loose, vague, lax, dissolute.
Licit, lawful, legal, legitimate.
Lie, falsehood, falsity, untruth, fabrication, fiction, invention, mendacity.
Life, animation, vivacity, spirits; good cheer.
Lifeless, dead, inanimate.
To Lift, heave, hoist; raise, elevate, erect, exalt.
Light (to supply), illuminate, illumine, illume, enlighten, lighten.
Lightness, ease, facility; levity, flightiness, volatility, giddiness; unsteadiness, mutability, inconstancy.
Like, uniform, equal, alike.
Likeness, resemblance, similarity; representation, similitude, picture, image, effigy.
Likelihood, probability.
Likewise, also, too.
Limit, extent, boundary, bound, border.
To Limit, bound, circumscribe, restrict, confine.
Lineage, family, house, race, generation.
To Linger, tarry, loiter, lag, saunter.
Liquid, fluid; liquor, juice, humor.
To Liquidate, lessen, decrease, lower, abate, diminish.
List, roll, catalogue, register.
To Listen, hearken, attend to.
Listless, indolent, supine, careless.
Literature, letters, learning, erudition.
Little, small, diminutive.

To Live, exist, subsist.
Livelihood, living, subsistence, maintenance, support, sustenance.
Lively, active, agile; alert, brisk, nimble, quick, sprightly, prompt, jocund.
Living at the same time with another, coeval, cotemporary, contemporary, contemporaneous.
Load, freight, cargo, lading, burden; weight.
Loath, reluctant, backward, unwilling, averse.
To Loathe, abhor, detest, abominate.
To Lodge, harbor, shelter, entertain.
Loftiness, dignity; haughtiness, pride.
Lofty, high, tall, elevated, exalted.
To Loiter, linger, tarry, lag, saunter.
Lonely, solitary, lonesome.
To Long for, desire, hanker after.
To Look, behold, view, eye, inspect.
Look, air, manner, mien, appearance, aspect; glance.
Looker on, spectator, beholder, observer.
To Look for, expect, await.
Looking into, inspection, insight.
Looking at things past, retrospect, retrospection.
Loose, vague, lax, slack; dissolute, licentious, unrestrained, wanton.
Loquacity, garrulity, talkativeness, babbling.
Lordly, imperious, overbearing, domineering.
Lord's supper, eucharist, communion, sacrament.
Loss, damage, detriment.
Lot, destiny, fate, doom.

Loud, noisy, clamorous, streperous, turbulent, tumultuous, blustering, vehement, vociferous.
Love, affection, attachment, fondness; friendship.
Lovely, amiable, charming, delightful.
Lover, suiter, wooer.
Loving, amorous, fond, affectionate.
Low, humble, lowly; base, abject, mean.
To Lower, reduce, humble, humiliate, degrade, debase, abase.
Lucky, fortunate, prosperous, successful.
Lucre, gain, profit, emolument.
Ludicrous, laughable, ridiculous, comical, droll.
Lunacy, madness, derangement, insanity, mania.
Lustre, brightness, splendor, brilliancy.
Lusty, corpulent, stout.
Luxuriant, exuberant.
Luxury, voluptuousness, sensuality.

M

Madness, derangement, insanity, lunacy, mania, phrensy; franticness, mental aberration, rage, fury.
Magisterial, majestic, stately, pompous, august, dignified.
Magnificence, grandeur, splendor, pomp.
Magnitude, size, bulk, greatness.
Majestic. See Magisterial.
To Maim, mutilate, mangle, cripple.
Main, chief, principal.
To Maintain, assert, vindicate, support, sustain.
Maintenance, livelihood, living, subsistence, sustenance, support.

To MAKE, create, form, produce; do, act.
To MAKE game, jest, sport, joke, mimic.
To MAKE amends, compensate, recompense, remunerate, requite.
MALADY, disease, distemper, disorder.
MALEDICTION, curse, imprecation, execration.
MALEFACTOR, criminal, culprit, felon, convict.
MALEVOLENT, malignant, malicious.
MALICE, spite, rancor, grudge, pique, ill-will.
MALICIOUS, malevolent, malignant.
MALIGNITY, malevolence, ill-will, mischievousness, maliciousness.
To MANAGE, contrive, concert; direct.
MANAGEMENT, care, charge, economy, direction.
MANDATE, command, order, injunction, precept.
MANFUL, manly, bold, daring.
To MANGLE, mutilate, maim, lacerate, tear.
MANIA, derangement, insanity, lunacy, madness.
To MANIFEST, discover, declare, reveal, make known, evince.
MANIFEST, open, apparent, visible, obvious, clear, plain.
MANNER, air, look, mien, aspect, appearance; habit, custom, way.
MANNERS, morals, habits, behavior.
MANY, several, sundry, divers, various, numerous, manifold.
MARGIN, border, edge, rim, brim, brink, verge.
MARINER, seaman, sailor.
MARK, print, impression, stamp, sign, note, symptom, token, indication; trace, vestige, track; badge, stigma; butt.

To MARK, note, notice, observe, remark; show, point out, indicate; impress, imprint, stamp, brand, stigmatize.
MARRIAGE, wedding, nuptials; matrimony, wedlock.
MARRIAGE (relating to), connubial, conjugal, matrimonial, nuptial, hymeneal.
MARTIAL, warlike, military, soldier-like.
MARVEL, wonder, miracle, prodigy, monster.
MASK, cloak, veil, blind.
MASSACRE, carnage, slaughter, butchery.
MASSIVE, bulky, heavy, weighty, ponderous.
MASTER, possessor, proprietor, owner.
MATERIAL, corporeal; important, momentous.
MATRIMONY, marriage, wedlock, nuptials.
MATTER, affair, business, concern; material.
MATURE, ripe, perfect, complete.
MAXIM, adage, aphorism, apophthegm, proverb, saying.
MAZE, labyrinth; uncertainty, perplexity.
MEAGRE, lean; poor, hungry.
MEAN, low, abject, vulgar, vile, contemptible, despicable; sordid, penurious, niggardly.
To MEAN, design, purpose, intend, contemplate; signify, imply, import, express, denote.
MEANING, signification, import, sense.
MEANS, way, manner, method, mode, course.
MECHANIC, artist, artisan, artificer, operative.
To MEDIATE, intercede, interpose.
MEDIUM, mean.
MEDLEY, difference, variety, diversity, mixture, miscellany.
MEEK, mild, gentle, humble, soft.

MEET, apt, fit, suitable; expedient.
MEETING, assembly, congregation, auditory, company.
MELANCHOLY, dejection, depression.
MELODY, harmony, accordance, unison.
MEMOIR, anecdote, annal, chronicle, narrative.
MEMORABLE, signal, worthy of remembrance.
MEMORIAL, monument, remembrancer, memento.
MEMORY, retention, recollection, remembrance, reminiscence.
MENACE, threat.
To MEND, amend, correct, emend, better, improve, rectify, reform.
MENDACITY, falsehood, untruth, lying, deceit.
MENIAL, servant, domestic.
MENTAL, intellectual, ideal.
MERCENARY, venal, hireling.
MERCHANT, trader, tradesman.
MERCHANDISE, goods, ware, commodity.
MERCIFUL, gracious, benignant, kind.
MERCILESS, cruel, unmerciful, hard-hearted.
MERCY, clemency, lenity, pity.
MERELY, barely, only, scarcely.
MERIT, worth, desert; claim, right.
MERRIMENT, mirth, joviality, jollity, hilarity.
MERRY, cheerful, mirthful, joyous, gay, sprightly, lively, blithe, blithesome, vivacious, jocund, sportive.
MESSAGE, mission, errand.
MESSENGER, carrier, harbinger, forerunner, precursor.
METAMORPHOSIS, change, transformation.
METAPHOR, figure, allegory, emblem, symbol.
METHOD, order, rule, regularity, system; way, manner, mode, course, means.

MIEN, look, air, aspect, appearance.
MIGHTY, powerful, potent.
MILD, soft, meek, gentle.
MILITARY, martial, warlike, soldier-like.
To MIMIC, ape, imitate, counterfeit, mock.
To MIND, heed, attend to, regard, notice.
MINDFUL, regardful, observant, attentive.
To MINGLE, mix, blend; compound; confound.
MINISTER, agent, official, employée; clergyman, parson, priest.
To MINISTER, administer, contribute, supply.
MIRACLE, wonder, marvel, prodigy.
MIRTH, festivity, joy, gladness, merriment, jollity, joviality, hilarity, gayety, vivacity, cheerfulness, fun.
MISCARRIAGE, failure, abortion, mishap.
MISCELLANY, mixture, medley, diversity.
MISCHANCE, calamity, disaster, misfortune, mishap.
MISCHIEF, evil or ill, misfortune; harm, injury, damage, hurt.
To MISCONSTRUE, misinterpret.
MISDEED, offence, trespass, transgression, misdemeanor, crime.
MISERABLE, unhappy, wretched.
MISERLY, avaricious, parsimonious, niggardly, penurious.
MISFORTUNE, harm, ill, mishap, calamity, disaster, nuisance.
To MISINTERPRET, misconstrue.
To MISS, lose; fail.
MISSION, message, errand.
MISTAKE, error, blunder, misconception.
To MISUSE, abuse, maltreat.
To MITIGATE, allay, soothe, appease, assuage.

To Mix, mingle, blend, confound.
To Moan, groan, grieve, deplore.
Mob, populace, mobility.
To Mock, mimic, imitate, ape; banter, deride, ridicule.
Mode, way, manner, method, course, means.
Model, copy, pattern, specimen.
Moderation, mediocrity; modesty, temperance, sobriety.
Modern, novel, new, recent.
Modest, bashful, diffident, reserved; chaste, virtuous.
To Molest, annoy, incommode, vex, tease, inconvenience, disturb, trouble.
Moment, signification, avail, importance, consequence, weight.
Monarch, prince, sovereign, potentate.
Monument, memorial, remembrancer.
Mood, humor, temper, frame.
Morals, manners, behavior.
Morbid, sick, sickly, diseased.
Moreover, besides, likewise, also.
Morose, gloomy, sullen, splenetic.
Mortal, deadly, fatal.
Mortification, vexation, chagrin.
Motion, movement.
Motive, cause, reason, principle.
To Mould, form, shape, fashion.
To Mount, arise, rise, ascend; climb, scale.
To Mourn, grieve, lament, fret.
To Move, actuate, impel, induce, stir, instigate.
To Move round, turn, revolve, circulate, whirl.
Moving, affecting, touching, pathetic.
Mulct, fine, penalty, forfeiture.
Multitude, crowd, throng, swarm.
Munificent, beneficent, bountiful, bounteous, generous, liberal.

To Murder, kill, assassinate, slay.
To Murmur, complain, repine.
To Muse, meditate, contemplate, think, reflect, wonder.
To Muster, collect, assemble.
Mutable, alterable, inconstant, changeable, fickle, variable, unstable, wavering, unsteady, irresolute.
To Mutilate, maim, mangle.
Mutinous, tumultuous, turbulent, seditious.
Mutual, reciprocal.
Mysterious, dark, obscure, hidden, occult, latent, dim, mystic.

N

Naked, bare, uncovered, unclothed; rude.
To Name, denominate, entitle, style, designate, characterize, term, call.
Name, appellation, denomination, title, cognomen; reputation, character, credit.
To Nap, sleep, doze, slumber, drowse.
Narration, narrative, account, description, relation, recital, detail, explanation.
Narrow, contracted, confined, straitened, limited.
Nasty, filthy, foul.
Natal, native, indigenous.
Native, intrinsic, real, genuine; indigenous.
Naturally, in course, consequently.
Naval, marine, maritime, nautical.
Nausea, disgust, loathing.
Nautical. See Naval.
Near, nigh, close, adjacent, contiguous, vicinal.
Necessary, expedient, essential, requisite, needful.
To Necessitate, compel, force, oblige.

NECESSITY, occasion, need; exigency, emergency.
NEED, poverty, indigence, want, penury.
To NEED, want, lack.
NEFARIOUS, wicked, unjust, iniquitous.
To NEGLECT, disregard, slight, contemn; omit.
NEGLIGENT, remiss, careless, heedless, inattentive.
NEIGHBORHOOD, vicinity, adjacency, vicinage.
NEVERTHELESS, however, yet, notwithstanding.
NEW, novel, fresh, modern, recent.
NEWS, tidings, intelligence.
NICE, exact, particular, precise; fine, delicate, dainty.
NIGGARDLY, avaricious, miserly, penurious, parsimonious, saving, sparing, thrifty.
NIGH, near, close, adjacent, contiguous, vicinal.
NIGHTLY, nocturnal.
NIMBLE, active, brisk, lively, expert, quick, agile, prompt.
NOBLE, exalted, elevated, illustrious, great, grand.
NOCTURNAL, nightly.
NOISE, cry, outcry, clamor.
NOISOME, hurtful, pernicious, noxious.
NOISY, loud, high sounding, clamorous.
NOMENCLATURE, dictionary, lexicon, catalogue, vocabulary.
To NOMINATE, name; entitle, call.
NOTE, mark, sign, symptom, token, indication; remark, observation, comment, annotation.
NOTED, distinguished, conspicuous, eminent, illustrious, celebrated, renowned, notorious.
NOTICE, advice, intelligence, information, warning.
To NOTICE, attend to, mind, regard, heed; mark, note.

NOTION, conception, perception, idea, opinion, sentiment.
NOTORIOUS, noted, distinguished, conspicuous, renowned.
NOTWITHSTANDING, however, yet, nevertheless.
NOVEL, new, fresh, recent, modern.
To NOURISH, nurture, cherish, support, maintain.
NUMB, benumbed, chill, torpid, motionless.
To NUMBER, calculate, compute, reckon.
NUMERAL, numerical.
NUPTIALS, marriage, wedding.
To NURTURE, cherish, nourish.

O

OBDURATE, hard, callous, hardened, unfeeling, insensible, unsusceptible.
OBEDIENT, dutiful, respectful, submissive, obsequious, compliant.
OBJECT, aim, end, subject.
To OBJECT, oppose, except to.
OBJECTION, difficulty, exception; demur, doubt, hesitation.
OBLIGATION, duty.
To OBLIGE, bind, engage, compel, force, necessitate.
OBLIGING, civil, complaisant.
To OBLITERATE, blot out, expunge, efface, erase, cancel.
OBLIVION, forgetfulness.
OBLOQUY, reproach, odium, contumely.
OBNOXIOUS, offensive; subject, liable, exposed.
OBSCURE, dim, dark, mysterious.
OBSEQUIOUS, obedient, submissive.
OBSERVANCE, form, ceremony, rite.
OBSERVANT, mindful, regardful.
OBSERVATION, observance; remark, comment, note.

To Observe, keep, fulfil; notice, remark, watch.
Observer, spectator, looker on, beholder.
Obsolete, old, ancient, antique, antiquated, old-fashioned, out of date.
Obstacle, difficulty, impediment.
Obstinate, perverse, pertinacious, contumacious, refractory, stubborn, inflexible, resolute, opinionated, headstrong, heady.
Obstinacy, perverseness, contumacy, stubbornness, inflexibility, pertinacity.
Obstreperous, loud, clamorous, noisy, vociferous, turbulent.
To Obstruct, hinder, prevent, impede.
To Obtain, acquire, attain, gain, procure; win, earn.
To Obtrude, intrude.
Obvious, apparent, open, visible, clear, plain, evident, manifest.
To Occasion, create, cause.
Occasion, opportunity, necessity.
Occasional, casual, irregular.
Occult, hidden, secret, latent.
Occupancy, occupation, holding possession.
Occupation, business, avocation, calling, employment, engagement, office, trade, profession.
To Occupy, hold, possess.
Occurrence, event, incident, adventure, casualty, contingency.
Odd, particular, singular, eccentric, strange; fantastical, whimsical, comical, droll.
Odious, hateful, detestable, abominable.
Odor, smell, scent, perfume, fragrance.
Offence, affront, insult, outrage, indignity; misdeed, trespass, transgression, misdemeanor.
To Offend, despise, vex.
Offender, delinquent, culprit.
Offensive, rude, saucy, impertinent, insolent, abusive, reproachful, scurrilous, opprobrious, insulting, obnoxious.
To Offer, present, exhibit, bid, tender, propose.
Offering, oblation, presentation.
Office, business, function, duty, charge; benefit, service.
Officious, active, busy.
Offspring, issue, progeny.
Often, frequently.
Old, aged, senile; ancient, antique, antiquated, old-fashioned, obsolete.
Older, senior, elder.
Omen, presage, prognostic.
Onset, attack, encounter, assault.
Onward, forward, progressive.
Opaque, dark, cloudy.
Open, candid, frank, ingenuous free, sincere, undissembling.
Opening, aperture, cavity.
Operation, work, action, agency.
Opinionated, opinionative, conceited, egotistical.
Opinion, sentiment, notion.
Opponent, adversary, antagonist, enemy, foe.
Opportunity, occasion.
To Oppose, combat, contradict, deny, object, resist, withstand, thwart.
Opposite, adverse, contrary, inimical, repugnant.
Opprobrious, abusive, reproachful, scurrilous, insolent, insulting, offensive.
Opprobrium, infamy, ignominy.
To Oppugn, oppose, attack, confute, refute, disprove.
Option, choice.
Opulence, affluence, riches, wealth.

ORAL, verbal, vocal.
ORATION, address, speech, harangue.
ORATORY, elocution, rhetoric.
ORB, circle, globe, sphere.
To ORDAIN, appoint, order, prescribe.
ORDER, class, rank, degree; succession, series; method, rule; command, injunction, precept, mandate.
To put in ORDER or rank, arrange, range, dispose, regulate, adjust, classify; digest.
To put out of ORDER, confuse, derange, perplex, disorder, disarrange, confound, disturb, displace, unsettle, ruffle, discompose.
ORDERLY, regular, systematic, methodical.
ORDINARY, common, vulgar, mean.
ORIFICE, perforation.
ORIGIN, original, beginning, rise, source.
ORIGINAL, primary, primitive, pristine.
To ORNAMENT, adorn, beautify, embellish, deck, decorate.
OSTENSIBLE, colorable, specious, plausible, feasible.
OSTENTATION, show, parade; vaunting, boasting.
OUTRAGE, affront, insult, offence.
OVERBALANCE, outweigh, preponderate.
To OVERBEAR, bear down, overpower, overwhelm, subdue.
OVERBEARING, imperious, lordly, domineering.
To OVERCOME, conquer, vanquish, subdue, surmount.
To OVERFLOW, inundate, deluge.
To OVERPOWER, overbear, bear down, overwhelm; defeat, overthrow, subdue, rout.
To OVERRULE, supersede.
OVERRULING, prevailing, predominant, prevalent.
To OVERRUN, overspread, ravage.

OVERSIGHT, inadvertency, inattention; inspection, superintendence.
To OVERTHROW, overturn, beat, defeat, rout; subvert, invert, reverse.
To OVERWHELM, overbear, bear down, overpower, subdue, crush.
OUTCRY, cry, clamor, noise.
To OUTDO, exceed, excel, surpass.
OUTLINES, sketch, draught.
To OUTLIVE, survive.
OUTSIDE, appearance, semblance.
OUTWARD, outer, external, exterior; extrinsic, extraneous.
To OUTWEIGH, overbalance, preponderate.
To OWN, acknowledge, confess, recognise.
OWNER, possessor, proprietor, master.

P

PACE, step, gait.
PACIFIC, peaceful, peaceable, mild, gentle.
To PACIFY, appease, calm, quiet, still.
PAGAN, gentile, heathen.
PAIN, anguish, agony, distress, suffering.
To PAINT, color, represent, depict, describe, delineate, sketch.
PAIR, couple, brace.
PALATE, taste, relish.
PALE, pallid, wan; fair.
PALINODE, palinody, recantation.
To PALLIATE, extenuate, gloss, cover, varnish.
PALLID, pale, wan.
To PALPITATE, flutter, pant, gasp.
PANEGYRIC, encomium, eulogy.
PANG, pain, anguish, agony, distress.
To PANT, palpitate, gasp.
PARABLE, allegory, similitude.

PARADE, show, ostentation, vainglory.
PARASITE, flatterer, sycophant.
To PARDON, forgive, absolve, remit, acquit; discharge, set free, clear.
PARDONABLE, venial, excusable.
To PARE, peel; diminish.
PARSIMONIOUS, avaricious, niggardly, miserly, penurious.
PART, portion, share, piece, division.
To PART, separate, divide, disunite.
To PARTAKE, participate, share.
PARTICULAR, peculiar, appropriate, exclusive; exact, nice, punctual, specific; circumstantial, minute.
PARTICULARLY, especially, principally, chiefly.
PARTISAN, adherent, follower, disciple.
PARTNER, colleague, coadjutor, associate.
PARTNERSHIP, association, company, society.
PARTY, confederacy, faction, detachment.
PASSAGE, course, race.
PASSIONATE, hot, hasty, irascible, angry.
PASSIVE, unresisting, quiescent; submissive, patient.
PASTIME, amusement, diversion, entertainment, recreation, sport, play.
PATCH, part, piece.
PATHETIC, moving, touching, affecting.
PATIENCE, endurance, resignation.
PATIENT, enduring, passive; an invalid.
To PAUSE, demur, hesitate, deliberate.
PAY, allowance, stipend, hire, salary.
PEACE, quiet, calm, tranquillity.
PEACEABLE, peaceful, tranquil, quiet, undisturbed, serene, mild, still, pacific.
PEASANT, countryman, swain, hind, rustic, clown.
PECULIAR, appropriate; particular, exclusive.
PEEL, skin, rind.
To PEEL, pare, strip, skin.
PEEVISH, captious, cross, fretful, petulant.
PELLUCID, transparent, clear.
PENALTY, fine, mulct, forfeiture.
To PENETRATE, pierce, perforate, bore.
PENETRATING, acute, sagacious, discerning.
PENETRATION, acuteness, sagacity; discernment, discrimination.
PENITENCE, repentance, contrition, compunction, remorse.
PENMAN, writer, scribe.
PENURIOUS, sparing, niggardly, parsimonious.
PENURY, poverty, indigence, want, need.
To PERCEIVE, discern, distinguish, observe.
PERCEPTION, idea, notion, conception, sentiment, sensation.
PEREMPTORY, absolute, positive.
PERFECT, complete, finished, consummated.
PERFECTION (to bring to), perfect, finish, complete, consummate; fulfil, accomplish.
PERFIDIOUS, faithless, treacherous.
To PERFORATE, pierce, bore, penetrate.
To PERFORM, effect, produce, execute, fulfil.
PERFORMANCE, production, work, deed, achievement, exploit, feat.
PERFORMER, actor, player.
PERFUME, odor, scent, fragrance, smell.
PERIL, danger, hazard.
PERIOD, time, age, date, era, epoch.

To Perish, decay, die, expire.
To Perjure, forswear, suborn.
Permanent, durable, lasting.
Permission, leave, liberty, license.
To Permit, admit, allow; consent, suffer, tolerate; yield.
Pernicious, destructive, ruinous, hurtful, noxious, noisome.
To Perpetrate, commit.
Perpetual, continual, lasting, constant, incessant, unceasing, uninterrupted.
To Perplex, embarrass, harass, confuse, entangle; molest.
Perplexity, anxiety, distraction; entanglement.
To Persevere, continue, persist, pursue, prosecute; insist.
Persons, people, folks, individuals.
Perspicuity, clearness, transparency, translucency.
To Persuade, exhort, urge, entice, prevail upon.
Pertinent, relevant, apposite.
Perverse, awkward, cross, untoward, crooked, froward.
Pest, bane, plague, ruin.
Peremptory, absolute, arbitrary, despotic.
To Possess, have, hold, occupy.
Possession, occupancy, occupation, holding.
Possessions, goods, property.
Possessor, proprietor, owner, master.
Possible, practicable.
Post, place, situation, station, position.
Posterior, after, subsequent.
To Postpone, delay, defer, procrastinate, prolong, protract, retard.
Posture, action, gesture, gesticulation, position, attitude.
Potent, powerful, mighty.
Potentate, prince, monarch, sovereign.
Poverty, indigence, want, penury, need.

To Pound, break, bruise, crush.
To Pour, shed, spill.
Pouring out, effusion.
Power, authority, strength, might, dominion, influence, sway.
Powerful, mighty, potent, puissant; efficacious, forcible, cogent, strong.
Pestilential, contagious, epidemical, infectious; mischievous, pernicious, destructive.
Petition, prayer, request, entreaty, suit.
Petty, trifling, trivial, frivolous, futile.
Petulant, captious, cross, peevish, fretful.
Phantom, vision, apparition, spectre, ghost.
Phrase, sentence, proposition, period.
Phraseology, diction, style.
Phrensy, madness, fury.
To Pick, choose, select.
Picture, likeness, image, effigy, representation.
Piece, part, portion; patch.
To Pierce, penetrate, perforate, bore.
To Pile, heap, accumulate, amass.
Pillage, rapine, plunder.
Pillar, column.
To Pinch, press, squeeze, gripe.
To Pine, flag, droop, languish.
Pious, holy, godly, devout, religious.
Pique, malice, rancor, spite, grudge.
Piteous, doleful, woful, rueful, pitiable.
Pitiful, mean, sordid, contemptible, despicable.
Pity, commiseration, compassion; sympathy, condolence, mercy.
Place, situation, station, position, site, spot, post; office, charge, function.
To Place, put, set, lay; dispose, order.

PLACID, serene, calm.
To PLAGUE, annoy, vex, tease, harass, torment, tantalize, importune, molest.
PLAIN, even, level, smooth; apparent, visible, clear, obvious, evident, manifest, distinct; open, candid, free, frank, ingenuous.
PLAN, design, device, contrivance, scheme, project, stratagem.
PLAUDIT, acclamation, applause, exultation, shouting.
PLAUSIBLE, colorable, specious, ostensible, feasible.
PLAY, game, sport, pastime, amusement.
PLAYER, actor, performer.
To PLEAD, apologize, defend, justify, exculpate, excuse.
PLEASANT, pleasing, agreeable; facetious, jocular, jocose, witty.
To PLEASE, gratify, satisfy.
PLEASED, gratified, glad, cheerful, joyful, pleasing, pleasant, agreeable.
PLEASING, pleasant, agreeable.
PLEASURE, comfort, enjoyment; joy, delight, charm.
PLEASURE (one given up to), voluptuary, sensualist, epicure.
PLEDGE, earnest, security, deposit.
PLENIPOTENTIARY, ambassador, envoy.
PLENITUDE, fulness; repletion, exuberance, abundance.
PLENTEOUS, plentiful, abundant, copious, ample, exuberant.
PLENTIFUL, abundant, ample, copious, exuberant, plenteous.
PLIANT, pliable, flexible, supple, yielding.
PLIGHT, situation, condition, state, predicament, case.
PLOT, cabal, conspiracy, combination; form, scheme, plan.
To PLUCK, pull; draw, tug.
PLUNDER, rapine, pillage, booty, spoil.

To PLUNGE, dive.
To POINT, aim, level.
To POINT out, show, mark, indicate.
To POISE, balance, equiponderate.
POLITE, polished, refined, genteel, civil.
POLITENESS, gentility, civility, courteousness, courtesy, affability; good breeding, good manners.
To POLLUTE, corrupt, contaminate, defile, taint, infect, vitiate.
POMP, magnificence, splendor, grandeur, show, state.
POMPOUS, magisterial, stately, august, dignified, lofty.
To PONDER, think, muse, reflect.
PONDEROUS, heavy, burdensome, weighty.
POOR, indigent, needy, necessitous, distressed.
POPULACE, people, mob, mobility.
PORT, harbor, haven.
To PORTEND, augur, presage, forebode, betoken, threaten.
PORTION, part, division, share, quantity.
POSITION, place, situation, station, post; action, gesture, gesticulation, posture, attitude; tenet.
POSITIVE, actual, real, certain; confident.
PRACTICABLE, practical, possible.
PRACTICE, custom, habit, manner.
To PRACTISE, exercise.
To PRAISE, commend, extol, eulogize, applaud.
PRAISE, encomium, eulogy, panegyric, applause, commendation.
PRAISEWORTHY, laudable, commendable, deserving praise.
PRANK, frolic, gambol.
To PRATE, babble, chat, chatter, prattle.

PRAYER, petition, request, entreaty, suit.
PRECARIOUS, doubtful, dubious, uncertain, equivocal.
PRECEDENCE, priority, pre-eminence, preference.
PRECEDENT, example.
PRECEDING, antecedent, anterior, previous, prior, former, foregoing.
PRECEPT, command, injunction, mandate, order; doctrine, principle; maxim, rule, law.
PRECIOUS, valuable, costly, uncommon.
PRECIPITANCY, rashness, temerity, hastiness.
PRECISE, accurate, correct, exact, nice.
To PRECLUDE, prevent, obviate, hinder, shut out.
PRECURSOR, forerunner, harbinger.
PREDICAMENT, situation, condition, state, plight, case.
To PREDICT, foretell, prophesy, prognosticate.
PREDOMINANT, prevailing, prevalent, overruling.
PRE-EMINENCE, priority, precedence.
PREFACE, prelude, introduction, proem.
To PREFER, choose; encourage, advance, promote, forward.
PREFERENCE, priority, precedence.
PREGNANT, big, large, enceinte.
PREJUDICE, prepossession, bias; disadvantage, injury, hurt, detriment.
PRELIMINARY, preparatory, introductory, previous.
PRELUDE, preface, introduction, proem.
PREMEDITATION, forethought, forecast.
To PREPARE, fit, equip, qualify, make ready.
PREPARATORY, introductory, preliminary, previous.

To PREPONDERATE, overbalance, outweigh.
PREPOSSESSION, bias, prejudice, bent.
PREPOSTEROUS, irrational, foolish, absurd.
PREROGATIVE, privilege, immunity.
PRESAGE, omen, token, prognostic.
To PRESCRIBE, appoint, ordain, dictate.
PRESCRIPTION, usage, custom.
PRESENT, gift, donation, benefaction.
To PRESENT, offer, exhibit, give, introduce.
To PRESERVE, keep, save; protect, spare.
To PRESS, squeeze, gripe, pinch.
PRESSING, urging, emergent, importunate.
PRESUMING, presumptive, presumptuous, forward, arrogant.
PRETENCE, pretension, pretext, excuse.
To PRETEND, feign, affect, simulate.
PRETENSION, claim, assumption.
PRETEXT, pretence, pretension, excuse.
PRETTY, beautiful, fine, handsome.
PREVAILING, prevalent, ruling, overruling, dominant.
To PREVENT, impede, obviate, preclude, hinder, obstruct; anticipate.
PREVIOUS, introductory, preliminary; anterior, prior.
PREY, booty, spoil.
PRICE, cost, charge, expense; value, worth.
PRIDE, arrogance, hauteur, haughtiness, assumption, vanity, insolence, conceit, ostentation, loftiness.
PRIMARY, primitive, pristine, original.
PRINCIPAL, chief, main.

PRINCIPALLY, especially, mainly, particularly, chiefly.
PRINCIPLE, doctrine, element; motive.
PRINT, mark, impression, stamp.
PRIOR, antecedent, anterior, previous, preceding, former.
PRIORITY, precedence, pre-eminence, preference.
PRISTINE, primitive, original.
PRIVACY, retirement, seclusion.
PRIVILEGE, immunity, prerogative, right, claim, exemption.
To PRIZE, value, esteem.
PROBABILITY, chance, likelihood.
PROBITY, honesty, uprightness, integrity.
To PROCEED, advance; arise, issue, emanate.
PROCEEDING, transaction; process, course, progress, progression.
PROCESSION, train, retinue.
To PROCLAIM, advertise, announce, publish, declare, promulgate.
PROCLAMATION, decree, edict.
To PROCRASTINATE, delay, defer, postpone, prolong, protract, retard.
To PROCURE, obtain, acquire, gain; win, earn.
PRODIGAL, extravagant, lavish, profuse.
PRODIGIOUS, enormous, monstrous.
PRODIGY, wonder, miracle, marvel, monster.
To PRODUCE, yield, give, impart, communicate.
PRODUCT, production, produce; performance, work.
PROFANE, impious, irreligious.
To PROFESS, declare.
PROFESSION, business, occupation, avocation, office, employment, engagement.
PROFICIENCY, advancement, progress, improvement.
PROFIT, gain, advantage, benefit, lucre.

PROFLIGATE, abandoned, corrupt, vitiated, depraved, vicious, wicked.
PROFUNDITY, depth.
PROFUSE, extravagant, prodigal, lavish.
PROGENITOR, forefather, ancestor, predecessor.
PROGENY, offspring, issue.
PROGNOSTIC, omen, presage.
To PROGNOSTICATE, foretell, predict, prophesy, vaticinate.
PROGRESS, advancement, progression; improvement, proficiency.
PROGRESSION, progress, advancement.
PROGRESSIVE, onward, forward, advancing.
To PROHIBIT, forbid, interdict, proscribe.
PROJECT, design, plan, scheme
PROLIFIC, fertile, fruitful.
PROLIX, diffuse, long, tedious.
To PROLONG, delay, protract, procrastinate; postpone, retard.
PROMINENT, conspicuous.
PROMISCUOUS, indiscriminate.
PROMISE, word, engagement.
To PROMOTE, encourage, advance, prefer, forward.
PROMPT, quick, active, agile, assiduous, alert, brisk, nimble, lively, sprightly.
To PROMULGATE, promulge, publish, proclaim, advertise.
PRONENESS, inclination, tendency, propensity.
To PRONOUNCE, articulate, speak, utter; declare, affirm.
PROOF, reason, argument, demonstration; evidence, testimony; experience, experiment, trial, test.
PROP, staff, stay, support.
To PROPAGATE, speed, circulate, diffuse, disseminate.
PROPENSITY, inclination, bias, proneness, tendency.
PROPER, right, just.

PROPERTY, goods, possessions; quality, attribute.
PROPITIOUS, favorable, auspicious.
To PROPHESY, foretell, predict, prognosticate, vaticinate.
To PROPITIATE, appease, conciliate, reconcile.
PROPORTION, rate, ratio; symmetry.
PROPORTIONATE, adequate, commensurate, equal.
To PROPOSE, purpose, intend; offer, bid, tender.
PROPOSITION, sentence, period, phrase.
PROPRIETOR, possessor, owner.
To PROROGUE, adjourn; postpone, defer.
To PROSCRIBE, forbid, prohibit, interdict.
To PROSECUTE, continue, pursue, persevere, persist.
PROSELYTE, convert.
PROSPECT, view, survey, landscape.
To PROSPER, flourish, thrive, succeed.
PROSPERITY, well-being, welfare, happiness.
PROSPEROUS, successful, flourishing, fortunate, lucky.
To PROTECT, support, cherish, harbor, shelter, foster, guard, defend, shield, cover, countenance, patronize, encourage, vindicate.
PROTECTION (a place for), asylum, sanctuary, refuge, shelter, retreat.
To PROTEST, assert, affirm, declare, asseverate, aver, assure, vouch.
To PROTRACT, delay, defer, prolong, retard, postpone.
To PROVE, evince, demonstrate, manifest, argue.
PROVERB, adage, maxim, aphorism, apophthegm, saying, saw, by-word.

To PROVIDE, procure, furnish, supply.
PROVIDENT, careful, cautious, economical.
PROVISION, fare.
To PROVOKE, aggravate, irritate, exasperate, tantalize, excite, incite.
PRUDENCE, judgment, discretion, wisdom, providence.
PROUD, vain, lofty, arrogant, presumptuous, assuming, haughty, conceited.
To PRY, scrutinize, look into.
PRYING, curious, inquisitive.
To PUBLISH, proclaim, advertise, announce, declare, promulgate; disclose, reveal.
PUERILE, youthful, juvenile, childish.
To PULL, draw, drag, haul, hale, tug.
PUNCTUAL, exact, nice, particular.
PUNGENCY, acridness, acrimoniousness, smartness, keenness.
To PUNISH, chastise, correct, chasten, discipline.
PUPIL, scholar, disciple.
To PURCHASE, buy, bargain.
PURGATIVE, abstergent, abstersive, cleansing.
PURPOSE, design, intention, view, aim, drift, end; sake, account, reason.
To PURSUE, follow; continue, persevere, persist, prosecute.
PUSILLANIMITY, cowardice, timidity, fear.
To PUT, place, lay, set.
To PUT down, suppress, repress; reduce, subdue; restrain.
To PUT off, postpone, defer, delay, protract, procrastinate, retard.
To PUTREFY, corrupt, rot.
To PUZZLE, perplex, confound, embarrass, bewilder, entangle.

Q

QUACK, mountebank, empiric, charlatan.
To QUAKE, shake, tremble, quiver, shudder.
QUALIFICATION, acquirement, acquisition.
QUALIFIED, competent, fitted, adapted.
To QUALIFY, fit, equip, prepare, adapt; temper, humor.
QUALITY, property, attribute; fashion, distinction.
QUANTITY, deal, portion, part.
QUARREL, dispute, contest, contention, broil, brawl, altercation, tumult, feud, affray.
QUARRELLING, dissension, strife, faction, contention, discord, altercation, wrangling, dispute.
QUARTER, district, region.
QUERY, question, inquiry, interrogatory.
To QUESTION, doubt, dispute; ask, interrogate, inquire.
QUICK, nimble, agile, active, brisk, lively, prompt, expeditious.
To QUICKEN, accelerate, hasten, expedite, despatch.
QUICKNESS, speed, velocity, celerity, swiftness, rapidity, fleetness, nimbleness, briskness; expedition, despatch; agility, activity.
QUICKNESS of intellect, acuteness, sharpness, sagacity, penetration, shrewdness.
To QUIET, appease, calm, pacify, still.
QUIET, ease, rest, repose, calm, tranquillity.
To QUIT, relinquish, leave, give up, resign.
To QUIVER, shake, tremble, quake.
To QUOTE, cite, adduce.

R

RACE, course, passage; family, house, lineage, breed, generation.
To RACK, break, rend, tear.
RADIANCE, brilliancy, lustre, brightness.
To RADIATE, shine, glitter, glare, sparkle.
RAGE, anger, choler, fury.
To RAISE, heighten, aggravate, lift, exalt, elevate, erect.
To RALLY, deride, mock, ridicule, banter.
RAMBLE, excursion, tour, trip, jaunt.
To RAMBLE, wander, stroll, move, roam, range.
RANCOR, hatred, enmity, ill-will, malice, spite, grudge.
To RANGE, class, place, rank; wander, stroll, rove, roam, ramble.
RANK, order, degree, class.
To RANSOM, redeem, free, manumit.
RAPACIOUS, ravenous, voracious, greedy.
RAPIDITY, quickness, swiftness, fleetness, celerity, velocity, speed, agility.
RAPINE, plunder, pillage.
RAPTURE, ecstasy, transport.
RARE, scarce, singular, uncommon, incomparable.
To RASE, blot out, efface, expunge, erase, obliterate, cancel; demolish, dismantle, destroy, subvert, ruin.
RASH, foolhardy, thoughtless.
RASHNESS, temerity, precipitance, precipitancy, precipitation, hastiness.
RATE, proportion, ratio, quota, degree; tax, assessment, impost; value, worth, price.
To RATE, estimate, value, appraise; scold.
RATIO, rate, proportion, degree, quota.
RAVAGE, desolation, devastation.
RAVENOUS, rapacious, greedy, voracious.
RAY, glimmer, gleam, beam.

To Reach, stretch, extend.
Ready, apt, prompt, dextrous; easy, facile.
Real, actual, positive, certain; genuine.
To Realize, accomplish, achieve, fulfil, effect, complete, excite, consummate.
Realm, state, kingdom.
Reason, argument, proof; cause, motive; sake, account, purpose, end.
Reasonable, rational, just, honest, equitable, fair.
Void of Reason, irrational, foolish, silly, unreasonable, absurd, preposterous, ridiculous.
Rebellion, insurrection, sedition, revolt; contumacy.
To Rebound, recoil, reverberate.
To Rebuff, repel, reject, beat back, oppose.
To Rebuke, reprimand, reprove, check, chide.
To Recant, abjure, retract, recall, revoke.
To Recapitulate, repeat, recite, rehearse.
To Recede, retire, retreat, withdraw, retrograde.
Receipt, reception.
To Receive, accept, take.
Recent, fresh, new, novel, modern.
Reception, receipt.
Reciprocal, mutual, alternate.
Reciprocity, interchange, exchange.
Recital, account, narrative, description, relation, detail, explanation, narration.
To Recite, repeat, rehearse, recapitulate.
To Reckon, compute, calculate, estimate, count, number; esteem, account.
Reckoning, account, bill, charge.
To Reclaim, reform, recover, correct.
To Recline, repose, lean, rest.

To Recognise, acknowledge, avow, confess, own.
To Recoil, rebound, reverberate, rush back.
Recollection, memory, remembrance, reminiscence.
To Recompense, make amends, compensate, compense, remunerate, requite.
Recompense, compensation, remuneration, requital, satisfaction, amends, gratuity.
To Reconcile, conciliate; propitiate.
To Record, enroll, register.
To Recount, relate, describe, enumerate.
To Recover, refrain, retrieve; repair, recruit.
Recovery, restoration.
Recreation, amusement, diversion, sport, pastime, entertainment.
To Recruit, repair, recover, retrieve.
To Rectify, amend, correct, emend, better, mend, reform, improve.
Rectitude, uprightness.
To Redeem, ransom, rescue, recover.
Redress, remedy, relief, amendment.
To Reduce, diminish, curtail, shorten, lower; subdue; degrade.
Redundancy, excess, superfluity.
To Reel, stagger, totter.
To Refer, allude, hint, glance at, intimate, suggest.
Refined, polite, polished, genteel, elegant.
Refinement, cultivation, civilization.
To Reflect, consider, think, ponder, muse; censure, reproach.
Reflection, consideration, meditation, cogitation.

To REFORM, amend, emend, mend, correct, better, rectify, improve, restore.
REFORMATION, reform, amendment, correction.
REFRACTORY, unruly, ungovernable, perverse, obstinate, contumacious.
To REFRAIN, abstain, forbear, withhold.
To REFRESH, revive, renovate, renew; refrigerate, cool.
REFUGE, asylum, shelter, retreat.
To REFUSE, deny, reject, decline.
REFUSE, dregs, sediment, dross, scum.
To REFUTE, confute, oppugn, disprove.
REGAL, royal, kingly.
REGARD, concern, care, attention; respect, reverence.
To REGARD, attend to, mind, heed; consider; esteem, respect, reverence.
REGARDFUL, mindful, heedful, attentive, observant.
REGARDLESS, indifferent, unconcerned, careless, unobservant.
REGIMEN, food, diet.
REGION, district, quarter.
To REGISTER, enroll, record.
REGISTER, list, catalogue, roll, record, archive, chronicle, annal, memoir.
To REGRET, complain, lament, repent, grieve.
To REGULATE, direct, dispose, adjust; govern, rule.
To REHEARSE, repeat, recite, recapitulate.
REIGN, empire, dominion; power, influence.
To REJECT, refuse, decline, repel, rebuff.
To REJOICE, exult, exhilarate.
REJOINDER, answer, reply, response, replication.
To RELATE, recount, narrate, detail, describe; refer, respect, regard, concern.
RELATED, connected, combined.
RELATION, account, narrative, description, recital, detail, narration, explanation.
RELATIVE. See RELATION.
RELATIONSHIP, kindred, consanguinity, affinity.
To RELAX, slacken, loose; mitigate, remit.
RELENTLESS, implacable, unrelenting, unpitying.
RELEVANT, pertinent, to the purpose, apposite, fit, proper.
RELIANCE, dependence; trust, confidence, repose.
RELICS, remains, leavings.
RELIEF, redress, alleviation, mitigation.
To RELIEVE, aid, help, succor, assist, alleviate.
RELIGIOUS, pious, devout, holy.
To RELINQUISH, give up, forego, renounce, quit, abdicate, resign.
RELISH, taste, flavor, savor.
RELUCTANT, averse, backward, unwilling, loth.
To REMAIN, abide, stay, continue, tarry, sojourn, await.
REMAINDER, rest, remnant, residue.
REMAINS, leavings, relics.
REMARK, annotation, note, comment, observation.
REMARKABLE, extraordinary, observable, distinguished, worthy of note.
To REMARK, observe, notice.
A REMARK, observation, comment, annotation, note, notice.
REMEDY, cure, reparation.
REMEMBRANCE, memory, recollection, reminiscence.
REMEMBRANCER, memorial, monument, memento.
REMINISCENCE, recollection, remembrance.
REMISS, inattentive, heedless, negligent, careless, thoughtless.

To REMIT, absolve, pardon, forgive; liberate, give up.
REMNANT, rest, residue, remainder.
To REMONSTRATE, expostulate.
REMORSE, repentance, penitence, contrition, repugnance.
REMOTE, distant, far.
REMUNERATION, compensation, satisfaction, recompense, requital.
To REND, break, rack, tear.
To RENEW, renovate, revive, refresh.
To RENOUNCE, abandon, forsake, abdicate, relinquish, resign, give up, quit, forego.
RENOWN, fame, notoriety, reputation, celebrity.
To REPAIR, restore, recover, amend, retrieve.
REPARATION, restoration, restitution, amends.
REPARTEE, retort.
To REPAY, restore, return.
To REPEAL, abolish, abrogate, revoke, annul, cancel; destroy, annihilate.
To REPEAT, tell over, recite, recapitulate, rehearse.
REPENTANCE, penitence, contrition, remorse, compunction.
REPETITION, tautology.
To REPINE, complain, murmur.
REPLICATION, answer, reply, rejoinder, response.
REPLY. See the preceding word.
REPORT, fame, rumor, hearsay.
REPOSE, ease, quiet, rest.
To REPOSE, recline, rest.
REPREHENSIBLE, blamable, culpable, reprovable, censurable.
REPREHENSION, reproof, blame, reproach.
REPRESENTATION, show, exhibition, sight, spectacle.
To REPRESS, restrain, suppress, subdue.
To REPRIEVE, respite.
To REPRIMAND, check, chide, reprove, rebuke.

REPRISAL, retaliation.
To REPROACH, blame, reprove, upbraid, censure, condemn; vilify, revile.
REPROACHFUL, abusive, scurrilous, opprobrious, insolent, insulting, offensive.
REPROBATE, abandoned, vitiated, profligate, corrupt, depraved, castaway, wicked.
To REPROBATE, censure, condemn.
REPROOF, reprehension, censure, blame.
To REPROVE, check, chide, reprimand, rebuke.
REPUGNANCE, aversion, dislike, antipathy, hatred.
REPUGNANT, adverse, contrary, opposite, inimical, hostile.
REPUTATION, character, fame, renown, credit, repute.
To REQUEST, ask, solicit, entreat, demand.
In REQUEST, repute, credit, demand.
REQUEST, prayer, petition, entreaty, suit.
To REQUIRE, demand, need.
REQUISITE, necessary, essential, expedient.
REQUITAL, compensation, satisfaction, amends, remuneration, recompense; retribution.
To RESCUE, deliver, set free, save.
RESEARCH, examination, inquiry, investigation, scrutiny.
RESEMBLANCE, likeness, similarity, similitude.
RESENTFUL, revengeful, vindictive.
RESENTMENT, anger, indignation, ire, wrath.
RESERVATION, reserve, retention.
To RESIDE, dwell, inhabit, sojourn, abide.
RESIDENCE, habitation, abode, dwelling, domicile.
RESIDUE, rest, remainder, remnant.

To Resign, give up; renounce, relinquish, forego, abdicate.
Resignation, patience, endurance, submission.
To Resist, withstand, oppose; thwart.
To Resolve, determine, purpose; solve, analyze, reduce.
Resolute, decided, determined, fixed; firm, constant, steady.
Resolution, courage, fortitude, firmness.
To Resort to, frequent, haunt.
Resource, resort, means, expedient.
To Respect, esteem, regard, honor, venerate, revere; value, prize.
Respect, deference, regard, consideration, esteem, estimation.
Respectful, obedient, dutiful.
Respite, reprieve; interval.
Response, answer, reply, rejoinder, replication.
Responsible, answerable, accountable, amenable.
Rest, cessation, stop, intermission; ease, quiet, repose; remainder, residue, remnant.
To Restore, return, give back, repay.
Restoration, restitution, retribution, reparation, compensation, requital, amends.
To Restrain, repress, coerce, restrict.
To Restrict, bound, limit, confine, circumscribe.
Result, effect, consequence, issue, event.
To Retain, hold, keep, detain, reserve.
Retaliation, reprisal, repayment.
To Retard, delay, defer, protract, prolong, postpone, procrastinate, hinder.
To Retire, recede, retrograde, retrocede, retreat; withdraw, secede.

Retirement, privacy, seclusion.
Retort, repartee.
To Retract, recall, revoke, recant, abjure.
Retreat, asylum, shelter, refuge.
To Retreat. See Retire.
Retribution, requital, repayment.
To Retrieve, recover, repair, recruit, regain.
To Retrocede. See Retire.
To Retrograde, go backward. See Retire.
Retrospect, review, survey.
To Return, revert; restore, repay.
To Reveal, divulge, disclose, make known, communicate, open, impart.
To Revenge, avenge, vindicate.
Revengeful, vindictive, resentful.
To Reverberate, rebound, recoil.
To Revere, reverence, adore, venerate.
Reverence, awe, dread; honor, respect.
To Reverse, invert, overturn, subvert, return.
Revery, dream.
Review, retrospect, survey; revisal, revision.
To Revile, vilify.
Revisal, revision, review.
To Revive, refresh, renew, renovate.
To Revoke, recall, retract; abolish, abrogate, annul, repeal, cancel, destroy, annihilate.
Revolt, insurrection, sedition, rebellion.
Reward, compensation, amends, satisfaction, remuneration, recompense, requital.
Rhetoric, elocution, eloquence, oratory.
Riches, wealth, opulence, affluence.
To Ridicule, laugh at, deride,

mock, satirize, lampoon, rally, banter.
RIDICULE, satire, sarcasm, burlesque, irony, banter.
RIDICULOUS, absurd, preposterous, ludicrous, droll.
RIGHT, straight, direct; just, proper; claim, privilege, immunity.
RIGHTEOUS, upright, just, honest, virtuous, incorrupt, equitable, godly.
RIGID, rigorous, austere, stern; harsh, severe.
RIM, border, edge, brim, brink, margin.
RIND, skin, peel, hide.
RIPENESS, maturity, perfection, puberty.
To RISE, arise, mount, ascend, climb, scale.
RISE, origin, source, original.
RITE, form, ceremony, observance.
RIVALRY, emulation, competition.
ROAD, way, route, course, path.
To ROAM, rove, wander, stroll, ramble, range.
ROBBERY, depredation, theft, plunder.
ROBUST, strong, firm, sturdy.
ROLL, list, register, catalogue.
ROMANCE, fable, tale, novel.
ROOM, space, extent; chamber, apartment.
ROOMY, capacious, ample, spacious.
To ROOT out, eradicate, exterminate, extirpate.
To ROT, putrefy, decay, corrupt.
ROTTEN, putrefied, putrid, decayed, corrupt, carious.
ROTUNDITY, roundness, circularity.
To ROVE, wander, stroll, ramble, roam, range.
ROUGH, rugged, rude, harsh, severe.
ROUND, circuit, tour, sphere, orb, globe.

ROUNDNESS, circularity, rotundity, globosity, sphericity.
To ROUSE, awaken, stir up, excite, provoke.
To ROUT, beat, defeat, overpower, overthrow.
ROUTE, way, road, course.
ROW, tumult, broil, commotion, riot, disturbance, affray, uproar.
ROYAL, regal, kingly.
To RUB, chafe, fret, gall.
RUDE, coarse, rough; uncouth, unpolished; impertinent, saucy, impudent, insolent.
RUEFUL, piteous, doleful, woful.
RUGGED, rough, rude, harsh.
RUIN, destruction; bane, pest.
RUINOUS, pernicious, destructive.
RULE, order, method; law, maxim, precept, guide, regulation, government.
RULING, prevailing, prevalent, predominant.
RUMOR, fame, report, bruit.
RUPTURE, fracture, fraction.
RURAL, rustic.
RUSTIC, rural; countryman, peasant, swain, hind, clown.

S

SACRAMENT, Lord's supper, eucharist.
SACRED, holy, divine.
SAD, sorrowful, mournful, melancholy, dull, dejected, depressed, gloomy, cheerless.
SAFE, secure, fearless; trusty, trustworthy.
SAGE, sagacious, sapient, wise, prudent; grave.
SAGACITY, acuteness, discernment, penetration.
SAILOR, mariner, seaman.
SALARY, allowance, stipend, pay, wages, hire.
SAKE, account, reason, purpose, end.
SALUBRIOUS, salutary, healthy, wholesome.

SALUTARY, advantageous. See also SALUBRIOUS.
SALUTATION, greeting, address.
SALUTIFEROUS, healthy.
SAMENESS, identity.
To SANCTION, countenance, support.
SANCTITY, holiness.
SANE, sound, healthy.
SANGUINARY, bloody, bloodthirsty.
To SAP, undermine, subvert.
SAPIENT, sagacious, wise, sage.
SARCASM, satire, ridicule, irony.
To SATIATE, satisfy, glut, cloy.
SATIRE, ridicule, irony, sarcasm; wit, humor, burlesque.
SATISFACTION, compensation, amends, remuneration, recompense, requital, reward; contentment.
To SATISFY, please, gratify; satiate, glut, cloy.
SAUCY, impertinent, rude, impudent, insolent.
SAVAGE, cruel, inhuman, brutal, barbarous; ferocious, fierce.
To SAVE, rescue, deliver; spare, protect; preserve.
SAVING, economical, sparing, frugal, thrifty; penurious, niggardly, stingy.
To SAUNTER, linger, loiter, lag, tarry.
SAVOR, taste, flavor, relish.
To SAY, speak, tell.
SAYING, adage, maxim, aphorism, apophthegm, proverb, by-word, saw.
To SCALE, rise, mount, ascend, climb.
SCANDAL, discredit, disgrace, reproach, infamy.
To SCANDALIZE, accuse falsely, asperse, calumniate, defame, detract, slander, vilify, offend.
SCARCE, rare, singular; hardly, scantily.
SCARCITY, dearth, penury.
To SCATTER, spread, disperse, dissipate.

SCENT, smell, odor, perfume, fragrance.
SCHEME, design, plan, project.
SCHOLAR, disciple, pupil.
SCHOOL, academy, seminary.
SCIENCE, knowledge, learning, erudition.
To SCOFF, gibe, jeer, sneer.
SCOPE, drift, aim, tendency.
To SCORN, contemn, despise, disdain.
To SCREAM, shriek, cry, screech.
To SCREEN, cover, shelter, shield.
SCRIBE, writer, penman.
To SCRUPLE, hesitate, doubt, fluctuate.
SCRUPULOUS, conscientious.
To SCRUTINIZE, pry, dive into, examine, investigate, inquire into, search.
SCUM, dregs, sediment, refuse, dross.
SCURRILOUS, abusive, reproachful, opprobrious, insolent, insulting, offensive.
SEA, ocean, main.
SEAMAN, sailor, mariner.
SEARCH, scrutiny, inquiry, investigation, examination, research, quest, pursuit.
SEASONABLE, timely, opportune.
To SECEDE, recede, retire, withdraw, retreat.
SECLUSION, privacy, retirement.
SECONDARY, second, inferior, subordinate.
SECRECY, concealment, privacy.
SECRET, clandestine, concealed, hidden, occult, latent, mysterious.
SECULAR, temporal, worldly.
To SECURE, make sure, certain, guarantee.
SECURE, certain, sure, safe.
SECURITY, deposit, pledge; fence, guard.
SEDATE, composed, calm, quiet, serene, unruffled, still.
SEDIMENT, dregs, dross, refuse, scum.

SEDITION, insurrection, rebellion, revolt.
SEDITIOUS, factious; tumultuous, turbulent, mutinous, rebellious.
To SEDUCE, allure, attract, decoy, entice, tempt, abduct.
SEDULOUS, diligent, assiduous.
To SEE, look, behold, view, eye; perceive, observe.
To SEEK, search, explore, examine.
To SEEM, appear.
SEEMLY, fit, suitable, meet, becoming, decent.
To SEIZE, catch, snatch, apprehend, lay hold on, take.
SEIZURE, capture.
To SELECT, choose, pick.
SELF-CONCEIT, self-sufficiency, vanity.
SEMBLANCE, show, outside appearance.
To SEND away, dismiss, discharge, discard, despatch.
SENIOR, elder.
SENSATION, perception, sentiment.
SENSE, feeling, perception; judgment; signification, meaning, import.
SENSIBILITY, feeling, susceptibility.
SENSITIVE, sensible, sentient.
SENSUALIST, voluptuary, epicure.
SENTENCE, decision, judgment; proposition, period, phrase.
To SENTENCE, condemn, doom.
SENTIENT, sensible, sensitive.
SENTIMENT, sensation, perception; opinion, notion.
SENTINEL, guard.
SEPARATE, distinct, different, unconnected.
To SEPARATE, detach, sever, divide, disjoin, disunite, disengage, part, sunder.
SEPULCHRE, grave, tomb.
SEPULTURE, burial, interment, inhumation.
SEQUEL, close, conclusion.

19

SERENE, calm, tranquil.
SERIES, course; successive order.
SERIOUS, earnest, grave, solemn.
SERVANT, domestic, menial, drudge.
To SERVE, aid, assist, help, succor, minister to, furnish, provide.
SERVICE, advantage, benefit, avail, use, utility.
SERVITUDE, slavery, bondage.
To SET, put, place, lay.
To SET free, liberate, loose; acquit, clear; pardon, forgive.
To SET apart, dedicate, devote; consecrate, hallow.
To SETTLE, adjust, compose; regulate, arrange, determine, fix, establish.
To SETTLE firmly, confirm, establish, corroborate.
SETTLED, determinate, definitive, decisive, conclusive.
To SEVER, separate, disjoin, detach.
SEVERAL, different, divers, sundry, various.
SEVERE, rigid, austere, rigorous, harsh, stern, rough.
SEVERE in remark, keen, cutting, sarcastic, satirical.
SEX, gender.
SHACKLE, fetter, manacle, chain.
SHADE, shadow.
To SHAKE, agitate, tremble, shudder, shiver, quiver, quake.
To SHAME, abash, confuse, confound.
SHAME, dishonor, disgrace.
SHAMELESS, immodest, impudent, indecent, indelicate.
SHAMEFUL (grossly), infamous, scandalous, disgraceful, opprobrious, ignominious.
To SHAPE, form, fashion, mould.
To SHARE, divide, distribute, apportion, participate, partake.
SHARP, acute, keen, shrewd.
SHARPNESS, penetration, shrewd-

ness, acuteness, sagacity; sourness, acidity, acrimony.
To SHED, pour, spill.
SHELTER, asylum, refuge, retreat.
To SHELTER, cover, screen, harbor, lodge.
SHIFT, evasion, subterfuge; expedient, resource, alternative.
To SHINE, radiate, glitter, glisten, gleam, glare, sparkle, coruscate.
SHINING, brilliant, splendid, resplendent, bright, radiant, glittering.
To SHOCK, offend, disgust; appall, dismay, terrify, affright, disturb.
SHOCKING, formidable, dreadful, terrible.
To SHOOT forth, sprout, bud, germinate.
To SHOOT out, project, protrude.
SHORT, brief, concise, compendious, summary, succinct, laconic.'
To SHORTEN, curtail, contract, abridge, reduce.
SHOUTING, declamation, applause, plaudit, exultation.
SHOW, outside appearance, semblance; exhibition, representation, sight, spectacle; parade, ostentation.
To SHOW, exhibit, discover, display; direct, point out, instruct, inform.
SHOWY, ostentatious, gaudy, fine, gay, splendid, pompous, sumptuous, magnificent, stately, grand.
SHREWD, acute, keen, penetrating.
To SHRIEK, cry, scream, screech.
To SHUDDER, shake, tremble, quake, quiver.
To SHUFFLE, equivocate, prevaricate, quibble, cavil, evade, sophisticate.
To SHUN, avoid, elude, eschew, evade.

To SHUT, close.
SICK, sickly, diseased, morbid, ill, indisposed.
SIGHT, show, exhibition, representation, spectacle.
SIGN, omen, prognostic, presage, bodement, signal, token; mark, sign, note, symptom.
SIGNAL, memorable, remarkable, eminent, distinguished.
SIGNIFICANT, expressive.
SIGNIFICATION, meaning, import, sense; avail, importance, consequence, moment, weight.
To SIGNIFY, denote, imply, express, declare, testify, utter, betoken, intimate.
SILENCE, taciturnity; stillness.
SILENT, dumb, mute, speechless.
SILLY, simple, foolish.
SIMILARITY, likeness, resemblance, similitude.
SIMILE, similitude, comparison.
SIMILITUDE, likeness, resemblance, similarity.
SIMPLE, silly, foolish; single, singular.
SIMULATION, dissimulation, feint, pretence.
SINCERE, unvarnished, honest, undissembling, upright, true, uncorrupt; plain, frank.
SINGLE, only, sole, singular, particular.
SINGULAR, particular, odd, eccentric, strange, rare, scarce.
To SINK, droop, drop, fall, tumble.
SITE, place, spot, situation, locality.
SITUATION, condition, state, plight, case, predicament; place, site, station, position, post, locality.
SIZE, greatness, magnitude, bulk.
To SKETCH, depict, delineate, portray, paint.
SKETCH, outline, draught.
SKILFUL, clever, expert, dextrous, adroit.
SKIN, hide, peel, rind, pelt, husk

SLACK, loose, relaxed.
To SLANDER, accuse falsely, asperse, calumniate, defame, detract, scandalize, vilify.
SLAVERY, servitude, bondage, captivity.
SLAUGHTER, carnage, massacre, butchery.
To SLAY, kill, murder, assassinate.
To SLEEP, slumber, nap, doze, drowse.
SLEEPY, drowsy, lethargic.
SLENDER, slight, slim, thin.
To SLIDE, slip, glide.
SLIGHT, slender, slim; cursory, hasty, desultory; neglect, contempt, scorn.
To SLIP, slide, glide.
SLOTHFUL, lazy, inactive, sluggish, inert.
SLOW, dilatory, tardy, tedious, dull.
SLUGGISH, inactive, inert, lazy, slothful.
To SLUMBER, sleep, doze, nap, drowse.
SLY, cunning, crafty, subtle, wily.
SMALL, little, diminutive, minute.
SMARTNESS, quickness, liveliness, briskness; pungency, tartness.
To SMEAR, daub, besmear.
SMELL, scent, odor, perfume, fragrance.
SMOOTH, even, plain, level.
To SMOTHER, stifle, suppress, suffocate.
SNARLING, cynical, snappish, waspish.
To SNATCH, catch, seize, grasp, gripe.
SNEAKING, crouching, servile.
To SNEER, scoff, gibe, jeer.
To SOAK, steep, imbrue; drench, macerate.
SOBER, moderate, abstemious, abstinent, temperate; grave.
SOBRIETY, moderation, temperance, modesty.

SOCIAL, sociable, convivial, conversable, familiar, companionable.
SOCIETY, association, company, community, fellowship.
SOFT, flexible, supple, ductile, pliant, lithe, pliable, yielding, compliant, docile, tractable; mild, gentle, meek.
To SOIL, stain, sully, tarnish.
To SOJOURN, dwell, reside, inhabit; tarry, stay.
SOLACE, consolation, comfort, recreation.
SOLE, solitary, single, only, alone.
SOLEMN, grave, serious.
To SOLICIT, ask, request, crave, entreat, beg, beseech, implore, supplicate.
SOLICITATION, importunity, invitation.
SOLICITUDE, care, anxiety.
SOLID, hard, substantial, firm, stable.
SOLITARY, sole, only, alone, single, lonely; retired, remote; desolate, desert.
To SOLVE, resolve, explain, clear up.
SOME, any.
SOON, early, betimes; quickly, promptly.
To SOOTHE, allay, appease, assuage, compose, calm, tranquilize, pacify, mitigate.
To SOPHISTICATE, adulterate, corrupt, vitiate.
SORDID, mean, covetous, niggardly, gross.
SORROW, affliction, grief.
SORRY, grieved, hurt, afflicted, affected, mortified, vexed, chagrined.
SORT, species, kind.
SOVEREIGN, prince, monarch, potentate.
SOUND, healthy, hearty, sane; tone.
SOUR, acid, sharp, tart, acrimonious, acetose, acetous.

Sourness of manner, acrimony, asperity, harshness.
Source, origin, rise, spring, fountain.
Space, room.
Spacious, ample, capacious.
To Spare, afford, give, impart, communicate.
Sparing, economical, saving, thrifty.
Spark, gallant, beau.
To Sparkle, shine, glitter, glare, radiate, coruscate.
To Speak, say, tell, talk, converse, discourse, utter, articulate, pronounce.
To Speak to, accost, address, discourse.
Special, specific, particular.
Species, kind, sort.
Specific, particular, special.
Specimen, model, pattern, sample.
Specious, colorable, ostensible, plausible, feasible.
Speck, stain, spot, flaw, blemish.
Spectacle, show, sight, exhibition, representation, pageant.
Spectator, looker-on, beholder, observer.
Spectre, ghost, phantom, apparition.
Speculation, theory, scheme.
Speech, oration, address, harangue.
Speechless, dumb, silent, mute.
To Speed, hasten, accelerate, expedite, despatch.
To Spend, expend; exhaust, dissipate, squander, waste.
Sphere, circle, globe, orb.
To Spill, pour, shed.
Spirited, lively, animated, vivacious, ardent, active.
Spirits, animation, life, vivacity; courage, enterprise.
Spiritual, immaterial, incorporeal.
Spite, rancor, malice, malevolence, malignity; pique, grudge.

Splendor, lustre, brightness, brilliancy; magnificence, pomp, pageantry.
Splenetic, morose, gloomy, sullen.
To Split, break, burst; crack.
Spoil, booty, prey.
Spontaneously, voluntarily, willingly.
Sport, amusement, diversion, entertainment, recreation, pastime; play, game.
Sportive, lively, jocund, sprightly, vivacious, merry.
Spot, place, site, locality; speck, stain, flaw.
Spotless, unspotted, unblemished; blameless, irreproachable.
To Spread, scatter, expand, diffuse, disperse, distribute, circulate, propagate, disseminate, dispensate.
Sprightly, active, agile, assiduous, alert, brisk.
Spring, fountain, source.
To Spring, arise, issue, proceed, flow, emanate.
To Sprinkle, bedew, besprinkle; scatter.
To Sprout, bud, germinate, shoot forth.
Spruce, finical, foppish, dandyish.
Spurious, counterfeit, supposititious, not genuine.
Spy, emissary.
To Squander, spend, expend, waste.
Squeamish, fastidious, over-nice, finical.
Squeeze, press, pinch, gripe.
Stability, fixedness, firmness, steadiness.
Staff, stick, crutch; prop, stay, support.
To Stagger, reel, totter.
To Stagnate, stand, stop, rest.
Stain, blot, blemish, spot, speck, flaw.
To Stain, color, dye, tinge.

To Stain or dirt, blot, maculate, spot, foul, soil, tarnish, sully, pollute.
To Stammer, stutter; hesitate, falter.
Stamp, mark, impression, print.
To Stand, stop, rest, stagnate.
Standard, criterion, rule, test.
To Stare, gape, gaze.
To Start, startle, shrink.
State, condition, situation, position, predicament, case, plight.
Station, situation, position, post, place.
Stately, magisterial, majestic, pompous, dignified, august.
Stay, staff, support, prop.
To Stay, remain, abide, continue.
State in life, station, situation, condition, circumstances, rank, degree, post.
Steadiness, constancy, firmness, stability.
To Steal away, withdraw, abscond.
To Steep, soak, drench.
Sterility, unfruitfulness, barrenness, aridity.
Stern, austere, severe, rigid, rigorous.
To Stick, hold, cleave, fasten, adhere, attach, fix.
Sticking to, adherent, adhesive, tenacious.
Sticking together, cohesion, agglutination.
To Stifle, suppress, smother; suffocate, choke.
Stigma, mark, badge.
To Still, quiet, calm, lull, allay, pacify, assuage, appease; subdue, suppress.
To Stimulate, animate, incite, encourage, impel, urge, instigate, irritate, exasperate, incense.
Stipend, allowance, pay, wages, salary, hire.
To Stir up, awaken, rouse, incite, animate, excite, stimulate, provoke.
Stock, store, fund, supply, accumulation, hoard, provision.
Stop, cessation, rest, intermission.
To Stop, check, hinder, impede.
Store. See Stock.
Storm, blast, tempest, hurricane.
Story, tale, anecdote, memoir, incident.
Stout, corpulent, lusty.
Straight, right, direct.
Strait, narrow.
Strange, particular, odd, singular, eccentric.
Stranger, foreigner, alien.
Stratagem, artifice, trick, finesse, deception, cheat, imposture, delusion, fraud, deceit, imposition.
To Stray, deviate, wander, swerve, rove, ramble, err.
Stream, current, tide.
Strength, power, force, authority.
To Strengthen, fortify, invigorate, animate.
Strenuous, bold, zealous, vehement, vigorous, ardent.
To Stretch, extend, reach.
Strict, accurate, exact, nice; rigorous, severe.
Stricture, animadversion, criticism, censure.
Strife, dissension, contention, discord.
To Strike, hit, beat.
A Striking together, collision, clashing.
To Strip, bereave, deprive, divest; rob, plunder, pillage.
To Strive, contend, vie; endeavor, aim, struggle.
Stroke, blow, knock.
To Stroll, wander, ramble, rove, roam, range.
Strong, forcible, cogent, potent, efficacious; powerful, vigorous, stout, robust, hardy, firm, muscular.

STRUCTURE, edifice, fabric.
To STRUGGLE, contend, contest, strive, endeavor, labor.
STUBBORN, obstinate, contumacious, unyielding, headstrong, heady.
STUDY, attention, application.
STUPID, dull, doltish.
STURDY, strong, firm, robust.
To STUTTER, stammer, hesitate, falter.
STYLE, diction, phraseology.
To STYLE, name, denominate, entitle, characterize, designate.
SUAVITY, urbanity, sweetness.
To SUBDUE, overbear, overpower, overcome, surmount, conquer, vanquish, subjugate.
SUBJECT, matter, materials, object; exposed, liable, obnoxious; subordinate, subservient, inferior.
To SUBJECT, subjugate, subdue.
To SUBJOIN, affix, attach, connect, add to.
SUBLIME, great, grand, exalted, lofty, elevated.
SUBMISSIVE, compliant, yielding, obedient, obsequious; humble, modest, passive.
To SUBMIT, comply, yield.
SUBORDINATE, subject, inferior, subservient.
To SUBORN, perjure, forswear.
SUBSEQUENT, consequent, posterior.
SUBSERVIENT, subject, subordinate, inferior.
To SUBSIDE, abate, intermit.
To SUBSIST, exist, to be.
SUBSISTENCE, living, livelihood, sustenance, support, maintenance.
SUBSTANTIAL, solid; strong, stout, bulky; responsible.
To SUBSTITUTE, change, exchange.
SUBTERFUGE, evasion, shift, quirk.
SUBTLE, cunning, crafty, sly, wily.

To SUBTRACT, deduct, withdraw.
To SUBVERT, overturn, overthrow, invert, reverse.
To SUCCEED, follow, ensue; obtain one's object.
SUCCESSFUL, fortunate, lucky, prosperous.
SUCCESSION, series, order.
SUCCESSIVE, alternate.
SUCCINCT, brief, short, concise, compendious, summary, laconic.
To SUCCOR, aid, assist, help, relieve, cherish.
SUDDEN, unexpected, unanticipated, unlooked-for.
To SUFFER, bear, endure, support, sustain; admit, allow, permit, tolerate.
SUFFICIENT, enough, competent, adequate.
To SUFFOCATE, stifle, smother, choke.
SUFFRAGE, vote, voice.
To SUGGEST, allude, hint, refer to, glance at, intimate, insinuate.
To SUIT, answer, fit, serve; agree, accord.
SUIT, prayer, request, petition.
SUITABLE, fit, apt, meet, becoming, expedient, seemly; agreeable, conformable; convenient.
SUITOR, wooer, lover.
SULLEN, gloomy, morose, splenetic.
To SULLY, stain, tarnish, soil.
SUMMARY, brief, short, compendious, succinct, laconic.
To SUMMON, call, cite, bid, invite.
SUNDRY, different, several, various, diverse.
SUPERFICIAL, shallow, flimsy.
SUPERFICIES, surface.
SUPERFLUITY, excess, redundancy.
SUPERIORITY, excellence, pre-eminence.
SUPERINTENDENCY, inspection, oversight, superintendence.

SUPERSCRIPTION, direction, address.
To SUPERSEDE, overrule, set aside.
SUPINE, indolent, listless, careless.
SUPPLE, flexible, pliant, bending.
To SUPPLICATE, beg, solicit, beseech, entreat, implore, crave.
To SUPPLY, furnish, provide, administer, minister, contribute.
To SUPPORT, sustain, stay, prop, uphold, maintain; assist, countenance, favor, second, forward, patronize, promote, encourage; nurture, nourish, cherish, protect, shield, defend.
To SUPPOSE, conceive, apprehend, imagine, think, believe, deem.
SUPPOSITION, conjecture, surmise, guess.
SUPPOSITITIOUS, spurious, counterfeit, not genuine.
To SUPPRESS, repress, restrain, put down, stifle, smother.
SURE, infallible, certain, indisputable; safe, secure; confident.
SURFACE, superficies.
SURGE, wave, billow, breaker.
SURMISE, conjecture, supposition.
To SURMOUNT, rise above, overcome, subdue, vanquish, conquer.
To SURPASS, excel, exceed, outdo, outstrip.
SURPRISE, wonder, astonishment, admiration, amazement.
To SURRENDER, give up, deliver, yield, cede.
To SURROUND, environ, encompass, encircle; enclose, invest.
SURVEY, review, retrospect; view, prospect.
To SURVIVE, outlive.
SUSCEPTIBILITY, sensibility, feeling.
SUSPENSE, doubt, indetermination.

SUSPICION, jealousy, distrust, diffidence.
To SUSTAIN, support, maintain, bear up.
SUSTENANCE, living, livelihood, subsistence, support, maintenance.
SWAIN, countryman, peasant, rustic, hind, clown.
To SWALLOW up, absorb, imbibe, ingulf, engross, consume.
SWARM, multitude, throng, crowd.
SWAY, influence, authority, ascendency, rule.
To SWELL, heave; rise, protuberate, enlarge.
To SWELL out, extend, enlarge, expand, dilate.
SWELLING, turgid, tumid.
To SWERVE, deviate, wander, stray.
SWIFTNESS, quickness, fleetness, rapidity, celerity, velocity.
SYCOPHANT, flatterer, parasite.
SYMBOL, emblem, figure, type; metaphor.
SYMMETRY, proportion, harmony.
SYMPATHY, compassion, commiseration, condolence; fellow-feeling; agreement.
SYMPTOM, mark, note, sign, token, indication.
SYNOD, assembly, meeting, convocation, diet, congress, congregation, convention.
SYSTEM, method; scheme.

T

TACITURNITY, silence.
To TAINT, contaminate, defile, pollute, corrupt, infect, vitiate.
To TAKE, accept, receive; seize.
To TAKE heed, guard against.
To TAKE from, deduct, subtract, abstract.
To TAKE out, extract.
TALE, anecdote, story, fable, incident, memoir, narrative.
TALENT, ability, faculty, gift, endowment.

TALK, conversation, colloquy, discourse, chat, dialogue, conference, communication.
TALKATIVENESS, garrulity, loquacity.
TALL, high, lofty.
TAME, gentle.
To TANTALIZE, aggravate, provoke, irritate, vex, tease, taunt, torment.
TARDY, slow, dilatory, tedious.
To TARNISH, stain, sully, soil.
To TARRY, await, loiter, continue, linger, saunter.
TARTNESS, acrimony, asperity, acerbity, harshness.
TASK, work, labor, toil, drudgery.
TASTE, judgment, discernment, perception, sensibility; savor, relish, flavor, goût.
To TAUNT, tease, vex, tantalize, torment.
TAUTOLOGY, repetition.
TAX, impost, tribute, contribution, duty, toll, rate, assessment, custom.
To TEACH, inform, instruct.
To TEAR, rend, rack, break.
To TEASE, vex, tantalize, plague, torment, mortify, chagrin.
TEDIOUS, slow, dilatory, tardy; wearisome, tiresome.
TEGUMENT, covering.
To TELL, make known, communicate, impart, reveal, disclose, inform, acquaint, report.
To TELL over, repeat, recite, rehearse, recapitulate, enumerate.
TEMERITY, rashness, precipitancy, heedlessness.
TEMPER, disposition, temperament, constitution; frame, mood, humor.
To TEMPER, gratify, humor, modify; soften, assuage, mollify, soothe, calm.
TEMPERAMENT, frame, constitution, temper.
TEMPERANCE, moderation, sobriety, modesty.

TEMPERATE, moderate, abstinent, abstemious, sober.
TEMPEST, blast, gale, storm, hurricane.
TEMPORAL, worldly, secular.
TEMPORARY, transient, transitory, fleeting.
TEMPORIZING, time-serving.
To TEMPT, allure, attract, decoy, entice, seduce; try.
TENDENCY, inclination, propensity, proneness; drift, scope, aim.
To TENDER, offer, propose, bid.
TENDERNESS, benignity, humanity, benevolence, kindness.
TENET, doctrine, opinion, principle, position.
TERM, condition, stipulation; limit, boundary; word, expression.
To TERMINATE, complete, finish, close, end.
TERRIBLE, terrific, fearful, dreadful, shocking, frightful, horrible.
TERRITORY, domain.
TERROR, alarm, fright, consternation.
TEST, criterion, standard; experience, experiment, trial, proof.
To TESTIFY, declare, signify, utter.
TESTIMONY, proof, evidence.
THEORY, speculation.
THEREFORE, consequently, accordingly.
THICK, dense, close, compact, solid; gross, coarse.
THIN, lean, meagre, slim, slender, rare, slight.
To THINK, cogitate, consider, reflect, ponder, deliberate, contemplate, meditate, muse; conceive, imagine, suppose, opine, believe, deem, fancy.
THOUGHT, imagination, conception, fancy, idea; conceit, notion, supposition, consideration, meditation, reflection, contemplation, cogitation, deliberation.

THOUGHTFUL, considerate, deliberate, attentive, careful, wary, circumspect, discreet; reflective, contemplative.
THREAT, menace.
THREATENING, imminent, impending.
THRIFTY, economical, saving, sparing, careful, penurious.
To THRIVE, flourish, prosper.
THRONG, multitude, crowd, swarm.
To THROW, cast, hurl.
To THROW back, reject, retort; reflect.
To THROW in, inject.
To THWART, oppose, resist, withstand.
TIDE, current, stream.
TIDINGS, news, intelligence.
TILLAGE, cultivation, husbandry.
TIME, duration; period, age, date, era, epoch; season.
TIMELY, seasonably, opportune.
TIME-SERVING, temporizing.
TIMID, timorous, fearful, afraid.
TIMIDITY, pusillanimity, fear, cowardice.
To TINGE, dye, color, stain.
TINT, hue, color.
To TIRE, weary, jade, harass.
TIRED, fatigued, wearied, jaded, harassed.
TIRESOME, tedious, wearisome.
TITLE, denomination, name, appellation.
TOIL, labor, drudgery.
TOKEN, mark, sign, note, symptom, indication.
To TOLERATE, admit, allow, permit, suffer.
TOLL, tax, custom, duty, impost, contribution.
TOMB, grave, sepulchre.
TONE, sound.
TONGUE, language, speech, idiom, dialect.
TORMENT, torture.
To TORMENT, tease, vex, tantalize, taunt, torment.

TORPID, benumbed, numb.
To TOSS, shake, agitate.
TOTAL, gross, whole, entire, complete.
To TOTTER, stagger, reel.
TOUCH, contact.
TOUCHING, affecting, moving, pathetic.
TOUR, circuit, round, excursion, ramble, trip, jaunt.
To TRACE, derive, deduce.
TRACE, mark, track, vestige.
TRACT, essay, treatise, dissertation; district, region, quarter.
TRACTABLE, docile, ductile.
TRADE, business, profession, occupation, calling, office, avocation, employment; commerce, dealing, traffic.
TRADER, merchant, tradesman.
To TRADUCE, disparage, detract, depreciate, degrade, decry.
TRAFFIC, commerce, exchange, barter, dealing, truck, trade.
TRAIN, retinue, procession.
TRAITOROUS, treacherous, treasonable.
To TRANQUILLIZE, appease, allay, assuage, compose, soothe, calm, pacify.
TRANQUILLITY, peace, quiet, calm, repose.
To TRANSACT, negotiate, treat for, or about.
TRANSACTION, proceeding.
To TRANSCEND, exceed, surpass, excel, outdo.
To TRANSCRIBE, copy.
To TRANSFIGURE, transform, metamorphose.
TRANSGRESSION, offence, infringement; misdemeanor, misdeed, affront.
TRANSIENT, transitory, temporary, fleeting.
TRANSPARENT, pellucid, translucent, transpicuous, diaphanous, pervious.
To TRANSPORT, bear, carry, convey.

Transport, ecstasy, rapture.
Travel, journey, tour.
Treacherous, faithless, perfidious, insidious.
Treasonable, treacherous, traitorous.
To Treasure, hoard, deposit, lay up.
Treat, feast, banquet, carousal, entertainment.
To Treat for, or about, negotiate.
Treatment, usage; entertainment.
Trembling, tremor, trepidation, shaking, shivering, quivering.
Tremendous, dreadful, frightful, terrible, terrific, horrid, horrible.
Tremor. See Trembling.
Trepidation, agitation, tremor, disturbance, emotion, trembling.
Trespass, offence, transgression, misdemeanor, misdeed.
Trial, experiment, proof, test; attempt, endeavor, effort.
Tribute. See Tax.
Trick, artifice, stratagem, wile, fraud, cheat, juggle, finesse, sleight, deception, imposture, delusion, imposition.
Trifling, trivial, futile, petty, frivolous, unimportant, inconsiderable, light, slight, worthless.
Trip, excursion, ramble, tour, jaunt.
Trivial. See Trifling.
To Trouble, afflict, distress, harass, perplex, disturb, molest.
Troubles, distress, affliction, adversity, calamity, misfortune; difficulties, embarrassments, perplexities, vexations, anxieties, sorrow, misery.
Troublesome, vexatious, perplexing, harassing, annoying, disgusting, disturbing, irksome, afflictive.

To Truck, exchange, barter, commute.
True, sincere, honest, upright, plain.
Trust, belief, credit, faith, confidence; hope, expectation.
Trusty, faithful.
To give in Trust, intrust, commit, confide, consign, charge.
Truth, veracity, honesty, faithfulness, fidelity.
To Try, attempt, endeavor, essay; tempt.
To Tug, haul, pull, pluck, hale.
To Tumble, fall, sink, drop, droop.
Tumid, turgid, bombastic.
Tumult, uproar, commotion, riot.
Turbulent, tumultuous, riotous, seditious, mutinous.
Turgid, tumid, bombastic.
Turn, gyration, meander; cast, bent, character.
To Turn, revolve, circulate, whirl, twirl, wheel; bend, twist, distort, wring, wrest, contort.
To Twist. See Turn.
Type, symbol, figure, emblem.
Tyrannical, absolute, arbitrary, despotic, imperious.

U

Ultimate, last, latest, final.
Umpire, arbiter, arbitrator, judge.
Unanticipated, unexpected, unlooked-for; sudden.
Unavoidable, not to be avoided, inevitable.
Unbelief, disbelief; infidelity, incredulity, skepticism.
Unblemished, blameless, spotless, unspotted, irreproachable.
Unbodied, incorporeal, immaterial, spiritual.
Unbounded, boundless, infinite, unlimited, illimitable, interminable.

UNBURY, disinter, disentomb, exhume, exhumate.
UNCEASINGLY, uninterruptedly, always, constantly, continually, perpetually, ever.
UNCERTAIN, doubtful, dubious, precarious; equivocal.
UNCOMMON, rare, scarce, unique, choice, singular.
UNCONCERNED, indifferent, regardless.
UNCONQUERABLE, invincible, insuperable, insurmountable.
UNCOUTH, odd, strange, awkward, clumsy, unhandy, unpolite.
To UNCOVER, discover, strip, denude.
UNDAUNTED, bold, fearless, intrepid.
UNDENIABLE, indubitable, indisputable, incontrovertible, unquestionable, irrefragable.
UNDER, below, beneath, subjacent, lower.
To UNDERMINE, sap.
To UNDERSTAND, comprehend, conceive, apprehend.
UNDERSTANDING, intellect, intelligence, faculty; comprehension, apprehension, perception, conception.
UNDERTAKING, enterprise, attempt, engagement.
UNDETERMINED, unsettled, unsteady, irresolute, unresolved, hesitating, doubtful, fluctuating, wavering.
UNEXPECTED, sudden, unlooked for, unanticipated.
UNFAITHFUL, perfidious, treacherous; undutiful, disloyal.
UNFEELING, insensible, unsusceptible, callous, obdurate.
To UNFOLD, develop, divulge, unravel, expand.
UNFRUITFULNESS, barrenness, sterility, aridity.
UNGOVERNABLE, unruly, refractory, obstreperous.

UNHANDY, awkward, clumsy, uncouth, untoward.
UNHAPPY, miserable, wretched, distressed, afflicted; unfortunate, calamitous.
UNIFORM, equal, even, equable, alike.
UNIMPORTANT, insignificant, immaterial, inconsiderable, trivial, trifling, petty.
UNINTERRUPTEDLY, unceasingly, incessantly, unintermitting.
UNISON, accordance, agreement, harmony; melody.
To UNITE, join, combine, connect, coalesce.
UNIVERSAL, general.
UNLEARNED, illiterate, unlettered, ignorant.
UNLIKE, dissimilar.
UNLIMITED, boundless, unbounded, illimitable, infinite.
UNLOOKED-FOR, unanticipated; sudden.
UNMERCIFUL, merciless, hardhearted, cruel.
UNOFFENDING, inoffensive, harmless.
UNQUESTIONABLE, indubitable, indisputable, incontrovertible, irrefragable, undeniable.
To UNRAVEL, unfold, develop; disentangle, extricate.
UNRELENTING, relentless, implacable, inexorable.
UNRULY, ungovernable, refractory.
UNSEARCHABLE, inscrutable.
To UNSETTLE, disconcert, discompose, disarrange, derange, displace, ruffle, disorder, confuse.
UNSETTLE, undetermined, unsteady, wavering.
UNSPEAKABLE, ineffable, unutterable, inexpressible.
UNSPOTTED. See SPOTLESS.
UNSTABLE, infirm, changeable, mutable, wavering.
UNSTEADY. See UNSETTLED.

UNSUSCEPTIBLE, unfeeling, insensible, hard, callous.

UNTIMELY, premature, inopportune, unseasonable.

UNTOWARD, awkward; uncouth; froward, perverse.

UNTRUTH, falsehood, falsity, lie, mendacity.

UNUTTERABLE. See UNSPEAKABLE.

UNWILLING, averse, backward, loth, reluctant.

UNWORTHY, worthless; mean, contemptible, vile.

To UPBRAID, blame, reprove, reproach, censure, condemn.

UPRIGHTNESS, rectitude, integrity, probity, honesty.

UPROAR, bustle, tumult, disturbance.

URBANITY, suavity, affability, complaisance, courtesy.

To URGE, animate, incite, impel, instigate, stimulate; encourage.

URGENT, pressing, importunate.

USAGE, custom, prescription; treatment.

USE, usage, practice, habit; avail, advantage, utility, benefit, service.

USUALLY, generally, commonly.

To USURP, arrogate, assume, appropriate.

UTILITY, advantage, benefit, service, avail, use.

To UTTER, speak, articulate, pronounce, express.

UTTERED by the mouth, oral, vocal, verbal.

V

VACANCY, vacuity, chasm, inanity.

VACANT, empty, void, devoid; idle.

VACUITY. See VACANCY.

VAGUE, loose, lax.

VAIN, idle, fruitless, ineffectual.

VALE, valley, dale, dingle, dell.

VALEDICTION, farewell, taking leave.

VALOR, bravery, courage, gallantry, boldness, intrepidity; fearlessness.

VALUABLE, precious, costly, estimable.

VALUE, worth, rate, price; account, estimation, appreciation.

To VALUE, compute, rate, calculate, appraise, assess; appreciate, estimate; esteem, respect, regard, prize.

VANITY, pride, conceit.

To VANQUISH, conquer, subdue, surmount, overcome.

VARIABLE, changeable, fickle, wavering, versatile, unsteady.

VARIATION, change, vicissitude, variety.

VARIETY, difference, diversity, change, medley.

VARIOUS, different, divers, several, sundry.

To VARNISH, gloss, palliate.

To VARY, change, alter; differ, disagree, dissent.

VAST, enormous, huge, immense.

To VAUNT, glory, boast, brag.

VAUNTING, boasting, ostentation, vain-glory, parade.

VEHEMENT, ardent, hot, eager, firm, passionate, impetuous, violent.

VEIL, mask, cloak, blind, covering.

VELOCITY, quickness, swiftness, fleetness, celerity, rapidity.

VENAL, mercenary, hireling.

To VENERATE, adore, revere, reverence.

VENIAL, pardonable.

VENTURE, hazard, risk.

VERACITY, truth, integrity.

VERBAL, vocal, oral.

VERGE, border, edge, rim, brim, brink, margin.

VESTIGE, mark, trace, track.

To VEX, tease, plague, tanta-

lize, torment, mortify, chagrin, offend.
VEXATION, chagrin, mortification; uneasiness, trouble.
VICE, imperfection, defect, fault; crime.
VICINITY, neighborhood.
VICIOUS, corrupt, depraved, profligate, wicked.
VICISSITUDE, change, variation.
VICTOR, conqueror, vanquisher.
To VIE, contend, strive.
To VIEW, look, see, behold, eye.
VIEW, survey, prospect; landscape.
VIGILANT, watchful, wakeful.
VIGOR, energy, force, strength, efficacy.
VIGOROUS, strong; active, agile, alert, brisk, nimble, sedulous, diligent.
VILE, base, mean, worthless, despicable, wicked.
To VILIFY, accuse falsely, asperse, calumniate, defame, detract, scandalize, slander.
To VINDICATE, defend, protect; clear.
VINDICTIVE, resentful, revengeful.
To VIOLATE, infringe, transgress; injure; hurt; ravish, deflower.
VIOLENT, forcible, vehement, boisterous, turbulent, furious, impetuous, passionate.
VISAGE, face, countenance.
VISIBLE, apparent, obvious, clear, plain, evident, discernible, manifest, distinct.
VISION, apparition, phantom, spectre, ghost.
VISIONARY, imaginary, fantastical; enthusiast, fanatic.
VISITANT, visiter, guest.
To VITIATE, contaminate, taint, defile, pollute, infect, sophisticate.
VITIATED, corrupt, depraved, debased, wicked.

VIVACIOUS, animated, lively, sprightly, sportive, jocund, merry.
VIVACITY, life, animation, spirits, lightness, volatility.
VIVID, clear, lucid, bright; lively, quick, sprightly, active; striking.
VOCABULARY, dictionary, nomenclature, lexicon, glossary.
VOCAL, verbal, oral.
VOID, empty, vacant, devoid.
VOLATILITY, lightness, levity, giddiness, flightiness.
VOLUNTARILY, spontaneously, willingly, gratuitously.
VOLUPTUARY, sensualist, epicure.
VORACIOUS, rapacious, ravenous, greedy.
VOTE, suffrage, voice.
To VOUCH, obtest, attest, warrant; asseverate, affirm, aver, protest, assure.
VULGAR, common, ordinary, mean, low.

W

WAGES, stipend, salary, hire, allowance, pay.
WAKEFUL, watchful, vigilant, observant.
WALK, carriage, gait.
To WALK unsteadily, stagger, reel, totter.
WAN, pale, pallid.
To WANDER, stroll, ramble, rove, roam, range.
WANT, poverty, penury, indigence, necessity, need, lack.
WARE, commodity, goods, merchandise.
WARINESS, caution, circumspection, scrupulousness, care.
WARLIKE, martial, military, soldier-like.
WARM-HEARTED, cordial, sincere, hearty.
WARMTH, fervency, fervor, ardor,

zeal, cordiality; vehemence, heat; glow.

WARNING, caution, admonition, notice.

To WARRANT, answer for, guaranty, secure.

WARY, cautious, circumspect, guarded, watchful.

To WASTE, spend, expend, dissipate; squander, consume, lavish, destroy.

WASTE, devastation, ravage, spoil, desolation, havoc, destruction; consumption, dissipation.

WASTEFUL, profuse, extravagant, prodigal, lavish.

WATCHFUL, vigilant, attentive, cautious, observant, circumspect, wakeful.

WATERY, aqueous.

WAVE, billow, surge, breaker.

To WAVER, hesitate, fluctuate, scruple.

WAY, method, system, mode, means, manner, form, fashion; road, route, course.

WEAK, feeble, infirm, enfeebled, debilitated, enervated.

WEAKNESS, debility, languor, feebleness, infirmity, imbecility, frailty, impotence; failing, foible.

WEALTH, riches, opulence, affluence.

WEARINESS, lassitude, fatigue.

WEARISOME, tiresome, tedious, fatiguing, troublesome, annoying, vexatious.

To WEARY, tire, fatigue, harass, jade, subdue; vex, annoy.

WEDDING, marriage, nuptials.

WEDLOCK, marriage, matrimony.

WEEKLY, hebdomadal.

WEIGHT, gravity, heaviness, ponderousness; burden, load; signification, avail, importance, consequence, moment.

WEIGHTY, heavy, burdensome, ponderous; onerous.

WELCOME, acceptable, agreeable, grateful.

WELL-BEING, welfare, prosperity, happiness.

WELFARE. See the preceding word.

To WELTER, wallow.

To WHEEDLE, coax, cajole, fawn.

WHIM, freak, caprice.

WHIMSICAL, capricious, fanciful, fantastical.

To WHIRL, twirl, turn, wheel, revolve, circulate.

To WHITEN, blanch, bleach.

WHOLE, all; entire, complete, integral, total, undivided, perfect.

WICKED, unjust, nefarious, irreligious, profane, impious.

WICKED in a high degree, atrocious, heinous, flagrant, flagitious, villanous, enormous, monstrous.

WILLINGLY, voluntarily, spontaneously.

To WIN, obtain, gain, procure, get, earn.

WILY, subtle, sly, crafty, cunning.

To WIND, turn, whirl, twirl.

WISDOM, sapience, knowledge; prudence.

WISE, sage; sapient, sagacious; learned, skilled; judicious; discreet, prudent.

To WISH, desire, long for, hanker after.

WIT, ingenuity; humor, satire, irony, burlesque; contrivance, stratagem, invention.

To WITHDRAW, retreat, retire, recede, retrograde, go back.

To WITHHOLD, keep back, let, hinder; refrain, forbear.

To WITHSTAND, oppose, resist, thwart.

WITNESS, deponent, evidence.

WOFUL, piteous, doleful, rueful.

WONDER, surprise, astonishment.

admiration, amazement; miracle, marvel, prodigy.
WOOER, suitor, lover.
WORD, term, expression; promise, argument.
WORK, employment, occupation; operation, performance; toil, labor, drudgery, production.
WORLDLY, secular, temporal.
WORSE (to make), impair, deteriorate; injure, damage.
To WORSHIP, adore, revere; honor.
WORTH, desert, merit; value, excellence; rate, price.
WORTHLESS, unworthy, valueless.
WORTHY, deserving, meritorious, estimable.
To WRANGLE, jangle, jar.
WRATH, anger, ire, fury, resentment, indignation.
To WRENCH, wrest, turn, bend, twist, distort.
WRETCHED, unhappy, miserable.
To WRING. See WRENCH.
WRITER, penman, scribe; author.
WRONG, injury, injustice.

Y

YEARLY, annual.
To YIELD, impart, give, communicate; produce; give up, comply, cede, concede, surrender; conform.
YIELDING, compliant, submissive.
YOUTH, juvenility, adolescence, puerility.

Z

ZEAL, ardor, enthusiasm.
ZEALOUS, ardent, earnest, solicitous, anxious, warm, fervent, enthusiastic.

INDEX.

INTRODUCTION.

PART I.

CLASSIFICATION OF WORDS. PAGE

CHAP. I. Words of different orthography, but of similar orthoepy. 9
" II. Words of similar orthoepy, but of different orthography
(17 classes), ... 19
" III. Words of equivocal signification, ... 35
" IV. Words,—colloquial improprieties, ... 44
" V. Words,—Rule of Orthography, ... 46

PART II.

CHAP. I. Derivation and composition 48
        Prefixes, ... 50
        Suffixes, ... 53
        Words from Latin, ... 57-171

A.

1. Acer—*acerbity.*
2. Ager—*agrarian.*
3. Ago, actum—*act.*
4. Alienus—*alien.*
5. Alo—*aliment.*
6. Alter—*altercation.*
7. Altus—*altitude.*
8. Ambulo—*amble.*
9. Amo—*amateur.*
10. Amplus—*ample.*
11. Ango—*anger.*
12. Angulus—*angle.*
13. Animus—*animal.*
14. Annus—*annual.*
15. Annulus—*annular.*
16. Antiquus—*antiquary.*
17. Aperio—*aperient.*
18. Apto—*apt.*
19. Aqua—*aquatic.*
20. Arbiter—*arbitration.*

21. Arbor—*arbor.*
22. Arceo—*coerce.*
23. Ardeo—*ardent.*
24. Arguo—*argue.*
25. Arma—*arm.*
26. Aro—*arable.*
27. Ars—*art.*
28. Articulus—*article.*
29. Asper—*asperity.*
30. Audio—*audible.*
31. Augeo—*augment.*
32. Avis—*aviary.*

B.

33. Bacchus—*bacchanal.*
34. Beatus—*beatific.*
35. Bellum—*belligerent.*
36. Bibo—*bibber.*
37. Bis—*bisect.*
38. Bonus—*bounty.*
39. Brevis—*brevity.*

C.

40. Cado—*cadence.*
41. Cædo—*excision.*
42. Caleo—*calid.*
43. Calx—*calcine.*
44. Candeo—*candle.*
45. Canis—*canine.*
46. Cantus—*chant.*
47. Capio—*capable.*
48. Caput—*capital.*
49. Carcer—*incarcerate.*
50. Caro—*carnal.*
51. Carpo—*carp.*
52. Castigo—*castigate.*
53. Catena—*concatenation.*
54. Causa—*cause.*
55. Caveo—*caution.*
56. Cavus—*cave.*
57. Cedo—*cede.*
58. Celeber—*celebrate.*
59. Celer—*celerity.*
60. Cella—*cellar.*
61. Celo—*conceal.*
62. Cælum—*celestial.*
63. Censeo—*censor.*
64. Centum—*centennial.*
65. Cerno—*certain.*
66. Certo—*concert.*
67. Certo—*certain.*
68. Cieo—*cite.*
69. Cingo—*cincture.*
70. Cinis—*cinder.*
71. Circus—*circle.*
72. Civis—*civic.*
73. Clam—*clandestine.*
74. Clamo—*clamor.*
75. Clarus—*clarion.*
76. Classis—*class.*
77. Claudo—*close.*
78. Clemens—*clement.*
79. Clino—*incline.*
80. Clivus—*acclivity.*
81. Codex—*code.*
82. Colo—*colony.*
83. Comes—*comity.*
84. Concilium—*council.*
85. Coquo—*concoct.*
86. Cor—*core.*
87. Cornu—*cornet.*
88. Corona—*crown.*
89. Corpus—*corporate.*
90. Costa—*coast.*
91. Cras—*procrastinate.*
92. Credo—*credit.*
93. Creo—*create.*
94. Crepo—*decrepit.*
95. Cresco—*crescent.*
96. Crimen—*crime.*
97. Crudus—*crude.*
98. Crux—*cross.*
99. Cubo—*encumber.*
100. Culpa—*culpable.*
101. Cumulus—*cumulative.*
102. Cura—*cure.*
103. Curro—*current.*
104. Curvus—*curve.*
105. Custos—*custody.*
106. Cutis—*cutaneous.*

D.

107. Damnum—*damage.*
108. Debeo—*debt.*
109. Decem—*decimal.*
110. Decet—*decent.*
111. Dens—*dental.*
112. Densus—*dense.*
113. Deterior—*deteriorate.*
114. Deus—*deity.*
115. Dexter—*dexterity.*
116. Dico—*dedicate.*
117. Dico—*diction.*
118. Dies—*diary.*
119. Digitus—*digit.*
120. Dignus—*dignity.*
121. Dimidium—*demigod.*
122. Disco—*disciple.*
123. Divido—*divide.*
124. Do—*donor.*
125. Doceo—*doctor.*
126. Doleo—*doleful.*
127. Dominus—*dominion.*
128. Domo—*indomitable.*
129. Domus—*dome.*
130. Dormio—*dormant.*
131. Dorsum—*dorsal.*
132. Dubious—*dubious.*
133. Duco—*duct.*
134. Duo—*dual.*
135. Durus—*durable.*

E.

136. Ebrius—*ebriety.*
137. Ædes—*edifice.*

FOL   304   INF

138. Edo—*edible.*
139. Ego—*egotism.*
140. Emo—*exempt.*
141. Æmulus—*emulation.*
142. Eo—*exit.*
143. Equus—*equestrian.*
144. Æquus—*equal.*
145. Erro—*err.*
146. Æstimo—*estimate.*
147. Ævum—*coeval.*
148. Exemplum—*example.*
149. Exterus—*exterior.*

F.

150. Faber—*fabric.*
151. Facies—*face.*
152. Facio—*fact.*
153. Fallo—*false.*
154. Fama—*fame.*
155. Fames—*famine.*
156. Familia—*family.*
157. Fanum—*fane.*
158. Fatus—*fate.*
159. Farina—*farinacious.*
160. Fessus—*confess.*
161. Febris—*fever.*
162. Fœdus—*federal.*
163. Felix—*felicity.*
164. Femina—*feminine.*
165. Fendo—*defend.*
166. Fera—*fierce.*
167. Fero—*ferry.*
168. Ferrum—*ferruginous.*
169. Ferveo—*fervor.*
170. Festus—*festal.*
171. Fido—*fidelity.*
172. Fixum—*fix.*
173. Filius—*filial.*
174. Filum—*filament.*
175. Fictum—*fiction.*
176. Finis—*finish.*
177. Firmus—*firm.*
178. Fiscus—*fiscal.*
179. Flagro—*flagrant.*
180. Flamma—*flame.*
181. Flecto—*flexible.*
182. Fligo—*afflict.*
183. Flatum—*inflate.*
184. Flos—*floral.*
185. Fluxum—*efflux.*
186. Folium—*foliage.*

187. Forma—*form.*
188. Fors—*fortune.*
189. Fortis—*fortitude.*
190. Fossa—*fosse.*
191. Fractum—*fracture.*
192. Frater—*fraternal.*
193. Fraus—*fraud.*
194. Frigus—*frigid.*
195. Frons—*front.*
196. Fruor—*fruition.*
197. Fugio—*fugacious.*
198. Fulgeo—*fulgency.*
199. Fumus—*fume.*
200. Fusum—*fuse.*
201. Fundus—*foundation.*

G.

202. Gelu—*gelid.*
203. Gestum—*gesture.*
204. Genitum—*genius.*
205. Gladius—*gladiator.*
206. Glutio—*glut.*
207. Gradior—*gradation.*
208. Grandis—*grand.*
209. Granum—*grain.*
210. Gratus—*grateful.*
211. Gravis—*grave.*
212. Gregis—*gregarious.*
213. Gubernator—*gubernatorial.*
214. Gusto—*gust.*

H.

215. Habeo—*have.*
216. Hæro—*adhere.*
217. Hæres—*heritage.*
218. Halo—*exhale.*
219. Haustum—*exhaust.*
220. Homo—*human.*
221. Honor—*honor.*
222. Hortus—*horticulture.*
223. Hospes—*hospitable.*
224. Hostis—*host.*
225. Humus—*inhume.*

I.

226. Idem—*identity.*
227. Ignis—*ignite.*
228. Imago—*image.*
229. Impero—*imperative.*
230. Inanus—*inanity.*
231. Index—*indicate.*
232. Inferus—*inferior.*

233. Insula—*insular.*
234. Integer—*integral.*
235. Intus—*interior.*
236. Ira—*ire.*
237. Iter—*itinerant.*

J.

238. Jaceo—*jacent.*
239. Jaceo—*ejaculate.*
240. Jocus—*joke.*
241. Judico—*judicatory.*
242. Jungo—*junction.*
243. Juro—*jury.*
244. Jus—*just.*
245. Juvenis—*juvenile.*

L.

246. Labor—*laborious.*
247. Lapsus—*lapse.*
248. Lapidus—*lapidary.*
249. Latus—*latitude.*
250. Lateris—*lateral.*
251. Laus—*laud.*
252. Lego—*legate.*
253. Lectum—*lecture.*
254. Lenis—*lenient.*
255. Levis—*levity.*
256. Legis—*legal.*
257. Liber—*liberal.*
258. Libri—*library.*
259. Libro—*deliberate.*
260. Licet—*license.*
261. Ligo—*ligament.*
262. Limen—*eliminate.*
263. Lingua—*language.*
264. Linquo—*delinquent.*
265. Linum—*linen.*
266. Litis—*litigation.*
267. Litera—*literature.*
268. Locus—*local.*
269. Longus—*long.*
270. Loquor—*loquacity.*
271. Lucrum—*lucre.*
272. Luctor—*reluctance.*
273. Ludo—*ludicrous.*
274. Luna—*lunar.*
275. Lutum—*ablution.*
276. Lucis—*lucid.*

M.

277. Magister—*magistrate.*
278. Magnus—*magnitude.*

279. Malus—*malice.*
280. Mando—*mandate.*
281. Mansum—*mansion.*
282. Manus—*manual.*
283. Mare—*marine.*
284. Mater—*maternal.*
285. Maturus—*mature.*
286. Medeor—*medicine.*
287. Medius—*medium.*
288. Mel—*mellifluous.*
289. Melior—*ameliorate.*
290. Memini—*memory.*
291. Mens—*mental.*
292. Mergo—*merge.*
293. Mercis—*commerce.*
294. Metior—*mete.*
295. Migro—*migration.*
296. Miles—*militia.*
297. Mille—*millennium.*
298. Mineo—*imminent.*
299. Minister—*ministry.*
300. Minor—*minority.*
301. Mirus—*miracle.*
302. Mixtum—*mix.*
303. Miser—*misery.*
304. Mitis—*mitigate.*
305. Missum—*mission.*
306. Modus—*mode.*
307. Molior—*mole.*
308. Mollis—*mollify.*
309. Moneo—*monitor.*
310. Mons—*mount.*
311. Monstro—*monster.*
312. Morbus—*morbid.*
313. Mordeo—*morsel.*
314. Mors—*mortal.*
315. Mos—*moral.*
316. Moveo—*move.*
317. Multus—*multitude.*
318. Mundus—*mundane.*
319. Munis—*ammunition.*
320. Munus—*municipal.*
321. Murus—*mural.*
322. Musa—*muse.*
323. Muta—*mutable.*

N.

324. Nascor—*native.*
325. Nato—*natation.*
326. Navis—*navy.*
327. Necto—*connect.*

328. Nego—*negation*.
329. Negotium—*negotiate*.
330. Neuter—*neutral*.
331. Nihil—*nihility*.
332. Noceo—*innocent*.
333. Norma—*normal*.
334. Notum—*note*.
335. Novus—*novel*.
336. Noctis—*nocturnal*.
337. Nuptum—*nuptials*.
338. Nudus—*nudity*.
339. Nullus—*nullify*.
340. Numerus—*numeration*.
341. Nuncio—*enunciate*.

O.

342. Oculus—*ocular*.
343. Odi—*odious*.
344. Oleo—*olfactory*.
345. Omnis—*omnipotent*.
346. Onus—*onerous*.
347. Opinor—*opine*.
348. Opto—*option*.
349. Opus—*operate*.
350. Orbis—*orb*.
351. Ordo—*order*.
352. Orior—*orient*.
353. Orno—*ornate*.
354. Oro—*orator*.
355. Os—*ossify*.
356. Ovum—*oval*.

P.

357. Pagus—*pagan*.
358. Pando—*expand*.
359. Pango, pactum—*compact*.
360. Pallium—*pall*.
361. Par—*parity*.
362. Pareo—*apparent*.
363. Pario—*parent*.
364. Paro, paratum—*apparatus*.
365. Pars—*part*.
366. Pasco, pastum—*pastor*.
367. Pater—*paternal*.
368. Patior—*patience*.
369. Pax, pacis—*peace*.
370. Pecco—*peccancy*.
371. Pectus—*pectoral*.
372. Pecus—*peculate*.
373. Pello, pulsum—*pulse*.
374. Pendeo—*pendent*.

375. Pene—*penult*.
376. Pœna—*penal*.
377. Penitus—*penetrate*.
378. Penna—*pen*.
379. Persona—*person*.
380. Pes, pedis—*pedal*.
381. Peto—*petulant*.
382. Pilo—*compile*.
383. Pingo, pictum—*picture*.
384. Pio, piatum—*expiate*.
385. Piscis—*piscatory*.
386. Placeo—*placid*.
387. Planta—*plant*.
388. Planus—*plane*.
389. Plaudo—*plaudit*.
390. Plebs—*plebeian*.
391. Pleo—*plenary*.
392. Plico—*accomplice*.
393. Ploro—*deplore*.
394. Plumbum—*plumb*.
395. Plus, pluris—*plural*.
396. Polio—*polish*.
397. Pomum—*pomace*.
398. Pondus—*pound*.
399. Pono, positum—*position*.
400. Populus—*people*.
401. Porta—*portal*.
402. Porto—*porter*.
403. Possum—*possible*.
404. Posterus—*posterior*.
405. Postulo—*expostulate*.
406. Poto—*potion*.
407. Precor, precatus—*deprecate*.
408. Præda—*predatory*.
409. Prehendo—*apprehend*.
410. Premo, pressum—*press*.
411. Pretium—*price*.
412. Primus—*prime*.
413. Privus—*private*.
414. Probo—*probity*.
415. Prope—*propinquity*.
416. Proprius—*appropriate*.
417. Puer—*puerile*.
418. Pugnus—*pugnacious*.
419. Pulvis—*pulverise*.
420. Pungo—*pungent*.
421. Punio—*punish*.
422. Puto—*compute*.

Q.

423. Qualis—*quality*.

424. Quantus—*quantity.*
425. Quatio, quassum—*quash.*
426. Quatuor—*quart.*
427. Queror—*quarrel.*
428. Quæro—*quest.*
429. Quies—*quiet.*
430. Quinque—*quintuple.*
431. Quot—*quota.*

R.

432. Rabies—*rabid.*
433. Radius—*radiate.*
434. Radix—*radical.*
435. Rado—*abrade.*
436. Ramus—*ramify.*
437. Rapio—*rapine.*
438. Rego—*regal.*
439. Reor, ratus—*rate.*
440. Repo—*reptile.*
441. Res—*real.*
442. Rideo—*ridicule.*
443. Rigeo—*rigid.*
444. Rigo—*irrigate.*
445. Rivus—*rivulet.*
446. Robur—*robust.*
447. Rogo, rogatum—*abrogate.*
448. Rota—*rotary.*
449. Rudis—*rude.*
450. Ruga—*corrugate.*
451. Rumpo, ruptum—*rupture.*
452. Rus, ruris—*rural.*

S.

453. Sacer—*sacred.*
454. Sagus—*sage.*
455. Sal, salis—*salad.*
456. Salio—*assail.*
457. Salus—*salutary.*
458. Sancio, sanctum—*saint.*
459. Sanguis—*sanguinary.*
460. Sanus—*sane.*
461. Sapio—*sapient.*
462. Sapo, saponis—*saponaceous.*
463. Satis—*satiate.*
464. Scala—*scale.*
465. Scando—*scan.*
466. Scindo—*rescind.*
467. Scio—*science.*
468. Scribo—*scribe.*
469. Scrutor—*scrutiny.*
470. Seco—*secant.*

471. Seculum—*secular.*
472. Sedeo—*sedentary.*
473. Semen, Seminis—*seminary.*
474. Semi—*semi-annual.*
475. Senex, senior—*senior.*
476. Sentio—*sentiment.*
477. Sepelio, sepultum—*sepulture.*
478. Septem—*September.*
479. Sequor—*sequel.*
480. Sero—*series.*
481. Serpo—*serpent.*
482. Serra—*serrated.*
483. Servo—*serve.*
484. Severus—*severe.*
485. Sex—*sextant.*
486. Sidus—*sidereal.*
487. Signum—*sign.*
488. Similis—*similar.*
489. Sinister—*sinister.*
490. Sinus—*insinuate.*
491. Sto, statum—*state.*
492. Socius—*sociable.*
493. Sol—*solar.*
494. Solidus—*solid.*
495. Solor—*console.*
496. Solus—*sole.*
497. Solvo—*solve.*
498. Somnus—*somnific.*
499. Sonus—*sound.*
500. Sopor—*soporific.*
501. Sors—*sort.*
502. Spargo, sparsum—*sparse.*
503. Spatium—*space.*
504. Specio, spectum—*aspect.*
505. Spero—*despair.*
506. Spiro—*spirit.*
507. Splendeo—*splendid.*
508. Spondeo, sponsum—*sponsor.*
509. Stella—*stellar.*
510. Sterno—*consternation.*
511. Stilla—*instil.*
512. Stipo—*constipate.*
513. Stirps—*extirpate.*
514. Stringo, strictum—*strict.*
515. Struo, structum—*structure.*
516. Suadeo, suasum—*persuade.*
517. Suavis—*suavity.*
518. Sudo—*exude.*
519. Sui—*suicide.*
520. Sum, esse—*essence.*
521. Sumo—*assume.*

522. Super—*superior*.
523. Surgo—*surge*.

T.

524. Taberna—*tabernacle*.
525. Taceo—*tacit*.
526. Tango—*tangent*.
527. Tego—*tegument*.
528. Tempus—*temporal*.
529. Tendo—*tend*.
530. Teneo—*tenure*.
531. Tento—*tempt*.
532. Tenuis—*attenuate*.
533. Tergo, tersum—*terse*.
534. Terminus—*term*.
535. Tero, tritum—*trite*.
536. Terra—*terrestrial*.
537. Terreo—*terror*.
538. Testis—*testify*.
539. Texo—*text*.
540. Timeo—*timid*.
541. Tingo—*tinge*.
542. Tollo—*extol*.
543. Torpeo—*torpid*.
544. Torqueo—*torture*.
545. Totus—*total*.
546. Trado—*tradition*.
547. Traho, tractum—*tract*.
548. Tremo—*tremble*.
549. Tres—*triple*.
550. Tribuo—*tribute*.
551. Trudo—*intrude*.
552. Tuber—*tubercle*.
553. Tueor—*intuition*.
554. Tumeo—*tumid*.
555. Tundo, tusum—*obtuse*.
556. Turba—*turbid*.
557. Turgeo—*turgid*.
558. Turris—*turret*.

U.

559. Ultimus—*ultimate*.
560. Umbra—*umbrage*.
561. Unda—*undulate*.
562. Unguo—*unguent*.
563. Unus—*unity*.
564. Utor, usus—*use*.
565. Vado—*evade*.
566. Vagus—*vagary*.
567. Valeo—*valid*.
568. Veho—*vehicle*.
569. Vello, vulsum—*avulsion*.
570. Velo—*veil*.
571. Vendo—*vend*.
572. Venio—*event*.
573. Venter—*ventriloquist*.
574. Ventus—*vent*.
575. Verbum—*verbal*.
576. Vereor—*revere*.
577. Vergo—*verge*.
578. Vermis—*vermin*.
579. Verto—*advert*.
580. Verus—*verity*.
581. Vestigium—*vestige*.
582. Vestis—*vesture*.
583. Vetus—*veteran*.
584. Via—*deviate*.
585. Viscis—*vicar*.
586. Video, visum—*vision*.
587. Vigeo—*vigor*.
588. Vinco—*convince*.
589. Vindex—*vindicate*.
590. Vinum—*vine*.
591. Vir—*virtue*.
592. Viris—*virulence*.
593. Vito—*inevitable*.
594. Vitrum—*vitreous*.
595. Vivo—*vivacity*.
596. Voco—*vocal*.
597. Volo—*volatile*.
598. Volo—*voluntary*.
599. Volupta—*voluptuous*.
600. Volvo—*evolve*.
601. Voro—*voracity*.
602. Voveo—*avow*.
603. Vulgus—*vulgar*.
604. Vulnus—*vulnerable*.

CHAP. III. WORDS DERIVED FROM THE GREEK . . . Pp. 169-200.
GREEK ALPHABET.

A.

1. Academia, ακαδημια—*academy*.
2. Achos, αχος—*ache*.
3. Akme, ακμη—*acme*.
4. Akouo, ακουο—*acoustic*.
5. Akron, ακρον—*acropolis*.
6. Adelphos, αδελφος—*adelphic*.
7. Aer, αηρ—*air*.
8. Ago, αγω—*demagogue*.
9. Agon, αγων—*agony*.
10. Algos, αλγος—*cephalalgy*.
11. Allaxis, αλλαξις—*parallax*.
12. Alpha, αλφα—*alphabet*.
13. Anemos, ανεμος—*anemometer*.
14. Aner, ανηρ, ανδρος—*android*.
15. Angello, αγγελλω—*angel*.
16. Anthos, ανθος—*anthology*.
17. Anthropos, ανθρωπος—*misanthrope*.
18. Arche, αρχη—*anarchy*.
19. Arktos, αρκτος—*arctic*.
20. Argos, αργος—*lethargy*.
21. Aristos, αριστος—*aristocracy*.
22. Arithmos, αριθμος—*arithmetic*.
23. Aroma, αρωμα—*aromatic*.
24. Askeo, ασκεω—*ascetic*.
25. Astron, αστρον—*astral*.
26. Athlos, αθλος—*athletic*.
27. Atmos, ατμος—*atmosphere*.
28. Aulos, αυλος—*hydraulic*.
29. Autos, αυτος—*autocrat*.

B.

30. Ballo, βαλλω—*emblem*.
31. Baptizo, βαπτιζω—*baptize*.
32. Basis, βασις—*base*.
33. Baros, βαρος—*barometer*.
34. Beta, βετα—*alphabet*.
35. Biblos, βιβλος—*bible*.
36. Bios, βιος—*biology*.
37. Botane, βορανη—*botany*.
38. Boucolos, βουκολος—*bucolic*.

C.

39. Kakos, κακος—*cacophony*.
40. Kalupto, καλυπτο—*apocalypse*.
41. Kanon, κανων—*canonical*.
42. Kaio, καιω, καυσω—*caustic*.

43. Kardia, καρδια—*cardiac*.
44. Kentron, κεντρον—*centre*.
45. Kephale, κεφαλη—*cephalic*.
46. Keras, κερας—*monoceros*.
47. Chaos, χαος—*chaos*.
48. Charis, χαρις, χαριτος—*charity*.
49. Cheir, χειρ—*chirography*.
50. Chole, χολη—*choler*.
51. Choreo, χωρεω—*anchorite*.
52. Christos, χριστος—*Christ*.
53. Chroma, χρωμα—*chromatic*.
54. Chronos, χρονος—*chronic*.
55. Chrusos, χρυσος—*chrysolite*.
56. Konche, κονχη—*conch*.
57. Kopto, κοπτω—*syncopate*.
58. Kosmos, κοσμος—*cosmogony*.
59. Kranion, κρανιον—*cranium*.
60. Kratos, κρατος—*democracy*.
61. Krites, κριτης—*critic*.
62. Krupto, κρυπτω—*cryptogamy*.
63. Kuklos, κυκλος—*cycle*.
64. Kuon, κυων—*cynical*.
65. Kustis, κυστις—*cyst*.

D.

66. Deka, δεκα—*decalogue*.
67. Demos, δημος—*democracy*.
68. Despotes, δεσποτης—*despot*.
69. Didasco, διδασκω—*didactic*.
70. Doxa, δοξα—*doxology*.
71. Drama, δραμα—*drama*.
72. Dromos, δρομος—*dromedary*.
73. Dunamis, δυναμις—*dynasty*.
74. Dus, δυς—*dyspepsy*.

E.

75. Oikos, οικος—*economy*.
76. Hedra, ιδρα—*sanhedrim*.
77. Hegesis, ηγησις—*exegesis*.
78. Emeo, εμεω—*emetic*.
79. Entera, εντερα—*entrails*.
80. Entomos, εντομος—*entomology*.
81. Epos, επος—*epic*.
82. Eremos, ερημος—*eremite*.
83. Ergon, εργον—*energy*.
84. Eso, εσω—*esotery*.
85. Aither, αιθηρ—*ether*.

86. Ethos, εθος—*ethics.*
87. Ethnos, εθνος—*ethnology.*
88. Etumon, ετυμον—*etymology.*
89. Eu, ευ—*eulogy.*

G.

90. Galax, γαλαξ—*galaxy.*
91. Gameo, γαμεω—*bigamy.*
92. Gaster, γαστηρ—*gastric.*
93. Ge, γη—*geology.*
94. Gennao, γενναω—*genesis.*
95. Glotta, γλωττα—*glottis.*
96. Glupho, γλυφω—*glyph.*
97. Gnome, γνωμη—*gnostics.*
98. Gonia, γωνια—*goniometer.*
99. Grapho, γραφω—*graphic.*
100. Gumnos, γυμνος—*gymnasium.*
101. Gune, γυνη—*gynarchy.*
102. Guros, γυρος—*gyral.*

H.

103. Hebdomos, ἑβδομος—*hebdomad.*
104. Hekaton, ἑκατον—*hecatomb.*
105. Helios, ἡλιος—*heliacal.*
106. Hellen, Ἑλλην—*hellenic.*
107. Haima, αἱμα—*hemorrhage.*
108. Hemera, ἡμερα—*ephemeral.*
109. Hemi, ἡμι—*hemisphere.*
110. Hepta, ἑπτα—*heptagon.*
111. Heteros, ἑτερος—*heterodox.*
112. Hex, ἑξ—*hexagon.*
113. Hippos, ἱππος—*hippodrome.*
114. Hieros, ἱερος—*hierarchy.*
115. Homilos, ὁμιλος—*homily.*
116. Homos, ὁμος—*homogeneous.*
117. Hora, ὡρα—*horal.*
118. Horizo, ὁριζω—*horizon.*
119. Hudor, ὑδωρ—*hyra.*

I.

120. Ichthus, ιχθυς—*ichthyology.*
121. Idios, ιδιος—*idiom.*
122. Idos, ειδος—*cycloid.*
123. Isos, ισος—*isosceles.*

L.

124. Laos, λαος—*laity.*
125. Lethe, ληθη—*lethean.*

126. Lexis, λεξις—*lexicon.*
127. Lithos, λιθος—*lithography.*
128. Logos, λογος—*logic.*
129. Lusis, λυσις—*paralysis.*

M.

130. Machomai, μαχομαι—*monomachy.*
131. Manteia, μαντεια—*necromancy.*
132. Martur, μαρτυρ—*martyr.*
133. Mathema, μαθημα—*mathematics.*
134. Mechanao, μηχαναω—*mechanism.*
135. Melos, μελος—*melody.*
136. Meteoros, μετεωρος—*meteor.*
137. Motron, μετρον—*metre.*
138. Mikros, μικρος—*microscope.*
139. Misos, μισος—*misanthropy.*
140. Mneme, μνημη—*mnemonics.*
141. Monos, μονος—*monad.*
142. Morphe, μορφη—*amorphous.*
143. Muthos, μυθος—*mythic.*

N.

144. Narke, ναρκη—*narcotic.*
145. Naus, ναυς—*nausea.*
146. Neos, νεος—*neology.*
147. Nesos, νησος—*peloponnesus.*
148. Neuron, νευρον—*neuralogy.*
149. Nomos, νομος—*anomaly.*
150. Nosos, νοσος—*nosology.*

O.

151. Ode, ωδη—*ode.*
152. Odos, ὁδος—*exodus.*
153. Odous, οδοντος—*odontalgy.*
154. Suffix *oid.*
155. Oligos, ολιγος—*oligarchy.*
156. Onoma, ονομα—*anonymous.*
157. Optomai, οπτομαι—*optics.*
158. Orama, οραμα—*diorama.*
159. Ornis, ορνιθος—*ornithology.*
160. Orthos, ορθος—*orthodox.*
161. Osteon, οστεον—*osteology.*
162. Oxus, οξυς—*oxyd.*

P.

163. Paideia, παιδεια—*pedant.*
164. Pan, παν, παντος—*panacea.*
165. Pathos, παθος—*pathetic.*

166. Pente, πεντε—*pentagon.*
167. Pepto, πεπτω—*peptic.*
168. Petalon, πεταλον—*petal.*
169. Petra, πετρα—*petrify.*
170. Phago, φαλω—*esophagus.*
171. Phaino, φαινω—*phase.*
172. Pharmakon, φάρμακον—*pharmacy.*
173. Phemi, φημι—*blaspheme.*
174. Phero, φερω—*metaphor.*
175. Philos, φιλος—*philanthropy.*
176. Phone, φωνη—*phonology.*
177. Phos, φως—*phosphate.*
178. Phrazo—φραζω—*phrase.*
179. Phren, φρην—*phrenzy.*
180. Phusis, φυσις—*physics.*
181. Peirao, πειραω—*empiric.*
182. Plane, πλανη—*planet.*
183. Plasso, πλασσω—*plastic.*
184. Pneo, πνεω—*pneumatics.*
185. Polemos, πολεμος—*polemic.*
186. Poleo, πωλεω—*monopoly.*
187. Polis, πολις—*police.*
188. Polus, πολυς—*polygon.*
189. Potamos, ποταμος—*hippopotamus.*
190. Pous, πους, ποδος—*antipode.*
191. Prasso, πρασσω—*practice.*
192. Protos, πρωτος—*protocol.*
193. Psuche, ψυχη—*psychology.*
194. Pur, πυρ—*pyre.*

R.
195. Rheo, ῥεω—*diarrhœa.*

S.
196. Sarx, σαρξ—*sarcasm.*

197. Skeptomai, σκεπτομαι—*skeptic.*
198. Schisma, σχισμα—*schism.*
199. Schole, σχολη, *school.*
200. Skopeo, σκοπεω—*scope.*
201. Sitos, σιτος—*parasite.*
202. Sophia, σοφια—*sophism.*
203. Spao, σπαω—*spasmodic.*
204. Statis, στατις—*system.*
205. Stello, στελλω—*apostle.*
206. Stenos, στενος—*stenographer.*
207. Stereos, στερεος—*stereometry.*
208. Stikos, στιχος—*acrostic.*
209. Strophe, ςτροφη—*apostrophe.*

T.
210. Taphos, ταφος—*epitaph.*
211. Taxis, ταξις—*tactics.*
212. Techne, τεχνη—*technical.*
213. Tessares, τεσσαρες—*tesselated.*
214. Theomai, θεομαι—*theatre.*
215. Thesis, θεσις—*thesis.*
216. Theos, θεος—*theism.*
217. Tome, τομη—*tome.*
218. Tonos, τονος—*tone.*
219. Topos, τοπος—*topic.*
220. Treis, τρεις—*three.*
221. Tropos, τροπος—*trope.*
222. Tupos, τυπος—*type.*

X.
223. Xulon, ξυλον—*xylography.*

Z.
224. Zoon, ζωον—*zoology.*

		PAGE
CHAP. IV. MISCELLANEOUS TABLES.		
1. Corresponding derivations,	. . .	202
2. Plurals of words from Latin and Greek,	.	203
3. Latin words, ...	.	204
" phrases, ...	.	205
4. French words, ...	.	209–10
" phrases, . . .	.	211
Italian "	.	213
5. Abbreviations, ...	.	213
6. Derivations from classical proper names,	.	216–19
Geographical derivations, . .	.	220–22

PART III.

ENGLISH SYNONYMS, ... 223–301

CATALOGUE

OF

Approved School and College Text-Books.

PUBLISHED BY E. H. BUTLER & CO.,
137 South Fourth Street, Philadelphia.

Goodrich's Pictorial History of the United States.
A Pictorial History of the United States, with notices of other portions of America. By S. G. GOODRICH, author of "Peter Parley's Tales." For the use of Schools. Revised and improved edition, brought down to the present time (1860). Re-written and newly illustrated. 1 vol. 12mo., embossed backs. Upwards of 450 pages.

Goodrich's American Child's Pictorial History of the United States. An introduction to the author's "Pictorial History of the United States."

Goodrich's Pictorial History of England. A Pictorial History of England. By S. G. GOODRICH, author of "Pictorial History of the United States," etc.

Goodrich's Pictorial History of Rome. A Pictorial History of Ancient Rome, with sketches of the History of Modern Italy. By S. G. GOODRICH, author of "Pictorial History of the United States." For the use of Schools. Revised and improved edition.

Published by E. H. BUTLER & CO., Philadelphia.

Goodrich's Pictorial History of Greece. A Pictorial History of Greece; Ancient and Modern. By S. G. GOODRICH, author of "Pictorial History of the United States." For the use of Schools. Revised edition.

Goodrich's Pictorial History of France. A Pictorial History of France. For the use of Schools. By S. G. GOODRICH, author of "Pictorial History of the United States." Revised and improved edition, brought down to the present time.

Goodrich's Parley's Common School History of the World. A Pictorial History of the World; Ancient and Modern. For the use of Schools. By S. G. GOODRICH, author of "Pictorial History of the United States," etc. Illustrated by engravings.

Goodrich's First History. The First History. An Introduction to Parley's Common School History. Designed for beginners at Home and School. Illustrated by Maps and Engravings. By S. G. GOODRICH, author of the Pictorial Series of Histories, etc.

Goodrich's Pictorial Natural History; Embracing a View of the Mineral, Vegetable, and Animal Kingdoms. For the use of Schools. By SAMUEL G. GOODRICH. 300 engravings, 1 vol. 12mo.

Geographie Elementaire a l'Usage des Ecoles et des Familles. Illustrée par 15 cartes et 30 Gravures. Par PETER PARLEY.

Histoire des Etats Unis d'Amerique, avec Notices des autres parties du Nouveau Monde. Par SAMUEL G. GOODRICH.

Petite Histoire Universelle a l'Usage des Ecoles et des Familles. Par S. G. GOODRICH.

Mitchell's First Lessons in Geography. First Lessons in Geography: for young children. Designed as an Introduction to the author's Primary Geography. By S. AUGUSTUS MITCHELL, author of a Series of Geographical Works. Illustrated with maps and numerous engravings.

Published by E. H. BUTLER & CO., Philadelphia.

Mitchell's New Primary Geography. (The second
book of the Series.) An Easy Introduction to the Study of Geography. Introductory to the New Intermediate Geography. Illustrated by nineteen colored Maps and nearly one hundred Engravings. By S. AUGUSTUS MITCHELL. 1 vol. small 4to This is an entirely new and beautiful book.

Mitchell's New Intermediate Geography. An
entirely new work. The maps are all engraved on copper, in the best manner, and brought down to the present date. It is profusely illustrated with beautiful engravings, and is the most complete quarto Geography ever issued in the world.

Mitchell's New School Geography and Atlas. En
tirely new.—Text, Maps, Illustrations,—ready January 1st, 1865.

Mitchell's New Ancient Geography. An Ancient
Geography, Classical and Sacred. By S. AUGUSTUS MITCHELL. An entirely new edition, drawn from the best authorities, ancient and modern. Designed for the use of Schools and Colleges. Illustrated with numerous Engravings. 12mo muslin.

Mitchell's Primary Geography (Old Series). An
Easy Introduction to the study of Geography. Designed for the instruction of children in Schools and Families. Illustrated by nearly one hundred Engravings and sixteen colored Maps. By S. AUGUSTUS MITCHELL.

Mitchell's School Geography and Atlas (Old Series).
New Revised Edition. A System of Modern Gegography, comprising a description of the present state of the World, and its five great divisions, America, Europe, Asia, Africa, and Oceanica, with their several Empires, Kingdoms. States, Territories, etc Embellished by numerous engravings. Adapted to the capacity of youth Accompanied by an Atlas containing thirty two maps, drawn and engraved expressly for this work. By S. AUGUSTUS MITCHELL.

Published by E. H. BUTLER & CO., Philadelphia.

Mitchell's Ancient Geography and Atlas (Old Series).

First Edition. Designed for Academies, Schools, and Families. A System of Classical and Sacred Geography, embellished with engravings of remarkable events, views of ancient cities, and various interesting antique remains. Together with an Ancient Atlas, containing maps illustrating the work. By S. AUGUSTUS MITCHELL.

Mitchell's Geographical Question Book (Old Series).

Comprising Geographical Definitions, and containing questions on all the maps of Mitchell's School Atlas; to which is added an Appendix, embracing valuable Tables in Mathematical and Physical Geography.

Mitchell's Biblical Geography. Sabbath School

Geography, designed for instruction in Sabbath School and Bible Classes, illustrated with colored maps and wood-cut engravings. By S. AUGUSTUS MITCHELL.

Hows' Primary Ladies' Reader. Primary Ladies'

Reader, a choice collection of Prose and Poetry, adapted to the capacities of young children.

Hows' Junior Ladies' Reader. A choice and varied

collection of Prose and Verse, with a synopsis of the Elementary Principles of Elocution; expressly adapted for the use of the young, and designed as an introduction to the Ladies' Reader. By JOHN W. S. HOWS, Professor of Elocution.

Hows' Ladies' Reader. Designed for the use of

Ladies' Schools and Family Reading Circles; comprising choice selections from standard authors, in Prose and Poetry, with the essential Rules of Elocution, simplified and arranged for strictly practical use. By JOHN W. S. HOWS, Professor of Elocution.

Hows' Ladies' Book of Readings and Recitations.

The Ladies' Book of Readings and Recitations: a collection of approved Extracts from Standard authors, intended for the use of Higher Classes in schools and seminaries, and for Family Reading Circles. By JOHN W. S. HOWS, author of "The Ladies' Reader," "The Junior Ladies' Reader," "The Ladies First Reader," etc., etc., etc.

Published by E. H. BUTLER & CO., Philadelphia.

Coppee's Elements of Logic. Elements of Logic.

Designed as a Manual of Instruction. By HENRY COPPEE, A. M., Professor of English Literature in the University of Pennsylvania; and late Principal Assistant Professor of Ethics and English Studies in the United States Military Academy at West Point.

Coppee's Elements of Rhetoric. Elements of

Rhetoric. Designed as a Manual of Instruction. By HENRY COPPEE, A. M., author of "Elements of Logic," etc. New edition, revised.

Coppee's Academic Speaker. Containing a large

number of new and appropriate Pieces, for Prose Declamation, Poetical Recitation, and Dramatic Reading, carefully selected from the best authors, American, English, and Continental. Arranged in a rhetorical order, and adapted to the wants of classes in Schools, Academies and Colleges. By HENRY COPPEE, A. M., Professor of English Literature in the University of Pennsylvania. 1 vol. 8vo.

Tenney's Geology. Geology; for Teachers, Classes,

and Private Students. By SANBORN TENNEY, A. M., Lecturer on Physical Geography and Natural History in the Massachusetts Teachers' Institutes. Illustrated with Two hundred Wood Engravings.

Stockhardt's Chemistry. The Principles of Chemis-

try, illustrated by Simple Experiments. By Dr. JULIUS ADOLPH STOCKHARDT, Professor in the Royal Academy of Agriculture at Tharand, and Royal Inspector of Medicine in Saxony. Translated by C. H. PEIRCE, M. D. Fifteenth Thousand.

Reid's Essays on the Intellectual Powers of Man.

Essays on the Intellectual Powers of Man. By THOMAS REID, D. D., F. R. S. E. Abridged, with notes and illustrations from Sir WILLIAM HAMILTON and others. Edited by JAMES WALKER, D. D., President of Harvard College.

Stewart's Philosophy of the Active and Moral

Powers of Man. The Philosophy of the Active and Moral Powers of Man. By DUGALD STEWART, F. R. SS. Lond. and Ed. Revised, with omissions and additions, by JAMES WALKER, D. D., President of Harvard College.

Published by E. H. BUTLER & CO., Philadelphia.

Hart's Constitution of the United States. A Brief
Exposition of the Constitution of the United States, for the use of Common Schools. By JOHN S. HART, LL. D., Principal of the Philadelphia High School, and Professor of Moral, Mental, and Political Science in the same.

Hart's English Grammar. Part. 1. An Introduc-
tion to the Grammar of the English Language. By JOHN S. HART, LL. D. 1 vol 12mo.

Hart's English Grammar. English Grammar, or
An Exposition of the Principles and Usages of the English Language. By JOHN S. HART, A. M., Principal of the Philadelphia High School, and Member of the American Philosophical Society.

Hart's Class Book of Poetry. Class Book of Poetry,
consisting of Selections from Distinguished English and American Poets, from Chaucer to the present day. The whole arranged in chronological order, with Biographical and Critical Remarks. By JOHN S. HART, LL. D., Principal of the Philadelphia High School.

Hart's Class Book of Prose. Class Book of Prose,
consisting of Selections from Distinguished English and American Authors, from Chaucer to the present day. The whole arranged in Chronological order, with Biographical and Critical Remarks. By JOHN S. HART, L L. D., Principal of the Philadelphia High School.

Smith's English Grammar. English Grammar on
the Productive System: a method of instruction recently adopted in Germany and Switzerland. Designed for Schools and Academies. By ROSWELL C. SMITH.

Comstock's Elocution. A System of Elocution, with
special reference to Gesture, to the treatment of Stammering and Defective Articulation; comprising numerous diagrams and engraved figures illustrative of the subject. By ANDREW COMSTOCK, M. D., Principal of the Vocal and Polyglott Gymnasium. Twentieth edition, enlarged.

Published by E. H. BUTLER & CO., Philadelphia.

www.ingramcontent.com/pod-product-compliance
Lightning Source LLC
Chambersburg PA
CBHW030754230426
43667CB00007B/966